MANUAL

OF

HOUSING LAW

AUSTRALIA
Law Book Co.
Sydney

CANADA and USA
Carswell
Toronto

HONG KONG
Sweet & Maxwell Asia

NEW ZEALAND
Brookers
Wellington

SINGAPORE and MALAYSIA
Sweet & Maxwell Asia
Singapore and Kuala Lumpur

MANUAL
OF
HOUSING LAW

By

ANDREW ARDEN Q.C.
and
ANDREW DYMOND

Barristers of Arden Chambers

Eighth Edition

First Edition 1978 (HOUSING: Security and Rent Control)
Second Edition 1983
Reprinted 1983
Reprinted 1984
Third Edition 1986
Reprinted 1987
Reprinted 1988
Fourth Edition 1989
Fifth Edition 1992
Reprinted 1994
Sixth Edition 1997
Seventh Edition 2003
Eighth Edition 2007

Published in 2007 by
Sweet & Maxwell Limited
100 Avenue Road
Swiss Cottage
London, NW3 3PF
Typeset by LBJ Typesetting Ltd of Kingsclere
Printed in England by MPG Books, Cornwall

British Library Cataloguing in Publication Data

A catalogue record for this book is available from the British Library

ISBN 978–1–84703–069–6

INTRODUCTION

Until the mid-1970s, the term "housing law" was in scant use: it was a term applied to a sub-division of planning law, and on occasion merited a mention in landlord and tenant. The subject covered the powers and duties of local authorities, mainly in relation to slum clearance (by area or individual unit), the provision of public housing and such related matters as improvement grants. Housing law was confined to a study of the powers exercisable in the public interest in relation to what was statutorily identified as housing.

Reflecting the growth of legal aid, the introduction of law centres and the underlying social demand for "rights", housing law began to develop—largely through the pages of the *Legal Action Group Bulletin* (as *Legal Action* was then called) and subsequently through the *Encyclopedia of Housing Law*—with a somewhat wider focus on the law, as it affected the use of property as a home, whether derived from private rights or from the public powers and duties conferred or imposed on local authorities, whether formally identified as housing or because they impacted on housing in practice.

The topics thus taken into the subject included the Rent Acts (governing private sector security and harassment/illegal eviction), leasehold enfranchisement and extension, matrimonial law so far as it affected the family home on domestic breakdown, environmental health (statutory nuisance and other provisions affecting housing), social security, rating, mobile homes, judicial review (enjoying its own period of unprecedented growth, itself in part a reflection of the same rise in rights awareness), as well as some planning law, compulsory purchase, conveyancing, contract and tort.

From these acorns have grown eight editions of this book (including the first, under the title *Housing: Security and Rent Control*).

The first edition coincided with the first homelessness Act. Since, we have seen the arrival (1980 Act) of security of tenure for public and quasi-public sector tenants, together with the right to buy, followed by the wholesale removal of housing associations into the private sector, and the concurrent diminution in their tenants' rights (1988 Act), only to see the "right to acquire" offered back to them (1996 Act), their identities changed by the same Act to "registered social landlords", and some sort of security parity re-achieved by means of the so-called "probationary" or "starter" tenancy, in the form of introductory tenancies under the Housing Act 1985 and shorthold tenancies under the Housing Act 1988; the former entirely new with, and the latter substantially recast by, the 1996 Act.

Over the 1980s, we watched the fall from grace of the Rent Acts (1915-1988) and the rise in their place of the assured tenancy—the same class of security into which housing association tenants were moved. Full security was tempered by the shorthold, initially a landlord's option, more recently (1996 Act) the presumptive form of letting to which full security has become the exception.

Meanwhile, housing improvement grants, mandatory since 1959, have—with but a few exceptions—been reduced to a discretionary status, and are now subsumed into a much broader discretionary system of "housing assistance" (Regulatory Reform (Housing Assistance) (England and Wales) Order 2002).

There have been many, many other changes, including the introduction of housing benefits followed by tight controls to prevent advantage being taken of their availability, and large-scale stock transfers.

The 1996 Act also revised homelessness law, a cornerstone of housing law as it had defined itself. That reduction of rights was reversed in part by the 2002 Act.

Fittingly, perhaps, from the perspective of this giddy review, that Act introduced a requirement for authorities to carry out homelessness reviews and formulate strategies for dealing with homelessness that is strongly reminiscent (at least for those with longer memories) of the function in s.91 of the Housing Act 1957—dating back to the Housing, Town Planning, etc. Act 1919—of preparing plans for providing new housing (backing up the consideration of housing conditions and review of information which survived through to, and survives in, the 1985 Act).

Along the way, rates departed, poll-tax (individual-based) came and went, and the replacement council tax took local taxation back to a property base. General (rate) fund subsidy for council tenants was abolished and replaced with a requirement to budget to balance the Housing Revenue Account. Other changes to local government law also had an impact, with greater access to information and less access to money, a Chief Financial Officer and a

Monitoring Officer to keep authorities on the straight-and-narrow, and cross-party committees to help take the politics out of local decision-making. That too changes gear—and direction—with the formal split between an authority's executive and their full authority.

The introduction of the Human Rights Act 1998 has meant that decisions of public authorities are subject to ever-closer scrutiny by the courts, a development which has already impacted on most housing issues and which may be considered the highest form yet of the rights-based movement with which modern housing law began, although not a basis for altering the balance of rights struck by the legislature (at any rate, in relation to security of tenure), i.e. it has been held not to comprise a form of security legislation in itself.

Since the seventh edition of this book, there has been a number of further developments. Increasingly, local authorities and other social landlords are expected to take action to combat antisocial behaviour through antisocial behaviour injunctions and antisocial behaviour orders. The Housing Act 2004 has introduced a whole new approach to regulation of standards of accommodation in the private sector. The Housing Health and Safety Rating System comprises an entirely new approach to the assessment of housing standards, and affords local authorities with significantly greater powers to deal with poor housing. In addition, the 2004 Act introduces licensing for HMOs, selective licensing of other residential accommodation, and empty dwelling management orders, allowing authorities to bring long-term vacant accommodation back into use.

It would be possible to continue to illustrate at length, and the Law Commission proposals for change to the mutliplicity of tenures under which housing is occupied, and its replacement with two basic "types" of occupation agreement (*Renting Homes: The Final Report* (*CP297*)) has not yet been touched on—although, at the time of writing, there is little sign that the government proposes to touch on it either. The point is nonetheless clear: housing law is a subject in a state of constant evolution (if not revolution) and if this history is anything to go by, is probably destined so to remain.

That makes it difficult to keep up with. Furthermore, law is rarely retrospective (although the Law Commission may yet fracture the mould with its "big bang" proposal to introduce its new tenures in place of *most*—but not *all*—existing tenures at one fell swoop—see *CP297*, para.2.4). Accordingly, one set of rules does not replace another, so much as: two (or ten) sets co-exist for a period. As this is about where people live, that usually means decades, rather than years.

This gives rise to difficult "policy" decisions as to what should be included in a book like this, without jeopardising its description as a Manual, and how to structure it to ensure that it reflects contemporary concerns.

A number of topics continue not to be touched upon at all: conveyancing, house construction, planning law, compulsory purchase, mobile homes, council tax.

Other subjects are treated briefly, e.g. owner-occupation (including the rights to buy and acquire) and domestic breakdown will almost invariably require the assistance of a solicitor, and—so far as this book is of use to law students—these are topics conventionally covered extensively in law courses.

Financial assistance, by way of housing benefit, is merely mentioned because the provisions and details change so frequently that what would be written here would almost certainly be out of date by the time it is read (and there are other annual works which are available and accessible both to lawyers and to non-lawyers).

The underlying approach, however, has remained the same since the first edition, even if the structure and emphasis have changed with the times. That approach is to start with the task of identifying the principal housing "status" of a tenant or other occupier. The inherent thesis is that in almost every case it will be impossible to determine what are the respective rights and liability of a party to a housing arrangement without first determining what is the status of the occupier in law.

The first chapter is therefore the child of the common law. Only once common law status has been identified does it become possible to turn to the work of Parliament and consider the many different categories of occupier which now exist by statute. The reader, then, is accordingly urged to bear with the first chapter, largely devoid as it is of substantive rights and duties, for without it the remainder of the book will be of little practical value, and the risk of its missapplication will be very real indeed.

For enlargement of detail and for the other areas of housing law which have not been covered in this Manual, the reader is referred to Arden and Partington's *Housing Law* (Sweet & Maxwell, looseleaf); for the source material, the reader may refer to the *Encyclopedia of Housing Law*, and the *Housing Law Reports*, both also published by Sweet & Maxwell; Sweet & Maxwell likewise publish the *Journal of Housing Law* in which many issues are given a more detailed, and commonly more discursive, examination than is commonly available in the other titles. For a more detailed treatment of homelessness and allocations, see the Legal Action Group book, *Homelessness and Allocations*.

The law is stated as at May 4, 2007.

Andrew Arden Q.C.

Arden Chambers
2 John Street
London WC1N 2ES
May 2007

TABLE OF CONTENTS

TABLE OF CASES

TABLE OF STATUTES

TABLE OF STATUTORY INSTRUMENTS

CIVIL PROCEDURE RULES

ABBREVIATIONS

Statutes

Matrimonial Causes Act 1973	MCA 1973
Criminal Law Act 1977	CLA 1977
Protection from Eviction Act 1977	PEA 1977
Family Law Act 1996	FLA 1996
Trusts of Land and Appointment of Trustees Act 1996	TLTA 1996
Protection from Harassment Act 1997	PHA 1997
Commonhold and Leasehold Reform Act 2002	CLRA 2002
Civil Partnership Act 2004	CPA 2004

Statutory Instruments

Civil Procedure Rules 1998	CPR 1998

Others

Anti-Social Behaviour Order	ASBO
Empty Dwelling Management Order	EDMO
European Convention on Human Rights	ECHR
Houses in Multiple Occupation	HMO
Housing and Regeneration Community Association	HARCA
Housing Health and Safety Rating System	HHSRS
Large-Scale Voluntary Transfer	LSVT
National Asylum Support Service	NASS
Notice of Proceedings	NOP
Notice of Seeking Possession	NSP
Registered Social Landlords	RSL
Rent Assessment Committee	RAC
Rent Assessment Panel Committee	RAPC
Retail Price Index	RPI
Right to Manage Company	RTM Company
Tenancy Relations Officer	TRO

CHAPTER ONE

The Classes of Occupation

Introduction

1.01 The starting-point of status. The starting-point of any study of housing law is the "status" of a person in premises, that is to say the "class" of occupation he enjoys. In turn, that involves two questions. First, there are classes of occupation rights—or means of identifying when they are absent—which have been developed over many years and are embodied in the common law. This gives us the existing legal concepts on which statutes bite. Moving on from there, the second part of the status issue is to identify within (or across) these common law classes of occupation those to whom the benefits of each body of statutory protection apply.

1.02 Law Commission. It is only when this exercise has been carried out that it is possible to say which substantive right—or duty—binds which occupiers and/or landlords. There is much scope for criticism of such a complex approach to housing rights, and the Law Commission—the body charged with proposing major reforms to the law—has recently issued proposals for a substantially simpler system of "Type I" and "Type 2" rights of occupation, meaning those with full and those with only restricted security, which is intended to do away with some, if not all, of this common law starting-point: see *Renting Homes: The Final Report, Commission Consultation Paper No.297.*

1.03 Two stages. Until that report is accepted, however, it remains necessary to approach status in the two stages described above. In this chapter, we are concerned (only) with the first stage—common law classes of occupation. In the next six chapters, we then consider these classes in the context of the numerous statutes which govern them.

1.04 Principal occupation classes. There are four principal ways in which a person can come to use premises as a residence:

- Owner-occupation;
- Trespass;
- Licence; and
- Tenancy.

1.05 Particular arrangements. In addition, however, there are particular categories or combinations of circumstances, some of which must also be considered:

- Tied accommodation;
- Sub-tenants;
- Joint tenants;
- Tenants of mortgagors;
- Assignees; and
- Change of landlord.

1.06 Minor arrangements. There is also a number of minor arrangements which do not fit comfortably or easily within either the classes of occupation considered in this chapter, or the specific classes of protection considered in the following chapters: for example, "shared ownership", where a person pays "rent" which is partly for use and occupation, and partly towards purchase. There are also "co-ownership" schemes, where member-tenants pay rent, but have an interest in the capital value of, usually, a block of flats. The complexity of such schemes, and the relatively few people affected, put the details of them beyond the scope of this book.

Outline

1.07 Owner-occupation

- Owner-occupiers may have a freehold, long-leasehold or commonhold interest.
- Owner-occupiers may mortgage their homes.
- Jointly owned property is held on trust.
- Trusts may also arise where a person contributes to the purchase, even though he is not the legal (named) owner.

- The courts have powers under the Trusts of Land and Appointment of Trustees Act 1996 to declare the extent of the trust and to order sale of the property.

1.08 Trespass

- Someone occupying a property without permission is a trespasser.

- Trespassers or "squatters" may be given permission to remain, in which case they become licencees.

- A trespasser may become entitled to ownership of the land through the law of adverse possession.

- A new class of trespass—"tolerated trespass"—has been recently identified by the courts in order to cope with those whose landlords have permitted them to remain in occupation after an order for possession has become effective, without re-acquiring their original rights.

- Trespass can sometimes be a criminal offence.

1.09 Licence

- A person with permission to occupy accommodation but who does not have a tenancy will occupy under a licence.

- Licences may arise in a number of circumstances—family arrangements; sharing arrangements; long-stay hotels; hostels; acts of kindness; and, genuine lodging arrangement.

- A tenancy rather than a licence will arise if the occupier has exclusive possession at a term for a rent.

- Even if an agreement is called a licence, it will be a tenancy if these elements are all present.

- Before a licensee can be evicted, the licence must be properly brought to an end; if a fixed-term contractual licence, the fixed-term must expire; if a periodic contractual licence, reasonable notice must be given.

1.10 Tenancy

- Tenancy is the normal arrangement by which one person occupies premises which are owned by another.

- There are four essential elements of tenancy—identifiable parties; identifiable premises; period of tenancy; and, exclusive possession.

- There are two common forms of tenancy—periodic and fixed term.

- A periodic tenancy is one which is granted to run from period to period, e.g. week to week.

- It can be terminated at common law by either the landlord or the tenant serving notice to quit.

- There are strict rules about the content and service of notices to quit.

- A fixed-term tenancy is one which is granted for a specific period of time, e.g. six months.

- It is brought to an end by the period running out.

- Tenancies may also be brought to an end by the tenant surrendering the tenancy but only if the landlord is willing to accept the surrender.

- A fixed-term tenancy can also be terminated before the term has run out, by the landlord obtaining forfeiture of the lease for breach of the agreement.

- Tenants may apply to the court for relief from forfeiture.

1.11 Other circumstances

Tied accommodation

- An occupier of accommodation which is provided in the course of employment may be a service tenant or a service occupier.

- A person living in tied accommodation is a service occupier if it is necessary for him to live in the premises in question in order to carry out the employment duties.

- A service occupier's licence is terminable on the cessation of employment without any requirement of notice.

Sub-tenancies

- Where a tenant's landlord is himself a tenant, the tenant is a sub-tenant; the sub-tenant's landlord is referred to as a mesne (pronounced "mean") tenant.

- Particular difficulties arise for sub-tenants when the mesne tenancy is brought to an end.

- Provided the sub-tenancy is lawful, some statutory protection for sub-tenants is available.

- A sub-tenancy is unlawful if there is a prohibition in the mesne tenancy on sub-letting; prohibitions may be absolute or qualified, i.e. it may require the consent of the head landlord.

- If the mesne tenancy includes a qualified prohibition on sub-letting, the head landlord generally cannot withhold consent unreasonably.

Joint tenants

- A joint tenancy arises where two or more persons share the tenancy.

- Service of a notice to quit by one joint tenant is sufficient to terminate the tenancy.

- Where accommodation is shared, but there is only one named tenant, other occupiers will generally be his sub-tenants or licensees.

- Groups of sharers may occupy under "non-exclusive occupation agreements" which, if genuine, means that they are only licensees.

Tenants of mortgagors

- Tenants of landlords who have mortgaged the property may be evicted by the mortgage company if the company repossesses the property on default of payment by the landlord, and if the tenancy was created in breach of the mortgage deed.

Assignment

- Most tenancies include a prohibition on assignment.

- Where assignment is permitted, certain formalities, including a written document, must be completed for it to be effective.

New landlords

- Where a landlord purchases a property with existing tenants, he takes it subject to those tenancies.

Owner-occupation

1.12   Unmortgaged freehold. A person who owns the freehold of the house in which he lives, untrammelled by any mortgage, is the principal "model" for owner-occupation. Such a person has the fullest rights of occupation and protection of all. The right to occupy the house can only be interfered with in limited circumstances. For example, if a local authority or some other public body should purchase the house compulsorily, perhaps for some new development; or else, if the property falls into considerable disrepair, the local authority might place a closing order or demolition order on the house, as a result of which it will become illegal to live in it.

1.13   Another way in which such an owner-occupier might lose the right of occupation is if he goes into bankruptcy and the trustee in bankruptcy forces the sale of his home. Some of these incidents are outside the scope of this book: prohibition and demolition orders, and clearance by a local authority, are dealt with in Chapter 12. We shall consider one further way in which a freehold owner might come to lose the right to occupy his home, which is as a result of a court order made in the course of the breakdown of a relationship: this is dealt with in Chapter 9.

1.14   Mortgaged freehold. Many people who have a freehold interest in their homes, however, do so under mortgage. A mortgage is a loan against the security of property, i.e. a house or a flat. The money is usually borrowed in order to buy the property, although sometimes it may be needed for carrying out repairs or improvements. Sometimes people raise money by way of mortgage simply because they are in other financial difficulties. If a person falls into arrears with his mortgage repayments, eviction may follow: see Chapter 2.

1.15   Long leaseholders. A freehold interest is one which is unlimited in time: there is no "superior" interest or landlord who can claim the property in the future. The opposite of freehold is the term which is limited in time. Strictly, all such terms are tenancies, whether they are on a lease for 999 years or a periodic weekly tenancy. In practice, however, to treat these last two occupiers in the same class of occupation would fly in the face of reality.

1.16   Accordingly, we include in "owner-occupation" those who do not have a freehold interest in their home, but who have a long leasehold interest, meaning one which is for a term of at least 21 years, which in normal circumstances will have been "bought" by a premium no different in quality (even if somewhat in quantity) than the purchase price paid for the acquisition of a freehold house. The first category of those are leaseholders who have been able to acquire their homes without a mortgage, who will pay what is usually a small, annual ground rent to a landlord, who is, at least in theory, entitled to reclaim the property at the end of the lease.

1.17 Termination. In practice, on the expiry of the lease, most long-leasehold occupiers have rights of occupation similar to those enjoyed by other tenants and, in some circumstances, a leasehold occupier may be able to compel the landlord to sell him the freehold or extend the lease. These rights will also be considered in Chapter 2. If the leaseholder breaches the terms of the lease, however, the landlord may seek to repossess through the forfeiture procedure. This procedure is considered below (1.131–1.146).

1.18 Mortgaged leasehold. Leasehold interests may be held under mortgage, although usually it will not be possible to obtain a mortgage on a leasehold property unless there is at least a 30-year period to run on the lease. This is because mortgage companies need security for their loans and must calculate what they can recover by resale of the property, should the occupier fall into arrears on the mortgage at any given point in time. If the occupier falls into arrears in the last few years, the mortgage company does not have much to resell, although the debt is correspondingly lower. If the occupier falls into arrears soon after the mortgage is granted, there is time enough on the lease for the mortgage company to recoup its loan.

1.19 Leasehold by assignment. Many people do not acquire a leasehold interest directly from the freeholder who originally granted it. They acquire it instead from the existing leaseholder, commonly the existing occupier who is selling his interest. During the course of such a transaction, the freeholder usually has little or nothing to do with the arrangements, save perhaps that his consent to them may be required (but is normally easily obtainable). Where a would-be occupier under leasehold purchases from an outgoing leaseholder, the transaction is called an assignment, but it is in all other respects much like a straightforward purchase. It does not matter how much time there is to run on the lease: the incoming occupier steps into the shoes of the outgoing occupier. It is the length of the interest itself, i.e. the lease, not the length of occupation left under it, which determines the quality of the class of occupation.

1.20 Commonhold. The Commonhold and Leasehold Reform Act 2002 ("CLRA 2002") introduced a new form of ownership for flats. Because of the need to have enforceable agreements about who is to maintain the common parts and provide common services, flats have traditionally been sold on a leasehold basis, with a freeholder owning the common parts and remaining responsible for their upkeep and that of the block, subject to payment of a service charge by the leaseholders. As noted above (1.18), however, this means that leaseholders have a "wasting asset" which may over time become unmortgageable.

1.21 Commonhold association. Under the commonhold system, however, all the common parts of the building are owned by a "commonhold association". The association is a company whose members are the owners of the flats. The flats are then owned on the equivalent of a freehold basis, i.e. without any limitation of time, and may be mortgaged as such (1.14). The rights and obligations of the flat owners and the commonhold association are dealt with in a document called the "commonhold community statement". Commonhold, therefore, is a form of collective freehold, applicable to flats.

1.22 Trust. The common law doctrine of trust deals with the position which arises at law whenever property is held in the name of one person but is intended for the benefit of another. Such property is held on trust, and the ownership is no longer the untrammelled ownership of any other freeholder or leaseholder but is subject to the trust, meaning the purposes of the trust and the interests of the beneficiaries. Property can be held on trust for the benefit of a number of individuals including one of the trustees himself. A person, for example, could buy a house and put it on trust for the use of himself and his spouse and/or children. The person could not subsequently dispose of the property, unless all the beneficiaries consented to the proposed arrangements.

1.23 Trusts of land. Property is automatically considered to be held on trust whenever two or more people own land or premises jointly. Such a trust is now governed by the Trusts of Land and Appointment of Trustees Act 1996 ("TLTA 1996"), which regulates all trusts of land.

1.24 The effect of a trust of land is that any of the joint owners (trustees) can apply to force the property to be sold, even against the wishes of the other party. This is a necessary provision, for the value of a half-share in a house will be non-existent if it is not possible to force a sale at will, nor as a matter of land policy would it be desirable to allow any kind of land—including housing—to be "locked" between parties in dispute. These rights are additional to the special provisions available to married partners, and are of most relevance where people have been cohabiting without being married, or where non-cohabitants purchase property together.

1.25 Powers of the courts. Whenever property is held on trust, or is alleged to be held on trust, the High Court or the county court has power to declare whether or not it is held on trust, and in what proportions or for whose benefit, and can also make orders which affect what should happen to the property in question.

1.26 It is not only the parties who can apply to the High Court, but also someone else with an interest, e.g. a mortgagee (TLTA 1996 s.14). In deciding what order to make (including whether the property should be sold), the court must take into account the following (TLTA 1996 s.15):

- the intention of the person or persons who created the trust;
- the purposes for which the property is held, e.g. is it as a family home?;
- the welfare of any children living in the property; and
- the interests of any mortgagee of the property.

1.27 How trusts arise. A trust sometimes arises under a formal deed. It may also arise if one person buys property, but for the benefit of another. It also arises if one person buys property either wholly or in part with someone else's money. In the case of a house or flat, this might arise because, for example, a woman has made direct contributions such as putting up all or part of the purchase price of the property, or all or part of the deposit on a property purchased under mortgage, or has simply contributed to the mortgage repayments, or if she has contributed to maintenance or improvement of the property in such a way as to increase its value.

1.28 Where there is such a direct contribution, but it was made without any common intention—on the part both of owner and contributor—to share an interest in the property, the trust is known as a resulting trust (*Lloyds Bank Plc v Rosset*, 1991). Where the common intention was that the contribution would result on a share of the property, the trust is known as a constructive trust, even if there was no common intention as to the extent of the shares (*Drake v Whipp*, 1995). A common intention is one that is shared and expressed between the parties, as distinct from an intention which one or other party had in his or her own mind, but that was never communicated to the other (*Springette v Defoe*, 1992).

1.29 Declaration of trust. It follows that if a woman living with a man, whether or not married to him, has made such a direct contribution, the law has power to intervene at a time of break-up, and make an appropriate declaration: for example, that the house is held for the benefit of the woman, or that she has an interest in it—in the case of a resulting trust, proportionate to such direct contributions (*Pettitt v Pettitt*, 1991), and in the case of a constructive trust, proportionate not only to such direct contributions but to indirect contributions such as household expenses (*Gissing v Gissing*, 1971). Other evidence may, however, be available, to suggest that the parties intended shares to be in a proportion other than confined to (direct or indirect) contributions (*Midland Bank Plc v Cooke*, 1995).

Trespass

1.30 Absolute trespass. From those with the greatest rights of occupation to those with the least. A trespasser is one who occupies premises without any permission at all to do so. Permission given by anyone in a position to grant the authority will prevent someone being a trespasser.

1.31 Permission. For example, an owner may obviously give permission to occupy property, but so also may his agent, or a director of a company which owns property, or even someone who is himself no more than a tenant. A tenant is in a position to give permission because so long as his tenancy lasts, it is the tenant, rather than the landlord or the owner, who has possession of the premises. It follows, therefore, that an owner or a landlord could not give someone else permission to occupy premises if he has already let them to a tenant.

1.32 Squatting. Squatting is a common term for occupying property as a trespasser. Sometimes people who enter as squatters are then given permission to remain. There is little popular distinction between those who squat without permission, and those who use short-life property with permission, but there is considerable difference in law: those without permission are trespassers; those who have permission are "licensees" (*GLC v Jenkins*, 1975; see also *Camden LBC v Shortlife Community Housing*, 1992).

1.33 The term "squatter" is not therefore one which it is appropriate to use in discussion of housing law, although in one case in which it was used (*McPhail v Persons Unknown*, 1973) the description given was consistent with trespass, rather than licence. This does not mean that all squatters are trespassers, but simply that if the term is to be used in law, it must be confined to those who squat without permission. As far as possible, the term "squatter" will not be used further in this book.

1.34 Criminal law. Trespassers may be committing criminal offences. These are considered further in Chapter 7.

1.35 Adverse possession. A trespasser can acquire the owner's interest in land if he has been in "adverse possession" of the land for a certain period of time. To be in adverse possession, a trespasser must have both factual possession of the land and an intention to possess it to the exclusion of the whole world, including the legal owner (*Pye v Graham*, 2002). In a residential context, if a trespasser replaces the existing locks to the front door so the owner cannot get in, he takes factual possession and demonstrates the necessary intention (*Lambeth LBC v Blackburn*, 2001). The fact that, if asked to do so, the trespasser would have been willing to pay for his occupation of the land does not show an absence of the requisite intention (*Pye, Blackburn*).

1.36 It is not necessary for the same person or group of persons to be in adverse possession for the whole period. As long as the period of adverse possession is continuous, the adverse possession of successive trespassers may be added together (*Asher v Whitlock*, 1865).

1.37 Tenants. If a tenant, however, takes possession of neighbouring land belonging to his landlord, he is not in adverse possession. Rather, he is said to be "encroaching" on his landlord's land and cannot acquire the landlord's interest (*Smirk v Lyndale Developments Ltd*, 1975).

1.38 Time required. The length of adverse possession required depends in part on whether land is "registered" or "unregistered" land (Land Registration Act 2002), a topic that is outside the scope of this book, although it may be said that most, if not all, urban land is by now registered, as is much rural land.

1.39 Unregistered land. If the land is unregistered land, the trespasser—either by his own or by successive occupation—must establish 12-years adverse possession of the land. If he does so, the owner cannot evict him and the trespasser becomes the owner of the land: Limitation Act 1980 ss.15 and 17. Although the European Court of Human Rights has held that this is a violation of the owner's right to quiet enjoyment of his possessions under Art.1, First Protocol, to the European Convention on Human Rights (*Pye v UK*, 2005), this does not affect the position in domestic law.

1.40 Registered land. The Land Registration Act 2002 ("2002 Act") changed the law in relation to registered land. The provisions of the 2002 Act are not retrospective, so it is necessary to consider the position before and after the date on which the Act came into force (October 13, 2003).

1.41 Pre-October 13, 2003 entitlement. If the trespasser was in adverse possession for 12 years before October 13, 2003, the owner was holding the title to the land on trust for him at that date. On that date, that trust was replaced by both a statutory right to be registered as the owner and a defence to any claim for possession (2002 Act, Sch.12 para.18). The "issue" on any such claim to registration or possession will be the same as in relation to unregistered land—has the trespasser accumulated 12 years of what is properly called adverse possession?

1.42 Post-October 13, 2003 entitlement. If the trespasser cannot establish 12-years adverse possession before October 13, 2003, he must apply to be registered as owner, which he may do after as little as 10-years adverse possession (2002 Act, Sch.6 para.1). The owner then has the option (2002 Act, Sch.6 para.3)—which he will normally take—of asking for the application to be dealt with under a special procedure (2002 Act, Sch.6 para.5), pursuant to which the trespasser will have to show not only adverse possession but one of a limited number of circumstances (to be found in 2002 Act, Sch.6 para.4) amounting to additional reasons as to why he should acquire the title, which are rarely likely to be fulfilled.

1.43 If successful in doing so, the trespasser will be entitled to registration. Even if unsuccessful, if left in occupation the trespasser can apply again after the full 12 years when he will not be required to show the additional circumstances. Usually, however, the trespasser's application after 10 years will prompt the owner to take possession proceedings against the trespasser before expiry of the additional two-year period.

1.44 Tolerated trespassers. In *Burrows v Brent LBC*, 1996, the House of Lords confronted the status of a former local authority tenant against whom a possession order had become effective, but whom the authority allowed to remain in occupation on terms. Such arrangements were—and are—common. Thus, when a tenant falls into arrears of rent, the court may make an order for possession, postponed so long as current rent plus an amount of the arrears is paid, to which terms the tenant may not adhere. In this case, the order will have become effective, but a landlord— particularly a local authority or registered social landlord—may still want to give the tenant "another chance" by way of a new agreement designed to clear the arrears. Even where an outright order is made, the landlord may be willing to do this.

1.45 At common law, such a person could not be described as a trespasser: so long as he complied with the agreement, he had the landlord's express permission to be there. He would therefore be a licensee (1.47). The "policy" difficulty for the courts was that local authority security of tenure applies as much to licensees as tenants (3.19). Accordingly, the House of Lords came up with a new, rather contradictory, term—"tolerated trespass".

1.46 These are mentioned here because of the term used to described them. They are not trespassers in the conventional sense, and it would be misleading—however correct at common law—to continue to refer to them as licensees (in the discussion which follows). They are considered further at 1.58–1.61, below.

Licence

1.47 Permission. While the normal arrangement whereby one person rents, as a home, property belonging to another is that of tenancy (1.93–1.108), there are a number of arrangements of less formality, which are known as licences. The term "licence" means "permission", whether used in connection with housing, driving a car, or selling alcohol (*Thomas v Sorrell*, 1673). In the housing context, it is used to describe one who is not a trespasser (because he has permission to occupy) but who is neither an owner-occupier nor a tenant. Were it not for "licences", there would be no term appropriate for such people as family, friends or casual guests.

1.48 Family. The most common example of licence is a person living in property which is either owned or rented by a member of the family, e.g. a parent. The non-owner, or non-tenant, is in this circumstance in law a licensee. Similarly, a cohabitant is a licensee of his partner, if it is the partner who owns or who is the tenant of the accommodation in which they live.

1.49 Technically, if one spouse is the owner or tenant of the matrimonial home, the other spouse is only his licensee, but it has been held that, both as a matter of practice and as a matter of good taste, it is inappropriate to consider one spouse as the licensee of another (*National Provincial Bank v Ainsworth*, 1965). The special position of both spouses and cohabitants will be considered in the context of break-up of a relationship in Chapter 9.

1.50 Sharing. Some people are quite obviously no more than licensees of another. Common sense dictates that a friend who comes to stay for a while is not to be considered a tenant, while at the same time he cannot be a trespasser because, of course, he is there by the host's invitation. This does not change simply because, for example, the guest is invited to stay for several weeks and even agrees to pay some sort of contribution towards the housekeeping expenses, or indeed, an amount of rent, although at this last stage the agreement is beginning to border on some sort of formal arrangement. Where two people move into accommodation, one named as tenant and the other not, it is likely that the latter will be viewed as no more than a sharer, and therefore licensee, of the other (*Monmouth BC v Marlog*, 1994).

1.51 Long-stay hotel occupation. There are other arrangements, however, where it is less immediately obvious whether a person is to be considered a licensee or a tenant. If someone goes to stay in a hotel for a few days, for example, it would not be considered that he had become a tenant of the hotel. But what if he had made his home over a number of years in the hotel? There are many who live for considerable periods of time in hotels (more commonly cheaper, long-stay hotels), who have nowhere else to live and who regard the hotel as a home. In *Luganda v Service Hotels*, 1969 the Court of Appeal considered that, nonetheless, such an occupier was only a licensee and did not become a tenant. A similar view was reached in *Brillouet v Landless*, 1996.

1.52 Hostels. In the same way, the occupier of a hostel is usually considered a mere licensee, e.g. a YWCA hostel, as in *R. v*

South Middlesex Rent Tribunal Ex p. Beswick, 1976, or one of the many hostels which exist not primarily to provide housing for people, but principally to help those who have had some sort of difficulty, such as drug addicts, mental patients, ex-prisoners, and only secondarily, in order to assist people to reach the point at which they can manage on their own, providing housing for some period or other: *Trustees of the Alcoholic Recovery Project v Farrell*, 1977.

1.53 The distinction which may be drawn between hostels and houses of bedsitting-rooms is that in a hostel there is normally a resident housekeeper or manager, and the occupier is bound to obey rules and regulations which interfere, far more than normal housing management rules do, with the occupier's way of life. See, for example, *Westminster CC v Clarke*, 1992, where a hostel provided accommodation for vulnerable single homeless men.

1.54 Old people's home. *Abbeyfield (Harpenden) Society v Woods*, 1968 affords another example. The society ran an old people's home, consisting of single rooms for which the old people paid a weekly rent. The project could only exist satisfactorily so long as each of the occupiers was self-sufficient. Once an elderly person required constant care and attention, it was no longer possible for him to go on living there. There were no facilities for the provision of such assistance and, clearly, in a house containing nothing but the elderly, the consequences could be serious. It was held that the occupier was a lodger, i.e. a licensee, not a tenant.

1.55 Acts of kindness. Acts of kindness or generosity are not acts from which tenancies spring. In *Booker v Palmer*, 1942, a city family were provided with accommodation in the country during the war. They later suggested that they had become tenants of the property, but the Court of Appeal applied what it termed a "golden rule" of interpretation of such matters: that the courts will not impute intention to enter into legal relations (including tenancy), where the spirit of the arrangement is family or friendly.

1.56 Holding over. This approach found some extension in the case of *Marcroft Wagons v Smith*, 1951. A woman had lived with her parents in a cottage for 50 years. Her father was the original tenant and, on his death, his wife was entitled, by the law then in force, to "succeed" to the tenancy. Only one such succession was, however, permitted, and on the death of her mother the daughter faced eviction. She asked for the tenancy to be granted to her but the landlords refused, though they permitted her to remain in occupation while she found somewhere else to live, during which period they continued to charge her the same weekly rent as her mother had been paying. It was (with some hesitation) held, in effect, that there had similarly been no intention to create a new contract. The court emphasised that this could only be the result where the would-be tenant was already in occupation of the premises at the time at which the arrangement was made; if an arrangement on those lines was offered to someone not living in the premises, this could still constitute a tenancy.

1.57   New tenancy v statutory protection. The result of *Marcroft*, and a number of cases which followed it, has been that when a tenancy came to an end, but the occupier stayed on for a period of time paying a weekly sum of money, the courts have not necessarily assumed a new tenancy agreement. If the reason why the occupier had gone on paying, and the landlord accepting, rent was because there was a statutory right to remain in occupation, i.e. "protection", the courts would assume that what was intended by the payment and acceptance of rent was the exercise of the statutory right to remain, rather than a new contractual tenancy (*Clarke v Grant*, 1950), with whatever statutory consequences the particular legislation has in mind (see Chapters 3–5).

1.58   Tolerated trespass. Where the statutory protection arises under the Housing Act 1985, however, the issues are somewhat different, as such protection attaches to both tenants and licensees (3.19). This was the genesis of the "tolerated trespasser" considered above (1.44), who would otherwise have been a licensee (because allowed to stay on) to whom security would have applied. It is now also likely to be the case that assured tenants under the Housing Act 1988 (Chapter 4) who are allowed to remain in occupation after a possession order becomes effective will be tolerated trespassers (*White v Knowsley Housing Trust*, 2007).

1.59 If the landlord obtains an outright order but allows the tenant to remain in occupation, a new tenancy or licence will only be created if that is what the parties intended to happen—which is unlikely in practice. If there is no such intention, then the former tenant is a tolerated trespasser, although the former tenancy can be revived by an application to the court by either party to vary the possession order (*Burrows v Brent LBC*, 1996).

1.60 In many cases, particularly those concerning rent arrears, the court will make a possession order but postpone the date for possession, so long as the tenant complies with certain conditions specified in the order. If the tenant breaches those terms, his tenancy comes to an end and the landlord can enforce the possession order. If the landlord allows the former tenant to remain in occupation, the former tenant does so as a tolerated trespasser (*Greenwich v Regan*, 1996; *Marshall v Bradford CC*, 2001), unless the circumstances show that a new tenancy has been created.

1.61 A new tenancy with a tolerated trespasser is difficult to establish. Merely allowing the tolerated trespasser to remain in occupation provided payments are made is not sufficient: *Hawkins v Newham LBC*, 2005. In *Lambeth LBC and Hyde Southbank Housing Association v O'Kane*, 2005, no new tenancy had been created, even though the landlord had sent the tolerated trespasser notices of rent increase. In contrast, in *Swindon BC v Aston*, 2005, a new tenancy was entered into where the tenant continued to make payments after he had paid off all the arrears due under the possession order, and the landlord issued him with a new tenancy agreement.

1.62 Disputed right to remain. Even if there was a dispute between the parties as to whether or not the occupier was entitled to remain in occupation, then—even if the occupier continued to pay the rent and the landlord to accept it—the courts might not assume a new tenancy (*Longrigg, Burrough and Trounson v Smith*, 1979).

1.63 The position today is that while it is true that the normal inference to be drawn from payment and acceptance of rent is that there is a tenancy (*Lewis v MTC (Cars)*, 1975; see also *Street v Mountford*, 1986), if there is some particular or peculiar explanation or "special circumstance" why the landlord is leaving an occupier in his premises, and on that account accepting money, other than an agreement to enter into a new contract, the courts remain likely to uphold a finding that there is no tenancy, and consequently only a licence.

1.64 The operative word is "agreement". When a person stays on after the termination of a tenancy without a new tenancy, "rent" is properly called "mesne profits", and landlords frequently declare that money will only be accepted as such, although such a declaration is not decisive as to whether or not a new tenancy has been created. The fact that the payment is called "rent" will also not be decisive (*Westminster City Council v Basson*, 1990).

1.65 Bedsitting-rooms. Returning to cases where there has been no prior tenancy, in *Marchant v Charters*, 1977, there was a house of bedsitting-rooms: each of the occupiers had cooking facilities and equipment in his own room, the rooms were furnished, and the occupiers lived wholly separate lives; that is to say there were no communal facilities. The house was expressed to be let and was actually let "to single men only", and there was a resident housekeeper with whom an arrangement could be made for the provision of evening meals, although this was not an obligatory part of the accommodation arrangement, and was not something agreed to by the occupier in question. None of these circumstances would individually cause the arrangement to be considered only a licence. Indeed, many would have thought that even taken together, there was nothing to distinguish the arrangement from a conventional bedsitting-room letting; such lettings have always been considered to constitute tenancies, rather than licences, and there is nothing exceptionable in the idea of a tenancy of a single room (*AG Securities v Vaughan*, 1988). Nonetheless, it was held that, in the individual circumstances of the case, the occupier was no more than a licensee.

1.66 The end of "intention". At the time, it was said that this was because the parties to the agreement would not have intended a tenancy, with all the formal consequences as to grant of separate possession (below) that this implied. This "intention" test was subsequently rejected by the House of Lords in the important decision of *Street v Mountford*, 1986, which caused a return to a much more traditional approach to the distinction between tenancy and licence, described as lying "in the grant of land"— including housing—"for a term at a rent with exclusive possession". In substance, the House of Lords was reiterating the proposition that "intention" did not mean the wishes or intentions of one or other—or even both—of the parties but the intention that the law would impute to the parties on the basis of the nature of the arrangement they had actually made.

1.67 A term, a rent, exclusive possession. The important statement of principle in *Street* is:

"In the case of residential accommodation there is no difficulty in deciding whether the grant confers exclusive possession. An occupier of residential accommodation at a rent for a term is either a lodger or a tenant. The occupier is a lodger if the landlord provides attendance or services which require the landlord or his servants to exercise unrestricted access to and use of the premises. A lodger is entitled to live in the premises but cannot call the place his own . . .

"If on the other hand residential accommodation is granted for a term at a rent with exclusive possession, the landlord providing neither attendance nor services, the grant is a tenancy; any express reservation to the landlord of limited rights to enter and view the state of the premises and to repair and maintain the premises only serves to emphasise the fact that the grantee is entitled to exclusive possession and is a tenant . . . There can be no tenancy unless the occupier enjoys exclusive possession; but an occupier who enjoys exclusive possession is not necessarily a tenant. He may be owner in fee simple, a trespasser, a mortgagee in possession, an object of charity or a service occupier. To constitute a tenancy the occupier must be granted exclusive possession for a fixed or periodic term certain in consideration of a premium or periodical payments. The grant may be express, or may be inferred where the owner accepts weekly or other periodical payments from the occupier."

1.68 Lodger or tenant? Attendance or services. The sort of attendances or services (see also 5.71–5.75, below) which would mean that the occupier was a lodger rather than a tenant might include daily room-cleaning, emptying of rubbish, changing sheets periodically, the provision of meals (see also 5.77) or other "housekeeping-type" activities (*Huwyler v Ruddy*, 1995).

1.69 Review of earlier decisions. The House of Lords in *Street* also analysed a number of the cases in which licence had been upheld, notwithstanding the grant of exclusive possession. It described *Booker v Palmer* (above) as a case only concerned with intention to create legal relations (rather than intention to create tenancy), and *Marcroft Wagons Ltd v Smith* (above) in the same way. *Abbeyfield (Harpenden) Society v Woods* and *Marchant v Charters* (above) were considered cases of "lodging":

"In order to ascertain the nature and quality of the occupancy and to see whether the occupier has or has not a stake in the room or only permission for himself personally to occupy, the court must decide whether upon its true construction the agreement confers on the occupier exclusive possession. If exclusive possession at a rent for a term does not constitute a tenancy then the distinction between a contractual tenancy and a contractual licence of land becomes wholly unidentifiable."

1.70 The three hallmarks of tenancy. The House of Lords identified three hallmarks of tenancy: exclusive occupation of residential accommodation, payment and term, i.e. periods or length of tenancy:

> "Unless these three hallmarks are decisive, it really becomes impossible to distinguish a contractual tenancy from a contractual licence save by the professed intention of the parties or by the judge awarding marks for drafting . . . The only intention which is relevant is the intention demonstrated by the agreement to grant exclusive possession for a term at a rent. Sometimes it may be difficult to discover whether, on the true construction of an agreement, exclusive possession is conferred. Sometimes it may appear from the surrounding circumstances that there was no intention to create legal relationships. Sometimes it may appear from the surrounding circumstances that the right to exclusive possession is referable to a legal relationship other than a tenancy. Legal relationships to which the grant of exclusive possession might be referable and which would or might negate the grant of an estate or interest in the land include occupancy under a contract for the sale of the land, occupancy pursuant to a contract of employment or occupancy referable to the holding of an office. But where as in the present case the only circumstances are that residential accommodation is offered and accepted with exclusive possession for a term at a rent, the result is a tenancy."

1.71 A fork by any other name. The question is determined not by what name the parties put on the agreement, but by what the agreement is considered to amount to in law:

> "It does not necessarily follow that a document described as a licence is, merely on that account, to be regarded as amounting only to a licence in law. The whole of the document must be looked at and if, after it has been examined, the right conclusion appears to be that, whatever label has been attached to it, it in fact conferred and imposed on the grantee in substance the rights and obligation of a landlord, then it must be given the appropriate effect, that is to say, it must be treated as a tenancy agreement as distinct from a mere licence . . . The important statement of principle is that the relationship is determined by the law, and not by the label the parties choose to put on it . . . is simply a matter of ascertaining the true relationship of the parties." (Jenkins L.J. in *Addiscombe Garden Estates v Crabbe*, 1958.)

1.72 Or, as it was put graphically in *Street*:

"[t]he manufacture of a five-pronged implement for manual digging results in a fork even if the manufacturer, unfamiliar with the English language, insists that he intended to make and has made a spade".

1.73 Paying arrangement. In every case, one should ask whether the arrangement is the normal arrangement by which one person comes to occupy premises belonging to another for use as a home, customarily paying rent in money for the right. If it is, then this is likely to be a tenancy however the parties have described it, and whatever they may have said that their intentions were:

"the courts must pay attention to the facts and surrounding circumstances and to what people do as well as to what people say" (*AG Securities v Vaughan*, 1988).

1.74 Once the occupier is paying for the accommodation, then there must be some overriding reason, such as those illustrated or referred to above or those considered below, which reduces the occupation to that of licence. Strictly, it is not even necessary to pay rent in order to establish that there is a tenancy (see most recently *Ashburn Anstalt v Arnold*, 1989), but the courts tend to look sceptically in this day and age at any arrangement purporting to be tenancy under which no rent is paid (*Heslop v Burns*, 1974) and will only be prepared to treat it as a tenancy if they can find some other consideration.

1.75 Evasion of protection. In addition to these questions, however, a person will be only a licensee if the rights which he has been given are not enough in law to amount to tenancy (*AG Securities v Vaughan*, 1988). The necessary elements of tenancy are considered below (1.95–1.108) and include the grant to the occupier of "exclusive possession" of the premises (1.103–1.108).

1.76 One device by which landlords sought to avoid the impact of Rent Act protection was the agreement which has come to be known as the "non-exclusive occupation agreement". This, too, is considered further below (1.214–1.220), although in practice such schemes have become less common because it is less necessary for landlords to rely on them since the advent of the assured shorthold tenancy under the Housing Act 1988.

1.77 Another device was "rental purchase", whereby a person was allowed into occupation as a licensee, paying money towards purchase but not enjoying the status of owner until the whole of the purchase price has been paid. Such schemes appear now to have fallen into almost total disuse and are therefore not considered.

1.78 Whatever the scheme, however, there is high authority (*AG Securities v Vaughan*, 1988, HL) for the proposition that the courts should lean against "pretences" designed to defeat statutory protection.

1.79 Trespassers, licensees and eviction. A person who is a trespasser but who is subsequently given permission, not amounting to tenancy, to remain on the premises becomes a licensee. A person whose licence is brought to an end becomes, technically, a trespasser. However, most of the recent laws relating to trespass do not affect those who entered as licensees but subsequently became trespassers.

1.80 Some licensees whose licences began before the commencement of Pt 1 of the Housing Act 1988 (January 15, 1989) are entitled to refer their contracts to the Rent Tribunal, which has power to register a reasonable rent for the premises, and which means that a court, and in the case of some now long-standing licences the Tribunal, has power to allow more time to leave premises occupied under licence. This is considered in greater detail in Chapter 6.

1.81 Eviction of licensees. Licensees may be termed "bare licensees", or may be termed "contractual licensees". One who is, by arrangement, paying a fixed sum of money for the right of occupation will be a contractual licensee. A friend, member of the family or cohabitant, even although he may be paying some amount by way of contribution to household expenses, will normally be considered a bare licensee.

1.82 This distinction may be relevant when the question of bringing a licence to an end arises. So long as the licence remains in existence, the licensee not only commits no offence by remaining on the premises, but cannot be turned off them without the person who does so himself committing an offence: see Chapter 7. Once the licence comes to an end, however, the person who is immediately entitled to possession of the premises in question, which may be the owner of the premises, a landlord or may even be only a tenant of the premises, can reclaim possession from the former licensee, save in the case of a licence which attracts security of tenure under the Housing Act 1985 (3.19).

1.83 In most circumstances, it is necessary to obtain a court order before evicting the former licensee, and an offence is committed if this is not done; in other circumstances, it may not be necessary to obtain a court order: see Chapters 7 and 8. But unless the licence has been duly brought to an end, the person who seeks possession is not entitled to reclaim it, with or without court proceedings.

1.84 Fixed-term licences. There are a few arrangements which may be described as "fixed-term" licences. That is to say, the period for which the right of occupation has been granted is fixed in advance. These arrangements require no notice to be given to bring them to an end because, in effect, the notice has been given at the outset of the arrangement.

1.85 Non-fixed term licences. Most licences, however, are not for a fixed period but exist from week to week, even from day to day, or perhaps as much as from month to month. In such cases, it is necessary to give notice in order to bring the arrangement to an end. It may be that some agreement about the length or form of notice has been reached while arranging the licence in the first place, e.g. one month's notice in writing. This is not a necessary element of a licence. If there is such an agreement, it would indicate that the licence was a contractual, not a bare licence. If there is such an agreement in force, then the licence cannot be determined except in accordance with it, for the law will not support a breach of contract (*Winter Garden Theatre (London) v Millennium Productions*, 1947).

1.86 Reasonable notice. Whether or not there is such agreement, however, the law additionally implies into every licence, whether bare or contractual, a term that it will not be brought to an end without "reasonable notice" being given. This means that a licence agreement which contractually provided for, e.g. one day's notice, would not be brought to an end in one day, unless the law considered one day a reasonable time (*Minister of Health v Belotti*, 1944).

1.87 Written notice. In the case of a periodic licence of a dwelling, other than in the case of what is called an "excluded licence" (8.22), the law now requires written notice of a minimum period of four weeks, which contains specified information. The information is the same as for a notice to quit for tenancies (see 1.124).

1.88 Reasonable time. What is a reasonable time is a question of fact. It will depend upon many circumstances: how long the licensee has been in occupation, how much furniture or property he has in the premises, size of family, what alternative arrangements have been or could be made, even the time of day or night could affect it. In addition, behaviour may affect what the law views as a reasonable time for determination of a licence. A violent licensee will not be given much time at all, e.g. a violent man who is cohabiting with the woman who is the tenant or owner-occupier cannot expect a matter of weeks in which to leave, even if he has lived in the property for years.

1.89 Alternative requirements. The rule may be shortly stated in this way: a licensee is entitled to a reasonable period of notice or a contractually agreed period of notice, or in the case of a periodic licence which is not an "excluded licence" (8.22) four weeks' notice, whichever is the longest. In most cases (other than excluded licences), court proceedings for eviction are required: see Chapter 8.

1.90 Alternative procedures. Proceedings in the civil courts are governed by the Civil Procedure Rules ("CPR"). CPR Pt 55 sets out the procedure for possession proceedings. A claim against a former licensee may be brought by ordinary possession action, or by a special, speedy form of procedure originally intended for trespassers, but also applicable to former licensees: CPR r.55.1(a). If these speedy proceedings are used, then the person seeking to evict the former licensee must establish that the licence had come to an end before the application was issued at the court (*GLC v Jenkins*, 1975). If normal proceedings are used, however, it is enough to show that the licence has expired by the time of the court hearing.

1.91 Licences and estoppel. In some cases, a rather different form of licence may be created which cannot be terminated but continues for the life of the occupier. This may occur where the occupier has incurred expenditure or otherwise acted to his detriment, in the belief that he had a right or interest in the property, and the owner of the land has encouraged that belief, so creating what is known as an estoppel. Thus, for example, an owner of a house may let a son into occupation, lead him to believe that the property will one day be transferred to him, and—in reliance on that belief—the son may expend money improving the property. In such circumstances, a trust will not arise because there is no intention to create an interest, nor a contribution to the purchase price (see 1.27). Instead, it is said that the father is "estopped" from denying the son's right to occupy.

1.92 Once the estoppel is established, it may be enforced by recognition of an irrevocable licence to occupy (*Inwards v Baker*, 1965; *Matharu v Matharu*, 1994). Where it becomes impossible for the licence for life to continue, e.g. because of an irretrievable breakdown in relations between the licensee and an owner with whom he is sharing the house, the courts adopt a flexible approach and seek the minimum equity to do justice (*Baker v Baker*, 1993).

Tenancy

1.93 The normal arrangement. Tenancy is the normal arrangement by which one person comes to occupy premises which are owned by another (see, generally, above 1.62–1.69, where the distinction between tenancy and licence is considered). It is customarily granted in exchange for a monetary payment, rent. It has been said (1.74) that this is not an essential element of tenancy but, except in the context of service tenancy (1.115–1.167), it is so likely that an arrangement under which no rent is paid will be considered a mere licence that this point will not be considered further here. Where someone has been a tenant, but stays on, whether this is because of a new tenancy or a mere licence, will have to be considered (1.56).

1.94 Landlord's interest. A tenancy may be created even where the landlord does not himself have a tenancy of the land but only a licence to occupy it, provided the hallmarks of a tenancy are present: *Bruton v London & Quadrant Housing Trust*, 1999. Thus in *Bruton*, the landlord only had a licence to occupy the land, and under the terms of the licence was not permitted to grant tenancies. The agreement entered into with the occupier had been said to be a licence. It was nonetheless held to be a tenancy because it gave exclusive possession of the premises to the occupier (1.103).

1. ESSENTIAL QUALITIES OF TENANCY

1.95 Four qualities. There are four essential qualities which will establish the existence of a tenancy. If one or more of them is missing, then the arrangement cannot be a tenancy, and for this reason will be that of a licence (*AG Securities v Vaughan*, 1988). The four qualities are as follows.

(i) *Identifiable parties*

1.96   A landlord and a tenant.   There must be a landlord and a tenant. This does not mean that the tenant must know the identity of the landlord, for this is frequently unknown, where, for example, agents have granted the tenancy on behalf of the landlord. It means that a person cannot be a tenant either of himself, or of premises or land which have no owner (*Rye v Rye*, 1962).

1.97   A person can, however, be a tenant of a company of which he is a director, or an employee, or even the major shareholder, and a person can be a tenant of a partnership of which he is one of the partners. In such a situation, it would be wrong to refer to the tenant alone as the owner: he is only the owner when taken together with the other partners. The same applies to trustees or joint owners (*Rye*).

(ii) *Identifiable premises*

1.98   A tenancy of premises.   There must be premises of which to constitute a tenancy. These premises can be as little as a single room, or as much as hundreds of acres of land. It is not, however, possible to be a tenant of only part of some premises, e.g. a shared room.

1.99   It is possible to be a joint tenant with another of premises (1.198–1.212), but if genuinely separate agreements have been independently reached with the landlord conferring a separate right to occupy on separate persons, e.g. a room, this cannot be tenancy because there is no identifiable part of the premises of which to have a tenancy. Even if the two—or more—individuals occupying were to divide up the room between themselves, they would still have to have access to the door in common.

1.100   In this connection it is important, however, to bear in mind the possibility that the arrangement may not be genuine, i.e. may be a sham (1.216–1.220).

(iii) *Period of tenancy*

1.101   Tenancy and time.   One cannot have a tenancy in respect of which there is no period of time involved. That is exactly what tenancy is: a slice of time in the exclusive use of the premises belonging to another. There must be both an ascertainable date of commencement, and an ascertainable period for which it is to run, both of which must be capable of being established before the lease takes effect (*Prudential Assurance Co Ltd v London Residuary Body*, 1992).

1.102 The need to identify the period of the tenancy does not mean that a tenancy cannot in practice be granted for an indefinite time, which is normally what happens when a periodic tenancy is granted. In these cases, the period for which the tenancy has been granted is the time of the periodic tenancy, e.g. one week, but the tenancy is automatically renewed from week to week until determined by notice to quit (see 1.113, below). If not periodic, tenancies must be of a fixed term, e.g. six or twelve months, or five years.

(iv) *Exclusive possession*

1.103 The tenant's use. Exclusive possession means that the arrangement in fact conveys to the tenant the use to the exclusion of all others of the premises in question. Exclusive possession is the most important, and on occasion (albeit now only rarely) the hardest to establish of the four essential qualities of tenancy. It is hard to establish because even a licensee can have exclusive occupation of premises and yet be considered no more than licensee, as in the circumstances described above (1.47).

1.104 Rights of entry. Exclusive use is not destroyed because the landlord retains some right to visit—for example, to inspect for disrepair, or to collect the rent—nor, for example, because under the terms of the tenancy the landlord provides cleaning of the premises, and a cleaner has occasional access to the premises to carry out his duties. Such functions are visits to the premises, or services performed to or in the premises, but they are not use of them. Indeed the express reservation of a right to enter for limited purposes emphasises that the occupier has exclusive possession: *Bruton v London & Quadrant Housing Trust*, above.

1.105 Unrestricted access. If, however, the extent of services is such that the access has to be unrestricted, i.e. not limited to particular times or occasions, the arrangement will be that of lodging, a form of licence (see 1.68).

1.106 The control test. It may be that in the normal management of a hotel or hostel, the landlord reserves the right to shift occupiers from room to room, as the occasion may demand. If so, the occupier cannot be described as having exclusive possession of the premises, even though he may have exclusive use of whatever room he is occupying for the time being. This is the "control" test: because the landlord controls even the internal use of the premises, the tenant cannot be described as having exclusive possession.

1.107 Sham. It is at this quality of tenancy that landlords have directed the most concerted attacks. The reservation of a right for the landlord himself to use the premises, not merely to visit them, or else a right to put some other person in to use them, would, if a genuine term of the arrangement, effectively destroy the idea of exclusive possession (*Somma v Hazelhurst*, 1978). Today, however, the courts are much quicker and more astute to appreciate that such terms may not be genuine but are a "sham" or "pretence" designed to avoid the protection that attaches to tenancies. In that case, the courts will not uphold the term (see 1.78).

1.108 Possession against all. If exclusive, possession is exclusive as against the whole world, including the person who granted the tenancy, so that even a landlord commits a wrong by contravening his tenant's exclusive possession without permission. Such a wrong is a trespass and is dealt with below (8.88–8.92).

2. PRINCIPAL TYPES OF TENANCY

1.109 Periodic and fixed-term tenancy. There are two main forms of tenancy: periodic tenancies and fixed-term tenancies. A periodic tenancy is one which is granted to run from period to period, e.g. week to week or month to month. A fixed-term tenancy is one which is granted for a specific period of time, e.g. three months, six months, or a year.

1.110 Need for writing. Neither sort of tenancy needs to be in writing, except for a fixed-term tenancy in excess of three years (Law of Property Act 1925 s.54(2)).

3. IDENTITY OF LANDLORD

1.111 Weekly tenancy. A landlord under a weekly tenancy (but no other) is obliged to provide a rent book or similar document, and commits a criminal offence if he does not do so (Landlord and Tenant Act 1985 ss.4, 7). Under that Act, any tenant can, in writing, ask the person who last received rent under the tenancy for the full name and address of the landlord. If the person to whom the demand is made fails to reply, also in writing, within 21 days, he commits an offence. This may be important information if, for example, the tenant wants to commence proceedings against an absentee landlord and cannot do so without first establishing his identity. Both of these offences should be reported to the council's Tenancy Relations Officer: see Chapter 8.

1.112 All tenancies. Under the Landlord and Tenant Act 1987 s.48, all landlords of premises which are, or include, dwellings must provide the tenant by notice with an address in England or Wales at which tenants' notices may be served on him, until compliance with which duty rent is not due: the notice must be in writing, but may be by means of inclusion in a tenancy agreement, or in a rent book (*Rogan v Woodfield Building Services Ltd*, 1994).

4. TERMINATION OF TENANCIES

1.113 Termination of periodic tenancy. The normal way a periodic tenancy is brought to an end is by service of a valid notice to quit.

1.114 Notice to quit and periodic tenancies. Notice to quit a tenancy is a formal and technical document, to which old common law rules apply, as well as modern regulations introduced by legislation. Notice to quit can be given by either landlord or tenant, although it is uncommon for a tenant to give notice to quit with sufficient degree of accuracy for it to qualify as such.

1.115 Invalid notice. An invalid notice to quit may be treated as valid by the party who receives it, at least in so far as the technicalities of the common law are concerned, and a landlord who receives an invalid notice from the tenant may treat this as a surrender. If the tenant subsequently changes his mind about departing, whether after notice to quit or surrender, the landlord will still have to take court proceedings to evict him and might not be able to do so (5.151).

1.116 Requirements of notice to quit. All notices to quit residential tenancies, other than "excluded tenancies" which began on or after the commencement of Pt 1 of the Housing Act 1988 (January 15, 1989) must be in writing, must be of a minimum length of four weeks (Protection from Eviction Act 1977 s.5; *Hounslow LBC v Pilling*, 1993), and must expire on either the last day or the first day of a period of the tenancy. The meaning of "excluded tenancy" is considered in Chapter 8 (8.20).

1.117 The final condition—expiry on last or first day of tenancy—is derived from the common law, as is the provision that the notice must also be of at least one full period's length of tenancy, so that a four-week notice to quit a monthly tenancy would be invalid, as a month is longer than four weeks. However, only six months' notice is required to terminate a yearly periodic tenancy. The four weeks include day of service or day of expiry (*Schnabel v Allard*, 1967). The rent day is normally the first day of the tenancy, in the absence of evidence that it is another day.

1.118 Saving clauses. A notice to quit which is of insufficient length will not become valid at a later, correct time, but will be wholly invalid. Because of this need for accuracy, many notices to quit, especially those from landlords to tenants, add a saving clause, which will read something like this: ". . . on the 13th day of December 2001 or at the end of the period of your tenancy expiring next four weeks after service of this notice upon you".

1.119 Such a saving clause is valid and if December 13, 2001 was neither the first nor the last day of a period of the tenancy, the notice to quit would take effect on the next of those two possible days, four weeks after service.

1.120 Service of notice to quit. Service of a notice to quit has to be personal. Most service is effected by post, although some service is carried out by leaving it at the premises. It is not validly served until the tenant himself receives it, or it is left with a tenant's spouse or some other person who may be treated as the tenant's agent for this purpose, i.e. someone left by the tenant in possession or control of the premises (*Harrowby v Snelson*, 1951).

1.121 If the tenancy itself expressly requires service of a notice to quit in order to determine it, however, it will be sufficient if the notice is left at the last known place of abode of the tenant (Law of Property Act 1925 s.196; *Wandsworth LBC v Attwell*, 1995; *Enfield LBC v Devonish*, 1996). The Local Government Act 1972 s.233, which permits postal service of notices required or authorised to be given "by or under any enactment", does not apply to common law notices to quit (*Enfield*).

1.122 Contents of notice to quit. A notice to quit must identify the premises which are the subject of the tenancy, so that a notice given for the wrong address will be invalid. Minor defects in description, such as specifying a back garden that does not exist, are unlikely to invalidate the notice; and if a notice to quit identifies the wrong address, it may be validated by a covering letter sent to the right one. In one case, a notice to quit two rooms was held invalid where the tenant was tenant of only one (*Jankovitch v Petrovitch*, 1977).

1.123 The notice must be addressed to the tenant, although if only the first name is wrong this will not be enough to invalidate it. It may be enough to specify only one of two or more joint tenants (1.198–1.212) and it is certainly enough to serve one only of the joint tenants. The notice must also state that it is given by or on behalf of the landlord, unless it is given by an agent acting in the normal course of his business on the landlord's behalf when serving the notice.

1.124 Prescribed information. In addition, a notice to quit from a landlord to a tenant must contain certain specified information, also in writing. Without this information the notice is invalid. The information is as follows (by virtue of the Notices to Quit, etc. (Prescribed Information) Regulations 1988 (SI 1998/2201)) although it does not have to be in the same form of words and will not be invalid if the different wording from earlier regulations is used (*Beckerman v Durling*, 1981; *Swansea CC v Hearn*, 1990):

(a) If the tenant or licensee does not leave the dwelling, the landlord or licensor must get an order for possession from the court before the tenant or licensee can lawfully be evicted. The landlord or licensor cannot apply for such an order before the notice to quit or notice to determine has run out.

(b) A tenant or licensee who does not know if he has any right to remain in possession after a notice to quit or a notice to determine runs out or is otherwise unsure of his rights, can obtain advice from a solicitor. Help with all or part of the cost of legal advice and assistance may be available under the Legal Aid Scheme. He should also be able to obtain information from a Citizen's Advice Bureau, a Housing Aid Centre, a rent officer or a Rent Tribunal Office.

1.125 Special procedures for Housing Act secure, assured, and introductory tenancies. Note that the termination of a Housing

Act secure (public sector) tenancy (Chapter 3), of a Housing Act assured tenancy (Chapter 4), of an assured shorthold and of an introductory (public sector) tenancy (Chapter 6) are by their own special, and different, procedures. Termination is by the court, and different notice provisions apply.

1.126 Termination of fixed-term tenancy. The normal way a fixed-term tenancy comes to an end is because the time runs out.

1.127 Surrender. As well as notice to quit and expiry of fixed term, another common way of bringing a tenancy to an end is for the tenant to "surrender" it. It occurs, commonly, when a tenant wants to leave accommodation before the end of a fixed term and if so, will commonly conform to the legal requirement that a formal declaration of surrender be drawn up.

1.128 Surrender can also, however, happen by operation of law if the tenant performs some unequivocal act of surrender, such as returning the keys to the landlord, or removing from the premises all signs of occupation, including furniture, belongings and any family or friends—or animals—who were living with him (*Chamberlain v Scalley*, 1992). This may happen in the case of either a fixed-term or periodic tenancy, but it is most common in the latter case, when a periodic tenant wishes to quit without going through the formality of serving notice to quit.

1.129 In deciding whether there has been such an unequivocal act of surrender, the subjective intentions of the tenant, e.g. as to whether they intend to give up their rights to the tenancy are irrelevant; it is the objective conduct which is crucial (*Zionmor v Islington LBC*, 1997).

1.130 Acceptance of act. It is an essential feature of surrender by operation of law that the landlord accepts the acts as acts of surrender. The landlord is not obliged to do so and can continue to consider the tenant liable for rent and other responsibilities in the premises. Abandonment of occupation may be considered a surrender (*R. v Croydon LBC Ex p. Toth*, 1988), but only where the landlord unequivocally accepts it as such (*Preston BC v Fairclough*, 1982). The landlord's conduct as a whole must be taken into account (*Brent LBC v Sharma*, 1992). The grant of a new tenancy to someone else will evidence acceptance of a surrender of the previous tenancy (*Tower Hamlets LBC v Ayinde*, 1994). There can even be surrender, by clear agreement, without quitting occupation (*Dibbs v Campbell*, 1988).

1.131 Forfeiture. The other common way of bringing a tenancy to an end, and one which is also normally only used in connection with fixed-term tenancies, is forfeiture. It may be used in cases of fairly short fixed terms, e.g. 12 months, and also in cases of long leases (1.15).

1.132 There can be no forfeiture unless it is provided for in the tenancy agreement or lease. Forfeiture is commonly something the landlord can claim has occurred automatically once rent has been in arrears for a stated period of time, e.g. 14 days. It can also be part of an agreement that forfeiture will occur if some other breach of the tenancy takes place.

1.133 Re-entry. When there is a forfeiture in this way, the landlord claims to "re-enter" the premises, although he cannot in fact do so because of the rules governing eviction of residential tenants, and it is therefore effected by proceedings for possession. A court has power to order "relief" from forfeiture, if the breach of the tenancy has been remedied, e.g. arrears of rent have been paid off.

1.134 Service and administration charges. In the case of long leases, forfeiture is often invoked for the non-payment of service or administration charges. Forfeiture in such cases is now prohibited unless the amount of the charge has been agreed or admitted by the tenant or has been determined by a court, by a leasehold valuation tribunal or by arbitration (Housing Act 1996 s.81).

1.135 Breach of other term. Likewise, landlords of long leaseholders (1.15) cannot seek forfeiture unless the fact that there has been a breach of the lease has been admitted by the tenant or has been determined by a court, by a leasehold valuation tribunal or by arbitration (CLRA 2002 s.168).

1.136 Relief from forfeiture. All forfeitures of residential premises in which anyone is living must be by way of court proceedings (Protection from Eviction Act 1977). This includes forfeiture of tenancies of premises which are partly commercial and partly residential (*Patel v Pirabarakan*, 2006). It is normally in the course of these proceedings that relief is sought.

1.137 Where the forfeiture is for a reason other than arrears of rent, a preliminary notice must be served, identifying the breach, calling for remedy (if the breach is remediable) and demanding compensation (where applicable) (Law of Property Act 1925 s.146).

1.138 The courts are chary of laying down general principles governing relief (*Hyman v Rose*, 1912), although remedying the breach will usually be necessary, and will invariably be so if the breach is non-payment of rent (*Barton, Thompson & Co v Stapling Machines Co*, 1966), though time will be allowed in which to do this. There can be no relief from forfeiture for breach of a covenant not to use premises for an immoral purpose (*British Petroleum Pension Trust Ltd v Behrendt*, 1986). Relief from forfeiture is not available to a Housing Act assured tenant (*Artesian Residential Developments Ltd v Beck*, 1999; see 4.74).

1.139 Waiver. There will be no entitlement to forfeit if the breach has been waived, e.g. waiver of illegal sub-letting (*Cornillie v Saha*, 1996; see 1.179).

1.140 Effect of relief. Relief may be granted in the High Court, if that is where the forfeiture proceedings are brought, but may also be granted in the county court. The effect of relief is to reinstate the lease as if there had been no forfeiture (*Hynes v Twinsectra Ltd*, 1995; *Rexhaven Ltd v Nurse*, 1995). Relief may be granted in relation to only part of the premises that are subject of the lease (*GMS Syndicate v Elliott (Gary) Ltd*, 1982).

1.141 Arrears and relief. Where proceedings are brought in the county court, and the breach in question is non-payment of rent (including service charges explicitly reserved as rent in the lease— *Sinclair Gardens Investment (Kensington) Ltd v Walsh*, 1995), there is automatic relief if all the arrears and the costs of the action are paid into court at least five days before the hearing; otherwise, the order for possession must provide at least four weeks before it takes effect, and there will again be automatic relief if all the rent and costs are paid into court. These provisions do not apply if the forfeiture is for, or also for, any other breach (County Courts Act 1984 ss.138–140).

1.142 If not obtained automatically, relief for arrears may still be available, as a matter of discretion, on an application made within six months of execution, i.e. even if afterwards (s.138). Unless s.138 is complied with, all other relief is barred.

1.143 While relief—including for non-payment of rent—may also be sought in the High Court (Supreme Court Act 1981 s.38), that procedure cannot be used to secure relief after execution, so as to circumvent the six-month limitation (*Di Palma v Victoria Square Property Co Ltd*, 1985).

1.144 Relief—automatic or after execution—under s.138 may also be sought by a sub-lessee, who likewise cannot circumvent its provisions by seeking relief (outside the six-month period) by application to the High Court (*United Dominions Trust v Shellpoint Trustees*, 1993).

1.145 Long leaseholders and arrears. The CLRA 2002 s.167 limits forfeiture of long leases (1.17) for arrears of rent, service or administration charges. If the amount of arrears is less than £350 or has been owed for less than three years, the landlord will not be permitted to exercise his right of re-entry or forfeiture.

1.146 Relief and disrepair. There is additional power to apply for relief from a s.146 notice which is concerned with an alleged failure to comply with a covenant requiring internal decorative repairs (Law of Property Act 1925 s.147). In the case of a lease of at least seven years, with at least three years left to run, the Leasehold Property (Repairs) Act 1938 prevents forfeiture for such a breach without the prior leave of the court (11.129).

5. EVICTION OF TENANTS

1.147 Although at the end of a tenancy a tenant becomes, in strict common law, a trespasser, this is so untrue in practice as to be deceptive.

1.148 Housing Act secure and assured tenants. It has already been noted (1.125) that these tenancies cannot be terminated except by an order of the court, which will also govern the eviction itself.

1.149 Rent Act protected tenants. A tenant who is a Rent Act protected tenant becomes a statutory tenant on termination of the contractual tenancy and, in effect, can remain on in the premises indefinitely, or subject only to proof of one of a limited number of sets of circumstances, until a court orders him to leave: see Chapter 5.

1.150 Rent Act restricted tenants. A Rent Act restricted tenant is one who can refer his tenancy to the Rent Tribunal, in respect of rent registration, and who may also be able to secure some temporary relief from eviction, either from a court or from the Tribunal (6.104–6.138).

1.151 Other tenants. The general position of tenants who are neither Housing Act secure, Housing Act introductory, Housing

Act assured, Rent Act protected, nor Rent Act restricted, is considered in Chapter 7. With the exception of "excluded tenants" (8.20) whose tenancies began on or after the commencement (January 15, 1989) of Pt 1 of the Housing Act 1988, all tenants, therefore including this residual class, are protected from eviction without due process of law, i.e. without a court decision which orders them to leave (Protection from Eviction Act 1977 ss.1–3, as amended): see Chapter 8.

Other circumstances

1.152 In addition to the main common-law classes of occupation, there are a number of other circumstances which we must now consider. These are:

1. Tied accommodation;
2. Sub-tenants;
3. Joint tenants;
4. Tenants of mortgagors;
5. Assignees; and
6. New of landlords.

1. TIED ACCOMMODATION

1.153 Job-related accommodation. Many people who live in premises they do not own are occupying accommodation which "goes with the job". Such people are not merely the obvious classes of service occupier or tenant, such as resident housekeepers, porters, au pairs, live-in help, caretakers, etc. but also people such as the managers of pubs and many who work in off-licences, and employees of some industries and of local authorities, who may, e.g. offer accommodation to key workers, such as teachers and social workers, as an inducement to work in particular areas. The accommodation is often job-related and the right to it customarily ends when the job itself is brought to an end.

1.154 This section is concerned only with accommodation which is job-related, and not with accommodation offered as an inducement but which is not otherwise tied contractually to the employment.

1.155 An additional test. Job-related accommodation poses particular problems in terms of housing law. Clearly, occupiers are not trespassers, nor of course are they owner-occupiers, and so they must, of definition, be either tenants or licensees. There are, however, particular tests which apply to this distinction when job-related accommodation is in question, which are additional to those already discussed (1.47–1.108).

1.156 A person might appear to qualify as a tenant by application of one of the particular, job-related tests, and yet lack one of the four essential qualities of tenancy, or else be a licensee for some other reason, e.g. because on taking up new employment in a strange area, the employer offered to provide temporary accommodation as a pure favour. Unless, however, one of the prior tests applies, then the test which follows will determine whether occupation is by way of tenancy or licence.

1.157 A job-related occupier who is a licensee is called a "service occupier", while one who is a tenant is called a "service tenant".

1.158 A single arrangement. In all these circumstances, it is assumed that the employment and the housing arrangements were reached as part of an overall package and are connected. It is entirely possible that a tenant subsequently becomes his landlord's employee. The tenancy would not then normally become a service tenancy, any more than it would if someone subsequently rented accommodation from his employer.

1.159 It is possible, however, that a landlord who has become someone's employer will offer a new arrangement which, if accepted, could become one of a licence (*Scrimgeour v Waller*, 1980). In deciding whether the new arrangement is valid, the courts will not take into account the inequality of bargaining power between the parties (*Mathew v Bobbins*, 1980), although they will recognise that a mere statement of intention is not binding, and may have been signed by the occupier because he had little choice (*AG Securities v Vaughan*, 1988).

1.160 A number of recent cases involving tied accommodation have concerned changes in circumstances, but these have been in the context of rights under the Housing Act 1985, which are available both to tenants and licensees, so that these cases do not address the fundamental, common law distinction (3.19).

1.161 The test of necessity. A person living in job-related accommodation will be a service occupier if it is necessary for him to live in the premises in question in order to carry out the employment duties (*Smith v Seghill Overseers*, 1875; *Street v Mountford*, 1986), or—at least—if it is a requirement of the contract of employment that he do so, and that requirement is imposed at the least for the better performance of employment duties (*Fox v Dalby*, 1874; *Glasgow Corp v Johnstone*, 1965), not merely as an arbitrary regulation, or whim, on the part of the employer (*Gray v Holmes*, 1949).

1.162 The fact that it is merely convenient for the employee to reside in the premises in question is not sufficient to make it for the better performance of his duties (*Ford v Langford*, 1949; *Chapman v Freeman*, 1978).

1.163 If neither of the factors above applies, then the occupier will normally be a service tenant.

1.164 Agricultural and forestry workers. Employees who occupy tied accommodation in agriculture and forestry occupy a peculiar position of privilege. Briefly, given certain qualifications—including length of employment in agriculture or forestry (but not necessarily with the same employer)—and despite the fact that they would normally qualify as service occupiers, they may come to enjoy full Housing Act 1988 security as if they had Housing Act assured tenancies (Chapter 4), or Rent Act protection as if they had tenancies (Chapter 5).

1.165 Tied accommodation and rent. One common problem which occurs in connection with occupiers of tied accommodation lies in establishing whether or not they are paying rent for their accommodation. Some will actually be doing so, i.e. they will be handing over a sum of money which will normally be entered as received in a rent book. Others may have an agreement as to how much rent they are paying for their accommodation, but this may be deducted from their wages at source. So long as the amount is quantified, they will still be treated as paying rent even if it is deducted at source (*Montagu v Browning*, 1954).

1.166 Others may not have any agreed quantification of rent but receive lower wages than they would normally get for the job in question on account of the provision of accommodation. Whether rent is actually being paid or not should not affect whether they are considered tenants or licensees, contrary to the normal presumption that one who pays no rent is not a tenant (*Heslop v*

Burns, 1974), but it may affect whether or not they can enjoy statutory protection (4.31, 5.82).

1.167 Tied accommodation and termination. A service licence which is expressly terminable on the cessation of employment comes to an end without any requirement of notice (*Ivory v Palmer*, 1975). Notice in accordance with the Protection from Eviction Act 1977 (1.124) is not, therefore, required (*Norris v Checksfield*, 1991).

2. SUB-TENANTS

1.168 Mesne tenants. It is entirely possible that a person's landlord is himself no more than a tenant of another. In such a case, the "middle" tenant is known as a "mesne" (pronounced "mean") tenant, and the "lower" tenant as the sub-tenant.

1.169 Many more people are sub-tenants than realise it. In strict law, the owner who holds only on a long lease is a tenant, although has been considered here as an owner-occupier (1.15–1.16). There are major property holdings still in existence in which the interests are all held on leasehold. Indeed, it is not only possible but common for there to be many "intervening" interests by way of superior leasehold between an actual occupier and the ultimate freeholder.

1.170 Continuation of mesne tenancy. So long as the mesne tenancy continues to exist, the sub-tenant is in no different a position than any other tenant. His landlord (the mesne tenant) must serve notice to quit in the normal way, and the sub-tenancy may fall into any of the classes of protection which will be discussed in Chapters 3–6. The position remains the same even when the mesne tenant is a Rent Act protected tenant (Chapter 5) and his contractual tenancy comes to an end. The mesne tenant becomes what is known as a statutory tenant, but the sub-tenant is in practice unaffected by this unless, or until, the mesne tenant's statutory tenancy is determined.

1.171 Termination of mesne tenancy. Difficulties arise once the mesne tenant's interest comes to an end. In such a case, the question to be decided is whether the sub-tenant has any right to remain in occupation as against the superior landlord. This will depend upon two main factors:

1. whether there is statutory protection afforded to the sub-tenant (Chapters 4 and 5); and
2. whether or not the sub-tenancy is a legal or illegal sub-tenancy.

1.172 Sub-tenants and statutory protection: Housing Act 1988. In the case of a Housing Act assured tenancy (Chapter 4), it is unlikely that both mesne and sub-tenant will be Housing Act assured because they may both live in the same building (4.44–4.51). Otherwise, a Housing Act assured sub-tenant will become the tenant of a superior landlord if:

• the mesne tenancy is determined, and

• at the time the mesne tenancy comes to an end, the sub-tenancy is legal, even if the mesne tenancy was not Housing Act assured, unless

• the landlord is one whose tenants are not normally Housing Act assured (Housing Act 1988 s.18; see 4.41).

1.173 Sub-tenants and statutory protection: Rent Act 1977. In the case of a Rent Act protected tenant (Chapter 5), it may likewise be the case that the mesne tenant and sub-tenant live in the same building, so that the sub-tenant will not be Rent Act protected (5.43). If:

(a) both mesne tenant and sub-tenant are protected by the Rent Act, however, as can arise, (e.g. in the case of an older letting—see 5.60), and

(b) at the time the mesne tenancy comes to an end, the sub-tenancy is legal, the sub-tenant will become the tenant of the landlord directly (Rent Act 1977 s.137).

1.174 A sub-tenant who is not a Rent Act protected sub-tenant (*Stanley v Compton*, 1951), or one who is an illegal sub-tenant, whether or not Rent Act protected, cannot take advantage of Rent Act 1977 s.137 in order to become the tenant of the landlord direct.

1.175 The fact that the mesne tenant is himself not a Rent Act protected tenant but, e.g. a Housing Act secure tenant (Chapter 3), does not affect the position as between mesne and sub-tenant (*Lewis v Morelli*, 1948; *Stratford v Syrett*, 1958) but does mean that the Rent Act 1977 s.137 cannot apply.

1.176 The tenancy will be on the same terms as from the mesne tenant, with the result that if the sub-tenancy was statutory as opposed to contractual (5.24), so it will remain (*Keepers & Governors of the Free Grammar School of John Lyon v Jordan*, 1995).

1.177 A Rent Act protected tenant who creates a lawful Rent Act protected sub-tenancy is obliged to notify the landlord of this in writing, within 14 days of creating the sub-tenancy, stating details of the sub-tenancy, including the name of the sub-tenant and the rent he is paying under the sub-tenancy (Rent Act 1977 s.139). Where the sub-tenant becomes tenant direct of the landlord by operation of s.137, then the landlord is entitled to disclaim responsibility for the provision of furniture, if he does so in writing within six weeks of the sub-tenant becoming his tenant (s.138).

1.178 Sub-tenants and statutory protection—(3) Housing Acts 1985 and 1996. No special provision is made to enhance the status of sub-tenants of secure tenants under the Housing Act 1985 (Chapter 3), or introductory tenants under the Housing Act 1996 (Chapter 6), for which reason the normal rule will usually prevail (1.171): that the sub-tenancy ends with the mesne tenancy.

1.179 Illegal sub-tenancy. There is only an illegal sub-tenancy if the terms of the mesne tenancy include a prohibition on subletting. Most written tenancies include such a term, and many weekly or monthly tenancies granted in the last few years, and for which the terms are to be found in printed rent books provided by the landlord, will also be subject to such a prohibition. Even a rent book issued for a period subsequent to the grant may be used as evidence of a prohibition (*RC Glaze v Alabdinboni*, 1992).

1.180 Some prohibitions on sub-letting are absolute, i.e. they simply state that it is not permitted. Some are qualified, i.e. they state that it is not permitted without the consent of the landlord. The law implies into a qualified covenant a condition that such consent will not unreasonably be withheld and if unreasonably withheld will treat the consent as given (Landlord and Tenant Act 1927 s.19; *Balls Brothers Ltd v Sinclair*, 1931). This is, however, not so where the covenant is implied by the Housing Act 1988 s.15, into a Housing Act assured tenancy (4.159).

1.181 Withholding of consent. There can only be an unreasonable withholding if there has been a request, and a refusal before the sub-letting is granted (*Barrow v Isaacs*, 1891; *Eastern Telegraph Co v Dent*, 1899), which is extremely rare. It is withholding which is prohibited, however, so that if the tenant seeks consent, and the landlord fails to reply after a reasonable time, consent has been withheld (*Wilson v Fynn*, 1948).

1.182 The best tactic is to seek consent and, when it is withheld, seek a declaration from the court that the withholding is unreasonable (*Mills v Cannon Brewery Co*, 1920).

1.183 Whether or not a withholding is reasonable will turn on the facts of each case (*Lee v K Carter (K) Ltd*, 1949) including the impact of statutory protection (*West Layton Ltd v Ford*, 1979). The reasonableness of withholding consent is not confined to questions about the proposed sub-tenant, but can include consideration of the landlord's own interests, provided they are interests which a reasonable landlord would have regard to (*Leeward Securities Ltd v Lilyheath Properties Ltd*, 1983), e.g. questions of good estate management, rather than an attempt to extract some benefit outside of the tenancy, such as unanticipated surrender (*Rayburn v Woolf*, 1985). The burden is on the tenant to show unreasonable withholding of consent (*Rayburn*).

1.184 Landlord and Tenant Act 1988. If the tenant seeks consent in writing, then the position is additionally affected by the Landlord and Tenant Act 1988. This Act applies only where the covenant is a qualified covenant (1.180).

1.185 Where a written application is made, the landlord owes the tenant a duty to reply within a reasonable time, either consenting, or else giving written notice either of a refusal, in which case the reasons must be stated, or of a "conditional consent", in which case the conditions must be stated. An unreasonable condition is not permitted. Under this Act, the burden is on the landlord to show:

- that he replied within a reasonable time;

- that any condition attached is reasonable; and

- that a refusal is reasonable.

1.186 Waiver of illegality. Even if an illegal sub-tenancy is created, it is possible that it will subsequently be "legalised". This can happen because the landlord learns of the illegal sub-letting and yet "waives" the breach of the term of the tenancy by continuing to accept rent from the mesne tenant as if nothing had happened.

1.187 Waiver requires that the landlord knew there had been an actual sub-letting, not, e.g. merely that a friend had come to live with the mesne tenant, and the act of waiver must be established, which normally means something more than a single rent payment accepted very shortly after the landlord found out, when, perhaps, reaction to the sub-letting was still in process.

1.188 The knowledge of the landlord's employees, agents or officers is imputed to the landlord, so that if one such person knows of the illegal sub-letting and the landlord continues to accept rent, there will have been waiver (*Metropolitan Properties Co v Cordery*, 1979). In one case, the issue of proceedings to gain access to the flat to inspect it, pursuant to the terms of the lease, was held to have waived an existing breach of the covenant not to sublet, of which the landlord was already aware (*Cornillie v Saha*, 1996).

1.189 Once waiver has occurred, the sub-tenant becomes a legal sub-tenant as if in the first place he had been allowed in lawfully.

1.190 No advantage of own wrong. A mesne tenant who lets illegally cannot himself subsequently take advantage of it (*Critchley v Clifford*, 1962) by claiming not to be bound by it. It is, after all, his wrong, or breach, not that of the sub-tenant. It is no ground for eviction of a sub-tenant by the mesne tenant that the letting was illegal.

1.191 Surrender by mesne tenant. There is one exception to all of these limits on when a sub-tenancy can survive the mesne tenant, which arises if the mesne tenant surrenders (1.127) to the landlord, and the landlord accepts the surrender (*Parker v Jones*, 1910). In this case, the sub-tenant becomes a tenant of the landlord regardless of whether or not the sub-tenancy is illegal, and regardless of class of protection.

1.192 This arises by operation of common law and may also be said to operate by way of waiver, i.e. of the illegality, although it is a waiver that takes place even though the landlord does not know of the existence of the sub-tenant. By accepting the surrender, the landlord is deemed to have waived any breaches by the tenant and to have taken over the tenant's liabilities, which include the sub-tenancy.

1.193   This will not happen if the mesne tenancy was within the Rent Act and already a statutory tenancy (5.27), however, because a statutory tenancy is not a tenancy at common law (*Solomon v Orwell*, 1954).

1.194   Sub-tenants and licensees.   All of these provisions, however, depend on the sub-tenant being a tenant at all, not merely a licensee. Someone who is the licensee of a tenant will find that his licence comes to an end automatically, without the giving of any notice, on the determination of the tenancy (even where the tenancy is surrendered—*Kay v Lambeth LBC*, 2004), although it will still normally be necessary for court proceedings to be taken to evict him: see Chapter 8.

1.195   Whether or not a person is the licensee or sub-tenant of another will be a question of fact based on the normal considerations, but it is true to say that where the parties are living in the same premises, the court will look closely at the arrangement and, unless there is clear evidence of separate living, it is likely to be inclined to view another occupier as a sharer, or as a lodger, and therefore in either event a licensee, even though rent is paid, rather than as a sub-tenant (*Monmouth BC v Marlog*, 1994). Such clear evidence of separate living might be provided by a rent book, perhaps separate payment for gas and electricity, separate housekeeping, etc. This question of whether a person is a licensee of, for example, someone he is sharing a flat with, is considered further under the next heading.

1.196   Sub-tenancy terminating with mesne tenancy.   If the mesne and sub-tenancies are not both Rent Act protected, or if the sub-tenancy is not Housing Act assured, or if the sub-tenancy is illegal, so that neither Rent Act 1977 s.137 nor Housing Act 1988 s.18 applies (1.172–1.177) and if there is no surrender by the tenant (1.127), the sub-tenancy automatically determines, i.e. without notice or forfeiture, on the determination of the mesne tenancy (*Moore Properties (Ilford) v McKeon*, 1976).

1.197   Relief.   A sub-tenant, even one who is an illegal sub-tenant, can apply for relief (1.136–1.146) from forfeiture (Law of Property Act 1925 s.146(4)).

3. JOINT TENANTS

1.198   Shared tenancy.   A joint tenancy occurs wherever more than one person shares the tenancy. Joint tenants do not each have a different part of, for example, a flat or a house: they are all equally entitled to share possession of the whole of it.

1.199 Between them, they must establish the four essential qualities of tenancy (*AG Securities v Vaughan*, 1988); but need not establish them (and, in particular, exclusive possession) as against each other.

1.200 Rent liability. Joint tenants are, unless the agreement states to the contrary (*AG Securities v Vaughan*, 1988; *Demuren v Seal Estates*, 1978), each liable for the whole rent of the premises, so that if a landlord can only trace one of them, that one will be obliged to pay any and all rent outstanding, though he may subsequently be able to recover shares from any of the missing joint tenants. Where there is no joint liability for the rent this may prevent a joint tenancy arising, and the occupiers may only be licensees (*Mikeover Ltd v Brady*, 1989).

1.201 Acting in harmony. Married or cohabiting couples are frequently joint tenants, but so also are groups of friends. So long as they all remain together, acting, at least in relation to the landlord, in harmony, their position is exactly the same as that of a sole tenant.

1.202 If there is any application, e.g. for rent registration, then they must either all sign the application, or else one of them must sign as agent for the others (*Turley v Panton*, 1975; *R. v Rent Officer for Camden Ex p. Felix*, 1988).

1.203 Service of a notice to quit on one is good service (*Doe d. Aslin v Summersett*, 1830), although there is some doubt as to whether a notice to quit which identifies only one of the joint tenants as the tenant will be valid.

1.204 Termination by one of joint tenants. Problems arise when the joint tenants themselves wish to go their separate ways. If the tenancy is periodic, then one joint tenant can serve notice to quit and bring the contractual tenancy to an end (*Greenwich LBC v McGrady*, 1983; *Hammersmith & Fulham LBC v Monk*, 1991). The notice to quit must, however, be valid (1.116) if it is to have this effect (*Hounslow LBC v Pilling*, 1993), and cannot simply be "treated as valid" (1.115) by the landlord.

1.205 This is something only a joint periodic tenant can do. If the tenancy is fixed term, one of the joint tenants cannot surrender it without the consent of all the others (*Leek and Moorlands Building Society v Clark*, 1952).

1.206 This technique is commonly used where a local authority wants to re-house one of the joint tenants, together with the children, without leaving the other—usually the man—in accommodation now much larger than he needs (*Crawley BC v Ure*, 1995).

1.207 Interaction with family law. The right to serve a notice to quit is not affected by matrimonial homes and occupation rights under the Family Law Act 1996: *Harrow LBC v Johnstone*, 1997; see 9.16, below. See also 9.13 on preventing service of a notice to quit in matrimonial cases.

1.208 Human Rights Act. Even after the notice to quit has expired, the property remains the man's "home" for the purposes of Art.8 of the European Convention on Human Rights: *Quazi v Harrow LBC*, 2001. That does not, however, defeat the landlord's claim to possession. The relevance of Art.8 is considered in Chapter 7.

1.209 Rent Act tenancies. If the tenancy is Rent Act protected (Chapter 5), termination by one joint tenant will not affect the right to security of tenure of the other(s) (*Lloyd v Sadler*, 1978). If one joint tenant simply departs, then the tenancy "devolves" on the remaining joint tenants (*Lloyd v Sadler*, 1978).

1.210 Joint tenancy v sole tenancy. It is possible, however, that people who assume that they are joint tenants are not so in law. For example, a group of friends take a flat together but only one of them is named in, or signs, the agreement, if any, or only one of them is named on the rent book. At first sight, the law would assume that the named occupier was the sole tenant, and that his sharers were either sub-tenants or licensees.

1.211 It is possible to upset this first impression with evidence that the entry of one name only was either an oversight or intentionally inaccurate, by showing that the landlord was contracting with the whole group, and that it was clearly intended, as between themselves and as between them and the landlord, that they should all have equal rights in the premises. This might be witnessed by the fact that they each pay the rent for the whole of the premises to the landlord in turn.

1.212 Although not impossible, it is nonetheless hard to upset the first impression created by a written indication that the tenancy belongs to only one of the sharers (*Hanstown Properties Ltd v Green*, 1978).

1.213 Sub-tenancy v sharers (licensees). Will the remaining occupiers then be licensees or sub-tenants? Again, the initial inference is that if a group of sharers are not joint tenants, there will be a sole tenant with a group of licensees (*Monmouth BC v Marlog*, 1994). There is some merit to this attitude, for as between the group of occupiers it is infrequent indeed that they will have intended the formality of landlord and tenant. More likely, they are all sharing the outgoings, perhaps even buying food together, and living as one household. This would all suggest licence, rather than sub-tenancy. Sub-tenancy could be established, however, if there was clear evidence of separate living, as suggested under the last heading (1.195).

1.214 Non-exclusive occupation. Another problem has been caused by the use of the evasive device of "non-exclusive occupation agreements". The technique of such arrangements is that the landlord enters into a series of separate contracts with each occupier, granting to the occupier the right to use the premises in question in common with others, but not to use a particular part of the premises. In this way, the landlord seeks to avoid a finding of tenancy of some part of the premises as against him, and—because the agreements are all separate—seeks also to avoid a finding of joint tenancy of the whole of the premises between himself and the group.

1.215 Such evasive devices often purport to retain for the landlord a right to come and live in the premises himself, or else to select new occupiers as and when one or other of the original group departs. Such arrangements could be genuine, e.g. if the landlord was effectively running a small-scale "hostel", and choosing the occupiers himself. An arrangement, if genuine, would create a series of individual licences, or, if specific rooms were allocated to individual occupiers, could create separate tenancies of the individual, specific rooms (*AG Securities v Vaughan*, 1988).

1.216 Genuine or sham. Sometimes, however, these arrangements are not genuine. With the availability of assured shorthold tenancies, landlords are less inclined to use such devices. Nonetheless, they are still sometimes used.

1.217   Sham arrangements.   In *Street v Mountford*, 1986, three cases in which the courts had upheld non-exclusive occupation agreements as genuine were said to have been wrongly decided, and to be obvious sham arrangements which the courts should have treated as tenancies. A "sham" (or "false label" as it is sometimes called) arises when a document claims one thing, but the reality or actuality is, and was intended to be, something quite different, e.g. creating the (false) impression that a group of occupiers are not joint tenants.

1.218   Pretences.   The decision in *Street* did not, however, bring an end to litigation on such agreements. The matter was considered again by the House of Lords in *Antoniades v Villiers*; *AG Securities v Vaughan*, 1988.

1.219   Save where the agreement was, unusually, a genuine arrangement between the landlord on one hand, and separate individuals on the other, as in *Vaughan* itself, the House of Lords reiterated that "pretences" devised to get around statutory protection would not be upheld. The courts should look at all the circumstances, including the relationship between the occupiers before they approached the landlord, the negotiations and, so far as the written agreement is alleged to be a pretence or sham, even after they have taken up occupation. If the reality is that the occupiers are to use the premises as a home, together, paying a rent for it, then the arrangement must be construed as a (joint) tenancy, no matter what documents have been drawn up.

1.220   Subsequent cases.   There has been a number of subsequent Court of Appeal decisions which have sought to apply the principles laid down by the House of Lords. In two of them (*Stribling v Wickham*, 1989, and *Mikeover Ltd v Brady*, 1989), the court found that the arrangements were genuine licences, while in three others (*Nicolaou v Pitt*, 1989; *Aslan v Murphy*, 1989 and *Duke v Wynne*, 1989), the agreements were all found to be "pretences" and the occupiers held to be tenants.

1.221   Departing joint tenants.   Once joint tenancy is established, there can still be problems. Commonly, in the course of time, one or more of the original occupiers will drift on to alternative accommodation. What, then, is the position of new occupiers, assuming that they are selected by the occupiers themselves and not by the landlord? If a new occupier is selected by the landlord, this will afford the landlord evidence that he is in overall possession of the premises and that there is therefore no tenancy at all.

1.222 New occupiers. If the landlord consents, a new occupier may become a joint tenant with the others. If he does not, then the existing occupiers cannot impose a new party to the tenancy on the landlord against his will. The new occupier must be either the sub-tenant or licensee of the existing and remaining joint tenants and, given the remarks which have already been made, is likely to be no more than licensee. In the course of time, it may be that all the original occupiers will have left and there will only be such licensees in occupation. The only defence left is if the existing occupiers, or some of them, can show that by the acceptance of rent or by some other conduct, the landlord has accepted them as tenants, or as joint tenants (1.62–1.63).

4. TENANTS OF MORTGAGORS

1.223 Normal position. A person is a tenant of a mortgagor when his landlord owns the property, whether freehold or lease-hold, under a mortgage. If the landlord falls into arrears with mortgage repayments, the mortgage company may "foreclose" and, in effect, take the property over. It is in this situation that problems may arise for the tenant.

1.224 As long as the mortgagor remains in possession, the tenant's position is wholly unaffected by the existence of a mortgage on the property, even if the tenancy is granted in contravention of its terms (*Church of England Building Society v Piskor*, 1954). There are commonly such terms in a mortgage.

1.225 Prior tenancy. If a person owns property before taking a mortgage on it, then any tenancies existing at the date of the mortgage are unaffected by the deed (*Mornington Permanent Building Society v Kenway*, 1953), even where the tenant has consented to the mortgage (*Woolwich Building Society v Dickman*, 1996). In such a case, even if the deed prohibits the creation of tenancies, on foreclosure the tenant will become the tenant of the mortgage company.

1.226 Illegal tenants. Almost all mortgage deeds (except those specifically for "buy to let") prohibit the creation of tenancies, and as the majority of tenancies from mortgagors are in fact created after the mortgage, there are many tenants of mortgagors who are—in this sense—"illegal" tenants. This does not avail the mortgagor, or afford him any additional right to evict the tenant. If the mortgage company forecloses, however, then no matter whether the tenant is statutorily protected or not, he has no right of occupation as against the mortgage company, even though the mortgage company knew of the illegal tenancy but continued to accept repayments (*Dudley and District Benefit Building Society v Emerson*, 1949; *Britannia Building Society v Earl*, 1989).

1.227 New tenancy? The only possibility is that, after foreclosure, the mortgage company either actively agrees to accept the continued presence of the tenant and takes on the tenancy, or does so by implication by taking rent from the tenant over such a long period that the only inference that can properly be drawn is that it is treating the tenancy as binding upon itself (*Taylor v Ellis*, 1960; *Stroud Building Society v Delamount*, 1960).

5. ASSIGNEES

1.228 Permitted or prohibited? The term "assignment" has been used before, to describe the purchase of a long lease from the existing leaseholder (1.19). The same may occur in connection with lesser forms of tenancy; that is to say that one tenant may assign the tenancy to another. An assignee steps into the shoes of the outgoing tenant, and occupies on exactly the same terms.

1.229 If there is nothing in the terms of the tenancy or statute, e.g. Housing Act 1988 s.15 prohibiting assignment of a Housing Act assured tenancy without the consent of the landlord; (see 4.157), to prohibit this, then it is permissible. Most tenancy agreements and rent books do, however, include such prohibitions which, like sub-tenancies (1.180), may be absolute or qualified.

1.230 Statutory tenancy. Only a contractual tenancy can be assigned, i.e. not a Rent Act statutory tenancy (Chapter 5; *Jessamine Investment Co v Schwartz*, 1977).

1.231 Assignment by deed. Strictly, like a surrender, assignment should be by formal deed, but it can also operate if the transaction is in writing, in a document that sets out all the express terms, and which is signed (Law of Property (Miscellaneous Provisions) Act 1989 s.2).

1.232 An assignment not by deed, though binding as between the two tenants, will not bind the landlord unless he accepts the assignment, e.g. by payment and acceptance of rent, in much the same way and to the same extent as if he were to be deemed to have created a new tenancy (1.62–1.63) or at least to the extent that the law must consider that he is estopped from denying the validity of the assignment, i.e. that it would be inequitable to allow him to do so (*Rodenhurst Estates v Barnes*, 1936).

1.233 A purported assignment that is neither by deed, nor in writing, signed and setting out the express terms, cannot be effective against the landlord. For the assignee to sustain the tenancy as his own, it will be necessary to demonstrate surrender by operation of law, accepted by the landlord, coupled to what the law will recognise as the grant by the landlord, by his conduct, of a new tenancy (1.62–1.63).

6. NEW LANDLORDS

1.234 Purchase subject to existing interests.   When a person purchases property, he does so subject to existing interests in it. A tenancy is an interest in property as, indeed, is a sub-tenancy, and even an illegal sub-tenancy. Accordingly, a purchaser takes subject to existing tenancies. A contractual licence is not an interest in property; it is a personal right, and it does not bind a purchaser (*Ashburn Anstalt v Arnold*, 1989). In some circumstances, however, where the licence amounts to an estoppel (1.91), a purchaser may be bound by it (*Inwards v Baker*, 1965).

1.235   The new landlord takes subject to all the old landlord's rights, liabilities and duties. He also takes liable to any knowledge the old landlord had, e.g. such knowledge as would found a claim for waiver of an illegal sub-tenancy or assignment. A tenancy dates from its original grant, and there is no new tenancy on change of ownership.

1.236 Notification.   Before a tenant starts to pay rent to the new landlord, the old landlord should write to him, authorising the changeover, and will remain liable as landlord until either he or the new landlord does so (Landlord and Tenant Act 1985 s.3).

1.237 Change of ownership: special issues.   There are special provisions relating to change of ownership which determine whether or not a tenant still has a resident landlord for the purposes of either the Housing Act 1988 (Chapter 4) or the Rent Act 1977 (Chapter 5). In addition, there are special provisions governing the transfer of ownership from local and other public authorities to Housing Action trusts, and in some cases into private ownership, which are considered in Chapter 3.

CHAPTER TWO

Owner-occupation

Introduction

2.01 Owner-occupiers. In this chapter, we shall examine in outline the rights of occupation of those who were described in Chapter 1 as owner-occupiers, i.e. freeholders, long leaseholders, and commonholders.

2.02 It has already been remarked that the fullest status that anyone can enjoy is that of freehold owner-occupation, unencumbered by mortgage (1.12). He has to pay neither rent nor mortgage repayments and has an absolute right of occupation which can only be interfered with in the sorts of circumstances indicated (1.12–1.13).

2.03 The position of the freeholder, the leaseholder and the commonholder as regards mortgage repayments is substantially the same, and will be considered under the general heading of mortgages (2.89–2.104). First, however, the position of the leaseholder, whether or not the property is mortgaged, at or before the end of the lease, must be considered (2.07–2.21).

Outline

2.04 Leasehold rights

- The Landlord and Tenant Act 1954 and the Local Government and Housing Act 1989 allow long leaseholders to continue to occupy after the end of the lease.

- The Leasehold Reform Act 1967 allows long leaseholders of houses the right to enfranchise, i.e. to compel the freeholder to sell the freehold to them, or to extend the lease for a further 50 years.

- Long leaseholders and other tenants of flats enjoy a right of first refusal under Landlord and Tenant Act 1987, so that a freeholder who wishes to sell his interest must first offer it to the tenants.

- The Leasehold Reform, Housing and Urban Development Act 1993 contains two important rights for long leaseholders:
  - the right to collective enfranchisement of the freehold interest in the block; and
  - the individual right to acquire a new lease.

- The Commonhold and Leasehold Reform Act 2002 provides long leaseholders and other tenants with a right to manage a building containing flats.

- Recovery of service charges from leaseholders is regulated by the Landlord and Tenant Act 1985.

- Recovery of administration charges from leaseholders is regulated by the Commonhold and Leasehold Reform Act 2002.

2.05 Freehold rights

- Recovery of estate charges from freeholders is regulated by the Commonhold and Leasehold Reform Act 2002.

2.06 Mortgages

- There are two main types of mortgages: capital repayment and endowment.

- Where other parties, e.g. a spouse or cohabite, already have an interest in the home, they are not be bound by a later mortgage unless they agree to it.

- Where a person's agreement to a mortgage is obtained through undue influence, the mortgage is not binding on him unless the mortgage company has ensured that he received independent advice before entering into the mortgage.

- Where there are arrears in mortgage payments, there must be a formal demand for payment.

- The mortgage company may seek possession in the county court if the arrears are not paid off.

- The county court has power to suspend the order for possession if it is of the view that the arrears can be cleared within a "reasonable period".

Leasehold rights

1. LANDLORD AND TENANT ACT 1954; LOCAL GOVERNMENT AND HOUSING ACT 1989 SCHEDULE 10

2.07 Long leases. "Long leases" are those for more than 21 years: Landlord and Tenant Act 1954 ("1954 Act") s.2(4); Leasehold Reform Act 1967 ("1967 Act") s.3(1); Landlord and Tenant Act 1987 ("1987 Act") s.59(3); Local Government and Housing Act 1989 ("1989 Act") Sch.10 para.2(3); Commonhold and Leasehold Reform Act 2002 ("CLRA 2002") s.76(2) (although—except under 1954 or 1989—the expression can include a lease under the "right to buy" provisions of the Housing Act 1985, even if it is for less than 21 years. This is extremely rare.)

2.08 Although the lease must (normally) be for more than 21 years, that is not to say that the leaseholder must have been in occupation for that period, merely that the right under which he occupies is or was for that period, i.e. he may have taken an assignment (1.19).

2.09 Time runs from when the lease was originally granted (*Roberts v Church Commissioners for England*, 1972), and not from any earlier date to which it may have been backdated.

2.10 Premature termination. So long as a leasehold interest has not expired, an occupier has as full a right of occupation as a freeholder, and this can only be interfered with in the same ways referred to above (1.12–1.13). For this purpose, however, it is assumed that the lease runs its full length: leases can be terminated prematurely, e.g. because of breach of a term of the lease, or non-payment of charges. In such a case, the lease is susceptible to forfeiture proceedings, just like any other fixed-term tenancy, with the possibility of relief discussed in Chapter 1 (see 1.136–1.146).

2.11 Statutory continuation. Assuming continuation of the lease, then so long as the occupier is using the premises, or part of them, as his home at the end of the lease, the lease will not come to an end, and the occupier can remain in occupation indefinitely because it is automatically continued by statute (either under the 1954 or 1989 Act). This is not so, however, if the landlord under the lease is one of the public landlords whose tenants cannot be Housing Act assured (4.41) or Rent Act protected (5.85).

2.12 Pre-April 1, 1990 leases. If the tenancy commenced before April 1, 1990, but terminated before January 15, 1999, the protection available is that of a statutory tenant (5.25–5.30) under the Rent Act 1977, save that:

- There is an additional ground for possession, if the landlord can prove that he proposes to demolish or reconstruct the whole or a substantial part of the premises in question (1954 Act s.12); and

- While the other qualifying conditions (5.39) must be fulfilled, the fact that the tenancy is at a low rent is disregarded (1954 Act s.2(1), (5)).

2.13 Use as a home. The most essential element of protection under the 1954 Act is that at the end of the lease, the premises are being used by the tenant as his home, to the same extent as is necessary to sustain a Rent Act statutory tenancy (5.94–5.111). Protection may, however, extend to only part of the premises (1954 Act s.3(2)), e.g. if the tenant occupies only one part, and does not intend to resume possession of the remainder, perhaps a part which he has sublet (*Regalian Securities v Ramsden*, 1981).

2.14 Procedure. During the last year of a long lease, the landlord can take action in the county court to try to secure a predetermination of whether or not the tenant is going to enjoy protection (1954 Act s.2(2)). If he does not follow this procedure, then the tenancy automatically continues, at the old—and usually low—rent, until brought to end by notice from the landlord (1954 Act s.3), indicating either that he intends to seek possession on one of the available grounds (2.12), or propose a statutory tenancy to commence at a specified date (1954 Act s.4), identifying the proposed terms of the statutory tenancy, and dealing with the question of "initial repairs" (1954 Act s.7; see below, [11.84–11.88).

2.15 Once the statutory tenancy has come into existence, it may later be determined in exactly the same way as one which arises under the Rent Act 1977 (5.119–5.171).

2.16 Termination post-January 15, 1999. For tenancies which are terminated under the 1954 Act after January 15, 1999, the tenancy will not become statutory, but will fall to be dealt with in the same way as those commencing after April 1, 1990 (1989 Act Sch.10 para.3(2)).

2.17 Post-April 1, 1990 leases. The protection available to these leaseholders (as well as to those which commenced earlier but terminated before January 15, 1999) is (by the Local Government and Housing Act 1989) that of an assured tenancy under the Housing Act 1988.

2.18 Procedure. The 1989 Act continues the existing tenancy until the landlord serves a notice either proposing an assured monthly periodic tenancy or giving notice of seeking possession (1989 Act Sch.10 para.4(5)). A notice proposing a new tenancy must propose a new rent which must be sufficient to ensure that it is no longer at a "low rent", and must either state that it is to be on the same terms as the long tenancy or propose new terms (1989 Act Sch.10 para.4(5), (6)). The new rent may be above the level (£25,000 per annum; 4.27), which will accordingly take the tenant outside protection (*R. (Morris) v London RAC*, 2002).

2.19 Where a notice of seeking possession is served, it must state the ground or grounds. The landlord may rely on some of the Housing Act 1988 grounds, i.e. Ground 6 (4.98) and the discretionary Grounds 9 to 15 (4.109–4.122). In addition, the landlord may also claim possession on the basis that he requires the premises for occupation for himself, any child over 18 or his parents or parents-in-law, provided his interest was not purchased after February 18, 1966, and that he can show that it is reasonable to grant possession. To rely on this ground, however, he must satisfy the "greater hardship" test (5.163: 1989 Act Sch.10 para.5).

2.20 The notice proposing a new tenancy or seeking possession must give the tenant the option either to elect to remain or to indicate a willingness to give up possession. Any application for possession must be made within two months of the tenant's election, or, if there is no reply, within four months of the landlord's notice (1989 Act Sch.10 para.13). The tenant may at any time, regardless of whether he has elected to remain, give one month's notice to terminate the tenancy (1989 Act Sch.10 para.13(4)).

2.21 An interim monthly rent may be proposed by the landlord, which the tenant may appeal to the rent assessment committee

(1989 Act Sch.10 para.6). If the tenant wishes to dispute the proposed rent and terms of the new tenancy he must serve a notice on the landlord within two months, making his own proposals. If no agreement can be reached, the matter may be referred by either party to the rent assessment committee, which has similar powers as under the Housing Act 1988 (4.130: 1989 Act Sch.10 paras 11, 12).

2.   LEASEHOLD REFORM ACT 1967

2.22   Enfranchisement and extension of long leases. Under the Leasehold Reform Act 1967, a person who is a long leaseholder of a house, but not of a flat, can compel the landlord to extend the lease for a further 50 years beyond the date of its original termination, or may require the landlord to sell him the freehold (known as "enfranchisement").

2.23 These rights only apply to those houses which are not horizontally divided from any other premises, i.e. they do not, to any material extent, overlap or, as it were, underlap another property (1967 Act s.2). Whether a part of a house above or below another property is material depends on the relationship between the part in question and the house, rather than with the whole of the other property; it is a question of fact and degree in each case (*Malekshad v Howard De Walden Estates Ltd*, 2002).

2.24 The house need not, however, be free-standing: it may be in a row of terraced houses. The house can be sub-divided, and even sublet. Thus, a house which is also a shop can qualify (*Tandon v Trustees of Spurgeons Homes*, 1982); the question is whether the building can reasonably be called a house (*Lake v Bennett*, 1970). A property divided into two maisonettes with separate entrances, but otherwise is apparently a single residence, has been held to be a house for this purpose (*Malpas v St Ermin's Property Co Ltd*, 1992).

2.25 The Act formerly only applied to tenancies at a low rent, i.e. a rent which is not more than two-thirds of the rateable value or, if there is no rateable value, if the rent is less than £1,000 per annum in Greater London or £250 elsewhere (1967 Act s.4). This require-ment was abolished by the Commonhold and Leasehold Reform Act 2002, although whether the tenancy is at a low rent affects the purchase price for the freehold (but not an extended lease) (2.30). It still applies only to long leases (2.07).

2.26   Qualifying periods. A leaseholder must exercise these rights before the lease expires or while his tenancy is continued under statute (2.11 or 2.17), unless a period of two months has elapsed since the landlord served notice proposing a statutory or assured tenancy (1967 Act s.3(2) and Sch.3 para.2(1)). The right may, however, be exercised after an extension to the lease has been granted.

2.27 Occupation as residence. The former requirement* that the leaseholder occupied the premises as his residence was abolished by the Commonhold and Leasehold Reform Act 2002. There remains two exceptions: (a) where a house includes a flat let to a qualifying tenant for the purposes of the 1993 Act (2.59), and (b) where the tenant occupies under a business tenancy. In both cases the tenant does not have the right to enfranchise unless he has been occupying the house or part of it as his only or main residence for the last two years or for periods amounting to two years in the last ten years.

2.28 It is enough to occupy only part of the premises, e.g. if the occupier has the lease on a whole house, lives in part and lets out part this will suffice (*Harris v Swick Securities*, 1969), provided, where necessary, he occupies at least part as his only or main, not just a residence (1967 Act s.1; *Poland v Earl Cadogan*, 1980).

2.29 Purchase price. Failing agreement between the parties, the purchase price can be fixed by the leasehold valuation tribunal, and on appeal therefrom by the Lands Tribunal, but the procedure is complicated, and anyone intending to use it should consult a lawyer or surveyor.

2.30 Extension does not cost anything, although a new ground rent, i.e. low rent, which is appropriate to the value of the house as at the date when the new lease is to start, will take effect from that date (1967 Act s.15). Extension is provided mainly for those who cannot afford to enfranchise or who, perhaps being elderly and with no relatives to whom to leave any acquired interest, have no reason to do so. There are special grounds of opposition to enfranchisement or extension available to specified public landlords (1967 Act s.28).

2.31 Sooner is cheaper. Enfranchisement can be extremely cheap. If the tenancy is at a low rent (2.25), all that is being bought back is the benefit of a very small ground rent and the fairly remote possibility that the landlord will ever get the property back at all. If the tenancy is not at a low rent, the purchase prices also includes allowance for "marriage value", i.e. the increase in the value of property which is produced by the two separate interests (the freehold and the leasehold) coming to be owned by the same person. The longer there is to run on the lease at the time a notice indicating an intention to purchase is served, the cheaper the price will be, because the landlord's expectations are the most remote. It follows that if an occupier has to satisfy the residential qualification, he should exercise the power to enfranchise as soon as he has done so.

2.32 The price of enfranchisement bears no practical relation to current property values or even to the customarily lower-than-vacant-possession value at which many sitting tenants are permitted to buy from their landlords. It may be a figure of less than £100, or not much more. The advice of a surveyor will count for much more than that of a lawyer where prices in enfranchisement and extension are concerned.

3. LANDLORD AND TENANT ACT 1987

2.33 Additional rights. Long leaseholders also benefit from a range of rights contained in the Landlord and Tenant Act 1987 Pts 1, 3 and 4 which may most conveniently be considered in this chapter. Other tenants may also benefit from Pt 1. (Part 2—the appointment of a manager—is considered in Chapter 11, below.)

(i) *Part 1—first refusal*

2.34 Right of first refusal. Part 1 contains provisions designed to give the tenants (including long leaseholders) of blocks of flats a "right of first refusal" should the freeholder or a superior landlord wish to sell his interest in circumstances amounting to a "relevant disposal". The provisions apply only to flats, and there must be at least two flats in the building for them to operate. The block need not be purpose-built.

2.35 Exclusions. The provisions do not apply if the landlord is a resident landlord or an exempt landlord, or if less than 50 per cent of the flats are occupied by qualifying tenants, or if less than 50 per cent of the floor area of the building (excluding common parts) is not in (or intended for) residential use (1987 Act s.1).

2.36 Exempt landlords. "Exempt landlords" include local authorities, new town development corporations or the Commission for the New Towns, an urban development corporation, the

Housing Corporation, charitable housing trusts, registered social landlords and Housing Action Trusts (1987 Act s.58).

2.37 Resident Landlord. "Resident landlord" is defined (1987 Act s.58) in terms very similar to the definition in the Housing Act 1988 (4.44–4.51. Accordingly, the mere fact that the landlord lives in a purpose-built block of flats will not prevent the right of first refusal arising. Where the resident landlord exemption does apply, however, e.g. in a converted house, the landlord need not have been in residence since the commencement of the tenancy, but only for a period of at least one year before the prospective disposal. The residential test is not "a" residence (as under the Rent Act 1977: 5.46–5.51), but "only or principal residence" (as under the Housing Act 1985: 3.32–3.35).

2.38 Qualifying tenants. All tenants, including Rent Act statutory tenants (5.25), are qualifying tenants, except shorthold tenants (6.139), assured tenants (Chapter 4), those to whom the business security of Pt 2 of the Landlord and Tenant Act 1954 (3.39(14)) applies, and service tenants (1.153; 1987 Act s.3). If, however, a person has a lease of three flats in the building, i.e. someone who has prima facie acquired for sub-letting, or if a person is a sub-tenant whose landlord is himself a qualifying tenant, he cannot be a qualifying tenant (1987 Act s.3).

2.39 Relevant disposal. The right of first refusal arises only in relation to a "relevant disposal". This means the disposal of any interest in the whole or part of the building other than a schedule of classes of disposal which includes:

- the grant of a tenancy of a single flat;
- a disposal of an interest by way of mortgage;
- disposal under the Matrimonial Causes Act 1973 ss.23A, 24, or 24A (9.06);
- a disposal related to a compulsory purchase;
- a disposal under the collective enfranchisement provisions of the Leasehold Reform, Housing and Urban Development Act 1993 (2.56);
- a disposal by way of gift to a member of the landlord's family or to a charity;
- a disposal by will;

- a disposal to the Crown; and

- a disposal to a company which has been "associated" (as defined) with the landlord company for two years (1987 Act s.4).

2.40 A contract to dispose is a relevant disposal (1987 Act s.4A). A disposal by a mortgage company falls within the provisions, even if it has taken the property back from the landlord under the mortgage.

2.41 Requisite majority. The provisions of Pt 1 are highly technical and are only described in outline. Where a relevant disposal is proposed, the landlord has to offer the tenants the right of first refusal, identifying what is on offer and its terms, including price. "Propose" here means a state of mind somewhere between mere consideration of a course of action, and a fixed or irrevocable determination to pursue it (*Mainwaring v Trustees of Henry Smith's Charity*, 1996).

2.42 The offer can only be accepted by a "requisite majority" of the qualifying tenants, within a period of not less than two months (1987 Act s.5). "Requisite majority" means more than 50 per cent of the "available votes". "Available votes" means one vote for each flat involved (1987 Act s.18A). If the requisite majority accepts the offer, they have a further two months in which to identify a person to act on their behalf in the further transactions, and the landlord cannot sell to anyone else until the end of the "relevant period", which is defined to cover the designated procedure (1987 Act s.6).

2.43 One year restriction on disposal. If no one is nominated or the offer is not accepted, the landlord cannot dispose elsewhere for 12 months save on the same terms and at the same price (1987 Act s.7). (This is to prevent offers at an unnaturally high figure.)

2.44 Nominated person. Once a person has been nominated, the landlord may not dispose of the property except to that person, and must send out a contract within one month (1987 Act ss.8 and 8A). The nominated person then has two months in which to offer an exchange of contract (1987 Act s.8A).

2.45 Other provisions. Other provisions deal with withdrawals and deemed withdrawals (in cases where time limits are not complied with) by both landlord and nominated purchaser and where the original proposed sale is by auction. There are also provisions to deal with a disposal which has not complied with the right of first refusal, which include the possibility of forcing the purchaser to resell to the tenants (1987 Act ss.11, 12A–12D; *Belvedere Court Management Ltd v Frogmore Development Ltd*, 1995).

2.46 Criminal offences. It is a criminal offence for a landlord, without reasonable excuse, to make a relevant disposal of property to which Pt 1 of the 1987 Act applies (1987 Act s.10A), with liability to a fine up to level 5 on the standard scale. Landlords under a duty to inform tenants of an assignment of the property (see 1.236) must also inform qualifying tenants of their rights under the 1987 Act (Landlord and Tenant Act 1985 s.3A). Failure to do so is a criminal offence.

(ii) *Part 3—compulsory acquisition*

2.47 Preconditions. Part 3 of the 1987 Act permits a form of "compulsory purchase" by qualifying tenants. For this purpose a qualifying tenant must have a long lease (2.07). A "business tenant" cannot be a qualifying tenant, nor can a tenant whose lease comprises more than two flats, nor if his own landlord is a qualifying tenant (1987 Act s.26).

2.48 For the provisions to operate, a specified number of flats in a building must be occupied by qualifying tenants: if less than four flats, all of them; if four to ten, no less than all but one; if ten or more, at least 90 per cent (1987 Act s.25).

2.49 Exclusions. As under Pt 1 (2.33), the provisions do not apply if more than 50 per cent of the building (excluding the common parts) is non-residential, nor if there is an exempt or resident landlord (2.36–2.37).

2.50 Acquisition order. The "acquisition order" can only be made by a court, which must be satisfied that the preconditions (above) apply and:

- that one of two sets of further conditions applies; and

- that the conditions for making the order exist (1987 Act s.29).

2.51 Conditions. It is the conditions which define the purpose. The conditions are where the freeholder is (and is likely to remain) in breach of his obligations (in respect of repair, insurance, maintenance or management)—or would be if notice could be served on him—to such an extent that the appointment of a manager under Pt 2 (11.123) would not be a sufficient remedy, or else that there has been a Pt 2 manager for at least two years (1987 Act s.29).

2.52 Further provisions. Further provisions govern the terms of the acquisition if the landlord cannot be found (1987 Act ss.30–33), but a landlord can apply for discharge of the order if the tenants do not proceed within a reasonable time, or if the number of tenants wishing to proceed falls below the requisite majority (1987 Act s.34).

2.53 Procedure. Before an application can be made to the court, a "requisite majority" of tenants (defined in the same terms as for Pt 1: 2.41) must serve notice on the landlord of the intention to apply, identifying the grounds on which the application will be made, specifying what remedial steps might be taken to avert the application within a specified reasonable period, and containing such other information as might be prescribed by the Secretary of State (1987 Act s.27). The court can, however, waive the requirement of preliminary notice if it considers that it is not reasonably practicable to serve one. Unless the prior notice is waived by the court, no application can be made until the period specified for remedial action has expired (1987 Act s.28).

(iii) *Part 4—variation of leases*

2.54 Applications to vary. Finally, attention may be drawn to the provisions of Pt 4 of the Act, which are again confined to long leaseholders (2.07). These provisions permit individual lease-holders to apply to a leasehold valuation tribunal for a variation of the terms of a lease which fail to make satisfactory provisions governing repairs or maintenance of a flat or building or of facilities necessary to ensure that occupiers enjoy a reasonable standard of accommodation, insurance, repairs, the provision or maintenance or services, or the way service charges are computed (1987 Act s.35).

2.55 There is also provision for the variation of other leases within a building to ensure consistency (1987 Act s.36) and for "block applications" by a specified number of leaseholders in a building: two to eight flats, no less than all but one; nine or more flats, 75 per cent in support of the application, and the application is not opposed by more than ten per cent.

4.   LEASEHOLD REFORM, HOUSING AND URBAN DEVELOPMENT ACT 1993

2.56   Rights for leaseholders of flats.   The rights of leaseholders of flats were further extended by the Leasehold Reform, Housing and Urban Development Act 1993, to compensate for their inability to enfranchise under Leasehold Reform Act 1967 (above), i.e. because their homes are flats, not houses. Two rights were created by the 1993 Act:

1. the right to collective enfranchisement of the freehold interest in a block of flats by qualifying tenants;

2. the individual right to a new lease of a flat.

(i)   *Collective enfranchisement*

2.57   The right of collective enfranchisement is the right to have the freehold of the premises in which the flat is situated acquired on their behalf by persons appointed by them for the purpose (1993 Act s.1).

2.58   Qualifying premises.   The building to be acquired must contain two or more flats owned by qualifying tenants (2.59), who must between them own at least two-thirds of the total number of flats in the building (1993 Act s.3). Where the building is not primarily in residential use or where there is a resident landlord in a building containing not more than four units, the right to collective enfranchisement is excluded (1993 Act s.4).

2.59   Qualifying tenants.   Qualifying tenants have to have a long lease, broadly meaning one for more than 21 years (1993 Act s.7).

2.60   Excluded tenants.   Certain tenants are excluded: business tenants, tenants of charitable housing trusts, and those whose tenancies are illegal because granted by a mesne landlord in breach of a superior lease (1993 Act s.5).

2.61   Procedure.   To make a purchase, qualifying tenants are entitled to information from their immediate landlord about those with superior interests (1993 Act s.11). Once the tenants decide to proceed they must serve an initial notice on the freeholder; this initial notice must be on behalf of tenants of not less than half of the total number of flats in the building (1993 Act s.13). Those qualifying tenants who are parties to the initial notice thereby become participating tenants.

2.62 The initial notice must state the name and address of a nominee purchaser, and also a proposed price, which must include not only the freehold price but also a price for any intermediate interests. The freeholder must serve a counter-notice either admitting or denying the right. The right may be denied on the basis that the freeholder intends to redevelop the premises (1993 Act s.21). If the freeholder admits the right, he may dispute the purchase price in his counter-notice. If he fails to serve a counter-notice, the nominee purchaser is entitled to acquire the freehold on the terms set out in the initial notice (*Willingale v Global Grange Ltd*, 2001).

2.63 Nominee purchaser. At the moment, there is no requirement for a specific person or type of body to fulfil the role of nominee purchaser, although in practice a company is often set up specially for the purpose. Amendments under the 2002 Act provided that a specially constituted "RTE" (right to enfranchise) company would have to be used, but it is now considered unlikely that these amendments will be brought into force.

2.64 The price. If the price is not agreed, it is to be determined under statutory rules into which statutorily defined assumptions are built. The price has to comprise a number of elements: the freehold price, the price of any intermediate leasehold interest, and the price of other interests to be acquired. The freeholder is entitled to compensation for any loss in value to any other property he owns, including loss of development value (1993 Act Sch.6). Disputes regarding price are referable to the leasehold valuation tribunal (1993 Act s.24).

2.65 Enforcement. The right may be enforced through application to the county court. Where there are disputes about the terms of the purchase, however, these may be referred to the leasehold valuation tribunal.

(ii) *New lease*

2.66 Ninety-year lease. In addition, the 1993 Act gives individual tenants the right to acquire a new 90-year lease. To exercise the right, there must be a qualifying tenant of a flat, i.e. one held on a long lease (2.59).

2.67 Procedure. The tenant proceeds by means of an initial notice, to which the landlord must respond with a counter-notice admitting or denying the right. The right can be denied on the basis that the landlord intends to redevelop (1993 Act s.45). Disputes regarding the terms and price may be referred to the leasehold valuation tribunal. Other disputes regarding progress may be referred to the county court. The tenant may withdraw (1993 Act s.52); in some circumstances of inaction by the tenant, withdrawal may be deemed to have taken place (1993 Act s.53).

2.68 Price and grant. If the price is not agreed, the dispute may be referred to the leasehold valuation tribunal. The price is determined according to statutory assumptions, and includes compensation for the landlord (1993 Act Sch.13; 2.63). Once all the terms are agreed or determined, and the price being paid, the tenant is under an obligation to accept—in substitution for his present lease—a lease for a term which will amount to 90 years from what would have been the end of the current lease, at a "peppercorn" rent (1993 Act s.56(1)). In addition, the tenant must clear any arrears of rent or service charges which have accrued (1993 Act s.56(3)). The new lease is, in general, to be on the same terms as the original (1993 Act s.57).

2.69 Future leases. Once a lease has been granted, there is nothing to prevent another such new lease being granted or indeed the right to collective enfranchisement being exercised. However, all rights to statutory security of tenure (2.1) are lost (1993 Act s.59).

5. COMMONHOLD AND LEASEHOLD REFORM ACT 2002

2.70 Right to manage. The right to manage, in cases of default by the freeholder, was introduced by the Landlord and Tenant Act 1987 and is considered in Chapter 11 (11.123). The 2002 Act provides qualifying tenants of qualifying premises with a right to manage, irrespective of any fault on the freeholder's part.

2.71 Qualifying requirements. The same qualifying requirements as under the 1993 Act must be met as to premises and tenants (2002 Act ss.72, 75: see 2.58, 2.59).

2.72 RTM company. In order to exercise the right, the tenants must first establish a right to manage company—"RTM company"—which accords with the requirements of the 2002 Act ss.73 and 74. The RTM company then serves notice inviting participation by tenants in the company (2002 Act s.78). Provided membership of the RTM company includes qualifying tenants of at least half the number of flats in the building, notice claiming the right can be served on the landlord (2002 Act s.79). The landlord must respond with a counter-notice admitting or denying the right (2002 Act s.84).

2.73 Procedure. If there is no dispute, the right to manage arises on the date set out in the initial notice, which must be at least four months after the date of the notice. If it is denied, the matter may be determined by the leasehold valuation tribunal. If the tribunal determines that there is an entitlement to the right, the right to manage will arise three months from the determination (2002 Act s.90).

2.74 Rights. Once it has acquired the right to manage, the RTM company becomes responsible for management functions, i.e. those concerning services, repairs, maintenance, improvements, insurance and management (2002 Act s.96).

6. SERVICE CHARGES

2.75 Landlord and Tenant Act 1985. Many long leases and some shorter tenancies have provision for the landlord to levy service charges. Disputes commonly arise about the amount of service charges, and the quality of the work that the landlord carries out. The Landlord and Tenant Act 1985 ss.18–30 govern the levy and recovery of service charges.

2.76 Service charge. The Act applies to all charges payable for services, repairs, improvements, maintenance or insurance or the landlord's costs of management, which vary or may vary in accordance with their cost (1985 Act s.18).

2.77 Reasonableness. Service charges can only be recovered so far as they are reasonably incurred and the works or services are to a reasonable standard (1985 Act s.19). Leasehold valuation tribunals have jurisdiction to determine whether charges are reasonable.

2.78 Exclusions. There are provisions for excluding—or seeking to have excluded—from service charges:

- some costs that have been met with specified types of grant-aid;

- costs incurred more than 18 months before the demand for payment (and of which no notice was given within that time); and

- landlords' costs in connection with a dispute (1985 Act ss.20A–20C).

2.79 Consultation. Before carrying out larger scale building works or entering into long-term contracts, the landlord must consult the tenants and any recognised tenants' association (1985 Act s.20 and Service Charge (Consultation Requirement) (England) Regulations 2003 or Service Charge (Consultation Requirement) (Wales) Regulations 2004). In the case of building works, consultation is required where any tenant would have to pay more than £250 towards the works in question. In the case of long-term contracts, consultation is necessary before entering into a contract if it is to last for more than 12 months, and any tenant's contribution to the costs in a year would be more than £100. Such long-term contracts might include contracts for cleaning services or managing agents.

2.80 The consultation requirements in the Regulations are detailed and vary depending on a number of circumstances, e.g. whether the landlord is a public authority. In general terms, the process allows the tenants to have input into the choice of contractor, to be provided with a number of estimates for the relevant costs, and to be given reasons for the landlord's choice of contractor. If the landlord fails to comply with the Regulations, the service charge which he may recover from each tenant is limited to either £250 (for building works) or £100 (for long-term contracts). At any time, whether before commencement of the works or even after their completion, any or all of the consultation requirements may be waived by a leasehold valuation tribunal where it is reasonable to do so, e.g. in cases of urgency (1985 Act s.20ZA).

2.81 Statements of costs. Under the 1985 Act s.21, landlords must also provide a statement of relevant costs incurred during an accounting period when requested to do so. Amendments contained in the CLRA 2002 requiring an annual statement of account, showing the charges, the costs and any balances held, have yet to be brought into force. If they are brought into force, a new s.21A will permit leaseholders to withhold the payment of service charges if the statement has not been provided or does not conform to the statutory requirements.

2.82 Separate accounts. At present, where landlords hold receive service charges, they are deemed to be held on trust (Landlord and Tenant Act 1987 Act s.42). Under the 2002 Act, it is proposed to add a new s.42A, which will additionally require that any monies in the trust fund must be held in a separate, designated account.

2.83 Service charge demands. With effect from October 1, 2007, if a landlord demands payment of a service charge, that demand must—in England—be accompanied by a summary of the rights and obligations of both the landlord and the tenant in relation to service charges (1985 Act s.21B inserted by the 2002 Act). The wording of the summary is prescribed by the Service Charges (Summary of Rights and Obligations, and Transitional Provision) (England) Regulations 2007 (SI 2007/1257). If the summary is not included, the tenant is entitled to withhold payment. At the time of writing, no such provision had been made in Wales, but it is common for Welsh housing legislation to take the same approach as in England, even if at a different time.

7. ADMINISTRATION CHARGES

2.84 Commonhold and Leasehold Reform Act 2002. Many long leases require the tenant to pay the landlord's costs of granting approvals, e.g. to an assignment, or of providing information to third parties (prospective assignees) or to pay charges in the event of a breach of the lease, e.g. interest on late payment of rent or services or the landlord's costs of preparing a notice under s.146 of the LPA 1925 (1.137). Recovery of administration charges is governed by the 2002 Act.

2.85 Reasonableness. Administration charges can only be recovered so far as they are reasonable (2002 Act Sch.11 para.2). Leasehold valuation tribunals have jurisdiction to determine whether charges are reasonable. If the amount of the administration charge is fixed under the lease—whether in a specific amount or by reference to a formula—the tribunal has power to vary the amount or formula as it sees fit (2002 Act Sch.11 para.2).

2.86 Administration charge demands. With effect from October 1, 2007, if a landlord demands payment of an administration charge, that demand must—in England—be accompanied by a summary of the rights and obligations of both the landlord and the tenant in relation to administration charges (2002 Act Sch.11 para.4). The wording of the summary is prescribed by the Administration Charges (Summary of Rights and Obligations) (England) Regulations 2007 (SI 2007/1258). If the summary is not included, the tenant is entitled to withhold payment. See also the note on Wales at 2.83, above.

Freeholder rights

1. ESTATE CHARGES

2.87 Estate management schemes. Many of the properties enfranchised under either the 1967 or 1993 Acts, are situated on estates, in particular the estates of the large landlords in central London. Under both the 1967 and 1993 Acts, landlords are allowed to establish estate management schemes in order to maintain the estate's character. Most such schemes impose estate charges on freeholders; these are similar to service charges (2.75) and administration charges (2.84).

2.88 Reasonableness. Estate charges can only be recovered so far as they are reasonable (2002 Act s.159). Leasehold valuation tribunals have jurisdiction to determine whether charges are reasonable. If the amount of an estate charge is fixed under the scheme—whether in a specific amount or by reference to a formula—the tribunal has power to vary the amount or formula as it sees fit.

Mortgages

2.89 Nature of mortgages. Freehold, leasehold and commonhold owner-occupation can, and frequently will, be subject to a mortgage. Mortgages are a form of loan against the security of the property in question. There are two principal sorts of mortgage: capital repayment and endowment.

2.90 Capital mortgage. A capital repayment mortgage is a loan which requires repayment in periodic amounts. Although it is not an essential part of a capital repayment mortgage, most mortgage companies insist that there is included in the package an element of insurance, called the mortgage protection policy. This provides insurance against the death of the owner-occupier, in which case the insurance will pay off any outstanding mortgage and so leave the property unencumbered for the next-of-kin.

2.91 Capital and interest. The two essential parts of the repayments are capital repayment and interest (commonly at a variable rate, though it can be fixed or, e.g. fixed for a period of time). Monthly payments are assessed at an amount slightly larger than the interest due on the original capital loan. This means that at the beginning of a mortgage repayment period, most of the payment is interest, and only a small amount of it is capital repayment. As the capital decreases, however, a decreasing proportion of the repayments goes to interest (still based on the original loan) and an increasing amount on capital.

2.92 Endowment. The monthly payment under an endowment mortgage is a sum assessed in two parts only: interest and life assurance premium. Subject to fluctuations in the mortgage interest rate, both these amounts remain the same. There is no capital repayment. Instead, the life assurance premium is calculated to produce a sum that, either at the end of the period for which the mortgage has been taken out, or on the death of the mortgagor, will be sufficient to pay off the whole of the capital outstanding. There are other benefits which may be included in an endowment mortgage arrangement, but they are decreasingly popular because the sums produced by the premium have in recent years proved insufficient to pay off the capital.

2.93 Repossession and arrears. Although all mortgage deeds contain a variety of terms, e.g. not to create tenancies—or tenancies other than of a particular type, i.e. without security—in the property without permission, it is usually only when an occupier falls into arrears with the repayments that the company has the right to take action to evict him, and to dispose of the property.

2.94 Absent agreement, either the mortgage company or the mortgagor may apply for an order for the property to be sold (under the Law of Property Act 1925 s.91). Thus, if a mortgage company wishes instead to rent the property out until the market picks up, the mortgagor can apply to the court to force the mortgage company to sell in order to prevent interest continuing to accrue (*Palk v Mortgage Services Funding Plc*, 1992). Usually, an order for sale at the request of the mortgagor will be refused if the mortgage company can demonstrate a tangible benefit of which it will be deprived, but that will not include either its own policy considerations, or the power to conduct the sale through its own agents and solicitors (*Barrett v Halifax BS*, 1995).

2.95 Who is bound by the mortgage? The mortgage company will, however, have to be able to show that the mortgage is binding on those against whom it seeks possession. It will not be binding on someone with a prior interest, e.g. a tenant (1.223), or a spouse with a right of occupation under the Family Law Act 1996 (9.16), unless there has been an effective agreement to subordinate that right to the subsequent mortgagee (*Woolwich BS v Dickman*, 1996). Likewise, if there are joint owners on the face of the deeds, or as a result of a trust (1.23), all those who have an existing right must be shown to be bound by the mortgage before the company will be able to exercise its rights.

2.96 Securing someone else's loan. These issues commonly arise when a home is put up as security for a loan, which may not itself be for housing purposes but, e.g. for a business purpose. Where one person puts up his own home as security, then the position is no different than in any other case where one individual borrows against the security of his house or flat. Problems arise where one person—who wants to borrow the money—needs the agreement of a joint owner or someone else with a prior right to use the property as security.

2.97 Undue influence. Where the agreement to the loan has been procured by a third party (such as a husband, cohabitee or employer) using undue influence, misrepresentation or another legal wrong, it may not be binding if the lender has notice of the wrong. In some relationships, e.g. parent/child, solicitor/client, undue influence will automatically be presumed (and therefore the lender would be on notice of it) in any transaction which was to the disadvantage to the borrower, unless it can be shown that he entered into it with "full, free and informed thought". This presumption does not, however, automatically apply to husbands and wives. To show undue influence in such cases, it is necessary to have evidence that the transaction was wrongful "in that it constituted an advantage taken of the person subjected to the influence which, failing proof to the contrary, was explicable only on the basis that undue influence had been exercised to procure it" (*National Westminster Bank Plc v Morgan*, 1995; *Royal Bank of Scotland v Etridge*, 2001).

2.98   Effect on borrower.   To avoid being bound by the wrong, the lender will therefore have to show that he had taken reasonable steps to satisfy himself that the other party has entered into the arrangement freely and in knowledge of the true facts, which will normally mean warning him or her—at a meeting not attended by the borrower—of the amount of the potential liability, and of the risks involved, and advising him or her to take independent legal advice (*Barclays Bank Plc v O'Brien*, 1993). Even if the lender does not meet with the borrower, the lender will be protected against the wrongdoing if he has confirmed with the wife that she has a solicitor acting for her, and has confirmation from the solicitor that the borrower has been appropriately advised (*Royal Bank of Scotland*, above).

2.99   Demand for arrears.   Before legal proceedings are started, the mortgage company will normally make a written demand for any arrears of repayment. It is not obliged by law to do this, but in practice the court (which has discretionary powers which are described below) will not look kindly upon a mortgage company which has proceeded to exercise its full legal rights without warning the occupier and giving him a chance to redeem his position. If the arrears are paid off at that point, nothing further will normally happen. If an occupier has a bad history of arrears, however, the mortgage company may still decide to press on with the full legal procedure.

2.100   Demand for repayment.   After any demand for the arrears, there will be a formal demand for repayment of the whole of the outstanding debt. This will be for all capital outstanding and any accumulated interest. At this point, an occupier can, if he is in a position to do so, buy off the mortgage company entirely and retain possession of the property. There has to be such a formal demand, however, even if it is quite obvious that the occupier cannot comply with it.

2.101   Possession proceedings.   The next step is for the mortgage company to issue possession proceedings in the county court. The company cannot evict the occupier without court proceedings. The court is not obliged to grant the possession order immediately. It has power to grant an order suspended on condition that the occupier continues to pay current instalments under the mortgage, and a fixed amount per payment off the arrears, or it may stay execution or postpone the date for giving up possession. Once an order has been executed, however, there are no further powers of stay, suspension or postponement, unless there are grounds on which to set aside the warrant for possession, or it is considered to be an abuse of the process of the court, or oppressive to execute it (*Cheltenham & Gloucester BS v Obi*, 1994).

2.102 Suspended orders. The court will only exercise this discretion if it is of the view that the arrears can be cleared in a reasonable time (Administration of Justice Act 1970 s.36; *Town & Country Building Society v Julien*, 1991). If it does not think this can be done, then the order will be final, but will usually be suspended for at least 28 days to give the occupier time to start making alternative arrangements: see Chapter 10. While it has been said that an order may be deferred for a short period, e.g. three months, in order to enhance the prospects of sale by the occupier (*Target Home Loans Ltd v Clothier*, 1992), this is not a rule of law, and if there is evidence that a sale could take place in a longer period, there is no reason why a court should not allow it (*National & Provincial BS v Lloyd*, 1995).

2.103 Reasonable time to clear arrears. There is no formal definition of reasonable time. For some time, the courts normally considered one year a reasonable time in which to clear the arrears (*Cheltenham & Gloucester BS v Grant*, 1994). The current position is that a court should take as its starting point the full period of the mortgage, and determine whether or not it would be possible for the mortgagor to maintain payment of the arrears by instalments over that period. This approach will call for more detailed analysis than had become customary, and amongst the features the court will need to consider will be how much the borrower could reasonably afford to pay (currently and in the future); if a difficulty is temporary, for how long it is likely to last; what the reason was for the arrears; the remaining term; any relevant contractual terms; the type of mortgage; over what period it is reasonable to expect the lender to recoup arrears of interest; and any other reasons affecting the security which should influence the length of the period (*Cheltenham & Gloucester BS v Norgan*, 1995).

2.104 Consumer Credit Act 1974. Loans of less than £15,000, which are not made by local authorities or building societies (and certain other exempt organisations) are regulated by the Consumer Credit Act 1974. Where the creditor is seeking repayment or possession, the court may make a "time order" to reschedule payment of the debt (1974 Act s.129). The court must consider whether it is just to make the order, and where possession proceedings are involved this relates to the whole outstanding balance under the mortgage (*Southern & District Finance v Barnes*, 1995). The court also has power to alter the rate of interest (1974 Act s.136).

CHAPTER THREE

Housing Act Secure Tenancies

Introduction

3.01 Landlords whose tenants are secure. A range of "social landlords" provide "secure tenancies" within the Housing Act 1985 Act Pt 3 ("1985 Act"). These are primarily local authorities and registered social landlords, but in the latter case only where the tenancy was granted on or before January 14, 1989 (at which time, those landlords were known as housing associations). Later tenancies are "assured" under the Housing Act 1988 (see Chapter 4).

3.02 Other rights of secure tenants. Where tenants of social landlords are secure, they also gain a number of additional rights, including the right to buy.

3.03 Other tenants of social landlords. Tenants of social landlords who do not qualify as secure tenants under the Housing Act 1985 will normally qualify as assured tenants under the Housing Act 1988 and are considered in Chapter 4. The remaining tenants of social landlords, who do not qualify under either Act, will be considered in Chapter 7.

Outline

3.04 Social landlords

- Local authorities have specific powers to provide housing.
- Tenants of local authorities are secure, unless specific exceptions apply.
- Certain other defined landlords can also grant secure tenancies.

- Registered social landlords formerly granted secure tenancies, but have not been able to do so since January 15, 1989; their subsequent tenancies are assured (see Chapter 4).

3.05 Secure tenants. A secure tenant is one to whom residential accommodation is let as a separate dwelling, under a tenancy or licence, and under which both the landlord condition and tenant condition are fulfilled. There is, however, a schedule of exceptions which may exclude someone who would otherwise be a secure tenant:

- On the death of the secure tenant, there is a right to one succession to a secure tenancy by a spouse or family member.

- A dwelling let under a secure tenancy can only be repossessed by the landlord obtaining a court order, usually after service of a notice of seeking possession, which sets out the statutory ground on which possession is sought.

- Some grounds require the court to be satisfied that it is reasonable to grant possession; others that suitable alternative accommodation is provided; and yet others that it is both reasonable, and suitable alternative accommodation is provided.

- A court may terminate a secure tenancy under a demotion order where the tenant has been guilty of antisocial behaviour.

- If the landlord is a local authority or Housing Action Trust, the demotion order replaces the secure tenancy with a demoted tenancy; if the landlord is a registered social landlord, the replacement tenancy is a demoted shorthold assured tenancy.

3.06 Additional rights and issues

- Secure tenants have a number of additional rights:
    - the right to buy;
    - right to improve;
    - rights to sublet and take in lodgers;
    - the right to exchange;
    - the right to repair;
    - rights in relation to variation of terms of the tenancy; and

- — rights to be consulted in matters of housing management.

- Local authorities are bound to charge "reasonable" rents; what is reasonable is largely a matter for the discretion of the local authority.

- Pre-1988 Act housing association tenancies (which are therefore normally secure) are subject to the fair rent regime of the Rent Act 1977 (Chapter 5).

- Management of the stock is largely a matter for the social landlord, although local authorities may enter into management agency agreements and their tenants may seek to set up their own tenant management organisation.

- Transfer of local authority housing has been a government policy for the last 20 years, and a number of mechanisms exist to achieve this: these include voluntary transfer and Housing Action Trusts.

- Further financial protection and assistance is available to secure tenants.

Social landlords

3.07 Local housing authorities. Local authorities still remain the main providers of social rented housing, although current government policy is to seek to reduce the amount of rented stock they hold (see below for provisions governing transfer). Since 1980, most of their tenancies have been secure, and continue to remain so.

3.08 Local authorities for housing purposes are: district councils; county and county borough councils (in Wales); London borough councils and the Common Council of the City of London; although county councils may, with the consent of the Secretary of State, also exercise housing powers. Unitary authorities will likewise be housing authorities.

3.09 Provision of housing. Under the 1985 Act s.8, local housing authorities are bound to consider the housing needs of their areas. Part 2 of that Act contains their powers to own, manage and dispose of their housing accommodation, although it should be noted that there is no absolute requirement that they should hold any stock of accommodation if they do not choose to do so (1985 Act s.9(5)).

3.10   Detailed provision is made as to who may be allocated local authority accommodation; this is considered in Chapter 10.

3.11   Other social landlords.   New town commissions, urban development corporations and Housing Action Trusts all fulfil functions similar to those of local authorities, and their tenants are likewise normally secure. Tenancies of certain other public bodies, such as the police service, are also secure.

3.12   Registered social landlords.   Housing associations, housing trusts and similar bodies—known under the Housing Act 1996 ("1996 Act") as "registered social landlords"—qualify for public funding for their activities. These are registered under Pt 1 of the 1996 Act, with the Housing Corporation or with the National Assembly for Wales.

3.13   Between 1980 and 1988, registered housing associations and trusts were landlords whose tenants were normally secure. From 1989, by Pt 1 of the Housing Act 1988, however, their tenants were taken out of the Housing Act 1985 and placed into the same framework as private sector tenants, as assured tenants. That is the regime which governs all subsequent tenants of registered social landlords: see Chapter 4, below.

3.14   Pre- and post-January 15, 1989 registered social landlord tenants.   In this chapter, accordingly, we are concerned with the tenants of registered social landlord only if the tenancy began before the commencement (January 15, 1989) of Pt 1 of the Housing Act 1988 ("1988 Act").

3.15   Exceptions.   A tenancy granted by a registered social landlord on or after that date cannot be secure unless either:

1. **Pre-Act contract.** It was entered into, pursuant to a contract for its grant which preceded that date; or

2. **New tenancy to former tenant.** It is the grant of a new tenancy (not necessarily of the same premises) to a person who was a former tenant of the same landlord, or one of a number of joint (1.198) such tenants; or

3. **Suitable alternative accommodation.** It is the grant of a tenancy resulting from an order for possession against a secure tenant, on the ground of suitable alternative accommodation (3.124, 3.135); and

    (a) the premises in question are those which the court has found suitable; and

    (b) the court directs that the new tenancy should be a secure tenancy on the ground that an assured tenancy will not provide sufficient security; or

4. **New town corporation to housing association.** It falls within a small class of tenancy formerly held by a new town development corporation, and passed into housing association ownership before March 31, 1996; or

5. **Defective premises.** The tenancy is one granted under special provisions (Housing Act 1985 Pt 16) dealing with buying back premises that have been designated as defective in their design (not covered in this book): 1988 Act s.34.

3.16 So far as this chapter concerns housing association tenancies, it therefore applies mainly to tenancies already granted. Tenancies granted on or after the commencement of Pt 1 of the 1988 Act are, subject to its own schedule of exclusions, likely to be assured tenancies, and are considered in Chapter 4.

Secure tenants

3.17 Let as a separate dwelling. A secure tenant is one to whom residential accommodation is let as a separate dwelling under a tenancy or licence (1985 Act s.79), under which both the landlord conditions and the tenant conditions are fulfilled, and which is not excluded from security under the schedule of exceptions (1985 Act Sch.1).

3.18 The term "let as a separate dwelling" is considered in relation to the Housing Act assured tenancies (4.17) and the Rent Act protected tenancies (5.40), as the greatest attention has been paid to it in connection with the private sector (but see also 3.23). Under those Acts, it refers to a letting by way of tenancy but not by way of licence (1.47).

3.19 Application to licensees. This is not so under the Housing Act 1985, which also applies to licences, whether or not granted for a monetary payment (1985 Act s.79(3)).

3.20 Licences within the 1985 Act are, however, only those which effectively grant the occupier exclusive possession (*cf.* 1.67). Where the landlord retains the right to move tenants to other rooms, as is commonly the case in agreements for a letting of a room in a hostel, the licence will not be within the Act (*Westminster CC v Clarke*, 1992).

3.21 Temporary licenses. The inclusion of licences does not extend to a licence granted as a temporary expedient to a person who entered the premises the subject of the licence, or other premises, as a trespasser (1985 Act s.79(4)), e.g. those who illegally entered unused public sector property awaiting demolition but—to avoid unnecessarily leaving property empty—who were allowed to remain or else were offered somewhere else temporarily (1.32).

3.22 Throughout this chapter, save where a distinction is drawn, references to secure tenancy include licences brought into security by s.79.

3.23 Shared living accommodation. Another important distinction between private security under the 1988 and 1977 Acts, and the 1985 Act, is that, while the 1988 and 1977 Acts are specifically applied to those who share living accommodation (4.17, 5.70), there is no such provision in the 1985 Act.

3.24 The effect of this is that there cannot be a secure tenancy where living accommodation is shared because there is no letting "as a separate dwelling": *Central YMCA HA Ltd v Saunders*, 1990; *Curl v Angelo*, 1948).

3.25 Living accommodation for these purposes means a living-room, rather than a bathroom or lavatory (*Cole v Harris*, 1945) or, probably, a kitchen, unless it is big enough to eat in (*Neale v Del Soto*, 1945; *Central YMCA*; *Uratemp v Collins*, 2001. There remains some doubt about the position, where what is shared is a kitchen that is not big enough to sit and eat in). This exclusion tends to affect those in hostels and other shared accommodation.

3.26 For this purpose, it does not matter whether or not anyone else is actually sharing living accommodation at any particular time; it is sufficient if the terms of the letting are such that it is genuinely within contemplation—or there is a real prospect—that the occupier will have to share living accommodation with another at some future date (*Gray v Brown*, 1992).

3.27 Principal issues. Under this heading, we must consider:

• the landlord condition;

- the tenant condition;
- exceptions;
- succession;
- loss of security.

1. THE LANDLORD CONDITION

3.28 Secure landlords. The landlord condition is that the landlord under the tenancy is:

- a local authority;
- a New Town corporation;
- a housing action trust;
- an urban development corporation or a housing co-operative as defined (1985 Act s.80(1)).

3.29 The section only applies to housing co-operatives set up under a housing management agreement (as defined in 1985 Act s.27B) (1985 Act s.80(4)).

3.30 Former secure landlords. A number of other landlords were formerly listed in the 1985 Act s.80(1) until they were removed by the Housing Act 1988. They are:

- the Housing Corporation;
- a housing trust which is a charity;
- registered housing associations (other than co-operative housing associations); and
- unregistered housing associations which are co-operative associations (1985 Act s.80(1), (2), prior to amendment).

3.31 Tenants of such landlords whose tenancies were granted prior to commencement of Pt I of the 1988 Act (January 15, 1989) remain secure.

2. THE TENANT CONDITION

3.32 Occupation by individual as only or principal home. The tenant condition is that the tenant is an individual, as opposed to a corporate body, e.g. a company, and that the tenant occupies the dwelling-house as his only or principal home (1985 Act s.81).

3.33   This is a slightly different test (*Poland v Earl Cadogan*, 1980) from that of statutory residence under the Rent Act 1977 (5.95–5.111), and is, rather, closer to that to be found in relation to the Leasehold Reform Act 1967 (2.28).

3.34   Whether premises are occupied as a home at all, is, however, to be determined in the same way as the question whether they are occupied as a residence under the Rent Act 1977 (5.98).

3.35   Actual physical occupation may not be necessary (*Crawley BC v Sawyer*, 1987). Where the tenant is no longer in occupation, however, he is under the burden of establishing that he intends to return to the property, and must substantiate this through visible signs of that intention (*Ujima HA v Ansah*, 1997 and *Amoah v Baking & Dagenham LBC*, 2001).

3.36   Joint tenants.   If the tenancy is a joint tenancy, then at least one of the joint tenants must be an individual as opposed to a corporate body, and at least one of the joint tenants must be in occupation as an only or principal home (1985 Act s.81).

3.37   A tenant does not necessarily lose security if he ceases to occupy as an only or principal home, so long as he is doing so when the tenancy purports to end (*Hussey v Camden LBC*, 1994), i.e. he may be able to resume sufficient occupation between service and expiry of notice to quit. (Note: a tenant who ceases to sustain sufficient occupation ceases to be secure; accordingly, the notice of seeking possession ("NSP") procedure considered below is inapplicable, and notice to quit in the ordinary way has to be served: see below, 3.67. As a notice to quit needs time to take effect, if the tenant does return, he becomes secure again and—because he is not a secure tenant—it is the notice to quit which has become inapplicable.)

3.38   A tenant may acquire security if his own landlord surrenders (1.191) his tenancy, e.g. where an authority had let premises as a business (3.39(14)), part of which had been sublet residentially (*Basingstoke & Deane BC v Paice*, 1995).

3.   EXCEPTIONS

3.39   Exceptions from security.   There are numerous exceptions from security (1985 Act Sch.1):

1. **Long leases.** Long leases, i.e. leases for a period in excess of 21 years (para.1);

2. **Introductory tenancies.** Tenancies which are granted under an introductory tenancy regime, and which have not moved into security pursuant to those provisions (para.1A; see Chapter 6).

3. **Employee accommodation.** Premises occupied under a contract of employment which requires the tenant to occupy the dwelling-house for the better performance of his duties (1.155–1.157), and the tenant is an employee of the landlord, or of a local authority, a New Town development corporation, an urban development corporation or a Housing Action Trust. (Note: this allows one public sector landlord to house the employee of another.)

   Also within this exclusion are premises provided to policemen free of rent and rates under the Police Act 1964, and premises rented to firemen in consequence of employment, where their contract of employment requires the fireman to live close to a particular station (para.2).

   A requirement to occupy will not be implied, unless the occupation is in fact necessary for the tenant's employment duties to be carried out (*Hughes v Greenwich LBC*, 1993; *Surrey CC v Lamond*, 1998).

   If occupation continues after employment ceases, it will be a question of fact whether the tenancy is still referable to the employment in question, or whether there has been an agreed or intended change in the nature or purpose of the occupation (*South Glamorgan CC v Griffiths*, 1992; *Elvidge v Coventry CC*, 1993; *Greenfield v Berkshire CC*, 1994).

4. **Temporary use of employee accommodation.** Where premises have been occupied under the last exemption from security at any time in the previous three years, the landlord can let them out in other circumstances, without the occupier becoming secure, provided:

   (a) the landlord gives the occupier notice that this exception will apply; and

   (b) (i) in the case of a local authority landlord, the landlord has not notified the tenant that he is to become secure, and

   (ii) in the case of any other landlord, the tenancy, or tenancies, do not themselves extend more than three years beyond the last time when the premises were occupied under a para.2 exemption (para.2).

5. **Development land.** Premises on land acquired for development, being used pending development for temporary housing accommodation, i.e. short-life user (para.3).

6. **Homeless-persons accommodation.** A tenancy granted to a person under Pt 7 of the 1996 Act is not secure until the landlord notifies the tenant that he is to be a secure tenant (para.4).

7. **Asylum-seeker accommodation.** A tenancy granted to someone of accommodation under the National Asylum Support Service set up under the Immigration and Asylum Act 1999, Pt 6 is not secure until the landlord notifies the tenant that it is to be (para.4A).

8. **Job-mobility accommodation.** Temporary accommodation granted to a person not hitherto resident in the same district or London borough as the premises, granted for the purposes of enabling the tenant to take up employment or an offer of employment within that district or London borough, or within an adjoining district or London borough, while looking for permanent accommodation.

   Before the grant of the tenancy, the landlord must notify the tenant that this exception applies. In the case of a local authority landlord, the exemption lasts until the landlord notifies the tenant that he is to become secure. In the case of any other landlord whose tenants are secure, the exception only applies for one year, or less if during that year the landlord notifies the tenant that he is to be a secure tenant (para.5).

9. **Sub-leasing schemes.** Sub-lettings under leasing schemes are not secure. These are schemes under which the landlord takes a lease from a private sector landlord, i.e. one whose tenants would not be secure if granted a direct tenancy, which is either for a fixed term or else granted on terms that the lease will come to an end when required by the landlord (*Haringey LBC v Hickey*, 2006).

   This scheme enables public landlords to take lettings of residential accommodation which would otherwise be left vacant by the private sector landlord, in order to lease it on to others (para.6).

10. **Accommodation pending works for non-secure tenant.** Temporary accommodation provided to a tenant who is not

a secure tenant, while works are executed to his usual home, is not secure (para.7).

11. **Agricultural holdings.** Agricultural holdings within the Agricultural Holdings Act 1986 or farm business tenancies within the Agricultural Tenancies Act 1995 are not secure (para.8).

12. **Licensed premises.** Tenancies are not secure if of premises which consist of or include premises licensed for the sale of intoxicating liquor for consumption on the premises (para.9).

13. **Student lettings.** Student lettings are not secure if granted to enable the tenant to attend a designated course at an educational establishment and the landlord has, before the grant of the tenancy, notified the student that the exception applies.

A designated course is one designated by the Secretary of State for this purpose. This exception ceases at any time:

(a) in the case of a local authority landlord, if the landlord has notified the tenant that he is to become secure; and

(b) in the case of any other landlord, until six months after he ceases to attend the educational establishment, or— if the tenant fails to take up his place on the course— six months after the grant of the tenancy (para.10), or if the landlord notifies the tenant that he is to be a secure tenant.

14. **Business lettings.** Business tenancies within the Landlord and Tenant Act 1954 Pt 2 (see Chapter 6) are not secure (para.11).

It may be particularly difficult to decide whether this applies to those who occupy premises, part of which consist of, for example, a shop or business. The following points may be noted:

(a) It is not possible for a tenancy which was originally let for a business purpose to become a letting within the 1985 Act, for it will not have been let "as a dwelling" (*Webb v Barnet LBC*, 1988) unless there is an agreed change to residential use (*Russell v Booker*, 1982), but it is possible for a tenancy which was originally let as a dwelling under a secure tenancy to become a business letting and so move from 1985 Act protection into that of the Landlord and Tenant Act 1954 Pt 2 (1985 Act

Sch.1 para.11), which is the main legislation concerned with business lettings.

(b) This move will happen if the predominant use of the premises is, or becomes, business use (*Cheryl Investments Ltd v Saldanha*, 1978), or if the business purpose can be said to be more than incidental to the residential occupation (*Wright v Mortimer*, 1996).

(c) This move will not necessarily happen merely because there has been some amount of business use, perhaps ancillary to offices elsewhere (*Royal Life Saving Society v Page*, 1978), although it is not decisive (in favour of business use in the premises in question) that no business is carried out from elsewhere (*Wright*).

(d) Merely taking in lodgers will not have this effect (*Lewis v Weldcrest*, 1978).

(e) The business activity must be part of the reason for, and the aim and object in, occupying the house, not merely an incidental hobby which made some money (*Gurton v Parrot*, 1990). It is always a question of fact and degree.

(f) Where the main purpose of the tenancy is to provide a place from which the tenant can trade, the fact that it also provides him with a home does not prevent the tenancy from being a business tenancy (*Broadway Investments Ltd v Grant*, 2006).

15. **Almshouses.** Almshouses occupied under a licence from a charity are not secure (para.12).

4. SUCCESSION

3.40 Solitary succession. Under the Housing Act 1985, there can only be one statutory succession, which is to a surviving spouse or civil partner or to a member of the deceased tenant's family (1985 Act s.87).

3.41 In some circumstances, there may be no succession at all. Thus, if the secure tenancy was originally a joint tenancy, but one of the joint tenants has died or otherwise surrendered his interest, there will be no further succession (1985 Act s.88).

3.42 Qualifying successor. Only a qualifying person can succeed. A person qualifies if, at the time of the death of the secure tenant:

- the would-be successor was occupying the dwelling-house as his only or principal home (3.32); and

- he was either:
  - — the deceased tenant's spouse or civil partner; or
  - — another member of the deceased tenant's family (1985 Act s.87).

3.43 In the case of anyone other than a spouse or civil partner, it is also necessary to show that the would-be successor had been residing with the deceased tenant for at least 12 months before his death.

3.44 Residing with. "Residing with" means more than "living or staying at" the premises, although does not necessarily require so much as permanent or indefinite residence: *Swanbrae v Elliott*, 1987; *Hildebrand v Moon*, 1989.

3.45 A period of absence does not necessarily break the continuity of residence. It depends on the nature and extent of the continuing connection with the premises throughout the period of absence and the quality of the intention to return (*Camden LBC v Goldenburg*, 1996).

3.46 The qualification of 12 months' residence with the deceased tenant, applicable to would-be successors other than a spouse, does not have to have been at the property to which succession is being sought: *Waltham Forest LBC v Thomas*, 1992. Thus, if the tenant came to stay with, say, a child in that child's home, but—less than 12 months before the end of the tenant's life—parent and child moved back into the parent's home, the child will still be able to succeed.

3.47 Choice of successor. There can be no joint succession: *Newham LBC v Phillips*, 1997. Where there is a number of potential qualifying successors, the deceased tenant's spouse or civil partner takes precedence, but otherwise the qualifying persons must agree amongst themselves who is to take over the tenancy. If they cannot do so, the landlord is entitled to choose. There is, however, no obligation to notify the landlord on the agreed successor (*General Management v Locke*, 1980).

3.48 Member of family. Members of the family are defined (1985 Act s.113) as: spouses, parents, grandparents, children, grandchildren, siblings, uncles, aunts, nephews and nieces; including step-relations, half-relations and illegitimate children and persons living together as husband and wife.

3.49 "[L]iving together as husband and wife" means more than merely living together in the same household (*City of Westminster v Peart*, 1991).

3.50 A homosexual couple can be considered to be living together as husband and wife.

3.51 A minor can succeed to a secure tenancy: *Kingston upon Thames RLBC v Prince*, 1998. As a minor cannot hold a legal interest in land, however, the tenancy must be held on trust for him.

3.52 The list of family members is exhaustive; its limitations do not discriminate against more distant family members in such a way as to breach Arts 8 (right to respect for family life and home) or 14 (non-discrimination) of the European Convention on Human Rights: *Wandsworth LBC v Michalak*, 2002.

3.53 No qualifying successor. If there is no one qualified to succeed on the death of the tenant under the statutory rules, the tenancy may yet remain secure if a court orders its transfer under one of a number of family statutes governing both partners and children, e.g. where a court makes such an order in favour of a person who did not fulfil the residential requirements, or in favour of a former spouse (likewise not residing with the deceased tenant).

3.54 Otherwise, the tenancy will cease to be secure once it has vested—pursuant to the rules applicable to the devolution of property (including tenancies) on death—and it is known that the vesting is not pursuant to one of those statutes (1985 Act ss.89, 90). In the interregnum, it therefore remains secure.

5. LOSS OF SECURITY

3.55 Ways of losing security. Leaving aside for the moment an order for possession made by the court (3.147–3.166), there are several circumstances in which security can be lost.

3.56 First of all, security will be lost if there is a change of landlord, and the new landlord does not fulfil the landlord condition (3.28–3.29; see also transfer of public housing, below).

3.57 Secondly, security will be lost if the tenant ceases to occupy the premises as his only or principal home (3.32).

3.58 Loss of security by assignment. In addition, any assignment (1.228) of a secure tenancy causes security to be lost, unless either:

- the assignment is pursuant to an order of the court under one of a number of family provisions (Chapter 9), governing both partners and children; or
- it is to someone who qualifies as a successor (3.42–3.46); or
- it is pursuant to the "right to exchange" (1985 Act s.91) (below, 3.205).

3.59 If the secure tenant sublets the whole of the premises, either at one go or piecemeal, security is also lost, even if the sub-letting is to a person who qualifies as a successor (1985 Act s.93).

3.60 A mere licence arrangement, however, will not cause the loss of security (*Hussey v Camden LBC*, 1994).

3.61 In any of these cases, once security is lost it cannot be regained (1985 Act ss.91, 93), e.g. by evicting a sub-tenant or by reassignment. Security will not now normally be lost by bankruptcy.

Security of tenure

3.62 Contractual security. If a secure tenancy is a periodic tenancy (1.102), the landlord cannot bring it to an end at all: only the court can do so (1985 Act s.82(1)), only on specified grounds and only after the landlord has followed the appropriate preliminary procedure.

3.63 If the tenancy is a fixed-term tenancy (1.102), it can only be forfeited by court order, and even if it expires by effluxion of time, there will come into its place an automatic periodic tenancy, on the same terms as the preceding fixed-term tenancy, and of which the periods are the same as those for which rent was paid under the preceding fixed-term tenancy (1985 Act s.86).

3.64 The only exceptions to this latter proposition are:

- if the landlord and the tenant agree a new fixed-term tenancy to follow the first fixed-term tenancy;
- if the court orders possession to be given up at the end of the fixed-term, i.e. in forfeiture proceedings (note: on proceedings to forfeit (1.131–1.135) a fixed-term secure tenancy,

the court has a choice of orders: it may determine the fixed term, but not order the tenant out, in which case the periodic (and Housing Act secure) tenancy will follow (1985 Act s.86(1)); or, it may grant a possession order); and

- if the court orders a demotion order, in which case a periodic demoted tenancy or demoted assured shorthold tenancy (depending on the identity of the landlord) replaces the fixed-term tenancy (3.167).

1.   TERMINATION OF TENANCY BY POSSESSION

3.65   Continuation until possession.   In the case of a periodic tenancy, whether originally periodic or following a fixed term, the tenancy itself continues until the date the court orders the tenant to give up possession (1985 Act s.82) or makes a demotion order (3.167). In this and the next two sections, we consider possession proceedings.

3.66   Notice of seeking possession (NSP).   The court can only make an order for possession on specified grounds, and only if either:

- the landlord has followed the proper procedure; or
- the court considers it just and equitable to dispense with the requirement for a notice (1985 Act s.83).

3.67   This procedure is in place of notice to quit, and is commonly known as a "notice of seeking possession" or NSP. Whether or not it is just and equitable to dispense with the NSP depends on all of the facts and circumstances both in which there was an omission to serve the notice and otherwise affecting landlord and tenant (*Bradshaw v Balwin-Wiseman*, 1985; *Kelsey Housing Association v King*, 1995).

3.68   Effectiveness of NSP.   The NSP must normally specify a date after which legal proceedings may be issued (1985 Act s.83(4)(a)). The NSP then remains in force for one year following that date (1985 Act s.83(4)(b)).

3.69   The specified date must not be earlier than the date when the tenancy could have been brought to an end by notice to quit (1.116–1.117) (1985 Act s.83(5)).

3.70 There are special provisions which apply when reliance is placed—in whole or part—on Ground 2, Nuisance and Annoyance (3.103). In these cases, the notice must state that proceedings for possession may be commenced immediately, and must specify a date by which the landlord wants the tenant to give up possession (1985 Act s.83(3)). Again, that date must not be earlier than when the tenancy could have been brought to an end by notice to quit (1985 Act s.83(5)). The difference allows the landlord to start proceedings under Ground 2 earlier than in other cases.

3.71 NSP—further conditions. The court cannot entertain proceedings for possession in a case to which Ground 2 is relevant unless the NSP is still in force at the time the proceedings are begun (1985 Act s.83A(1)), which means one year after the date specified as that by which the landlord wants the tenant to give up possession (1985 Act s.83(3)).

3.72 In any other case, the court cannot entertain proceedings for possession unless the proceedings are commenced after the specified date (1985 Act s.83A(2)), and the NSP is still in force at the time the proceedings are begun, which is for one year from that date (1985 Act s.83(4)).

3.73 Domestic violence. Ground 2A allows recovery of property where there has been domestic violence leading to the departure of one of a couple (married, civil partners, or who have been living together as husband and wife or civil partners), one of whom is, or both of whom are, a tenant of it (3.112).

3.74 If this ground is to be used, the court is not to entertain proceedings for possession unless satisfied that the landlord has served—or has taken all reasonable steps to serve—a copy of the NSP on the partner who has left (1985 Act s.83A(3)).

3.75 If the case is one in which Ground 2 (above) is also specified, the court may dispense with this service requirement, however, if just and equitable to do so (1985 Act s.83A(5)).

3.76 Contents of notice. The NSP must be in the form prescribed by the Secretary of State, or substantially to the same effect, and it must specify the grounds on which the court will be asked to terminate the tenancy and make a possession order (1985 Act s.83(2)).

3.77 The particulars must be sufficient to enable the tenant to know what he has to do in order to put matters right, e.g. they must specify an amount of arrears (*Torridge DC v Jones*, 1985; *Mountain v Hastings*, 1993, *cf. Marath v MacGillivray*, 1995). In cases where Ground 2A (domestic violence: 3–112) is being relied on, the incidents of violence should be particularised: *Camden LBC v Mallett*, 2001.

3.78 An error in the particulars does not, however, invalidate the notice, provided it sets out what the landlord intends in good faith to prove (*Dudley MBC v Bailey*, 1990).

3.79 There is power (1985 Act s.84(3)) for the court to allow additional grounds to be specified, or the grounds to be altered, which imports power to alter or add to the particulars (*Camden LBC v Oppong*, 1996).

3.80 Domestic violence and service. If the new grounds include Ground 2A (domestic violence: 3.112), the court has to be satisfied that the landlord has served a notice on the partner who has left, or has taken all reasonable steps to do so (1985 Act s.83A(4)). Again, the court may dispense with this requirement, however, if just and equitable to do so, and if Ground 2 is also specified (1985 Act s.83A(5)).

3.81 Fixed-term tenancies. An NSP must also be served before possession can be sought of a fixed-term tenancy. The NSP has effect with respect to any periodic tenancy arising on the termination of the fixed term by virtue of the 1985 Act s.86 (3.62) (1985 Act s.83(6)) The specific provisions for notices in relation to Ground 2 (3.71) do not apply to notices served on fixed-term tenants (1985 Act s.83(6)).

2. GROUNDS FOR POSSESSION

3.82 The most significant element in security law is the grounds for possession. These fall into three classes (1985 Act s.84(2)):

1. ground plus reasonableness;

2. ground plus suitable alternative accommodation; and

3. ground plus suitable alternative accommodation plus reasonableness.

3.83 The grounds for possession are set out in the 1985 Act Sch.2. The Schedule provides an exhaustive code of the grounds on which a landlord may bring a secure tenancy to an end (*Islington LBC v Uckac*, 2006).

(i) Ground plus reasonableness

3.84 Reasonableness—additional requirement. In relation to this class of ground for possession, the landlord must satisfy the court:

- that the ground is itself made out; and
- that it is reasonable to make the order sought (1985 Act s.84)).

3.85 It is important always to bear in mind that this requirement is additional and must be considered in every case (*Peachey Property Corp v Robinson*, 1967).

3.86 Reasonableness—general principles. "Reasonable" has to be determined having regard to both the interests of the parties and also to the interests of the public: *Cresswell v Hodgson*, 1951; *Battlespring v Gates*, 1983. There is no general restriction, save relevance, as to what the court can take into account under this heading (*Cresswell*), which is to be considered as at the date of the hearing: *Rhodes v Cornford*, 1947.

3.87 Reasonableness—arrears. Even where arrears are of charges owed to a third party, such as water rates, it may nonetheless be reasonable to make an order for possession, and a judge should not limit himself to doing so only in "exceptional circumstances": *Lambeth LBC v Thomas*, 1997.

3.88 In *Lal v Nakum*, 1982, a tenant withheld rent on account of an alleged breach of repairing obligation by the landlord (Chapter 11), which allegation he did not sustain in court. He had, however, saved the withheld rent and could have paid it all at once: nonetheless, the court made an outright order for possession. The Court of Appeal set this aside.

3.89 Where, however, a tenant lost a counterclaim for disrepair and was unable to make any provision to pay off the arrears in *Haringey LBC v Stewart*, 1991, the Court of Appeal upheld the outright order for possession.

3.90 In *Woodspring DC v Taylor*, 1982, a couple had lived in their house for 24 years. The man lost his employment and suffered a heavy tax demand; the woman had diabetes and was attending a blood specialist. The Department of Health and Social Security took over their rent payments, and were paying £1 per week off the arrears. Until the recent difficulties, the Taylors had always been good tenants. The county court judge made an order for possession, but the Court of Appeal had "difficulty in understanding how anyone could have made an order turning them out of their home".

3.91 Rent arrears pre-action protocol. Before commencing possession proceedings, a social landlord (including a local authority, registered social landlord or Housing Act Trust) should comply with the pre-action protocol for rent arrears claims under the CPR. In general terms, this requires the parties to make efforts to reach agreements for the payment of the arrears without having to go to the court. The court may take into account any unreasonable failure by the tenant to comply with the protocol, when considering whether it is reasonable to make an order. Failure to comply by the landlord may result in his claim being dismissed.

3.92 Reasonableness—antisocial behaviour. In cases under Ground 2 (nuisance and criminal behaviour: 3.103), the court must always take into account the effect that the tenant's behaviour has had on neighbours, the continuing effect of that behaviour, and the effect that it would be likely to have if it is repeated: 1985 Act s.85A; *Woking BC v Bistram*, 1993; *Kensington & Chelsea RLBC v Simmonds*, 1996; *Darlington BC v Sterling*, 1996; *Newcastle CC v Morrison*, 2000; and *West Kent HA v Davies*, 1998.

3.93 The fact that the nuisance behaviour was carried out by someone other than the tenant does not mean it is not reasonable to grant possession: *Simmonds, Sterling; Camden LBC v Gilsenan,* 1998; *Portsmouth CC v Bryant*, 2000. This is so even where there are alternative remedies, such as an injunction (8.110), or an antisocial behaviour order (8.129) is available against the perpetrator: *Morrison; Manchester CC v Higgins*, 2006.

3.94 In severe cases, such as drug dealing from the premises or racial harassment, it will only be in exceptional circumstances that it is not reasonable to make an order: *Bristol CC v Mousah*, 1997; *Davies.*

3.95 Reasonableness—impact of homelessness. While it is right for a judge to consider the effect of a possession order in rendering a tenant homeless, it is wrong for the judge to consider the possible outcome of any application made by the tenant as a homeless person, e.g. that the tenant may be intentionally homeless (10.47): *Mousah; Sterling; Shrewsbury & Atcham BC v Evans,* 1997; *Lewisham LBC v Akinsola,* 1999; *Watford BC v Simpson,* 2000; *cf. Croydon LBC v Moody,* 1999.

3.96 Reasonableness—impact of ECHR, Article 8. In *Lambeth LBC v Howard,* 2001, the Court of Appeal considered the impact of Art.8 of the European Convention on Human Rights (respect for home) on the discretionary grounds for possession. It concluded that Art.8 would not lead the courts to reach substantially different decisions from those which they had been reaching for years, when applying the test of reasonableness.

3.97 Rent unpaid. The first ground is Ground 1: rent due from the tenant has not been paid, or an obligation of the tenancy has been broken or not performed.

3.98 There will be no arrears if the tenant has exercised the right to set-off an amount against the landlord's breach of his repairing obligations (11.105–11.109), although it has already been noted that if the tenant does so wrongly there will be a ground for possession (whether or not it is then likely that it will be reasonable to make the order depending on whether or not the tenant has the money to pay the arrears: 3.88–3.89).

3.99 It will usually be unreasonable to make the order if the tenant has paid off the arrears by the date of hearing (*Hayman v Rowlands,* 1957), although in some circumstances, e.g. a long history of non-payment, it may still be possible (*Bird v Hildage,* 1948).

3.100 Breach of term. There will be no breach of a term of the tenancy if there has been a waiver (1.186) of the breach.

3.101 It is only breach of a term of the tenancy which gives rise to the claim, not breach of some additional, ancillary agreement, e.g. a personal undertaking (*RMR Housing Society v Combs,* 1951).

3.102 In *Heglibiston Establishments v Heyman,* 1977, it was held that cohabitation did not amount to a breach of a covenant prohibiting immoral user. In *Sheffield CC v Jepson,* 1993, and *Green v Sheffield CC,* 1993, orders were made or upheld for breaches of terms prohibiting the keeping of pets in blocks of flats.

3.103 Nuisance and annoyance. Ground 2 (as amended by the Housing Act 1996) permits eviction—where reasonable to make the order—if the tenant or any person residing in or visiting the dwelling-house has been guilty of conduct causing or likely to cause a nuisance or annoyance to others residing, visiting or otherwise engaging in a lawful activity in the locality.

3.104 Nuisance here does not necessarily mean nuisance in a technical legal sense, but in a natural sense; in any event, annoyance is a term with a wider meaning, although it must be such as would annoy an ordinary occupier (rather than especially sensitive): *Tod-Heatly v Benham*, 1885; Harlow DC v Sewell, 2000.

3.105 Where the allegation is one of nuisance by members of the family or visitors, there need not be any personal fault on the part of the tenant (*Davies, Bryant*), although the extent of personal fault will be relevant to the question of "reasonableness" (3.92).

3.106 In *Manchester CC v Lawler*, 1998, the Court of Appeal held that locality may be part of, or the whole of an estate. In each case, it is a question of fact for the judge whether the place in which the conduct occurred is or is not within the locality of the dwelling. It would seem, though, that there must be a link between the behaviour and the fact that the family lived in the area; the link is the legitimate interest which the landlord authority have in requiring their tenants to respect the neighbourhood for the benefit of the authority's other tenants: *Northampton BC v Lovatt*, 1997.

3.107 Immoral and illegal use. Ground 2 also applies where the tenant or any person residing in or visiting the dwelling-house has been convicted either of using the dwelling-house or allowing it to be used for immoral or illegal purposes, or of an arrestable offence in, or in the locality (see last para.) of the dwelling.

3.108 Immoral use will normally lead to an order for possession, though not invariably (*Yates v Morris*, 1950).

3.109 "Arrestable offence" means (Police and Criminal Evidence Act 1984 Act s.24):

- any offence which bears a fixed penalty, e.g. murder;
- any offence for which a first offender of 21 or more could be sent to prison for five or more years; and

• any offence specifically identified as such.

3.110 Illegal use only applies when the use of the premises has something to do with the conviction, even if the offence was not one which as a matter of law necessarily involved the use of the premises. Nonetheless, the use of the premises must have been part of the facts leading to the conviction, rather than only incidentally the site of the commission of the offence (*S. Schneider and Sons v Abrahams*, 1925). (Note: a conviction for possession of cannabis at the premises will be unlikely to lead to an order, especially as it will mean the imposition of a double penalty: *Abrahams v Wilson*, 1971.)

3.111 Other powers. Secure landlords have other powers to combat antisocial behaviour which may be used as an alternative—or in addition—to possession proceedings. Instead of ordering possession, the court may make a demotion order so that the tenant loses security of tenure (3.167). Landlords may also obtain injunctions (8.110) or antisocial behaviour orders (8.129) to control the conduct of tenants, their families and visitors.

3.112 Domestic violence. Ground 2A applies where:

• the property was occupied—whether on their own, or together with others—by a married couple, civil partners, or a couple living together as husband and wife or as civil partners;

• one of whom is, or both of whom are, a tenant of it;

• one of whom has left because of violence or threats of violence towards (usually) her or a member of her family who was residing with her immediately before she left the other;

• the court is satisfied that the partner who has left, i.e. the victim of the violence, is unlikely to return. (See also the added requirements for notice: above, 3.73.)

3.113 Deterioration of premises or furniture. Grounds 3 and 4 concern deterioration of the premises or common parts, or of any furniture provided by the landlord in the premises or common parts, attributable to the acts, neglect or default of the tenant, or of someone living with him.

3.114 No order will be made on either of these grounds if the default was that of a sub-tenant or lodger, and before the hearing the tenant has taken such steps as are available in order to evict him.

3.115 Deception. Ground 5 is that the tenant is the person, or one of the persons, to whom the tenancy was granted, and the landlord was induced to grant the tenancy by a false statement knowingly or recklessly made by the tenant or by a person acting at the tenant's instigation, i.e. obtaining a tenancy by deception.

3.116 As such an allegation is of a quasi-criminal nature (and if the tenancy was granted under Pt 6, an actually criminal nature, *cf.* 10.234), it will accordingly require a high standard of proof. Once proved, however, the judge may, in deciding whether it is reasonable to grant possession, take into account the need to discourage dishonest applications generally: *Rushcliffe BC v Watson*, 1991 and see also *Shrewsbury & Atcham BC v Evans*, 1997; *Lewisham LBC v Akinsola*, 1999.

3.117 If the tenancy was granted to two persons, e.g. cohabitants, spouses, one of whom has departed, the ground is only available against the remaining tenant if he was guilty of the false statement or had instigated the deception by the departed tenant.

3.118 Once the tenancy has been assigned (3.58), this ground is no longer available: *Islington LBC v Uckac*, 2006.

3.119 Premium on exchange. Ground 6 relates to the "right to exchange" (3.205): it arises if the tenancy arose by exchange, to which either the tenant, or a member of his family (3.48) from whom he has taken over the tenancy, was a party and a premium, i.e. money or other pecuniary consideration, e.g. goods, was paid in connection with the exchange (whether to, or by the tenant or member of his family). In the case of a member of the family, he must still be living in the property with the tenant.

3.120 Conflict with other purposes. Ground 7 governs employment-related accommodation (not excluded from security, *cf.* 3.39), and arises where:

- the premises are part of, or in the grounds of, a building held by the landlord for non-housing purposes;
- the letting was in consequence of employment; and
- the tenant or someone residing in the property has been guilty of conduct, such that, having regard to the purposes

for which the main building is held, it would not be right for the tenant to remain in occupation.

3.121 Accommodation pending works. Ground 8 arises where the secure tenant of one set of premises is asked to move to another set of premises while works are carried out. The ground may be compared to Sch.1 para.7 of the 1985 Act of the exceptions to security (3.39(10)), excluding from security tenants who have similarly been moved, but from an insecure tenancy.

3.122 Ground 8 is only available if the terms of the move included an undertaking that the tenant would move back once works were completed, and the works are now completed and the original property ready for reoccupation.

3.123 The requirement of reasonableness allows the tenant to argue, e.g. that the works have not been done as agreed, or that they have taken so long that he has now set down new roots in the alternative property and ought not to have to move back again.

(ii) *Ground plus suitable alternative accommodation*

3.124 Suitable accommodation. Under this category of ground for possession, it is not necessary to show reasonableness in addition to the ground, but instead it is necessary to show that suitable alternative accommodation is available. In effect, these are estate management grounds.

3.125 Once satisfied on both points—ground and suitable alternative accommodation—the court has, accordingly, no discretion whether or not to make the order.

3.126 If the landlord is not the local authority, the certificate of the local authority that suitable accommodation will be provided by that authority will be conclusive evidence that alternative accommodation so provided is suitable (1985 Act Sch.2 Pt 4 para.4).

3.127 Otherwise, alternative accommodation will only be suitable if it is of premises to be let as a separate dwelling under a Housing Act secure tenancy, or under a Housing Act assured or a Rent Act protected tenancy, other than one subject to any of the mandatory grounds for possession (4.88–4.97; 5.122–5.141) including short-hold (Chapter 6; 1985 Act Sch.2 Pt 4 para.1).

3.128   The accommodation must, in the opinion of the court, be reasonably suitable to the needs of the tenant and his family. The court must, on this, have regard to:

- the nature of the accommodation usually provided by the landlord to persons with similar needs;

- distance from the place of work or education of the tenant or members of his family;

- distance from the home of the family or any member of the tenant's own family, e.g. relatives who require or provide support, if proximity is necessary to the well-being of either relative or tenant;

- the needs (as regards extent of accommodation, which can in an appropriate case include a garden: *Enfield LBC v French*, 1984) and means of tenant and his family;

- the terms of the accommodation; and

- if furniture has hitherto been provided, whether furniture is to be provided in the alternative accommodation, and its nature (1985 Act Sch.2 Pt 4 paras 1 and 2).

3.129   This schedule of matters to which regard is to be paid is not exhaustive; the weight to be given to each is a matter of degree in each case (*Enfield LBC*).

3.130   Overcrowded accommodation.   The first ground under this class is Ground 9, and arises when the dwelling currently occupied is overcrowded within the meaning of Pt 10 of the Housing Act 1985, in such circumstances as to render the occupier guilty of an offence (14.16–14.22). In relation to this ground only, it should be noted that alternative accommodation is not to be deemed unsuitable solely because it offends the space standard described in Chapter 14 (14.17(2); 1985 Act Sch.2 Pt 4 para.3).

3.131   Redevelopment.   Ground 10 is available when the land-lord intends, within a reasonable time of seeking possession, either:

- to demolish or reconstruct the building, or part of the building, which includes the dwelling in question; or

- to carry out work on the building, or on land let together with the building; and

- in either case, cannot reasonably do so without obtaining possession.

3.132 The landlord has to be able to show an established, settled and clearly defined intention to do the works, and that it needs possession in order to execute the works (*Wansbeck DC v Marley*, 1987).

3.133 Approved development area. Ground 10A was added in 1986, and applies when the landlord, within a reasonable period of obtaining possession, intends to sell with vacant possession, but it applies if, and only if, the property is in an "approved development area" (that is to say, approved by the Secretary of State or, in the case of a registered social landlord, by the Housing Corporation). There is provision for a dwelling which falls partly within, and partly outside of, such an area.

3.134 Conflict with charitable purposes. Ground 11 is available only to a landlord which is a charity within the meaning of the Charities Act 1993, and the tenant's continued occupation of the dwelling would conflict with the objects of the charity, i.e. where the charity has a specific purpose, such as the assistance of single parents, or the disabled, and neither the tenant nor anyone living with him any longer qualifies for such a description.

(iii) *Ground plus suitable alternative accommodation plus reasonableness*

3.135 Suitable and reasonable. In this class, the landlord must prove:

- that the ground is available and applicable; and

- that suitable alternative accommodation (as defined; 3.124–3.129) is available; and

- that it is reasonable to make the order sought, thus importing the court's discretion considered above (3.86–3.96).

3.136 Non-housing property required for employee. Ground 12 applies where:

- the property forms part of, or is in the grounds of, a non-housing building, or in the grounds of a cemetery; and

- was let in consequence of employment; and
- the property is now reasonably required for a new employee.

3.137 This ground is similar to Case 8 under the Rent Act 1977 (5.157).

3.138 Adapted housing. Ground 13 applies to dwellings which have features which are substantially different from ordinary houses, designed to make the house suitable for the occupation of a physically disabled person.

3.139 The ground is only available if there is no longer a physically disabled person of the class for whom it was provided in occupation (which need not be the tenant, but could be a member of his family), and the landlord requires it for occupation of one such disabled person.

3.140 Required for persons with special needs. Ground 14 is available only to housing associations or housing trusts engaged in letting property to specific categories of persons who, for reasons other than poverty, have particular difficulty satisfying their housing needs, e.g. ethnic groups, battered women, young people, the mentally handicapped.

3.141 This ground is only available when either there is no longer such a person in occupation (whether as tenant or not), or the local authority are offering the tenant a secure tenancy elsewhere, and in either case the landlord requires the dwelling for occupation by a person of the class they are engaged in assisting.

3.142 Sheltered accommodation. Ground 15 applies to "sheltered accommodation", i.e. houses or flats in a group which are in practice let to people with special needs, and in close proximity to which a social service or other special facility is provided, e.g. for elderly people, or the disabled.

3.143 As under the last two grounds, the ground is only available when there is no longer a person of the designated class in occupation, and the premises are required for occupation by such a person.

3.144 Under-occupation. Ground 16 is only available when the tenant has succeeded to the secure tenancy on the death of a previous tenant (3.40–3.54).

3.145 It is never available when the tenant is the spouse or civil partner of the deceased secure tenant.

3.146 It is only available when the accommodation afforded by the dwelling is more extensive than is reasonably required by the successor, and notice of seeking possession (3.66) was served both no earlier than six months after the death of the previous tenant and no later than 12 months after his death.

3. ORDERS FOR POSSESSION

3.147 Once the court is satisfied that a ground for possession has been proved and, as necessary, that it is reasonable to make an order for possession and/or that suitable alternative accommodation is available, it must make an order for possession.

3.148 There are three types of order: outright, postponed and suspended.

3.149 An order may only be postponed or suspended where possession is sought on any of the grounds in relation to which the court must also be satisfied that it is reasonable to make an order (Grounds 1–8: 3.97–3.123; and Grounds 12–16; 3.135–3.146) (1985 Act s.85(1)).

3.150 The power to postpone or suspend an order may not only be exercised for the benefit of the tenant but also for his spouse or ex-spouse, civil partner or former civil partner and some cohabitants and former cohabitants (Chapter 9) (1985 Act s.85(5), (5A)).

3.151 Outright orders. An outright order grants possession to the landlord after some finite period of delay, usually two weeks, but on occasion, in extreme hardship, sometimes stretched to a maximum of six (Housing Act 1980 s.89).

3.152 Once the period of delay granted by the court has run out, the landlord can issue a bailiff's warrant and there may be a further period of delay before any actual eviction.

3.153 Postponed order. There are two types of postponed order. First, the court may fix a date for possession, but postpone possession for as long as the tenant complies with specified terms, e.g. to pay the current rent and pay off rent arrears in instalments or not to commit specified acts of nuisance or annoyance to neighbours.

3.154 Secondly, in arrears cases, the court may postpone the date of possession to a subsequent date to be fixed by the court (*Bristol CC v Hassan*, 2006). The order will also specify requirements for the tenant to pay his current rent and pay off the rent arrears in instalments. If the tenant fails to keep to the terms of the order, the landlord may apply for a date for possession to be fixed by the court. The procedure for the application is set out in CPR Pt 55 PD 10.

3.155 The advantage to the tenant of the second type of postponed order is that if he fails to comply with the terms of his order, his tenancy continues. Where, however, a date for possession is fixed, his tenancy comes to an end no matter how minor the breach of the terms may be, and he becomes a tolerated trespasser (1.44, 1.58–1.61).

3.156 Suspended orders. For many years, the county court used a standard form of "suspended possession order", which was generally thought to have the effect of the first type of postponed order (3.153), i.e. the tenancy continued until the terms of the order were breached. In *Harlow DC v Hall*, 2006, however, the Court of Appeal held that the effect of that form of order was to bring the tenancy to an end on the date specified in the order, and merely suspend the landlord's right to enforce the order by bailiff's warrant until the terms of the order were breached. Accordingly, even if the defendant subsequently made all the payments required by the order, he was nevertheless only a tolerated trespasser (1.44, 1.58–1.61) and not a tenant.

3.157 Suspended possession orders are still made but the use of such orders is now less common. Courts are more likely to make a postponed possession in one of the two forms considered above.

3.158 Rent arrears—period of postponement or suspension. A court should not make an order producing an indefinite postponement or suspension, disappearing into the "mists of time" (*Vandermolen v Toma*, 1981; *Taj v Ali (No.1)*, 2001), although in *Lambeth LBC v Henry*, 2000, a period of 23 years was upheld by the Court of Appeal.

3.159 Postponed or suspended orders—antisocial behaviour. In cases under Ground 2 (3.103), it may be appropriate to postpone or suspend the order: *Kensington & Chelsea RLBC v Simmonds*, 1996; *Greenwich LBC v Grogan*, 2001; *Portsmouth CC v Bryant*,

2000; *Castlevale Housing Action Trust v Gallagher*, 2001. In considering whether postponement or suspension is appropriate, the judge must consider future conduct. There is, however, no point suspending an order if the inevitable outcome will be future breaches: *Canterbury CC v Lowe*, 2001. Even if the tenant's conduct has improved significantly by the time of the hearing, it may still be appropriate to make an outright possession order where the past conduct was serious (*Lambeth LBC v Howard*, 2001).

3.160 Warrant for possession. The powers to suspend or postpone can be exercised at any time before execution of the warrant for possession, but not thereafter, unless either the circumstances are such that there are grounds to set aside the original order, e.g. if the tenant had no notice of the proceedings, or if it was an abuse of the process or oppressive to proceed with the warrant (*Governors of Peabody Donation Fund v Hay*, 1986; *Leicester CC v Aldwinckle*, 1991; *Hammersmith & Fulham LBC v Hill*, 1994; *Barking & Dagenham LBC v Saint*, 1999; *Southwark LBC v Sarfo*, 1999; *Hammersmith & Fulham LBC v Lemeh*, 2001; *Lambeth LBC v Hughes*, 2001.

3.161 Oppression in the execution of a warrant requires unfair use of the court's procedures, or action by a person which is open to criticism as unfair use: *Jephson Homes HA v Moisejevs*, 2001.

3.162 Application to suspend warrant. Where a tenant applies to suspend a warrant for possession, it is open to the landlord to adduce evidence of a ground—or grounds—of possession different to those relied upon at the original hearing, even if those grounds had existed when the original order was made: *Sheffield CC v Hopkins*, 2001 (original order made on the grounds of rent arrears, evidence of nuisance adduced at application to suspend warrant). Where the new ground was already available at the time of the original possession action, the landlord will only be allowed to raise the matter if the tenant was warned that the landlord was only going to bother proceeding on the one ground, so that he will have been aware that the other could also still subsequently be used to give rise to eviction.

3.163 Conditions. Conditions may be imposed on any adjournment, stay, suspension or postponement. In all cases, however, unless it will cause exceptional hardship to the tenant, or would otherwise be unreasonable, the court will order payments of rent and of any arrears that there may be (1985 Act s.85(3)).

3.164 Variation of conditions. Where a postponed or suspended order is made under one ground for possession, e.g. rent arrears, and another ground for possession, e.g. antisocial behaviour, subsequently becomes available, it is not necessary for the landlord to commence new proceedings. The court has the power to add conditions in respect of the new ground to the existing order (*Manchester CC v Finn*, 2002).

3.165 If conditions are complied with, e.g. to clear arrears, it is worthwhile applying for discharge, rather than leaving on the court file an order which might later be activated erroneously and with inadequate warning to the tenant.

3.166 Orders and security. If possession is postponed to a specific date, or the possession order is suspended, on terms with which the tenant ceases to comply, the breach terminates the tenancy and entitles the landlord to obtain a warrant for possession (*Thompson v Elmbridge BC*, 1987; *Greenwich LBC v Regan*, 1996). The landlord may allow the former tenant to remain in the property as a tolerated trespasser. This is discussed at 1.58–1.61.

4. DEMOTED TENANCIES

3.167 Antisocial behaviour Act 2003. The Antisocial Behaviour Act 2003 introduced demoted orders in cases of antisocial behaviour. If the landlord is a local authority or Housing Action Trust, a demotion order replaces the secure tenancy with a demoted tenancy, which is governed by provisions in the Housing Act 1996. If the landlord is a registered social landlord, however, the secure tenancy is replaced by a demoted assured shorthold tenancy. Demotion is an alternative to possession proceedings. It replaces the existing secure tenancy with a tenancy which the landlord can end without having to establish grounds for possession. Demoted tenancies and demoted assured shorthold tenancies are considered in Chapter 6. In this section we consider how the landlord may apply for a demoted tenancy order against a secure tenant.

3.168 Preliminary notice. As for possession proceedings (3.65), unless the court considers it just and equitable to dispense with the requirement to do so, the landlord must serve the tenant with a notice. The notice must be in the form prescribed by the Secretary of State, or substantially to the same effect (1985 Act s.83). It must specify the date after which proceedings may be begun. The specified date must not be earlier than the date when the tenancy

could have been brought to an end by notice to quit (1.116·
The notice ceases to be in force 12 months after that date.

3.169 Antisocial behaviour. A demotion order can only be
made if the court is satisfied that the tenant, or a person residing
or visiting the dwelling has either:

- engaged in, or threatened to engage in, conduct capable of
  causing a nuisance or annoyance to any person which
  directly or indirectly relates to or affects the housing
  management functions of the authority; or

- engaged in conduct which involves using or threatening to
  use for an unlawful purpose housing accommodation owned
  or managed by a local authority, Housing Action Trust or a
  registered social landlord (1985 Act s.82A(4)).

3.170 Reasonableness. The court can only make an order
where it considers it reasonable to do so. Various factors are
relevant to this issue, many of which are also relevant to the
making of a possession order, e.g. effect on neighbours, severity of
the conduct and degree of fault on the tenant's part (3.92–3.94).
The effect on the tenant will be relevant, i.e. the fact that after the
order is made, the landlord can obtain possession not only for
further antisocial behaviour but for any reason, including rent
arrears.

Additional rights of secure tenants

1. RIGHT TO BUY

3.171 Entitlement. The best-known additional right of a secure
tenant is the "right to buy".

3.172 The right to buy arises only after a tenant has spent a
specified amount of time as a secure tenant or as another form of
public sector tenant, e.g. a tenant of a registered social landlord
(1985 Act Sch.4), although not necessarily with the same landlord,
in the same premises or continuously (1985 Act s.119). Following
amendments made by the Housing Act 2004, the qualifying period
is five years for tenants who first became public sector tenants on
or after January 18, 2005. Those who were already public sector
tenants at that date need only establish a period of two years.

3.173 The tenant has to be secure both when applying to buy and
throughout the process (*Sutton LBC v Swann*, 1985; *Jennings v*

Epping Forest DC, 1992; *Muir Group HA v Thornley*, 1992; *Bradford City MBC v McMahon*, 1993).

3.174 Once matters in relation to the purchase have been agreed or determined, the tenant may obtain an order to require the landlord to sell the property to him, under the 1985 Act s.138.

3.175 If, however, the landlord is at the same time seeking to evict the tenant, e.g. because of antisocial behaviour, it is up to the court to decide in which order it hears the two conflicting applications, to compel the sale and for possession: *Bristol CC v Lovell*, 1998. The sequence of events and the seriousness of the allegations made by the landlord will be relevant to how the court exercises its discretion: *Tandridge BC v Bickers*, 1998. Specific provision is made for suspension of the duty to proceed with the sale in antisocial behaviour cases (3.184).

3.176 Family members. The right may be exercised together with other members of the family whom the tenant identifies for this purpose (1985 Act s.123). If the tenant died after establishing the s.123 right, such other members of the family would be entitled to pursue the purchase, even if not otherwise entitled to succeed to the tenancy (3.40; *Harrow LBC v Tonge*, 1992).

3.177 Freehold or leasehold. If the dwelling is a house, and the landlord owns the freehold, the right to buy is a right to the freehold (1.12). Otherwise, i.e. if the property is a flat, or if the landlord only has a lease, the right is to a lease of, normally, 125 years, although it may be less if the landlord's own interest is itself not that long (1985 Act Sch.6).

3.178 Other matters. There are detailed provisions governing the definition of "house" and "flat" (1985 Act s.183) and the exercise of these rights by joint tenants (1985 Act s.118).

3.179 Exemptions. Some property is exempt from the right to buy (1985 Act Sch.5), including property belonging to a housing trust which is a charity, sheltered accommodation (*cf.* 3.142) and accommodation adapted for the physically disabled (*cf.* 3.138).

3.180 Discount. The right is to buy at a discount (1985 Act s.129), amounting to:

- For tenants who have to show two years as public sector tenants (3.172):

  — (in the case of a house) 32 per cent for up t
  as a secure tenant, plus one per cent per ye
  to a maximum of 60 per cent; or
  — (in the case of a flat), 44 per cent for up to three yeaᵣ₅,
  plus two per cent per year thereafter, to a maximum of
  70 per cent.

- For tenants who have to show five years as public sector
  tenants (3.172):

  — (in the case of a house) 35 per cent for up to three years
  as a secure tenant, plus one per cent per year thereafter,
  to a maximum of 60 per cent; or
  — (in the case of a flat), 50 per cent for up to three years,
  plus two per cent per year thereafter, to a maximum of
  70 per cent.

3.181 There are also maximum discounts set by the Secretary of State, under the 1985 Act s.131, which vary depending on the area in which the property is situated.

3.182 A discount will normally have to be repaid if the house or flat is subsequently sold within five years (1985 Act s.155). Where a sale is proposed within ten years of the purchase under the right to buy, a notice must be served on the landlord which allows it the opportunity to buy the property back (1985 Act s.156A).

3.183 Non-compliance with time limits. If the landlord fails to comply with the statutory time provision for handling the right to buy, would-be purchasers will be able to serve notices, the effect of which will be to "penalise" the landlord by treating rent payments during the periods of delay as deductions from the purchase price (1985 Act ss.153A, 153B).

3.184 Antisocial behaviour. A court can suspend a tenant's right to buy where the tenant is guilty of antisocial behaviour and the court considers that it is reasonable to make a suspension order (1985 Act s.121A). The standard of behaviour is the same as that which justifies a demotion order (3.169). If the landlord has applied for a demotion order, or a possession order based on Ground 2 (3.103), or a suspension order, it does not have to sell the property pending determination of the application.

3.185 Demolition. Where the landlord intends to demolish the premises, he may serve a demolition notice. There are two types of demolition notice: interim and final. A final notice must state that the property will be demolished by a specified date, which must be no later than two years after the date of the notice. An initial notice does not have to specify a date but must say that the landlord intends to demolish the property within a period not exceeding five years. While a final notice is in force, a tenant cannot apply to exercise the right to buy. If he has already made an application, the landlord is not obliged to sell him the property. While an interim notice is in force, a new application to exercise the right to buy can be made but any such application, or any existing application, is suspended.

3.186 Preserved right to buy. On a transfer of stock to the private sector (see further below), a secure tenant's right to buy is "preserved": 1985 Act ss.171A–171H. Where transfer is, as is most common, to a registered social landlord, it is the right to buy which is preserved, rather than the right to acquire given to assured tenants (4.162).

3.187 The preserved right to buy will be inapplicable if the right to buy as against the former landlord was unavailable because of paras 1–3, Sch.5 of the 1985 Act (charities and certain housing associations), or in such other cases as may be excepted by order of the Secretary of State: 1985 Act s.171A(3).

3.188 The right to buy is only preserved so long as the tenant occupies the premises as his only or principal home (3.32).

3.189 The right may be exercised by the tenant, or a qualifying successor, as defined, and may extend from the original premises to other premises to which the tenant has moved, and which are rented from the same landlord (or if a company, a connected company): 1985 Act s.171B.

3.190 By s.171F, a court is not to make an order for possession against a tenant or qualifying successor on the ground of suitable alternative accommodation without ensuring that the right to buy will be preserved (or that the tenant will be Housing Act secure as against the new landlord).

3.191 A subsequent disposal by the (new) landlord does not terminate the preserved right to buy, unless either the new landlord is a landlord whose tenants are Housing Act secure (so that there will be a new right to buy in any event), or the original landlord has failed to register the right as a notice on the register of land in accordance with the 1985 Act Sch.9A. If the tenant loses the right due to a failure to register, he may recover compensation for breach of the statutory duty under the 1985 Act Sch.9A.

3.192 The preserved right to buy may also be determined on the termination of the landlord's interest by a superior landlord, other than by merger, but where this occurs because of the intermediate landlord's act or omission, there is a right to compensation: s.171E.

3.193 Section 171C empowers the Secretary of State by regulation to modify Pt 5 of the 1985 Act for the purposes of the preserved right to buy, which he has done (SI 1993/2241, as amended).

2. IMPROVEMENTS

3.194 Right to improve. Secure tenants also enjoy a "right to improve". It is a term of all secure tenancies that the tenant will not make any improvement, without the written consent of the landlord, which consent is not unreasonably to be withheld (1985 Act ss.79–99). Although cast in a negative frame, the term substantively confers a positive entitlement to improve, where consent has been granted. A refusal of consent can be challenged in the county court (1985 Act s.110).

3.195 For these purposes, improvement includes addition or alteration to a dwelling, and external decorations (1985 Act s.97). If the landlord does refuse consent, he is obliged to provide a written statement of reasons, and in the course of any subsequent challenge by the tenant, the burden lies on the landlord to show that the refusal was reasonable, which it may do, amongst other ways, by showing that the improvement would make the dwelling, or neighbouring premises, less safe, or that it would cause him to incur additional expenditure, or that it would reduce the value of the house (1985 Act s.98).

3.196 Financial matters. Secure tenants may be entitled to compensation for certain improvements (1985 Act s.99A). Their rent is not to be increased on account of improvements they execute (1985 Act s.101), and the landlord has power to reimburse the tenant for the cost of any improvements carried out, on the tenant's departure (1985 Act s.100).

3. SUB-LETTING AND LODGERS

3.197 Rights to let. Secure tenants have an absolute right to take in lodgers, and a qualified right to sublet part of their premises (1985 Act s.93).

3.198 The right to sublet is expressed as a negative obligation: the secure tenant shall not sublet part without the written consent of the landlord (1985 Act s.93(1)(a)). This consent, however, is not unreasonably to be withheld, and if unreasonably withheld, is to be treated as given. Accordingly, the right is in substance a positive entitlement to sublet with consent (1985 Act s.94).

3.199 Consent. The exercise of a qualified right to sublet has been considered above (1.181–1.183) but it is worth restating that, no matter how well-founded may be the anticipation of refusal, a tenant will not be able to claim unreasonable withholding without first making the request (*Barrow v Isaacs*, 1891).

3.200 If the landlord fails to reply within a reasonable time, consent is deemed to have been withheld (1985 Act s.94(6)), but if the landlord does refuse, then a written statement of reasons for refusal must be provided (1985 Act s.94(6)).

3.201 Consent may, however, be sought after the sub-letting, and if given will then validate it (1985 Act s.94(4)).

3.202 No conditions may be attached to a consent (1985 Act s.94(5)).

3.203 When considering the reasonableness of a refusal, over-crowding will be relevant (14.09–14.15), as will any proposals for works which the landlord may have and which would affect the accommodation likely to be used by the sub-tenant (1985 Act s.94(3)).

3.204 The burden of proof lies always on the landlord to show that the withholding is reasonable (1985 Act s.94(2)), and the tenant may apply to the county court for a declaration that a withholding is unreasonable (1985 Act s.110).

4. EXCHANGE

3.205 Right to exchange. All secure tenants have the right to exchange their properties with another secure tenant, whether of the same landlord or not (1985 Act s.92(1)).

3.206 The right extends to include Housing Act assured tenants of the Housing Corporation, a registered housing association, or housing trust which is a charity, i.e. those landlords formerly within the 1985 Act (3.30; 1985 Act s.92(2A)).

3.207 There can even be three-way exchanges, provided all are Housing Act secure tenants or have a relevant assured tenancy, and the landlord of each has consented in writing (1985 Act s.92(2)).

3.208 Consent. A landlord has 42 days in which to consent, and can only refuse consent on one of a specified schedule of grounds (1985 Act s.92(4), (5)). The landlord loses the right to reply on any of the grounds unless he replies within 42 days.

3.209 If the landlord refuses consent on another ground, consent is to be treated as given.

3.210 This does not, however, mean that the exchange can necessarily take place. The landlord is entitled to attach one condition to any consent: if there are rent arrears, or there is another breach of a term of the tenancy, the landlord can require the arrears to be cleared, or the breach to be remedied (1985 Act s.92(5)).

3.211 The landlord may not, however, attach any other conditions to the consent, and any that are attached may be disregarded (1985 Act s.92(6)).

3.212 The grounds for refusing consent are (1985 Act Sch.3):

- the tenant or proposed assignee already is under a court order to give up possession;

- proceedings for possession have commenced, or NSP has been served (3.66), on any of the grounds for possession which require only that it is reasonable to make the order (3.84–3.123);

- where a court order is in force against the tenant or proposed assignee which is based on antisocial behaviour, e.g. a suspended possession order, an antisocial behaviour injunction (8.110), or an antisocial behaviour order (8.129);

- the accommodation would be too large for the prospective assignee, or otherwise not reasonably suitable to his needs;

- the premises were let in consequence of employment, and form part of, or are in the grounds of, a non-housing building or a cemetery (3.39, 3.136);

- the landlord is a charity and the proposed assignee's occupation would conflict with its objects (3.134);

- the property is designed for a physically disabled person, and if the proposed assignee moved in, there would be no such person in occupation (3.138);

- the landlord is a special needs housing association or trust, and if the proposed assignee moved in there would be no one with the relevant need in occupation (3.140);

- the accommodation is sheltered and, as above, if the proposed assignee moved in, there would be no one with the relevant needs in occupation (3.142).

5. REPAIR

3.213 Right to repair. The "right to repair" (1985 Act s.96) permits secure tenants to require local authority landlords to appoint a contractor when repairs are not carried out on time, and if there are further delays to receive compensation: the provisions are governed by regulations—see the Secure Tenants of Local Authorities (Right to Repair) Regulations 1994 (SI 1994/133).

6. HEATING CHARGES

3.214 Right to information. In addition, there is power for the government to introduce provisions which would entitle secure tenants to find out how their landlords have calculated heating charges included in the rent (1985 Act s.108). This power has not yet been brought into use.

Related provisions

1. VARIATION OF TERMS

3.215 A landlord may vary the terms of a secure tenancy by notice to take effect no sooner than the landlord could have served notice to quit (1.116–1.117). Before that date, the tenant may respond with notice to quit, in which case the variation will not take effect before the tenant's departure (1985 Act ss.102, 103). A term in the tenancy agreement which purports to prevent the landlord from exercising this right of variation is of no effect if the landlord is a local authority, as it would mean that the local authority would have "fettered their discretion" in relation to their power to change the terms, which public authorities are not allowed to do in relation to any of their powers (*R. (Kilby) v Basildon DC*, 2007).

3.216 Before any such notice is served, the landlord must serve a preliminary notice, outlining the intended variation, explaining its effect and inviting the tenant's comments.

3.217 This is not necessary, however, if the variation relates to the rent payable, or any amount in respect of rates, services or facilities provided by the landlord.

3.218 A notice of variation cannot vary the extent of the premises let under the tenancy.

2. CONSULTATION

3.219 Housing management. Where more general changes to housing management arrangements are intended, whether or not amounting to a variation of the terms of tenancies, local authorities and some other landlords under secure tenancies may be obliged to consult with their tenants (1985 Act s.105).

3.220 "Housing management" includes new programmes of maintenance, improvement or demolition, and changes in practice or policy, likely to affect the secure tenants of the landlord as a whole or a group of them (1985 Act s.105(3)), but excludes questions of rent, payments for services or facilities provided by the landlord (1985 Act s.105(2)).

3.221 All landlords bound by these consultation provisions (1985 Act s.114) must make and maintain consultation machinery or arrangements for notifying their tenants of proposed changes in matters of housing management, and ascertaining their views. They must publish details of these arrangements (1985 Act s.105(5)).

3.222 When the landlord seeks approval of an area for the purposes of a "redevelopment scheme" in connection with Ground 10A (3.133), however, different consultation provisions apply;

similarly, a disposal by a Housing Action Trust of a property subject to a secure tenancy (3.243) carries with it its own alternative consultation provisions.

3. INFORMATION

3.223 Information about terms. Landlords under secure tenancies must publish information which explains the effect of the express terms of their secure tenancies, the security provisions of the 1985 Act and other provisions considered in this chapter, the right to buy, and the provisions of the Landlord and Tenant Act 1985 s.11 (11.47–11.79; 1985 Act s.104).

3.224 Copies of this publication must be provided to secure tenants. Where the landlord is a local authority, the information regarding the right to buy and repairing obligations must be provided annually.

Rents

1. LOCAL AUTHORITY RENTS

3.225 Reasonable rents. Local authorities are bound to charge reasonable rents and to review their rent levels from time to time; in setting their rent levels, they are bound to have regard to the principle that rents of property of one class or description should bear broadly the same proportion to private sector rents as the rents of houses of any other class or description (1985 Act s.24).

3.226 Ring-fencing. Local authorities have a long history of discretion in relation to their decisions as to what comprises a "reasonable" rent. The provisions of the Local Government and Housing Act 1989 have, however, severely limited the theoretical freedom which local authorities enjoy over rent levels, by requiring an authority's Housing Revenue Account to be balanced (1989 Act s.76), and limiting what can be credited and debited to it (so as to exclude any contribution from an authority's general fund, i.e. by the body of local taxpayers generally: this is the policy known as "ring-fencing of the account"; see 1989 Act s.75 and Sch.4).

3.227 Challenging local authority rents. There been a number of attempts to challenge local authority rent levels in the courts (both by those who think they are too high, and by those who think they are too low), most of which have failed.

2. HOUSING ASSOCIATION RENTS

3.228 Fair rents. Tenancies which began before the commencement (January 15, 1989) of Pt 1 of the 1988 Act (3.14), from housing associations, housing trusts and the Housing Corporation, were excluded from Rent Act protection by ss.15 and 16 of the Rent Act 1977 (5.85). They were and are, however, subject to the same fair rent structure as those private sector tenants (Rent Act 1977 Pt 6).

3.229 The same is true of housing association tenancies which, although granted after that date will, for one of the reasons set out in 3.15 above, not become Housing Act assured tenancies but remain within all or part of an earlier regime of protection.

3.230 Register. Although there is a separate part of the register for housing associations and other such bodies (1977 Act s.87), the same general principles will apply (*Palmer v Peabody Trust*, 1975) on the determination of their fair rents as other Rent Act protected tenants (5.174–5.188).

3.231 Increase without termination of tenancy. Provision is made to allow housing associations to increase these rent without the need to go through the process of determining the tenancy and granting a new one at the higher rent. This they may do by serving notice of variation, similar to that already considered in relation to Housing Act secure tenants generally (3.215) (1977 Act s.93).

3.232 Operation of provisions. It is not necessary to consider the operation of the fair rent system in relation to housing association tenancies, for the system is largely the same as that to be considered in relation to the private sector, and variations in detail are relatively minor. It may, however, be noted that a registered rent forms the rent limit for a housing association tenancy (5.212; 1977 Act s.88).

3.233 Other housing association tenants. Housing association, etc. tenancies which are within the Housing Act 1988, i.e. as assured tenancies (Chapter 4), are subject to the same rent provisions as those applicable to other, private sector assured tenants.

Local authority housing management

3.234 Management powers. Prima facie, all housing management powers and duties are vested in the landlord authority and must be exercised by them.

3.235 Under ss.27–27AB of the 1985 Act, however, local authorities may, after consultation with their tenants, be authorised by the Secretary of State to enter into management agency agreements with another body, e.g. a registered social landlord, and may be obliged to enter into such agreements with a "tenant management organisation", i.e. a body formed by the tenants, complying with regulations (the Housing (Right to Manage) Regulations 1994 (SI 1994/627)).

3.236 Best value. Under the provisions of the Local Government Act 1999 Pt I, local authorities are obliged to secure continuous improvement in the delivery of their service, including housing management. This has, to date, been achieved through a regime of "best value" reviews and performance plans.

3.237 The achievement of best value is secured by an inspection framework. Inspections are carried out through the Housing Inspectorate—an arm of the Audit Commission. For registered social landlords, a similar regime on inspection of their housing management functions is carried out by the Housing Corporation.

Transfer of public housing

3.238 Transfer policy. As mentioned above (3.07), government policy is to try to reduce the size of the housing stock held by local authorities.

3.239 Two mechanisms to achieve this were introduced by the Housing Act 1988, but one of them—"Tenants' Choice"—under 1988 Pt 4 was repealed by the 1996 Act. The other is considered briefly below under its own heading (Housing action trusts).

3.240 In addition, local authorities may engage in voluntary stock transfer (1985 Act s.32). If part of a programme of 500 or more dwellings, such transfers will qualify as a Large-Scale Voluntary Transfer ("LSVT") under Leasehold Reform, Housing and Urban Development Act 1993 s.135.

3.241 Like any other disposal of local authority housing stock, such a transfer requires the consent of the Secretary of State. In the case of LSVT, this may lead to the payment of a "levy" under the 1993 Act s.136, designed to reimburse the Government, out of the receipts, for past housing subsidy paid on the property.

3.242 Consultation. Before any transfer (other than to another landlord whose tenants will be secure), a local authority must consult all their affected secure and introductory (6.37) tenants: 1985 Act s.106A and Sch.3A. The Secretary of State's consent will, again, be needed (1985 Act s.32) but, if it appears to him that a majority of the tenants do not wish the proposal to proceed, he cannot give it (1985 Act Sch.3A para.5).

3.243 Housing action trusts. Only six Housing Action trusts have ever been declared and it is not anticipated that there will be any more. For that reason, only a brief outline is included here.

3.244 Housing action trusts were intended not only to take over housing stock but also, in their designated areas, a number of other housing-related powers and duties (many of which are referred to in Chapters 12–14, below), either together with the local authority, or instead of. The proposals were intended to deal with parts of a local authority's area, not the whole of the area of each local authority.

3.245 The Secretary of State has power to transfer to a housing action trust: (a) certain housing powers under the Housing Act 1985 (1988 Act s.65); certain planning powers (1988 Act ss.66–67); certain public health powers (1988 Act s.68); certain powers in respect of highways (1988 Act s.69); and (b) land and housing belonging to a local authority in its area (1988 Act ss.74–76).

3.246 The Secretary of State could not designate a housing action trust without first carrying (or having carried) out a ballot or poll, and if a majority of the tenants who responded to the ballot or poll were opposed to it, he had to abandon the proposals (1988 Act s.61).

3.247 Among the considerations which could influence the Secretary of State when deciding whether or not (subject to ballot) to designate a housing action trust were the extent of local authority housing in an area, its physical state and design, the need for repair of accommodation in the area generally, the way in which the local authority housing was being managed, living conditions in the area, social conditions, and the environment (1988 Act s.60).

3.248 The principal objects of the housing action trust were to secure repair or improvement of the accommodation it took over, and its proper and effective management and use, and to encourage diversity in the ways in which people occupy accommodation (tenancy—public or private, owner-occupation), as well as generally to secure or facilitate the improvement of living conditions in the area, and social conditions and the general environment (1988 Act s.63).

3.249 The purpose was not for the housing action trust to replace the local authority indefinitely; it was intended to achieve its objects and wind itself up as soon as practicable (1988 Act s.88). Its purpose, rather, was to transfer the housing to others, whether owner-occupiers or landlords, (to both of whom a trust may give financial assistance: 1988 Act s.71).

3.250 Transferee landlords had to be approved for the purpose by the Housing Corporation: 1988 Act s.79. The Housing Corporation could not approve a public sector landlord, or a county council, or any body which it thought would be under the control or influence of the public sector landlord, county council or its officers or members (1988 Act s.79). For this purpose, public sector landlord means any local housing authority or a new town corporation. Although the primary function of a housing action trust was to transfer the housing to others, tenants nonetheless have the option in certain circumstances of transferring back to the local authority (1988 Act s.84A).

3.251 Because of the role of the Housing Corporation in approving landlords, it has power to provide legal assistance to a tenant transferred from a housing action trust to a private landlord (1988 Act s.82). The power only applies to someone who was a Housing Act secure tenant at the time of the transfer, or his surviving spouse.

Further financial protection and assistance

3.252 There are other forms of financial protection or assistance which may be applicable.

3.253 Premiums and deposits. Premiums and deposits are not specifically prohibited under the Housing Act 1985: cf. 5.215–5.226.

3.254 Accommodation agency charges. Accommodation agency charge provisions (4.164) are unlikely to be relevant as matters of practice.

3.255 Utility charges. The provisions governing the resale of utilities, i.e. gas and electricity (4.169), are also not likely to be relevant (but cf. 3.214).

3.256 Housing benefits. Under the Social Security Contributions and Benefits Act 1992, rent rebates and allowances, together with council tax rebates, are available to assist those on income support and others with low incomes with their housing costs. The details of these support schemes are so commonly varied that it is impracticable to consider them here. There are a number of annual publications which contain current provisions.

CHAPTER FOUR

Housing Act Assured Tenancies

Introduction

4.01 New status. The assured tenancy was introduced in 1988, by the Housing Act of that year ("1988 Act"), to replace:

- the Rent Act 1977 protected tenancy in the private sector (Chapter 5); and

- the Housing Act 1985 secure tenancy in relation to housing association tenancies (Chapter 3).

4.02 Commencement. These provisions applied from the commencement of Pt 1 of the 1988 Act, January 15, 1989.

4.03 Transitional cases. There is a small number of circumstances in which a letting commencing on or after January 15, 1989 may still fall within either the Rent Act 1977 (5.08) and/or the Housing Act 1985 (3.15).

4.04 Assured shorthold tenancies. Following the model of the "protected shorthold" tenancy under the Rent Act 1977 (6.139), the 1988 Act also included a class of assured tenancy known as the assured shorthold (1988 Act s.20), with considerably less security of tenure than fully assured tenants.

4.05 Initially, this was the legal exception rather than the norm, in the sense that there was a fully assured tenancy unless a notice was given, before the tenancy began, that it was to be shorthold.

4.06 In the fully private sector, however, shorthold rapidly became the most common form of letting, and, with changes in policy towards the homeless (see Chapter 10), shorthold lettings became, from February 28, 1997, the universal default form of letting, i.e. subject to a number of exceptions (4.58), all assured tenancies were to be assured shortholds unless and until notified that the tenancy was to be fully assured.

4.07 Despite this, most assured tenants of registered social landlords ("RSLs") are in fact notified that their tenancies will be fully assured before, immediately on, or within a fairly short period of time from the commencement of their tenancies. RSLs are engaged in the long-term function of providing rented accommodation, and do not seek to operate on the basis of being able to evict for anything other than the sort of good reason embodied in grounds for possession, whereas a fully private landlord may well wish to retain the freedom to evict for other reasons, e.g. to sell.

4.08 Where tenants are guilty of antisocial behaviour, however, an RSL may apply for an order, under which a fully assured tenancy is replaced by a demoted assured shorthold tenancy, so that the landlord may thereafter obtain possession without having to establish grounds. The demoted assured shorthold was introduced by the Anti-social Behaviour Act 2003.

4.09 Structure of chapter. Notwithstanding the shift to a presumptive shorthold, however, in view of:

- the almost complete absence of security of tenure enjoyed by the assured shorthold tenant; and

- the fact that most RSL tenants are not shorthold;

this chapter will therefore—as with earlier editions—continue to describe full assured security, leaving shorthold security to be dealt with in Chapter 6, along with other forms of letting which enjoy only limited security.

Outline

4.10 Assured tenants

- An assured tenant is one to whom residential accommodation is let as a separate dwelling under a tenancy (not a licence), which the tenant occupies as his only or principal home, and which is not excluded from security under the schedule of exceptions.

- A form of assured tenancy was introduced in 1980 and there are transitional provisions which apply to such tenancies.

- There are particular provisions which apply to agricultural and forestry workers.

- All new assured tenancies created on or since February 28, 1997 are automatically assured shorthold unless either:

    - the landlord indicates through notice or the tenancy agreement that the tenancy is to be fully assured; or
    - it arises out of an existing tenancy in one of a number of specified circumstances;

- There are limits on the grant of fully assured tenancies where the grant is of temporary accommodation to a homeless person.

4.11 Security of tenure

- There is provision for one statutory succession to an assured tenancy, but only by a "spouse".

- An assured tenancy can only be repossessed by the landlord by obtaining a court order, following service of a notice of seeking possession which sets out the statutory ground on which possession is sought.

- Where an assured tenancy is for a fixed term which terminates, the tenant will be entitled to remain in occupation, under the same terms, as a statutory periodic tenant.

- Some grounds require the court to be satisfied that it is reasonable to grant possession; others are mandatory.

- Social landlords may apply for a court order replacing a fully assured tenancy with a demoted assured shorthold tenancy.

4.12 Rent and other terms

- Where the tenancy agreement does not contain its own rent review clause, the 1988 Act provides a mechanism for rents of periodic assured tenancies to be varied on an annual basis.

- Variations under this procedure may be referred to the Rent Assessment Committee to determine the open market rent.

- Terms as to access—to carry out works—are automatically implied into the tenancy.

- Terms as to assignment and sub-letting may be implied into periodic assured tenancies.

4.13 Further financial protection and assistance

- Some assured tenants of registered social landlords have the "right to acquire" their homes.

- There are provisions as to accommodation agency charges, resale of utilities and welfare benefits which are relevant to assured tenants.

Assured tenants

4.14 Principal issues. The Housing Act 1988 assumes that all tenants to whom property is let as a separate dwelling (on or after the commencement of the 1988 Act Pt 1: January 15, 1989) are assured tenants if they fulfil the qualifying conditions, and unless there is some factor which takes them out of Housing Act assured protection (1988 Act s.1).

4.15 There is a number of issues:

- there must be a qualifying letting as a separate dwelling, which is not within any exclusion;
- 1980 Act assured tenancies;
- agricultural and forestry workers;
- assured or assured shorthold;
- temporary accommodation for the homeless.

1. QUALIFYING LETTING

4.16 Tenancy. For there to be an assured tenancy, there must be a tenancy (1.93), i.e. (and unlike secure status: 3.19) the Act does not apply to licences.

4.17 Separate dwelling. The tenancy must be of a dwelling-house let as a separate dwelling. Premises which are let with no element of shared living accommodation (3.23) will be a "dwelling" for these purposes, provided that the tenant occupies them as his home. It does not matter if they do not include any kitchen facilities, although the premises probably have to be big enough to sleep in, i.e. for a bed: *Uratemp Ventures Ltd v Collins*, 2001.

4.18 Sharing living accommodation. If living accommodation (3.23) is shared with someone other than the tenant's own landlord, however, this will not prevent the tenancy qualifying as assured, even although, strictly, there is no letting as a separate dwelling (3.17). This is, as with Rent Act protected tenancy (5.70), provided by statute (1988 Act s.3).

4.19 If the tenant shares, or may have to share, living accommodation with his landlord, however, there is no letting as a separate dwelling and no saving statutory provision.

4.20 This arrangement should not be confused with the position of a resident landlord, with his own separate home elsewhere in the same building, and which is subject to its own express exclusion (4.44). The proposition applies, rather, where the landlord and the tenant share living accommodation, i.e. neither of them has his own separate dwelling. In that case, there is no letting as a separate dwelling, no prima facie assured tenancy, and the resident landlord exclusion never comes into play, and need not be relied on.

4.21 There may be no letting as a separate dwelling, even if the landlord does not actually live in the premises, but - whether or not he has actually ever exercised the right or whether or not he has a current intention to do so - sharing with his tenant was in contemplation at the time of the letting, the right to do so was reserved, and there is, at the lowest, a real prospect of the landlord doing so at some future date (*Gray v Brown*, 1992).

4.22 Qualifying conditions. Not all residential lettings are included. There are two qualifying conditions which must also be fulfilled. They are (s.1(1)):

1. that the tenant is an individual rather than a company or other corporation, or if a joint tenancy, that all the joint tenants are individuals; and

2. that the tenant, or if a joint tenancy at least one of them, occupies the dwelling as an "only or principal home" (3.32).

4.23 Exclusions. There is a small number of exclusions from protection which are (a) rare enough in practice, and (b) are of sufficient particularity that they do not merit discussion: licensed premises and lettings of agricultural and/or substantial land.

4.24 The remaining factors which take a tenancy out of assured protection are as follows:

- **prior tenancy:** tenancies preceding commencement (1988 Act Sch.1 para.1);

- **high-rateable value or rent:** the rateable value or high rent of the premises (1988 Act Sch.1 para.2);

- **no or low rent:** whether any or how much rent is paid (1988 Act Sch.1 para.3);

- **business lettings:** whether it is a business letting (1988 Act Sch.1 para.4);

- **student lettings:** whether it is a student letting (1988 Act Sch.1 para.8);

- **holiday lettings:** whether it is a holiday letting (1988 Act Sch.1 para.9);

- **resident landlord:** whether there is a resident landlord (1988 Act Sch.1 para.10);

- **exempt landlords:** whether the landlord is exempt from assured protection (1988 Act Sch.1 paras 11, 12);

- **asylum-seeker accommodation:** accommodation provided for asylum-seekers (1988 Act Sch.1 para.12A).

- **other classes of protection:** a tenancy which remains a Rent Act protected, housing association, or Housing Act secure tenancy (1988 Act Sch.1 para.14).

4.25 Prior tenancy. A tenancy entered into before, or under a contract which pre-dates, the commencement of the Housing Act 1988 will be either Housing Act secure or Rent Act protected (3.15, 5.08).

4.26 High-rateable value or rent. Some premises have such a high-rateable value or rent that they are considered to be beyond the need for protection.

4.27 It is the part of the premises which the tenant occupies which must be valued, not the whole house in which the tenancy is situated. A block of flats will often, as a whole, have too high a rateable value for 1988 Housing Act purposes, but each individual flat will not.

4.28 A tenancy will not be a Housing Act assured tenancy if the premises have a rateable value in excess of £1,500 (Greater London) or £750 (elsewhere) (1988 Act Sch.1 para.2A). Where a tenancy has been granted after April 1, 1990 and is for a property which had no rateable value on March 31, 1990 it will be excluded if the rent is greater than £25,000 a year (1988 Act Sch.1 para.2).

4.29 No or low rent. The 1988 Act is not designed to apply to those who purchase long leases and pay only a small, annual ground rent (1988 Act Sch.1 para.3). These have been considered as owner-occupiers, and were dealt with in Chapter 2.

4.30 This exclusion applies where the annual ground rent is less than two-thirds of the rateable value of the premises (1988 Act Sch.1 para.3B) or in the case of a tenancy which has been granted after April 1, 1990 and is for a property which had no rateable value on March 31, 1990, where the rent is £1000 or less a year in Greater London or £250 or less elsewhere (1988 Act Sch.1 para.3A).

4.31 Specifically disregarded in ascertaining the rent is any part of the rent which is expressed to be payable in respect of rates, services, management, repairs maintenance or insurance, unless, even although so expressed, the rent could not have been regarded as so payable (1988 Act Sch.1 para.2(2)).

4.32 Tenancies at no rent are also excluded (1988 Act Sch.1 para.3).

4.33 Rent in money. It has been held that rent must mean payment of rent in money if the tenancy is to be brought within protection, i.e. not payment in goods or services (*Hornsby v Maynard*, 1925).

4.34 There is, however, some authority for the proposition that if goods or services represent a quantified, or agreed amount which would otherwise be payable by way of rent, the Act may apply (*Barnes v Barratt*, 1970).

4.35 Where there is a true service tenancy (1.155) and an amount of rent between a landlord/employer and his tenant/employee has been agreed but is merely deducted at source, this will be considered sufficient payment of rent for the purposes of protection (*Montague v Browning*, 1954).

4.36 Business lettings. Tenancies which are subject to the business protection of the Landlord and Tenant Act 1954, and are therefore outside of residential protection (under this Act, as under the Housing Act 1985—see 3.39—and the Rent Act 1977—see 5.14) have been described above (3.39(14)).

4.37 Student lettings. A tenancy will not be an assured tenancy if the landlord under the tenancy is a specified educational institution and the tenant is following or intends to follow a course of study at that or another specified educational institution (1988 Act Sch.1 para.8).

4.38 Holiday lettings. If the purpose of the tenancy is use as a holiday home, then the tenancy will not be assured (1988 Act Sch.1 para.9).

4.39 This is an exemption which had been widely used as a device to defeat the Rent Acts (see also 1.75, 5.17, 5.83). The mere fact that someone has been compelled to sign an agreement alleging falsely that the tenancy was for a holiday purpose does not make it so as a matter of law. The principles relating to sham will apply to determine whether the agreement was a mere device to exclude protection, although occupiers should be aware that once they have signed such an agreement, the courts will consider that the burden of proof is upon them to displace the inference that the tenancy is not protected: see *Buchmann v May*, 1976. It may, however, be enough to show that there is a "false label", which is a slightly less pejorative term, and was applied in *R. v Rent Officer for LB of Camden Ex p. Plant*, 1981, in which the landlord was found to have known, either before the first or the second of two consecutive "holiday" lettings, that the occupiers were students. What is a holiday is a question of fact and common sense.

4.40 Other classes of protection. Those cases where a letting will be Housing Act 1985 secure, notwithstanding that the letting follows the commencement of Pt 1 of the 1988 Act, have already been described (3.15) and those which remain Rent Act protected are described at 5.08. They are therefore not assured (1988 Act Sch.1 para.13).

4.41 Exempt landlords. Those landlords whose tenants are not assured are (1988 Act Sch.1 para.12):

- local authorities (including district and county councils, county borough councils, London Borough Councils, the

Common Council of the City of London and the Council of the Isles of Scilly);

- the Commission for the New Towns;
- an urban development corporation;
- a new-town development corporation;
- a waste disposal authority;
- a residuary body (under the Local Government Act 1985, which took over the residual affairs of an abolished council, i.e. the Greater London Council and the metropolitan counties);
- a fully mutual association housing association, i.e. where the rules restrict membership to people who are tenants or prospective tenants of the association, and preclude the grant or assignment of tenancies to persons other than members; and
- a housing action trust (3.243).

4.42 In addition, tenants of the Crown or a government department are not assured unless the tenancy is under the management of the Crown Estate Commissioners (1988 Act Sch.1 para.11).

4.43 Asylum-seeker accommodation. A tenancy granted to someone being accommodated under the National Asylum Support Service, set up under the Immigration and Asylum Act 1999 Pt VI, is not assured (1988 Act Sch.1 para.12A).

4.44 Resident landlords. The exclusion of the tenants of resident landlords was developed under the Rent Acts (5.43–5.59) and operates similarly under the Housing Act 1988 (1988 Act Sch.1 para.10).

4.45 The exclusion applies to premises let which are part of a building and, unless the dwelling itself forms part only of a flat, that building is not a purpose-built block of flats (4.48). At the time of the grant of the tenancy, the landlord must have occupied, as his only or principal home (3.32, 4.22), another dwelling forming part of the same building (or, where the dwelling forms part only of a flat, another part of the same flat).

4.46 For the landlord to take advantage of this exclusion he must establish that, since the commencement of the tenancy, he has at all times used the other part of the building or flat which he occupies as an only or principal home.

4.47 The two sets of homes must be within the same building. This will not cover, e.g. a terrace of houses, but may include a house which has had an extension added, even if there is no interconnection between the house and extension (*Griffiths v English*, 1981; *Lewis-Graham v Conacher*, 1991).

4.48 The term "purpose-built block of flats" means exactly what it says. A house converted into flats, no matter how long ago, or however separately the living units are now constructed (*Barnes v Gorsuch*, 1982), will not be a purpose-built block (*Bardrick v Haycock*, 1976; *Griffiths*), even if there are separate entrances.

4.49 If the building is a purpose-built block, however, then it avails the landlord not at all that he lives in one and the tenant lives in another flat.

4.50 A corporate landlord, e.g. a landlord which is a company, a trust of a partnership, cannot qualify as a resident landlord for these purposes because it cannot occupy as a home. It is, however, expressly provided that occupation by one of two or more joint owners/landlords is enough to keep the tenant from being a Housing Act assured tenant. There are also provisions to exclude security when "the landlord" is a trustee, and it is the beneficiary who is resident.

4.51 There are two circumstances when residence is treated as continuing, even though it is not:

- **Sale.** If the landlord sells the house, residence will be treated as continuing for a further 28 days. If, during that time, the new owner serves notice that he intends to move into the premises for use as a home, then he has a total of six months in which to do so, during which period residence by the landlord will likewise be treated as continuing. If, by the end of the six months, the new owner has not taken up residence, the tenant will become an assured tenant and will so remain, even when the owner moves in, for there will not have been continual residence (or deemed residence) since the start of the tenancy. During the deemed period, the landlord cannot evict otherwise than as if the tenant was assured, i.e. if there are grounds.

- **Death.** On the death of a resident landlord, the executors effectively have two years, during which the fact that there is no resident landlord will be disregarded. During this period, however, the landlord's executors may freely evict as if there was still a resident landlord.

  The two periods (two years under this paragraph, six months under the last) may be added together (*Williams v Mate*, 1982).

2. 1980 ACT ASSURED TENANCIES

4.52 The term "assured tenancy" was first used in the Housing Act 1980 and reflected a policy of encouraging the private sector to build housing for rent, with a system of protection modelled on the "new tenancy" mechanism applicable to business lettings under Pt 2 of the Landlord and Tenant Act 1954. The policy was not successful and, subject only to minor qualification and those lettings at the time being kept alive under the adapted 1954 Act, all Housing Act 1980 assured tenancies were converted into Housing Act 1988 assured tenancies from the commencement of Pt 1 of the 1988 Act (January 15, 1989) (1988 Act ss.1, 37).

3. AGRICULTURAL AND FORESTRY WORKERS

4.53 Under the Housing Act 1988 Pt 1 Chapter 3, agricultural—and forestry—tied workers, whose occupation commenced on or after January 15, 1989, enjoy a measure of protection, notwithstanding that they may well have licences rather than tenancies.

4.54 It is not possible in this book to consider these provisions in any detail, but the following points of distinction should be noted:

- Chapter 3 applies not only to service tenants but also to service occupiers (1988 Act s.24), i.e. licensees.
- The fact that such occupiers will not usually be paying rent does not take them out of protection (1988 Act s.24(2));
- It is usually necessary to show that the employee has been an agricultural worker (though not necessarily with the same employer) for 91 out of the 104 weeks preceding the date when it is claimed that the Act applies (1988 Act Sch.3).

4.55 The structure allows a landlord to make application to the local authority to provide re-housing "in the interests of efficient agriculture" for both assured agricultural occupiers and those protected by the Rent (Agriculture) Act 1976 (5.15) (1976 Act Pt IV).

4.56 Agricultural workers not within these provisions may get some temporary security for up to a year, under the Protection from Eviction Act 1977, by way of time granted by the court before a possession order takes effect.

4. ASSURED OR ASSURED SHORTHOLD

4.57 Tenancies created on or since February 28, 1997. As noted above (4.06) lettings granted on or since February 28, 1997 are automatically assured shortholds, unless (1988 Act s.19A and Sch.2A) certain conditions are fulfilled.

4.58 Those conditions are:

1. notice is served by the prospective landlord on the prospective tenant before the tenancy is entered into that it is not to be an assured shorthold; or

2. notice is served by the landlord on the tenant after the tenancy has been entered into that it is no longer to be an assured shorthold; or

3. the tenancy agreement itself contains a provision that it is not to be an assured shorthold; or

4. the tenancy falls within the transitional provisions considered below, governing new tenancies for existing tenants (4.64); or

5. the tenancy was a secure tenancy (Chapter 3) which is transferred to a registered social landlord and, accordingly, became an assured tenancy; or

6. it is an assured tenancy arising on the termination of a long lease (2.17); or

7. the grant is to a person who (or, if joint tenants, one of whom) immediately beforehand was an existing assured tenant (or one of a number of assured joint tenants) by someone who (or, if joint landlords, one of whom) is the existing landlord (or one of a number of joint landlords), even if in different premises. (Note: the purpose here is to protect such tenants against deprivation of rights, and

provision is accordingly made to allow voluntary removal of protection by means of a notice served on the landlord by the tenant, which must be served before the tenancy begins, and has to be in the prescribed form (in order to warn the tenant of what rights he may be giving up); or

8. a periodic assured tenancy comes into being following a fixed-term assured tenancy (4.75); or

9. the grant is of an assured agricultural occupancies (4.55).

4.59 Tenancies created prior to February 28, 1997. It may remain relevant to determine whether a tenancy created prior to February 28, 1997 was at that time fully assured or assured shorthold, as that can affect:

● whether or not the tenant, if still in occupation, is fully assured or assured shorthold; and

● the validity of any new agreement entered into, i.e. provisions to protect a fully assured tenant against being tricked into signing an assured shorthold tenancy (4.58(7)) will not operate if the tenant was already assured shorthold.

4.60 Where a tenancy was granted prior to February 28, 1997, and otherwise fulfilled all the requirements for an assured tenancy, it was fully assured unless the landlord had served notice on the tenant that it was to be an assured shorthold tenancy.

4.61 In addition to service of notice, the tenancy had to be for a fixed term of not less than six months (containing no power for the landlord to determine the tenancy within that period, other than by way of forfeiture).

4.62 When the initial shorthold tenancy came or comes to an end, a periodic tenancy came or comes into being, of the same or substantially the same premises, which was or is also an assured shorthold tenancy unless the landlord served or serves notice stating that it is no longer to be considered a shorthold tenancy (1988 Act s.20(4)).

4.63 In each case, "the landlord", in the case of joint landlords, means at least one of them.

4.64 To prevent a landlord persuading a Housing Act assured tenant to enter into a new arrangement which is shorthold, a tenancy will not be an assured shorthold if, immediately beforehand, the person to whom it is granted (or if joint tenants, one of them) was a fully assured tenant of the same landlord (even if in different premises) (1988 Act s.20(3)).

5. TEMPORARY ACCOMMODATION FOR THE HOMELESS

4.65 When seeking to house homeless families under the interim housing duties imposed on them by the Housing Act 1996 Pt 7 (Chapter 10), local authorities may seek to use accommodation provided by other landlords, whether RSL or wholly private.

4.66 In order to ensure that the homeless do not obtain any security when they are being housed under any of the temporary, interim housing duties, the 1996 Act s.209 provides that a tenancy granted in pursuance of arrangements with authorities in the discharge of one of the interim duties under Pt 7 (s.188: accommodation pending enquiries; s.190: accommodation for intentionally homeless; s.200: accommodation pending or following a local connection referral; s.204: accommodation pending appeal to county court—see further Chapter 10) is not assured at all for a period of 12 months (from notification of decision, or decision on review or appeal), unless the tenant is notified by the landlord that the tenancy is to be either assured or assured shorthold.

Security of tenure

4.67 A number of matters have to be considered under this heading:

- succession;
- loss of assured status;
- continuation and termination;
- grounds for possession; and
- demotion orders.

1. SUCCESSION

4.68 Single succession. There is a limited right of "statutory succession" to an assured tenancy, similar to (but not as extensive as) that available to Housing Act secure tenants under the Housing

Act 1985 (3.40–3.54) and to Rent Act protected and statutory tenants under the Rent Act 1977 (5.33–5.38).

4.69 On the death of an assured tenant, his spouse or civil partner can succeed, provided that immediately before his death she was occupying the dwelling-house as her only or principal home (4.22): 1988 Act s.17(1)(a). For these purposes, persons who have been living together as husband and wife or as if they were civil partners are included (see 3.49).

4.70 Limits on succession. There can be no statutory succession if the deceased was himself already a successor, whether by reason of this (or another: 5.34) statutory succession provision or because of inheritance (1988 Act s.17(2)). If the tenancy was a joint tenancy (1.195), and the deceased became the tenant on the death of his joint tenant, there can be no statutory succession (1988 Act s.17(2)). Statutory succession only applies to a sole tenancy (1988 Act s.17(1)); on the death of one joint tenant, the other or others become the sole tenant or remaining joint tenants, by right of survivorship.

4.71 Devolution by will or on intestacy. Where there is no statutory succession, a tenancy can pass under a will or on intestacy, and if the inheritor occupies as an only or principal home, the tenancy will still be assured, but as there is to be a mandatory ground for possession available against the successor (provided the proceedings are brought within time limits: 4.102) it is a succession potentially of little value.

2.   LOSS OF ASSURED STATUS

4.72 There is a number of circumstances in which a tenancy may cease to be assured:

- **Want of residence.** The assured tenancy ceases to be assured for want of continued use as an only or principal home, in which case the landlord can terminate the tenancy in the usual way (1.113–1.146).

- **Exclusions.** The exclusions from security do not necessarily apply once and for all; see, e.g. resident landlord (4.44), low rent (4.29). A tenancy may therefore move in to, or out of, assured status.

- **New landlord.** The premises are bought by one of the public landlords described above whose tenants are not assured (4.41). The tenancy will usually then become a secure tenancy: see Chapter 3.

- **Ground for possession.** The landlord establishes to a court, which will be the county court, that one of the stated sets of circumstances exists, as a result of which he is or may be entitled to an order of the court for possession.

3. CONTINUATION AND TERMINATION

4.73 Continuation by contract. Security of tenure under the Housing Act 1988 operates closer to the Housing Act 1985 than the Rent Act 1977, in so far as a periodic contractual tenancy cannot be brought to an end by the landlord other than by court order (1988 Act s.5), so that there is no division between a contractual and a "statutory" tenancy as in the case of a Rent Act protected tenancy (5.24). (Note: the periodic tenancy can, however, still be brought to an end by the tenant in the normal way, i.e. by notice to quit or surrender (1.113–1.130)). A possession order will only be available on specified "grounds" (see next heading). An assured tenancy can also be ended by a demotion order, which replaces the fully assured tenancy with a shorthold (4.126).

4.74 Fixed terms. In the case of a fixed-term assured tenancy which contains a forfeiture clause (1.132), the tenancy cannot be brought to an end by the landlord by the exercise of that power. Nor can the tenant apply for relief from forfeiture (1.136–1.144): *Artesian Residential Developments Ltd v Beck*, 1999.

4.75 Instead of forfeiture, the landlord has to obtain an order of the court to determine the tenancy as if it was a periodic tenancy. If the fixed term ends in any other way, e.g. because its time expires, then—unless the tenant voluntarily leaves—there will automatically come into being a "statutory periodic tenancy", which will continue until determined by a court, on specified grounds, in the same way as a tenancy that had been periodic all along.

4.76 There will be no statutory periodic tenancy, however, if the landlord and the tenant agree a new tenancy to start on the determination of the old, whether that is a new fixed term or a new period tenancy.

4.77 Notice of seeking possession. As under the Housing Act 1985 (3.66), in place of notice to quit, the landlord has to serve a notice of seeking possession, specifying the ground he intends to rely on, before he can seek an order for possession (1988 Act s.8).

4.78 Contents of notice. The notice must be in the form prescribed, and must inform the tenant that the landlord intends to bring proceedings on the grounds specified, and that the proceedings will begin no earlier than a date specified in the notice, but no later than 12 months from service of the notice. The discussion of contents of notices, relative to secure tenants, is equally applicable to assured tenants (3.76).

4.79 Domestic violence and service. There are added requirements where the domestic violence ground (Ground 14A) is relied on (1988 Act s.8A), analogous to those applicable to secure tenants (3.73).

4.80 Just and equitable. The court can, however, dispense with such a notice if it considers it just and equitable (3.67) to do so (other than when possession is sought on Ground 8: 4.105).

4.81 Commencement of proceedings. Proceedings cannot commence before the later of the following:

- two weeks; or
- if possession is sought on Grounds 1, 2, 5–7, 9 or 16, two months; or
- if a periodic tenancy, the earliest date when a notice to quit could have expired; or
- if reliance is placed on Ground 14, the date of service of the notice.

4.82 A notice of seeking possession can, however, be served during a fixed-term tenancy, to take effect in relation to the following statutory periodic tenancy.

4.83 Grounds. Unless the court dispenses with the notice, or the court gives permission to alter or add to the grounds, possession can only be ordered on a ground specified in the notice.

4. GROUNDS FOR POSSESSION

4.84 Discretionary and mandatory grounds. As under both the 1985 and the 1977 Acts, grounds for possession (1988 Act s.7

and Sch.2) are either discretionary or mandatory. The mandatory grounds are set out in Sch.2 Pt 1; the discretionary grounds are set out in Sch.2 Pt 2.

4.85 The discretionary grounds for possession are those where the landlord has to prove that it is reasonable to make the order: the law on this subject, and the burden of proof, are the same as under the Housing Act 1985 (3.86–3.96).

4.86 Powers of court. In the case of discretionary grounds, the court's powers to postpone, suspend or vary an order are the same as under the 1985 and 1977 Acts (3.153–159; 1988 Act s.9), and if an assured tenant breaches the terms of a postponed or suspended order, he becomes a tolerated trespasser (*White v Knowsley*, 2007; 1.44; 1.58–1.61). The court's powers are otherwise as limited as under those two Acts where no security attaches or where a mandatory ground is available (1980 Act s.89; 151).

4.87 Rent arrears. There are three rent-arrears grounds. One is mandatory (Ground 8; 4.103), while the other two are discretionary (Grounds 10 and 11; 4.119 and 4.121). Possession may be sought on both the mandatory and discretionary grounds in the same proceedings. If, on the face of the order, it has not been made on the mandatory Ground 8, however, the court will retain its added powers (4.86) to suspend the order or a warrant for possession: *Capital Prime Plus Plc v Wills*, 1998. When making an order under Ground 8 the court should therefore ensure that this is made clear on its face: *Diab v Countryside Rentals 1 Plc*, 2001.

(i) *Mandatory grounds*

4.88 There are eight mandatory grounds for possession, i.e. those which, if proved, leave the court no alternative but to make an order for possession, to take effect within two to six weeks (depending on hardship; 3.151), regardless of whether or not it is reasonable to make the order.

4.89 Absentee owner-occupiers. Ground 1 concerns absentee owner-occupiers, although it may be noted that for these purposes the landlord could himself be the tenant of another, while still qualifying as an "owner-occupier" in relation to his sub-tenant.

4.90 The ground is available to a landlord who has (or, if joint landlords, one of whom has) formerly occupied the property as his only or principal home (4.22). It is also available to a landlord who requires (or, in the case of joint landlords, one of whom requires) to occupy the property as his or his spouse's or civil partner's only or principal home, although this is not an available alternative if the would-be occupier bought the premises (for money or money's worth) with the tenant already in occupation.

4.91 This ground is only available to a landlord who has served notice no later than the beginning of the tenancy, warning the tenant that the ground might be used against him.

4.92 If the landlord fails to do so, however, the court may waive this requirement, if it thinks it just and equitable to do so, e.g. if the tenant had oral notice, although such other factors as mutual hardship and time in occupation are also relevant (*White v Jones*, 1993). Persistent late payment of rent may also be relevant (*Boyle v Verrall*, 1996).

4.93 Mortgaged property. Ground 2 is available when the property is subject to a mortgage granted before the beginning of the tenancy, and the mortgagee has become entitled to exercise the power of sale under the mortgage (Chapter 2) and requires possession in order to sell with vacant possession.

4.94 Again, there has to have been notice no later than the beginning of the tenancy that this ground might apply, unless the court uses its power to waive notice on the basis that it is just and equitable to do so.

4.95 Out-of-season holiday letting. An out-of-season fixed-term letting for not more than eight months, of premises occupied within the previous 12 months for a holiday (4.38), is subject to a mandatory ground for possession, providing notice was given no later than the beginning of the tenancy that the ground would apply (Ground 3). There is no power for the court to waive the notice requirement.

4.96 Off-season student letting. An off-season fixed-term letting for not more than one year, of premises occupied within the previous 12 months as a student letting (4.37), is likewise subject to a mandatory ground for possession, provided notice was given no later than the beginning of the tenancy that the ground would apply (Ground 4). There is no power for the court to waive the notice requirement.

4.97 Ministers of religion. Ground 5 is a special ground, applicable to property occupied or formerly occupied by ministers of religion.

4.98 Demolition. Possession can be obtained under Ground 6 by a landlord who intends to demolish or reconstruct the whole or a substantial part of the premises, or carry out substantial works on them, if the following conditions are fulfilled:

- The work cannot reasonably be carried out with the tenant in occupation either because the tenant will not agree to a variation in terms, such as would allow sufficient access and facilities to permit the work to be carried out, or no such variation is practicable in the light of the intended works; or

- The tenant will not agree to accept an assured tenancy of part only of the property, such as would permit the landlord to carry out the works, or no such "part-property" arrangement would be practicable.

4.99 The ground is similar to that available under the Housing Act 1985; in particular, a landlord's plans have to be clear and certain before the ground is available (3.132).

4.100 This ground is also available in the case of a registered housing association or charitable housing trust (3.30) where the person intending to do the works is not the landlord under the tenancy but a superior landlord.

4.101 This ground is not available, however, to a landlord who has bought the property for money or money's worth with the tenant in occupation, or when the assured tenant has become an assured tenant by succession under the Rent Act 1977 (5.34).

4.102 Inherited tenancy. Ground 7 is available in the case of a periodic tenancy (including a statutory periodic tenancy: 4.75), but not a fixed-term tenancy.

4.103 This ground applies when the tenancy has devolved not on statutory succession (4.68) but under the will of the tenant, or on the tenant's intestacy, and proceedings for possession are commenced no later than one year after the death of the former tenant (or, if the court so permits, one year after the court considers that the landlord—or in the case of joint landlords, one of them—became aware of the death of the former tenant).

4.104 It is expressly provided that if the landlord continues to accept rent from the successor, this will not amount to the creation of a new tenancy (1.56), unless there is a variation in the amount of rent, the terms of the tenancy, its periods or the property itself.

4.105 Two months' rent arrears. Ground 8 concerns rent arrears (*cf.* 3.97, 5.144). This mandatory ground is available if both at the date of service of the notice of seeking possession (4.77) and at the date of hearing of the action, there are at least eight weeks' or two months' rent arrears.

4.106 At the hearing, unless the tenant can raise a defence to the arrears, e.g. a set-off for disrepair (11.105), the court must order possession. In exceptional circumstances, it can, however, adjourn the proceedings. The fact that the arrears may be attributable to a local authority failing to process a housing benefit claim is not one such exceptional circumstance (*North British Housing Association v Matthews*, 2004)

4.107 There are also two discretionary grounds concerning rent arrears (4.119, 4.121). If no notice has been served pursuant to s.48 of the Landlord and Tenant Act 1987 (1.112), rent will not yet be due and, therefore, cannot be in arrears (*Marath v MacGillivray*, 1996). Nor will there be arrears if there is a valid set-off for disrepair (or other breach) (11.105), but there will be arrears (at the date of NSP) even if there is a counter-claim for disrepair (or other breach), although (arguably) not at (the end of) the date of hearing, i.e. if a (sufficient) award is made on the counter-claim.

(ii) *Discretionary grounds*

4.108 The discretionary grounds for possession are those in relation to which the court enjoys extensive powers, and in which the landlord must prove that it is reasonable to make the order, in addition to showing that the details of each ground are applicable (4.85). There are ten of them.

4.109 Suitable alternative accommodation. Ground 9 applies when suitable alternative accommodation is available or will be available for the tenant when the order takes effect.

4.110 Suitable alternative accommodation is defined in Pt 3 Sch.2 of the 1988 Act. A certificate from the local authority that the tenant will be re-housed by them is conclusive that suitable alternative accommodation will be available (although not necessarily that it is reasonable to make the order).

4.111 In the alternative, a landlord can himself provide another private tenancy, or obtain one for the tenant from another landlord. In this case, the Schedule regulates such details as suitability for the needs and means of the tenant and his family as regards extent and character, or its similarity to the existing accommodation, or its proximity to work (*Yewbright Properties Ltd v Stone*, 1980).

4.112 The character of the new premises can be a determining factor. In *Redspring v Francis*, 1973, it was held that premises on a busy road, next door to a fish and chip shop, were not suitable for a tenant who had hitherto been living in a quiet residential street. The extent of the facilities and amenities in an area, including shops, open space, transport, etc. will also influence a decision.

4.113 The new tenancy must either be assured, excluding tenancies in respect of which notices under Grounds 1–5 have been given, and excluding an assured shorthold (see Chapter 6), or else must afford security equivalent to that enjoyed by an assured tenant.

4.114 Alternative accommodation will never be suitable if it will result in overcrowding, even if the tenant's present premises are overcrowded.

4.115 Suitable alternative accommodation may consist of part only of a tenant's present premises, e.g. if one room is sublet or disused (*Mykolyshyn v Noah*, 1970). If the part of the premises which the landlord is seeking to recover is used at all, e.g. as a study or workroom or a spare room for visiting family, it is extremely unlikely that the court would allow this ground for possession to be used effectively in order to reduce the size of the tenancy (*MacDonnell v Daly*, 1969).

4.116 The landlord must still establish that it is reasonable to make the order. A court will frequently refuse, even where the alternative premises are apparently suitable, because of, e.g. the age of the tenant.

4.117 An order may well be made subject to undertakings from the landlord to do specific works to the new premises, or else to pay for various removal or other expenses.

4.118   If such undertakings are not fulfilled, the tenant can apply to the court to set aside or discharge the order, or else sue for the amount owing.

4.119   Arrears of rent.   Ground 10 is the first of the further grounds dealing with rent arrears, and applies when rent is in arrears both at the date when the proceedings for possession are commenced, and at the date of service of the notice of seeking possession (4.77), unless such notice is waived by the court (4.80).

4.120   It may be distinguished from the mandatory Ground 8 in that:

- there may be no arrears at the date of hearing; and

- there is no minimum amount.

4.121   Ground 11 is available where, regardless of whether there are current rent arrears, and regardless of whether there were arrears at date of service of notice of seeking possession, issue of proceedings or date of hearing, the tenant has persistently delayed paying rent. Whether or not there are arrears may be affected by the question of set-off or counter-claim for disrepair (or other breach) (3.98).

4.122   Remaining discretionary grounds.   The next series of grounds is familiar:

- Ground 12: broken obligation of tenancy (3.100, 5.144);

- Ground 13: deterioration of dwelling-house or common parts owing to acts of waste by, or the neglect or default of, the tenant or someone else residing in the property (whom no steps have been taken to try to remove) (3.113, 5.150);

- Ground 14: concerning nuisance, annoyance and convictions, as extended by the Housing Act 1996 (3.103);

- Ground 14A: is the domestic violence ground (3.112);

- Ground 15: concerning condition of furniture, with the same qualification in the case of default by someone residing in the premises other than the tenant (3.113, 5.151);

- Ground 16: concerning service tenancies (1.153–1.163)—it is available when the property was let to the tenant in consequence of his employment, and he has ceased to be in that employment;

- Ground 17: concerning tenancies induced by a false statement (3.115).

(iii) *Related issues*

4.123 Forfeiture. In the case of a fixed-term tenancy which contains a forfeiture clause (4.74), the court can only make an order for possession on the discretionary grounds in Sch.2, Pt II, other than Grounds 9 or 16, or Grounds 2 or 8 of the mandatory grounds in Sch.2 Pt I (1988 Act s.7), and then only if the forfeiture clause itself permits the lease to be ended on that ground.

4.124 The landlord does not need to bring a parallel claim for forfeiture, nor do the provisions for relief from forfeiture (1.136) apply: *Artesian Residential Developments Ltd v Beck*, 1999.

4.125 Misrepresentation. Where possession is ordered on any ground, and it can later be shown that the order was obtained by misrepresentation or concealment of a material fact, the landlord can be ordered to compensate the tenant (1988 Act s.12).

5. DEMOTION ORDER

4.126 An RSL may bring an assured tenancy to an end by obtaining a demotion order. The effect of the order is to replace the assured tenancy with a demoted assured shorthold tenancy.

4.127 Preliminary notice. As for possession proceedings (4.80), unless the court considers it just and equitable to dispense with the requirement, the landlord must serve the tenant with a notice. There is no prescribed form of notice but it must give particulars of the antisocial behaviour relied on and state that proceedings will not begin before a specified date; it must also state that proceedings cannot commence later than 12 months from service of the notice (1988 Act s.6A).

4.128 Antisocial behaviour. A demotion order can only be made if the court is satisfied that the tenant, or a person residing or visiting the dwelling has either:

- engaged in, or threatened to engage in, conduct capable of causing a nuisance or annoyance to any person which directly or indirectly relates to or affects the housing management functions of the authority; or

- engaged in conduct which involves using or threatening to use for an unlawful purpose housing accommodation owned or managed by a local authority, a housing action trust, or a registered social landlord (1988 Act s.6A(4)).

4.129 Reasonableness. The court can only make an order where it considers it reasonable to do so. Various factors are relevant to this issue, many of which are also relevant to the making of a possession order, e.g. effect on neighbours, severity of the conduct and degree of fault on the tenant's part (3.92–3.94). The effect on the tenant will be relevant, i.e. the fact that after the order is made, the landlord can obtain possession not only for further antisocial behaviour but for any reason, including rent arrears.

Rent and other terms

1. STARTING RENTS

4.130 Periodic tenancy. The starting point of such rent control as is applicable to assured tenancies is that what has been agreed is payable; there is no concept analogous to "registered rents" under the Rent Act 1977 (Chapter 5), by which an existing registration might override the rent agreed at the commencement of the tenancy.

4.131 Fixed-term tenancy. In the case of a fixed-term assured tenancy, there is no means for varying the rent, other than as the agreement itself provided, until such time as the agreement becomes a statutory periodic tenancy (4.75).

4.132 Statutory periodic tenancy. Under a statutory periodic tenancy, the terms are prima facie the same as under the fixed term, and its periods are the same as those for which rent was paid under the fixed term (1988 Act s.5).

4.133 Within one year of the termination of the fixed term, however, either the landlord or the tenant may serve notice on the other, in prescribed form, proposing different terms and, if considered appropriate, a variation of rent to reflect the variation of terms (1988 Act s.6).

4.134 Once such a notice has been served, the landlord or the tenant on whom it has been served has three months within which to refer it to a rent assessment committee (5.203; note: not the rent officer; rent officers have no role in relation to rent-fixing for assured tenancies) (1988 Act s.6).

4.135 If the notice is not so referred, then the proposed terms, and rent, become the terms (and rent) of the statutory periodic tenancy (1988 Act s.6(3)).

4.136 If there is a reference, the rent assessment committee has to consider the proposed terms, and determine whether they, or some other term (dealing only with the same subject-matter as the terms proposed) might reasonably be expected to be found in an assured periodic tenancy of such a property, presuming:

- that the tenancy began on the coming to the end of the former fixed term; and

- that the tenancy was granted by a willing landlord on the terms (other than those now under review) that apply to that tenancy (1988 Act s.6(4)).

4.137 The committee has to disregard the fact that there is a sitting tenant (1988 Act s.6(6))

4.138 Even if the notice proposing the new terms did not include a proposal for the variation of rent to reflect them, the committee is entitled to adjust the rent to take account of the adjustment of the terms (1988 Act s.6(5)).

4.139 Unless the landlord and tenant agree otherwise, the committee decides when the new terms and rent apply from, save that in the case of the rent, it cannot specify a date which is earlier than any proposed in the original notice (1988 Act s.6(7)).

4.140 The committee is not bound to continue with the process if the landlord and the tenant give notice in writing that they do not wish it to do so; nor need it continue if the tenancy ends before it reaches its determination (1988 Act s.6(8)).

2. VARIATION OF RENTS

4.141 In the case of a periodic assured tenancy, or in the case of a statutory periodic tenancy to which the foregoing provisions (4.132–4.140) do not apply, e.g. because no variation of terms is proposed or because the one-year time limit from the expiry of the previous fixed term has passed, a variation of rent procedure applies, although it can only be initiated by a landlord seeking an increase (1988 Act s.13).

4.142 This procedure is not available, however, if the periodic tenancy (not being a statutory periodic tenancy following a fixed term) itself contained its own provisions for determining increases, e.g. a procedure by which the landlord can increase it using an index-linked formula, or by reference to arbitration (1988 Act s.13(1)).

4.143 Statutory process for increase of rent. To obtain an increase by the statutory process—when applicable (periodic tenancy without its own provisions, or statutory periodic tenancy following a fixed term)—the landlord must serve notice on the tenant, in the prescribed form, proposing a new rent to take effect at the beginning of a period of the tenancy. The period must itself commence no earlier than:

- the minimum period (4.146) after service of the notice; and
- other than in the case of a statutory period tenancy, the date that falls 52 weeks after the date on which the tenancy began; and
- if there has been a previous increase under the statutory process, the appropriate date (1988 Act s.13(2)).

4.144 Appropriate date. The appropriate date is either:

- 52 weeks after the date on which the last increase took effect; or
- 53 weeks after that date if the 53rd week after the date of the last increase begins more than six days before the first increase after February 1993.

4.145 The point of this cumbersome 52/53–week rule is to allow landlords to increase rents on the same day in each year, e.g. the first Monday in April.

4.146 The "minimum period" is six months in the case of a yearly tenancy; one month in the case of a tenancy the periods of which are less than a month, e.g. weekly or four-weekly; or in any other case, e.g. quarterly tenancy or six monthly tenancy, one period of the tenancy (1988 Act s.13(3)).

4.147 Effect of notice. The new rent will take effect unless before the beginning of the (minimum) period specified, the tenant refers the notice to a rent assessment committee, by application in the prescribed form, or else the landlord and the tenant agree a different rent (1988 Act s.13(4)).

4.148 Decision. If the rent is referred to a rent assessment committee, the committee has to decide:

- what rent the property concerned might reasonably be expected to obtain on the open market;
- by a willing landlord letting an assured tenancy of the same periods;
- beginning at the period specified in the notice;
- the terms (other than rent) of which are the same; and
- in respect of which the same notices under Sch.2 Grounds 1–5 (mandatory grounds for possession; 4.88–4.96) have been served (1988 Act s.14(1)).

4.149 Disregards. The committee must disregard the fact that there is a sitting tenant.

4.150 The committee must also disregard:

- any increase attributable to a "relevant improvement" by a person who—at the time it was carried out—was the tenant (not necessarily the current tenant); and
- any reduction in value attributable to the tenant's failure to comply with the terms of his tenancy (the tenant's failure only applies to the current tenant and not any predecessor: *N & D (London) Ltd v Gadson*, 1991) (1988 Act s.14(2)).

4.151 An improvement is not to be disregarded, i.e. is not "relevant", if it was an improvement which the tenant was required to do under a term of the tenancy or any other "obligation" to the landlord (unless the obligation arose as a condition of consent given by the landlord on a request by the tenant to execute works) (1988 Act s.14(2)).

4.152 A "relevant improvement" is otherwise one carried out during the current tenancy, or carried out no more than 21 years before the date of service of the notice proposing the rent increase, during which 21 years the property has always been subject to an assured tenancy, on the termination of which the tenant (or if joint tenants, one of them) did not quit (1988 Act s.14(3)).

4.153   These are the only improvements to be disregarded: the tenant will have to pay for others, by way of increased rent.

4.154   Powers of committee.   When determining rent, the rent assessment committee is not concerned with any service charge within the Landlord and Tenant Act 1985 (2.75) (1988 Act s.14(4)), as this can be referred to a leasehold valuation tribunal under that Act, and must determine a rent which is exclusive of rates (1988 Act s.13(5)).

4.155   If there are both a notice seeking an increase in rent and a notice proposing a variation of terms (4.132–4.140) before the committee at the same time, and the notice proposing a variation of terms specifies a date no later than the proposed rent increase, the committee is entitled to hear the applications together, and when it does so is bound to decide the variation of terms before it decides the new rent (1988 Act s.14(6)).

4.156   Unless the landlord and the tenant otherwise agree, the new rent takes effect from the date specified in the notice of increase unless it appears to the committee that this would cause undue hardship, in which case the committee may determine a later date (but no later than their decision): 1988 Act s.14(7).

4.157   The committee is not bound to continue with the process if the landlord and the tenant give notice in writing that they do not wish it to do so; nor need it continue if the tenancy ends before it reaches its determination (1988 Act s.14(8)).

3.   OTHER TERMS

4.158   Access.   It is an implied term of all assured tenancies that the tenant should afford to the landlord access to the property and all reasonable facilities for executing repairs which the landlord is entitled to execute (1988 Act s.16).

4.159   Assignment and sub-letting.   With two exceptions, all assured periodic tenancies are subject to a prohibition on assignment of the tenancy, in whole or part, and on sub-letting under the tenancy in whole or part, without the consent of the landlord (1988 Act s.15(1)).

4.160 In the case of this implied prohibition, there is no qualification that the landlord's consent cannot unreasonably be withheld (1988 Act s.15(2); 1.180).

4.161 The first exception is if the tenancy agreement itself contains a prohibition, whether absolute or qualified (1.180, 1.228), in which case it is the agreement which determines what rights there are, not the Act. The second is if a premium is paid on the grant or renewal of the tenancy (1988 Act s.15(3)). "Premium" has the same meaning as under the Rent Act 1977 (1988 Act s.15(4); 5.215–5.224).

Further financial protection and assistance

4.162   Right to acquire.   The assured tenants of registered social landlords have the right to acquire their dwelling if it was provided with "public money", i.e. it was funded in whole or in part by a social housing grant (paid by the Housing Corporation) or was transferred to the registered social landlord from a landlord whose tenants are secure (3.28) (Housing Act 1996 s.16).

4.163   Operation.   The right to acquire essentially mirrors the right to buy (3.171–3.193), save that the Secretary may adapt or modify the provisions (see Housing Act 1996 s.17 and SI 1997/619).

4.164   Miscellaneous provisions.   To avoid other forms of exploitation of tenants, or ways of extracting more money from them than permitted, there are other forms of financial protection which may be applicable. In addition, housing benefits are as available for assured tenants as for secure tenants (see 3.256). (Unlike under the Rent Acts, there is no prohibition on premiums and deposits under the Housing Act 1988: cf. 5.215–5.226).

4.165   We shall therefore consider:

- accommodation agency charges; and
- resale of utilities, i.e. gas and electricity.

4.166   Accommodation agency charges.   Under the Accommodation Agencies Act 1953, it is a criminal offence either to demand or to accept any payment either for registering or undertaking to register the name and requirements of a person seeking a tenancy of premises.

4.167 It is also an offence under the same Act to demand or accept a payment simply for supplying or undertaking to supply addresses or other particulars of premises to let.

4.168 In *Saunders v Soper*, 1975, it was held that the purpose of the latter provision was to prohibit payments made simply for supplying addresses and particulars of property to let, and that it did not prohibit payment for actually finding somewhere for the prospective tenant to live.

4.169 It follows that an illegal payment has been made, and is therefore recoverable by the tenant, if the payment is made simply for the provision of addresses. It is also illegal if made for the provision of addresses, even though expressed to be returnable if the tenant does not accept a tenancy through the services of the agency. The payment is not illegal, however, if made after a tenancy has been found and accepted.

4.170 As well as constituting offences, such payments can be recovered as civil debts within six years of the payment being made (Limitation Act 1980).

4.171 Resale of utilities. The public electricity suppliers are entitled to publish a tariff, which may differ from area to area, indicating the maximum amounts which may be charged for the resale of electricity. This will usually be a figure that permits the landlord a small profit per unit, to cover, among other things, the cost of renting the electricity meter which monitors the occupier's use.

4.172 The public gas suppliers are under a duty to fix such maximum prices.

4.173 In either case, the amounts overcharged are recoverable by the occupier as a civil debt.

CHAPTER FIVE

Rent Act Protected Tenancies

Introduction

5.01 In this chapter, we shall examine the Rent Act 1977 ("1977 Act") protected tenancy, the rights of the protected tenant to security of tenure and regulation of rent, and some further financial protection.

5.02 No new Rent Act protected tenancies. Subject to a limited number of exceptions, it has not been possible to create any new Rent Act protected tenancies since the commencement of Pt 1 of the Housing Act 1988 ("1988 Act"), January 15, 1989.

5.03 It follows that, in this chapter, what is discussed either actually is, or is derived from, a letting arrangement that is some years old. It remains necessary to consider the Rent Acts, however, for a number of reasons.

- Tenancies can last not mere years, nor even mere decades, but generations. Although they will overwhelmingly have "settled down" as Rent Act protected tenancies (rather than, e.g. licences or holiday lettings or one of the other, sometimes well-known devices for defeating Rent Act protection that have been largely replaced since 1980 by security-free "shorthold" lettings—see 4.04; 6.139), there are still many people who occupy under them.

- Much residential security and rent law—perhaps most of it—was developed under the Rents Act. (They were the governing form of residential security from 1915 until 1988.) Often, it is only a subordinate part of a Rent Act decision which is still relevant; nonetheless, it cannot be fully comprehended without the context. (Thus, the proposition that for a room to be let as a separate dwelling, it had to comprise. In particular, cooking facilities was "received wisdom" even under Housing Act security—3.17; 4.17—until critically examined in its original Rent Act context in 2001; see *Uratemp Ltd v Collins*, 2001).

5.04 This chapter will accordingly read somewhat differently than earlier and later chapters. There is less detail about how an original Rent Act protected tenancy comes into being, and other information that is unlikely today to be of much relevance; and, because its purpose is in part to retain the origins of residential security (and rents) law, even what is left is of less obvious practical relevance. Nonetheless, it may safely be asserted that no one involved in private-sector housing advice or action will work for long before needing to come to grips with the tenure.

Outline

5.05   General principles

- Subject to exceptions, there have been no new protected Rent Act tenancies since January 15, 1989 (commencement of Pt 1 of the 1988 Act).
- Security under the Rent Acts applies to private landlords, not social landlords.
- Landlords have used a number of mechanisms to try and avoid security under the Rent Acts, in particular licences, but also holiday lettings and company lettings, although they are of decreasing importance with the passage of time.
- In deciding whether an agreement such as a licence evades Rent Act protection it is necessary to look at its substance and reality, not its form.
- There are two types of full-security tenancy under the Rent Act:
    - protected tenancies: those where the contract for the tenancy has not terminated; and
    - statutory tenancies, which arise on termination of the contractual protected tenancy.
- A spouse or same-sex partner can on the death of a protected or statutory tenancy succeed to a statutory tenancy, provided there has been no previous succession.
- If there has been a previous succession, a spouse may succeed to an assured tenancy under the Housing Act 1988 ("1988 Act").

- It there is no spouse entitled to succeed, a member of the family can succeed to an assured tenancy under the Housing Act 1988.

5.06 Rent Act protected tenants

- A tenant to whom a dwelling house was let as a separate dwelling prior to January 15, 1989, will be a protected tenant unless one of a number of exclusions applies.

- A protected tenant cannot be evicted unless the contractual tenancy is first brought to an end.

- Once the contractual tenancy is brought to an end a statutory tenancy will arise, provided the tenant occupies the dwelling as his residence.

- A court may only order possession of a protected or statutory tenancy on one of the grounds set out in the 1977 Act.

- Some grounds require the court to be satisfied that it is reasonable to grant possession, which are known as the discretionary grounds, while others are mandatory.

- A protected shorthold tenant is a particular type of protected tenancy, granted under the Housing Act 1980. This was a precursor to the Housing Act 1988 assured shorthold tenancy (4.04). Because, subject only to technical requirements, this meant that the tenant could be easily evicted after an initial two-year period, this conferred only limited security and it is therefore considered in Chapter 6.

5.07 Protection of rents and other financial protection and assistance

- Rent Act protected tenants may apply for a fair rent to be registered.

- A fair rent is a market rent adjusted for scarcity and the statutory disregards.

- A fair rent is initially set by a rent officer.

- In assessing the fair rent, the officer must ignore any scarcity of accommodation in the area and the personal circumstances of the tenant but must take into account the age, character, locality and state of repair of the dwelling.

- Once a fair rent has been registered, it applies to any subsequent Rent Act protected tenancy of the same premises.

- Applications can be made by either the landlord or the tenant to review a fair rent every two years.

- Appeals against the rent registered can be made to the Rent Assessment Committee.

- It is illegal to charge a premium on the grant, continuance or renewal of a Rent Act protected tenancy.

General principles
1.   EXCEPTIONS AND EVASIONS

5.08   Exceptions. Notwithstanding the general rule that there can be no new protected tenancies after commencement of Pt 1 of the 1988 Act (5.02), there can be a new Rent Act protected tenancy created on or after January 15, 1989, if the tenancy falls within one of the following exceptions:

- **Pre-Act contract.** It was entered into pursuant to a contract for its grant which preceded that date; or

- **New tenancy to former tenancy.** It is the grant of a new tenancy (not necessarily of the same premises) to a person who was a former protected or statutory (5.25) tenant of the same landlord, or one of a number of joint (1.198–1.207) protected or statutory tenants (not including a shorthold tenant (6.139)).

- **Suitable alternative accommodation.** It is the grant of a tenancy resulting from an order for possession on the ground of suitable alternative accommodation (5.169), the premises in question are those which the court has found suitable, and the court directs that the new tenancy should be a protected tenancy because it considers that an assured tenancy (Chapter 4) would not afford sufficient security of tenure.

- **New town corporation to private ownership.** It falls within a small class of tenancy formerly held by a new-town development corporation, and passed into the private sector prior to March 31, 1996: 1988 Act s.34.

5.09   New tenancies normally Housing Act assured. Tenancies granted on or after the commencement of Pt 1 of the 1988 Act are subject to its own schedule of exclusions, likely to be assured tenancies, and are considered in Chapter 4.

5.10 Tenants only. Only tenants can enjoy full Rent Act protection, not trespassers or licensees (see, e.g. *Marcroft Wagons v Smith*, 1951), nor, except as described in Chapter 2, owner-occupiers.

5.11 Landlord and Tenant Act 1987 Part 1. Rent Act protected tenants are included as "qualifying" tenants for the purposes of Pt 1 of the Landlord and Tenant Act 1987, i.e. the "right of first refusal" (2.34–2.46).

5.12 Private tenants. In the main, tenants whose landlords are not public bodies, such as local authorities, nor bodies such as housing trusts and registered social landlords, will be Rent Act protected tenants provided that their landlords do not live in the same building as themselves.

5.13 This short description can, however, be misleading, as some who would appear to qualify will not be Rent Act protected tenants, and others who would appear to be excluded may, for one reason or another, in fact enjoy full Rent Act protection.

5.14 Business lettings. As with Housing Act secure tenancies, business tenancies are excluded from protection (1977 Act s.24): see 3.39(14).

5.15 Agricultural and forestry workers. Under the Rent (Agriculture) Act 1976 ("1976 Act"), protection largely similar to that to be described in this chapter is available to agricultural- and forestry-tied workers whose rights of occupation precede the commencement of Pt 1 of the 1988 Act (January 15, 1989), i.e. those living in accommodation belonging to their employers (1.153).

5.16 It is not possible in this book to consider the 1976 Act in any detail, but the same points made in relation to assured agricultural occupancies are relevant here (4.53).

5.17 Rent Acts and evasion. Landlords commonly sought to avoid the effects of Rent Act protection by granting forms of letting which were not within the ambit of the 1977 Act.

5.18 The most common form of evasion was the licence agreement: we have already considered one form of licence; the non-exclusive occupation agreement (1.214–1.220). We have also considered how the law approaches the task of interpreting an agreement as licence or tenancy (1.67–1.74).

5.19 Substance and reality. In relation to the Rent Acts:

> "It has been said before, and it must be said again, that in the consideration of questions arising under the Rent Acts, the court must look at the substance and reality of a transaction, not its form" (Viscount Simonds, *Elmdene Estates v White*, 1960).

5.20 In an earlier case, *Samrose Properties v Gibbard*, 1958, Lord Evershed M.R. said that a court must always ask itself:

> "Whether the transaction, viewed as a whole and according to the substance of it, is in truth one which . . . is on that side of the line which frees the premises from the impact of the Acts, or whether, so regarded, the transaction is one which is of the mischief which the Acts were designed to avoid."

5.21 More recently, it has been said that:

> ". . . the manufacture of a five-pronged implement for manual digging results in a fork even if the manufacturer, unfamiliar with the English language, insists that he intended to make and has made a spade . . . The court should . . . be astute to detect and frustrate sham devices and artificial transactions whose only object is to disguise the grant of a tenancy and to evade the Rent Acts" (*Street v Mountford*, 1986. In *AG Securities v Vaughan*; *Antoniades v Villiers*, 1988, Lord Templeman said that the word "pretence" should be substituted for sham devices and artificial transactions.)

5.22 In this chapter, two further pretences, to which the same general principles are applicable, are considered in their most appropriate contexts: holiday lettings (5.83) and company lets (5.107).

5.23 The overriding principle should always be borne in mind: look at what the parties factually intended to be the arrangement (by which is meant what the law understands the parties to have intended), not how they have described it.

2. STATUTORY TENANCIES

5.24 Protected and statutory tenancy. The term Rent Act protected tenant technically refers to a tenant within Rent Act protection who is still a contractual tenant (1977 Act s.1), i.e. one whose contract of tenancy has not come to an end in one of the ways described (1.113–1.146).

5.25 This reflects the somewhat different approach to security under the Rent Acts than under the Housing Act 1985 ("1985 Act"; 3.62) and the Housing Act 1988 (4.73), where termination of the tenancy contract can only be effected by the courts. After the termination of a contractual Rent Act protected tenancy under the 1977 Act, security of tenure operates by providing a right to remain or "status of irremovability" which is known as a statutory tenancy (1977 Act s.2) and which the tenant can enjoy so long as he continues to occupy the property as "a" residence (not necessarily "only or principal" or "only or main").

5.26 If there were joint contractual tenants, each will acquire the personal right of statutory tenancy (*Daejan Properties Ltd v Mahoney*, 1995), and if only one remains, he will be able to sustain it alone (*Lloyd v Sadler*, 1978).

5.27 Terms of statutory tenancy. A statutory tenancy continues on exactly the same terms as the prior contractual tenancy save where such terms would be inconsistent with the idea of statutory tenancy (1977 Act s.3), e.g. a requirement to yield up vacant possession on termination of the contractual tenancy or a right to assign or sublet the whole of the premises (*Keeves v Dean*, 1924; *Atyeo v Fardoe*, 1978), and save as regards rent which, obviously, may be increased as the years pass (5.212).

5.28 Expiry of contractual tenancy. The distinction between a contractual tenancy and a statutory tenancy may not be without importance as regards both security of tenure and rent regulation. This is especially so if the contractual tenancy is a fixed-term tenancy.

5.29 Before any court proceedings to evict the tenant can be brought on one or other of the grounds described below, the contractual tenancy must have been brought to an end (1.113–1.146). Even if a tenant is in arrears of rent, then it will be necessary for the landlord to forfeit a fixed-term agreement, or serve valid notice to quit. Unless he does so, then no matter how great the tenant's default, the proceedings will be defective and no order will be made. (Note: the tenancy must have expired by the date proceedings are commenced, not just by the date of hearing.)

5.30 Fixed term and rent. The tenant may be able to derive an advantage as regards rent from a lengthy fixed-term tenancy. Even if the registered rent increases, the landlord will still be limited by the contractual rent, until such time as he can bring the contractual tenancy to an end; in the case of a fixed term they may not be for some time. (Note: for this reason, many fixed-term agreements came to say that the contractual rent would be a particular sum or the registered rent, if that is higher. Such a clause is valid.)

5.31 Periodic tenancy and rent. In the case of a periodic tenancy, however, a notice of increase of rent can double as a notice to quit so as to bring the tenancy to an end and allow a higher rent than originally agreed to be charged. To operate dually in this way, a notice of increase must be in the proper form (*Aristocrat Property Investments v Harounoff*, 1982) and specify a date for the increase to take effect no earlier than a notice to quit could have taken effect (1.116–1.117). It will then have the effect of converting the contractual tenancy into a statutory tenancy (1977 Act s.49).

5.32 Termination of statutory tenancy. Once the contractual tenancy has been brought to an end, howsoever this is done, there is no need for any further notice to be served to bring the subsequent statutory tenancy to an end before bringing proceedings, even if there is a gap of several years between termination and commencement of proceedings. No new contractual tenancy comes into being unless there is evidence that such was intended, e.g. because the landlord and the tenant agreed to vary some term of the tenancy other than rent, and it is sufficiently substantial to warrant description as a new tenancy (1.57). The tenant simply occupies as a statutory tenant until such time as a court orders possession to be given up to the landlord.

3. SUCCESSION

5.33 Statutory tenancy by succession. Normally, a tenant will be first a contractual tenant and subsequently a statutory tenant. This may not be the case, however, when a protected tenant dies and his widow succeeds to the tenancy (1977 Act s.2). In such circumstances, the successor becomes a statutory tenant at once, and the terms are the same, save as already mentioned, as those of the contractual tenancy of the person to whom the new tenant has succeeded.

5.34 Rent Act succession to Housing Act assured tenancy. Succession to a tenancy where the tenant died on or after the commencement of Pt 1 of the 1988 Act (January 15, 1989), is subject to the following rules:

- **Priority to spouse.** If the tenant who died was married, his spouse will have priority in the succession, provided she was living in the dwelling-house at the time of his death, but for this purpose the terms marriage and spouse includes a couple living together as husband and wife (1977 Act Sch.1 para.2, as amended by 1988 Act s.37 and Sch.4) and a same-sex couple (*Ghaidan v Godin-Mendoza*, 2004).

- **Member of family.** If there is no spouse to succeed, then any member of the family who was residing in the dwelling-house at the time of the tenant's death and for two years beforehand is entitled to succeed to the tenancy, but the tenancy will be a Housing Act assured tenancy (Chapter 4), not a Rent Act protected or statutory tenancy (1977 Act Sch.1 para.3, as amended).

- **Death of spouse successor.** On the death of a successor spouse, a member of the family (of both the original tenant and the successor) residing in the dwelling-house at the time of the successor's death and for two years beforehand is entitled to a "second succession", but likewise only to a Housing Act assured tenancy (1977 Act Sch.1 para.6, as amended).

5.35 Deemed residence. There were transitional provisions governing deaths within the first 18 months following the commencement of Pt 1 of the 1988 Act, under which a member of the family residing with the deceased for six months before the commencement date was treated as having resided for two years. "Residing" means more than staying at an address, even if the quality of the residence is not permanent or indefinite (*Swanbrae Ltd v Elliott*, 1986; *Hildebrand v Moon*, 1989).

5.36 Cohabitation. Prior to amendment by the Housing Act 1988, when persons living together as husband and wife were specifically defined as spouses, it had been held that a cohabitant of long standing could be treated as a member of the family for the purpose of succession: *Dyson Holdings v Fox*, 1976; *Watson v Lucas*, 1980 (even though still legally married to someone else). A lengthy period of cohabitation may not be needed if there is additional supporting evidence of the nature of the relationship (*Chios Investment (Property) Co v Lopez*, 1987), but in *Helby v Rafferty*,

1979, a man failed in his claim to succeed to his cohabitant's tenancy—they had been together only five years, lived relatively independent lives, and she retained her own name.

5.37 Member of the family. Member of the family is not statutorily defined and may be given a wide meaning. It is not used in any technical sense but in a popular sense (*Longdon v Horton*, 1951; *Brock v Wollams*, 1949). The hallmarks of family membership are essentially that there should be a degree of mutual interdependence, of the sharing of lives, of caring and love, of commitment and support. In respect of legal relationships these are presumed; in other relationships, these are capable, if proved, of creating membership of the tenant's family (*Fitzpatrick v Sterling HA*, 1999).

Rent Act protected tenants

5.38 Two main issues must be addressed:

1. who qualifies as a Rent Act protected tenant? and

2. security of tenure.

1. WHO QUALIFIES AS A RENT ACT PROTECTED TENANT

5.39 Let as a separate dwelling. The Rent Act assumes that all tenants to whom property was let as a separate dwelling before the commencement of Pt 1 of the 1988 Act (January 15, 1989) are Rent Act protected tenants unless there is some factor which takes them out of protection (1977 Act s.1).

5.40 The phrase "as a separate dwelling" has been considered in relation both to secure tenancies (3.17) and assured tenancies (4.16). Because of the provisions including sharers (5.70), it is of much less significance under the 1977 Act.

5.41 Exclusions. The exclusions from protection cover a range of matters:

- **resident landlord**: in respect of tenancies commencing on or after August 14, 1974, whether the landlord lives in the same building or not (Rent Act 1977 s.12);

- **old furnished lettings and resident landlord**: in respect of tenancies commencing before August 14, 1974, whether the tenancy was considered to be a furnished tenancy in law before that date, and whether the landlord has lived in the same building or not since August 14, 1974 (1977 Act Sch.24);

- **sharing living accommodation with landlord**: regardless of when the tenancy commenced, whether the tenant shares living accommodation with the landlord or not (1977 Act s.21);

- **attendances**: whether the tenant is provided with attendances (1977 Act s.7);

- **board**: whether the tenant is provided with board (1977 Act s.7);

- **low rent**: whether the rent is what the law knows as a "low rent" (1977 Act s.5);

- **student lettings**: whether it is a student letting (1977 Act s.8);

- **no rent**: whether any rent is paid (1977 Act s.5);

- **holiday lettings**: whether it is a holiday letting (1977 Act s.9);

- **identity of landlord**: the identity of the landlord (1977 Act ss.13–16);

- **high-rateable value**: the rateable value of the premises (1977 Act s.4);

- **agricultural land**: whether the property qualifies as an agricultural holding (1977 Act s.10);

- **other land**: whether the letting is with other land (exceeding two acres) (1977 Act ss.6, 26);

- **shared-ownership leases**: whether the letting qualifies as a shared-ownership lease, as defined (1977 Act s.5A);

- **licensed premises**: whether the premises qualify as licensed premises (1977 Act s.11).

5.42   The last four of these do not require further consideration.

(i)   *Tenancies commencing on or after August 14, 1974*

5.43   Resident landlord. When the Rent Act 1974 came into operation on August 14, 1974, it brought with it two major changes. One was that it extended full Rent Act protection to the tenants of furnished accommodation who had hitherto been excluded (but enjoyed restricted security: 6.104).

5.44   The other change was to substitute a new class of tenancy subject to the lesser jurisdiction of the Rent Tribunal: those were tenants with resident landlords, as defined. The definition applies where the landlord and the tenant occupy different parts of the same building (not being a purpose-built block of flats), or else (even if a purpose-built block of flats) that they occupy different parts of the same flat. These conditions are defined in the same way as under the Housing Act 1988 (4.44).

5.45   Continuous residence.   For a landlord to take advantage of this exception, he must establish that (subject to the provisions governing change of landlord described below), he has at all times since the commencement of the tenancy used the other part of the building which he occupies as a residence (1977 Act s.12).

5.46   Use as a residence.   Legal residence is discussed in greater detail below (5.95–5.111), as the same test applies to the question whether a statutory tenant has sufficient residence to maintain his right to the statutory tenancy (1977 Act Sch.2).

5.47   Briefly, residence means that premises are being used as a home, even if not the only home. A person may for short periods cease to use premises as a residence and still be treated as sustaining legal residence, provided both that he fully intends to return to live in the premises, and that he has left some physical sign of occupation in the premises, e.g. furniture, belongings, family.

5.48   The law accepts that a person may have more than one residence at a time, but a purely token residence will not suffice: a landlord cannot simply keep one room in a house, or in several houses, in order to keep his tenants out of protection.

5.49   The question that must be asked is not whether at all times the landlord has been in residence, or has resided in the part kept for himself, but whether the premises have been a legal residence of the landlord throughout the period in question, i.e. since the start of the tenancy.

5.50   When both landlord and tenant moved house together, over a period of about a week, the fact that the landlord happened not to move in until after the tenant did not disqualify him from claiming residence, as he had both the intention to move in, of which there were already signs (*O'Sullivan v Barnett*, 1994). This accords with the usual test of statutory residence (5.95–5.111).

5.51 It is likely that residence by one of two or more joint owners/landlords would be considered to be enough to keep the tenant out of protection (*cf.* 4.50).

5.52 Corporate landlords. Because of this requirement for residence, however, a corporate landlord, i.e. a landlord which is a company, a trust, a partnership, etc. cannot "reside" at all because such a landlord has no natural life (*Hiller v United Dairies (London)*, 1934).

5.53 Change of resident landlord. If a landlord sells the house, residence will nonetheless be treated as continuing for a further 28 days. If, during that time, the new owner serves notice that he intends to move into the premises for use as a home, then he has a total of six months in which to do so, during which period residence by the landlord will likewise be treated as continuing (1977 Act Sch.2).

5.54 If, by the end of the six months, the new owner has not taken up residence, the tenant will become a Rent Act protected tenant and will so remain, even when the owner moves in, for there will not have been continual residence since the start of the tenancy.

5.55 Termination of contractual tenancy during period of disregard. If the contractual tenancy comes to an end within this period, on the one hand no statutory tenancy will arise, but on the other, the landlord cannot during this period evict other than as if the tenant was a statutory tenant (1977 Act Sch.2). In these circumstances, even if he has not moved in, provided he gets a court order (Chapter 8) the (new) landlord can at the end of the period simply evict (*Landau v Sloane*, 1981).

5.56 Death of resident landlord. The position is somewhat different on the death of a resident landlord. In such circumstances, the executors effectively have two years in which the fact that there is no resident landlord will be disregarded (1977 Act Sch.2). The two periods (two years under this paragraph, six months above) may be added together (*Williams v Mate*, 1982). During this period, the landlord's executors may freely evict.

5.57 Former tenancy in same building. In certain circumstances, a tenant who would appear to have been excluded from protection because of a resident landlord may in fact be protected.

5.58 A landlord with good knowledge of the law might have been able to take protection away from a tenant, by moving into a house in which there is an existing protected tenant and offering him a new tenancy of the same or another part of the building, so as to claim that since the start of that tenancy, he has been resident.

5.59 The Rent Act 1977 s.12 provides that a tenant who was formerly a Rent Act protected tenant under a previous tenancy of the same or another part of the building remained a Rent Act protected tenant. This, however, is only so where the presence of the resident landlord would be the only reason for exclusion from protection, not where he is excluded for other reasons. (Likewise, it will not apply if he was not a protected tenancy under a previous tenancy, i.e. if he was excluded for some other reason—in particular, because the letting was furnished: 5.60.)

(ii)   *Tenancies commencing before August 14, 1974*

5.60 Old furnished lettings and resident landlords. The policy of the legislature is to allow people with protection to keep it (see also 5.59). It follows that questions can still arise as to whether or not the tenant was protected before the Rent Act 1974 came into force (*Mann v Cornella*, 1980). If not, then the question is whether there has been a resident landlord since that date, in the same way as already described, with the substitution of August 14, 1974 for the commencement of the tenancy (5.43–5.59).

5.61 Furnished lettings. Deciding whether or not premises were protected prior to August 14, 1974 is not easy business. The class exempted from protection was that of furnished tenancies.

5.62 The law did not, however, treat any amount of furniture, however small, as taking a tenant out of protection. The landlord had to provide enough furniture that the value to the tenant of the furniture formed a substantial proportion of the whole rent paid under the tenancy. (Note: it is the value to the tenant which has to be calculated, in calculating which regard may be had to the social conditions prevailing at the time, i.e. the fact that the tenant lost the valuable asset of a protected tenancy, while the landlord gained the ability to evict his tenant with little or no difficulty, so that even a lot of furniture could have little actual value to the tenant: *Woodward v Docherty*, 1974).

5.63 Valuation involves a valuation of the furniture, with a proportion (usually 20 per cent) representing a fair return to the landlord. This sum must then be compared to the rent, ascertained as at the commencement of the tenancy. Courts will normally view anything over 20 per cent as substantial, anything between 15 per cent and 20 per cent as probably substantial, anything between 15 per cent and 10 per cent as possibly substantial, and anything below 10 per cent as insubstantial (see *Nelson Developments Ltd v Toboada*, 1992).

5.64 Furniture or landlord's residence. If the tenancy—approached thus—was furnished, then it was not protected and, as noted (5.60), the test is whether the resident landlord test has been fulfilled since August 14, 1974. If not, then it was protected and the tenant remains protected, even though there has been a resident landlord in the building since August 14, 1974.

5.65 Neither insubstantial furniture nor want of residence will be relevant, however, if the tenant is excluded from protection by any of the conditions specified below (of which the next condition is of particular relevance).

(iii) *Sharing living accommodation with landlord*

5.66 Sharing living accommodation. If the tenant shares what the law recognises as living accommodation (3.23) with his land-lord, then regardless of when the tenancy commenced, it will not be a protected tenancy (*Neale v Del Soto*, 1945).

5.67 This is so even if no furniture at all was provided under the tenancy, and even if the degree of residence by the landlord leaves in some doubt whether he qualifies as a resident landlord in the normal way. What is comprised in sharing is considered in relation to assured tenancies (4.18).

5.68 The mere empty retention of a right to share living accom-modation, designed to defeat protection, would probably not succeed because it would essentially be a sham reservation (5.17).

5.69 Continuing relevance. This issue is extremely unlikely to arise in connection with a tenancy commencing after August 14,

1974, because it could only apply to a situation in which, on the one hand, the landlord used the premises, but, on the other, he did not establish sufficient residence to qualify as a resident landlord. It may, however, be relevant to an argument over whether or not the tenant was Rent Act protected at the beginning of the tenancy if the landlord took up residence shortly before August 14, 1974 and is trying to establish that the tenancy was not Rent Act protected at that date.

5.70   As with an assured tenancy (4.17), the fact that a tenant is sharing living accommodation with other tenants only, does not affect protection at all (1977 Act s.22).

(iv) *Attendances*

5.71   Attendances.   A tenancy will be a protected tenancy unless the tenant is, under the terms of the tenancy, provided with attendances, and the value to the tenant of the attendance forms a substantial proportion of the whole rent (1977 Act s.7). The substantiality test is the same as that applicable to that for furniture and the same principles will apply, although attendances may be somewhat harder to value (5.61–5.63).

5.72   Personal services.   Attendance means personal service performed in the premises in question for the tenant, e.g. room cleaning, changing the sheets, doing the tenant's laundry, etc. (*Palser v Grinling*, 1948; *Nelson Developments Ltd v Taboada*, 1992).

5.73   Attendances do not include the provision of gas or electricity, or hot water, nor does it include cleaning of the common parts of a house in multiple occupation, e.g. hallways, stairs, bathroom, lavatory, etc. (*King v Millen*, 1922).

5.74   The provision of a resident housekeeper does not mean that of definition the tenant is provided with attendances, although it is likely. The full amount of the wages of the resident housekeeper should not be attributed to the tenants, as a whole, even apportioned between them, for the presence of a resident housekeeper is considered to be of value also to the landlord.

5–75   Window-cleaning is another service which is considered to be partly of value to the landlord and partly an attendance upon the tenant (*Engvall v Ideal Flats*, 1945).

Note

5.76 Within jurisdiction of rent tribunal. All tenants whose tenancies precede the commencement of Pt 1 of the 1988 Act (January 15, 1989), and who are excluded from protection for one of the reasons described above, will be subject to the jurisdiction of the Rent Tribunal: Chapter 6.

(v) *Board*

5.77 Board. A tenant who, under the terms of his tenancy, is provided with any amount of board cannot be a Rent Act protected tenant.

5.78 Board means more than a mere morning cup of tea (*Wilkes v Goodwin*, 1923), but no more than a continental breakfast has been upheld as the provision of board for this purpose, provided that at least some services are involved in preparing it and it includes the provision of crockery and cutlery with which to eat it (*Otter v Norman*, 1988).

(vi) *Low rent*

5.79 Low rent. As under the Housing Act 1988, the 1977 Act is not designed to protect those who purchase long leases and pay only a small, annual ground rent (1977 Act s.5). A low rent is defined in the same way as under the 1988 Act (4.29).

(vii) *Student lettings*

5.80 Student lettings. A tenancy will not be protected if the landlord under the tenancy is a specified educational institution, and the tenant is following or intends to follow a course of study at that or another specified educational institution (1977 Act s.8).

Note

5.81 Possible jurisdiction of rent tribunal. Tenants whose tenancies precede the commencement of Pt 1 of the 1988 Act (January 15, 1989) and who are excluded from protection for any one of the last three reasons described above may come within the jurisdiction of the Rent Tribunal: see Chapter 6.

(viii) *No rent*

5.82 No rent. If no rent is paid under the terms of the tenancy, the tenancy cannot be protected (1977 Act s.5). The same issues as to the meaning of rent apply here, as under the 1988 Act (4.31).

(ix)   *Holiday lettings*

5.83   Holiday lettings.   If the purpose of the tenancy was used as a holiday home, then the tenancy will not be protected (1977 Act s.9).

5.84   This is an exemption which has been widely used as a device to defeat the Rent Acts (see also 1.75; 4.38), and is considered in relation to the same exemption which arises under the 1988 Act (4.38).

(x)   *Identity of landlord*

5.85   Identity of landlord.   The tenants of the following land-lords will not be Rent Act protected:

- local authorities;
- New-town corporations;
- registered social landlords;
- housing trusts;
- The Housing Corporation (1977 Act ss.14–15).

5.86   Most of these tenants will, however, if pre-Housing Act 1988, be secure tenants: see Chapter 3.

5.87   Tenants of the Crown and a government department will not be protected unless the property is under the management of the Crown Estate Commissioners (1977 Act s.13).

5.88   Tenants of a housing management co-operative (a body formed to manage or lease land belonging to, e.g. a local authority or housing association) will also not be protected (1977 Act s.16).

5.89   Other kinds of housing co-operative are usually registered social landlords and are therefore exempt (1977 Act s.15).

(xi)   *High-rateable value*

5.90   High-rateable value or rent.   This exemption operates in the same way as under the 1988 Act (4.26). Under the 1977 Act, this exception is presumed to be so unlikely to apply that it is assumed not to apply unless the landlord shows the contrary (1977 Act s.4(6)).

Note

5.91 No rent tribunal jurisdiction. None of the tenancies excluded from protection by any of the last three reasons referred to above will fall within the jurisdiction of the Rent Tribunal. They are, therefore, considered in Chapter 7.

2. SECURITY OF TENURE

5.92 Contractual Security. It has been noted (5.29) that no tenant can be evicted, whether lawfully in fact or by court proceedings, so long as the tenancy has not been brought to an end. In the case of a protected tenant, this means the contractual tenancy (5.24).

5.93 The contractual tenancy may have come to an end by expiry of a fixed term, by notice to quit that complies with the conditions described, by forfeiture or by notice of increase (5.31). It is unlikely to have come to an end by surrender (1.127) if the tenant is still living in the premises.

5.94 Statutory tenancy. Once the contractual tenancy has come to an end, the tenant has an absolute right to continue living in the premises indefinitely and as a statutory tenant on, by and large, the same terms as under the contractual tenancy (1977 Act s.3) until:

- the statutory tenancy itself terminates for want of continued residence; or

- the premises become overcrowded in law, or are subject to a closing or demolition order because of their condition; or

- the landlord establishes to a court that one of the stated sets of circumstances exists, as a result of which he is entitled to an order for possession; or

- the premises are bought by one of the public or registered social landlords described above (5.85) and the tenant is removed from protection. (Note: the tenancy will usually then become a secure tenancy or, in the case of registered social landlords, an assured tenancy: see Chapters 3 and 4.)

(i) *Statutory residence*

5.95 Statutory residence. The purpose of the Rent Act is to protect homes (*Skinner v Geary*, 1931). Once the contractual tenancy has come to an end, a statutory tenancy will only come into and remain in being, so long as the tenant is in statutory residence.

5.96 This requires exactly the same degree of residence as a landlord must sustain in order to qualify as a resident landlord (5.43–5.51).

5.97 This applies only during a period of statutory tenancy. During the contractual tenancy there is no obligation at all upon a tenant to do so much as set foot in the premises, although one who fails to do so may have a hard time later proving his residence during the statutory period.

5.98 Regular and personal use. Statutory residence, for these purposes as for the purposes of resident landlords, must be continuous although, again, this does not mean that the tenant must constantly be living in the premises, although he must still be able to claim that the premises are in his use as a home, even if not as an only home. Use as a home means "a substantial degree of regular personal occupation by the tenant of an essentially personal nature" (*Herbert v Byrne*, 1964).

5.99 If a tenant is absent from premises for a longish period of time, e.g. (and at least) a few months, there may, on the face of it, be a claim that he has abandoned use of the premises as a home (*Brown v Brash*, 1948), and if sufficiently prolonged may put the tenant to having to prove continued residence (*Roland House Gardens v Cravitz*, 1974).

5.100 The tenant may nonetheless still be using the premises as a home, even if he is also using somewhere else in the same way. The question is whether the tenant is keeping on the premises in question "as a mere convenience" (*Beck v Sholz*, 1953) or whether in fact he is using both places as homes, even if he only visits one or other of them infrequently (*Langford Property Co v Tureman*, 1949).

5.101 Intention to return. Regardless of whether a person is laying claim to two homes or not, a person who absents himself from premises for a longish period of time can still claim to be a statutory tenant of them so long as he intends to return at some time in the future to use the premises as a home, and leaves in the premises some visible signs of that intention (*Brown v Brash*, 1948). There must be both intention to return and some indication of it.

5.102 A tenant who claims that he intends to return subject to a condition, e.g. works by the landlord, which he has no reasonable expectation of being fulfilled, will not be considered a statutory tenant (*Robert Thackray's Estate Ltd v Kaye*, 1988).

5.103 Indication of intention could be belongings or furniture, or even leaving a friend in occupation to, as it were, "keep the place warm". But simply leaving a friend in occupation without any intention to return to live there himself will not be sufficient to allow them to maintain the claim to be a statutory tenant of the premises.

5.104 Residence and spouses. As an exception to the need to show intention to return, a tenant can be treated as still in occupation if he leaves his spouse living in the premises (*Wabe v Taylor*, 1952). This is so, however, only as long as the marriage lasts, and will therefore cease to apply on decree absolute (*Metropolitan Properties Co v Cronan*, 1982; *Lewis v Lewis*, 1985).

5.105 A non-tenant abandoned spouse should therefore take steps to have the tenancy transferred into his name before divorce proceedings are concluded: see Chapter 9.

5.106 There is no continued residence without intention to return if the only sign of occupation is by a former cohabitant (*Colin Smith Music Ltd v Ridge*, 1974).

5.107 Residence and companies. As with residence by a landlord, neither a company nor any other "artificial" body can lay claim to residence (*Reidy v Walker*, 1933).

5.108 This requirement that the occupant should not be a corporate body has given rise to yet a further (1.217; 5.17) evasive device, which will only be defeated on the usual principles applicable to sham (5.17).

5.109 In this exercise, a landlord lets not to the tenant, but to a limited company, as whose licensee the tenant occupies (*Firstcross Ltd v East West Ltd*, 1980; *Tetragon Ltd v Shidash Construction Co Ltd*, 1981; *Hilton v Plustitle Ltd*, 1988). In such a case, the court will probably only allow a statutory tenancy to arise if it believes that the company—to the landlord's knowledge—took as agent or nominee for the tenant, and even then this is not certain. The question to be asked in such a case is whether the company letting is genuine (*Kaye v Massbetter*, 1990).

5.110 Residence by another. In general, the courts will not permit abuse of the requirements of individual statutory residence by the Rent Act protected tenant by permitting the landlord to put the tenancy in one person's name but for the real use of another (*Cove v Flick*, 1954; *Dando v Hitchcock*, 1954), although it will only interfere to let the "true tenant" become the statutory tenant if the arrangement was a device (*Feather Supplies v Ingham*, 1971).

5.111 Thus, one person cannot suddenly step forward and say that he is the true tenant, and the named tenant no more than his agent, without this having been known to the landlord (*Hanstown Properties Ltd v Green*, 1977).

5.112 Effect of bankruptcy. As only the person who was the former Rent Act protected, i.e. contractual, tenant can become the statutory tenant, if the tenant goes bankrupt while it is still contractual, the contract of tenancy may vest in his trustee in bankruptcy. When then determined, the bankrupt cannot become the statutory tenant because immediately before determination he was not the tenant, i.e. the trustee was (*Smalley v Quarrier*, 1975).

5.113 If, however, the contractual tenancy was determined before bankruptcy, it does not vest in the trustee because it is not a true tenancy but only a "status of irremovability" (*Jessamine Investments Co v Schwartz*, 1977). Accordingly, the bankrupt can remain in possession as a statutory tenant (*Sutton v Dorf*, 1932).

5.114 At one time, contractual tenancies invariably vested in the trustee. The position today is that Rent Act protected tenancies will not do so unless the trustee elects to adopt the tenancy (1988 Act s.117), and the bankrupt tenant will be permitted to retain the tenancy in his own name. This averts the worst effects of this rule while retaining the trustee's right to vest the contractual tenancy in himself, e.g. if the rent is too high.

5.115 Nor does this provision apply where the tenancy is one in respect of which a premium may lawfully be charged (5.215), i.e. because it has a value which the trustee can realise.

5.116 Cessation of residence. Once the statutory residence ceases, the statutory tenancy comes automatically to an end. However, the possibilities of a mistake being made, especially whether the property has been abandoned or it is merely a question of the tenant being absent for a while, especially by a landlord who may be eager to reclaim the premises, are so high that most landlords will commence proceedings for a court order for possession before seeking to take over the premises, and they are well advised to do so.

(ii) Overcrowding and closing orders

5.117 Housing conditions. Even if statutory residence is sustained, and even if the contractual tenancy has not been brought to an end, the Rent Act will not apply to premises which are subject to a prohibition (12.51) or demolition (12.76) order because they are hazardous (12.19–12.25), or to premises which are being occupied by so many people that they are statutorily overcrowded (14.16–14.20).

5.118 Even where these exceptions apply, however, the landlord must still terminate the contractual tenancy before recovering possession (1.113–1.146; *Aslan v Murphy*, 1989).

(iii) Grounds for possession

5.119 Orders for possession. The most usual way for a person who does not voluntarily give up possession of premises subject to a Rent Act protected tenancy to leave the premises is because a court order for possession is made against him.

5.120 As under the Housing Act 1985 (3.82) and the Housing Act 1988 (4.84), the court may order possession only where the landlord makes out either a mandatory ground for possession (1977 Act s.98 and Sch.15 Pt 2) or a discretionary ground for possession (1977 Act s.98 and Sch.15 Pt 1), i.e. one where in addition to the provisions of the ground, the landlord must also provide that it is reasonable to make the order sought. Reasonableness has been considered in Chapter 3 (3.86–3.96).

5.121 Powers of court. In the case of discretionary grounds, the court's powers to postpone, suspend or vary an order are the same as under the 1985 and 1988 Acts (3.153; 1977 Act s.100); likewise, the court's powers are as limited as under those two Acts where no security attaches or a mandatory ground is available (1980, s.89; **3.151**). These powers may not only be exercised for the benefit of the tenant but also for his spouse or ex-spouse (Chapter 9).

5.122 Mandatory grounds. There are 10 mandatory grounds for possession, i.e. those which, if proved, leave the court no alternative but to make an order for possession, to take effect within two to six weeks (depending on hardship; 3.151), regardless of whether or not it is reasonable to make the order.

5.123   Under the Rent Act 1977 the grounds for possession are known as "Cases" (*cf.* Chapters 3 and 4, as "Grounds" under the Housing Acts 1985 and 1988). The mandatory grounds are Cases 11–20. Cases 15–18 are special grounds, applicable to property occupied or formerly occupied by ministers of religion, or people employed in agriculture, and it is not necessary to consider them any further here. Case 19 is shorthold (6.159–6.168). Cases 11, 12 and 20 may be considered as one group, Cases 13 and 14 as another.

5.124   Owner-occupiers.   Case 11 is available to absentee owner-occupiers, i.e. someone who before the letting had occupied the premises as a residence, although it may be noted that for these purposes the landlord may himself be a tenant, yet still qualify as an "owner-occupier" in relation to his sub-tenant (*cf.* 4.89).

5.125   This case is only available to a landlord who has served notice at the commencement of the tenancy, warning the tenant that the case might be used against him, although the court has power, if it thinks it just and equitable to do so, to waive this requirement (see further 3.67, 4.92 and 5.130).

5.126   The case is only available if the landlord has not let the property out since he last occupied the premises as a residence, other than on terms that include service of one such notice at commencement, although again this requirement may be waived by the court.

5.127   The requirement of former residence can be fulfilled by previous intermittent residence, or something less than permanent residence (*Naish v Curzon*, 1984). Such residence does not have to be as a home (*cf.* 5.98; *Mistry v Isidore*, 1990).

5.128   Retirement homes.   Case 12 is available to a landlord who has bought property and intends to retire to it once he ceases regular employment.

5.129   Again, notice must have been served at the commencement of the tenancy, warning the tenant that the case might be used, and again the property must not have been let out to another since the landlord bought it, without the service of such a warning notice, although, again, in each case the court has power to waive the requirements, if just and equitable to do so.

5.130 The court should not exercise this power unless the tenant knew at the outset that he had only limited security, i.e. it should only be used where the failure was largely technical (*Bradshaw v Baldwin-Wiseman*, 1985; see also *White v Jones*, 1993). The fact that the occupiers signed licence agreements, which the landlord later conceded amounted to the grant of a tenancy, is not sufficient on its own to make it just and equitable to dispense with notice (*Ibie v Trubshaw*, 1990).

5.131 Member of armed forces. Case 20 is available to a landlord who, both at date of purchase and of letting, is a member of the armed forces: the same requirements of notice, both to tenant and to anyone else to whom the property has been let other than the present tenant, are imposed, though may be waived by the court, again in limited circumstances.

5.132 Applicability of additional criteria. Assuming that a landlord falls within one of these three cases, he must go on to prove certain additional facts.

5.133 There are seven such additional facts, but they are not all equally available. Under Case 11, the landlord must be able to show the second, fourth, fifth, sixth or seventh; under Case 12, the landlord must be able to show the third, fourth, fifth, sixth or seventh; under Case 20, the landlord must be able to show the first, fourth, fifth, sixth or seventh.

5.134 The additional criteria. The additional factual qualifications are as follows:

1. The property is required as a residence for the owner.

2. The property is required as a residence for either the owner or for any member of his family who lived with him when last he occupied the property as a residence.

3. The owner has retired from regular employment and requires the property as a residence.

4. The owner has died, and the dwelling is required as a residence for a member of his family who was living with him at the time of his death.

5. The owner has died, and the dwelling is required by his successor in title, either to live in, or to sell with vacant possession.

6. The property is subject to a mortgage granted before the tenancy was granted, and the mortgagee requires vacant possession in order to sell the property under the power of sale, i.e. for default (by the landlord).

7. The dwelling is not reasonably suitable to the needs of the owner, having regard to his place of work, and he wants to sell it with vacant possession, and use the proceeds of sale to buy somewhere more suitable for himself (1977 Act Sch.15 Pt 5, added by 1980 Act Sch.7).

5.135   Requirement for residence.   Where the landlord is in fact two people, i.e. joint owners, the necessary qualifications can be fulfilled by just one of them (*Tilling v Whiteman*, 1980), so that, e.g. both do not need to show they want to come and live in the house.

5.136   In each case, the landlord need only show that he requires the property, rather than "reasonably requires" the property. "Requires" means no more than bona fide wants and genuinely intends to occupy as a residence either at once or at any rate within a reasonable time, but so wanted and intended whether reasonably or unreasonably, even from the landlord's point of view (*Kennealy v Dunne*, 1977).

5.137   Once his wish to return to the property has been established, it does not matter if the landlord can be shown to want to sell it as and when he can (*Lipton v Whitworth*, 1993).

5.138   Out of season holiday lettings.   Case 13 applies where the letting is for a fixed term of not more than eight months; the tenant must have been given notice at the commencement of the letting that the case could be used against him; and, within the 12 months preceding the commencement of the letting, the property was occupied under a holiday letting (5.83).

5.139   This case dealt, in effect, with "out-of-season" holiday lettings. In view of the time requirement, although in theory someone could have remained in occupation as a statutory tenant since, it is extremely unlikely that it will be applicable to any current tenants, and it has in practice expired.

5.140   Off-season student lettings.   Case 14 concerned property normally used for student lettings (5.80). The letting in question had to be for a fixed term of not more than 12 months; the tenant had to have been given notice at the commencement of the letting that the case may be used against him; and, within the 12 months preceding the commencement of the letting, the property was occupied under a student letting.

5.141 Again, for time reasons this case has for all practical purposes expired.

5.142 Discretionary grounds. The discretionary grounds for possession are those in relation to which the court enjoys extensive powers (3.153), and in which the landlord must prove that it is reasonable to make the order, in addition to showing that the details of each case are applicable (3.84).

5.143 Most of these grounds imply some degree of fault on the part of the tenant, although not all, and many have been reproduced in the Housing Act 1985 or the 1988 Act, and have already been described.

5.144 Rent arrears and breach of term of tenancy. Case 1 is available where either the tenant is in arrears with his rent, or the tenant has broken a term of the tenancy (see 3.97–3.102; 4.122, *cf.* 4.121).

5.145 Breach of a condition attached to a grant of consent to improve can constitute a breach of a term of the tenancy for these purposes (1980 Act s.83).

5.146 A clause limiting use to that of the tenant's residence will automatically and impliedly extend to allow residence by his partner (whether or not actually married) and family, in the absence of a clear prohibition to the contrary (*Blanway Investments Ltd v Lynch*, 1993).

5.147 Nuisance, annoyance, illegal or immoral user. Conviction for immoral, or illegal, user is also a ground for possession, as is nuisance and annoyance to adjoining occupiers (Case 2) (3.103; 4.122).

5.148 The nuisance or annoyance must be to an adjoining occupier but this does not mean that the occupier's property is necessarily physically contiguous: it means the same as "neighbour" (*Cobstone Investments Ltd v Maxim*, 1985).

5.149   This ground is narrower than the extended corresponding grounds in the Housing Acts 1985 (3.103) and 1988 (4.122).

5.150   Deterioration of premises or furniture.   Cases 3 and 4 concern deterioration of the premises, or of any furniture provided by the landlord, attributable to the acts, neglect or default of the tenant, or someone living with him (3.113). (Note: unlike the 1985 and 1988 Acts, these cases do not cover deterioration of common parts or furniture situated in common parts.)

5.151   Tenant's notice to quit.   Case 5 is peculiar to the Rent Act and is available when the tenant has given notice to quit the premises, in consequence of which the landlord has contracted to sell or let the property, or has taken any other steps as a result of which he would be seriously prejudiced if the tenant were to remain.

5.152   For the case to apply, the notice to quit must be wholly valid (1.113) (*De Vries v Smallridge*, 1927), which is relatively uncommon.

5.153   Assignment or sub-letting.   Case 6 is available when the tenant, without the consent of the landlord, has assigned (1.228) or sublet (1.168–1.190) the whole of the premises, whether the subletting is in one go, or bit by bit.

5.154   Commonly, although not inevitably, the tenant will in any event lose his statutory tenancy if he does this, for want of residence (5.95–5.103).

5.155   The case is available even if there was no prohibition in the tenancy agreement on sub-letting (*Regional Properties Co v Frankenschwerth*, 1951). Consent may, however, be express or implied, and may be before or even after the assignment or sub-letting, at any time before hearing (*Hyde v Pimley*, 1952), so that cases on waiver of illegal sub-letting (1.186) may be relied on by way of analogy.

5.156   Overcharging sub-tenant.   If the rent for the sub-tenancy has been registered (5.190–5.212), or if the Rent Tribunal has fixed a rent for the sub-tenancy (6.118–6.120), it is a ground for possession against the tenant that he has overcharged the sub-tenant, i.e. charged more than either class of rent (Case 10).

5.157   Required for employee.   Case 8 is available only in relation to a service tenant (1.153–1.163). The letting must have been in consequence of the employment, the tenant must have been in the landlord's employment, and the property must now be reasonably required (*cf.* 5.136) by the landlord for the occupation of someone else in his full-time employment, or someone with whom a contract of employment has been agreed, conditional upon the provision of accommodation (*cf.* 1985 Act, Ground 12, 3.136 and 1988 Act Ground 16, 4.122).

5.158 In one case, the landlord was one person, but the employer was a partnership, of which the landlord was but one member: it was held that the case did not apply (*Grimond v Duncan*, 1949).

5.159 Required by landlord. Case 9 is applicable where the property is reasonably required (*cf.* 5.136) by the landlord for occupation as a residence by himself, any of his children over the age of 18, his parents or his spouse's parents.

5.160 This case is not available if the landlord became the landlord by purchasing the property with the tenant already in occupation (*Newton v Biggs*, 1953). Purchase does not carry any technical meaning but covers what a reasonable person would consider a purchase (*Ammadio v Dalton*, 1991). It does not include a transfer "in consideration of mutual love and affection" (*Mansukhani v Sharkey*, 1992).

5.161 A landlord cannot use this case if his true intention is to gain vacant possession in order to sell, no matter how reasonably he wishes to do so. He must want the property for living in it (himself or for one of the other permitted occupiers) for some reasonable period, definite or indefinite (*Rowe v Truelove*, 1976).

5.162 Under this case (*cf.* 5.135), if the landlord is comprised of two or more joint owners, they must all wish to live there before it can apply (*Macintyre v Hardcastle*, 1948). It is not necessary, however, for any son or daughter for whom the property is required to be the child of both joint owners; it is sufficient if they are the child of any one of them (*Potsos v Theodotou*, 1991).

5.163 Greater hardship. This case is often referred to as "greater hardship" because the 1977 Act provides a particular defence to a claim under it, that—having regard to all the circumstances of the case, including the availability of other accommodation to either landlord or tenant—greater hardship would be caused by granting than by refusing the order (1977 Act Sch.15 Pt 3).

5.164 The court must consider hardship long term, so that if a tenant who is to be re-housed by a local authority (Chapter 10) will suffer some short-term inconvenience, it is unlikely to amount to "greater hardship" (*Manaton v Edwards*, 1985).

5.165 Burden of defence. The burden of proving the defence lies on the tenant (*Sims v Wilson*, 1946), and he must, at the lowest, produce evidence of attempts to find other accommodation in order to discharge it (*Alexander v Mohamadzadeh*, 1985).

5.166 Where there are joint tenants, hardship to all of them must be taken into account.

5.167 The extent to which either landlord or tenant may be eligible for re-housing under Pt 7 of the Housing Act 1996 (see Chapter 10), may well be decisive under this case.

5.168 Misrepresentation. If an order for possession is made under either Case 8 (5.157) or Case 9 (5.159), and it is later made to appear to the court that the landlord obtained the order by misrepresenting circumstances to the court or by concealing some material fact, the court has power to order the landlord to pay damages to the tenant (1977 Act s.102). This can be a difficult claim: a mere change of mind is not the same as a misrepresentation, and will not be enough.

5.169 Suitable alternative accommodation. The final "ground for possession", in relation to which reasonableness must still, and additionally, be shown, does not appear in the schedule of discretionary grounds (1977 Act Sch.15). It is that the landlord can provide or obtain suitable alternative accommodation for the tenant (1977 Act s.98).

5.170 The meaning of this phrase is, however, defined in Sch.15 Pt 4, and is in similar terms to the 1988 Act (4.109). The ground is subject to reasonableness, although this could include the need for works which cannot be carried out, e.g. for want of funds on the part of the landlord (*Trustees of Hungerford Charity v Beazeley*, 1993).

5.171 If the court seems likely to make an order on this ground, it will be in the tenant's interests to seek a ruling that the tenancy of the new premises should be Rent Act protected, rather than a Housing Act assured (Chapter 4) tenancy (5.08).

Protection of rents

5.172 Need for protection of rents. All Rent Act protected tenants, whether statutory or contractual, are entitled to protection of their rents. Indeed, statutory tenancy itself would be valueless if landlords could simply increase rents beyond what tenants can afford to pay, and protection of rents would be valueless if landlords could serve retaliatory notices to quit.

5.173 In this section we shall consider:

- what the fair rent is;
- how it applies to a tenancy; and
- the rent limit for regulated tenancies.

1. THE FAIR RENT

5.174 Rent officers. A fair rent is one that a rent officer—employed by the Rent Officer Service established by the Secretary of State—considers fair for the premises and tenancy in question. An appeal from the rent officer lies to a Rent Assessment Committee ("RAC"), which applies the same principles as the rent officer.

5.175 Statutory considerations. The Rent Act contains guidelines as to what should be considered a fair rent (1977 Act s.70).

5.176 The rent officer is obliged to take into account all the circumstances (other than personal circumstances) and in particular the age, character, and locality of the residential accommodation, its state of repair, if any furniture is provided for use under the tenancy, the quantity, quality and condition of the furniture, and any premium, or sum in the nature of a premium, which has been or may be lawfully required or received on the grant, renewal, continuance or assignment of the tenancy (5.219) (1977 Act s.70(1)). He must also assume that there is no scarcity of dwellings in the locality (1977 Act s.70(2)).

5.177 The rent officer must disregard disrepair or defects attributable to a failure by the tenant or his predecessor in title to comply with any terms of the tenancy, any improvements carried out, otherwise than under the terms of the tenancy, by the tenant or his predecessor in title, and—if furniture is provided—either any improvement to it or deterioration in its condition due to ill-treatment, attributable to the tenant or his predecessor in title (or, in the case of deterioration, attributable to ill-treatment by anyone living with the tenant) (1977 Act s.70(3)).

5.178 Adjusted market rent. Following the Housing Act 1988, there was, for the first time since the introduction of fair rents in 1965, the growth of a body of market rents (4.130). This impacted on Rent Act fair rents, which had hitherto functioned by comparison with other fair rents registered by rent officers (rather than with market demand). Indeed, "comparables" (as they were known) had been held to be the best evidence of a fair rent (*Mason v Skilling*, 1974).

5.179 Building on this new market, a number of judicial decisions in the following decade required more emphasis to be placed on the market, albeit adjusted to accommodate the statutory criteria, in place of an earlier focus on the existing body of comparable fair rents.

5.180 Following these decisions, it may be said that a fair rent had become the market rent for a property adjusted for scarcity (5.184) and having regard to (or disregarding) the matters specified in the statute: *Curtis v London RAC*, 1999; *Spath Holme v Greater Manchester & Lancashire RAC*, 1995. The expression is "fair" rent, which is not (necessarily) the same as a "reasonable" rent (*BTE Ltd v Merseyside & Cheshire RAC*, 1991; *Spath Holme*). Comparables remain an alternative approach only where there continues to be no, or an inadequate, market on the basis of which to proceed.

5.181 Maximum increases. The new approach led to substantial increases in rent and, in turn, to the Rent Acts (Maximum Fair Rent) Order 1999, made under the Landlord and Tenant Act 1985 s.31. This set a maximum increase on all fair rents registered since February 1, 1999, fixing them by reference to a formula using the RPI.

5–182 A challenge to the legality of the order was rejected by the House of Lords in *R. v Secretary of State for the Environment Ex p. Spath Holme Ltd*, 2000.

5.183 Current position. Accordingly, the current position is that the determination of the fair rent involves consideration of the market rent, followed by adjustment for the statutory considerations, followed by limitation (if needed) by the RPI–based formula. If there is no market on the basis of which to determine the rent, then comparison with other registered rents would remain a correct approach, but the RPI–based formula would still be applicable.

5.184 Statutory criteria. A failure to comply with the statutory criteria would mean that the registration exercise was invalid. The matters to be taken into account or disregarded are as follows:

1. **Disregard of personal circumstances.** The most common example of a personal circumstance is the tenant who is in straitened circumstances, or the landlord who claims that he cannot afford to keep the property in repair. Another example might be that of an elderly person who finds it more inconvenient to live at the top of a flight of stairs than would a hypothetical, average tenant; or a tenant with children who feels the lack of a garden.

   The presence or otherwise of a garden, or the fact that a flat is at the top of, perhaps, a long flight of stairs, will, however, affect the value of the premises themselves in any event, just not more so because of the particular characteristics or circumstances of the present tenant.

   The extent of a tenant's security of tenure, (e.g. notice under mandatory ground (5.124–5.131) or housing association landlord—to whose tenants these provisions in some circumstances also apply—(3.228–3.233; 7.72), is a personal circumstance if the approach being taken to assessment is by means of valuing the property (*Palmer v Peabody Trust*, 1975; *Spath Holme v Greater Manchester & Lancashire RAC*, 1995), although it is not if a comparables approach to valuation (5.180) is adopted (*Spath Home*).

2. **General conditions in locality.** Although it is not permissible to take into account the tenant's financial circumstances, it is possible for a rent officer to consider the general level of wages throughout a particular locality (*Guppy's (Bridport) Ltd v Carpenter*, 1973).

   It is up to the rent officer to determine just what he will consider the locality for the purposes of the determination (*Palmer v Peabody Trust*, 1975). This could benefit a tenant of whatever income, living in a working class district, but, equally, could act to the detriment of a poor tenant living in an area that is, or that has become, predominantly middle class.

3. **Age, character and locality.** Whether or not premises are on a noisy street is obviously relevant. Consideration of locality means more than just what part of town premises are in, but also whether they are near other amenities, such as parks and recreational facilities, public transport and good shopping centres. In other words, all the factors that would normally be considered as affecting the value of living in particular premises or that would tend to push rents up or down (*Metropolitan Property Holdings v Finegold*, 1975).

State of repair is very important indeed; if premises are in such a bad condition that they are not even habitable, or perhaps only in part habitable, then there is nothing to stop a rent officer determining a purely nominal rent for the premises as a whole, or attributing a purely nominal amount to the uninhabitable part (*McGee v London RAPC*, 1969) although he is not obliged to do so (*Williams v Khan*, 1981).

4. **Disregard of tenant's improvements.** The rent officer must disregard, in addition to personal circumstances, any improvements done by the tenant (other than improvements which he is obliged to do under the terms of the tenancy), and any damage or disrepair attributable to the tenant's default.

5. **Scarcity value.** The major element which the rent officer must disregard, that forms the cornerstone of the fair rent system, is "scarcity value".

It is scarcity, more than anything else, which pushes up the price of property and rents. In order to avoid scarcity value, the rent officer is obliged to adopt the assumption that there are not substantially more people seeking any particular sort of accommodation in the locality than there is such accommodation available (1977 Act s.70(2)).

The locality for these purposes is very much larger than that relevant for ascertaining the general market rent in the locality under s.70(1) (5.184(3)): *Queensway Association v Chiltern, Thames and Eastern RAC*, 1998.

5.185 Rent register. The rent officer service is obliged to maintain a rent register, which is open for public inspection. This contains details of all rent registrations in force.

5.186 Normally these are rents which will have been registered by a rent officer since 1965, when the fair rent system was introduced (Rent Act 1965). There is one exception to this. Prior to August 14, 1974, furnished tenancies were subject to the Rent Tribunal (5.44) and rents may have been registered in respect of them with the Rent Tribunal (see Chapter 6). When the Rent Act 1974 came into force, such rent registrations were deemed to be fair rents and were included in the register (1977, Sch.24).

5.187 Comparables. The rent register contains the documentary part of the experience which the rent officer will apply to any particular application. In the past, the practice of rent officers was to look at the register to see if there were any previous registrations for properties of similar size, in similar areas, and with any other similarities. These were what has been referred to above (5.178) as "comparables", formerly considered the best evidence of a fair rent (*Mason v Skilling*, 1974).

5.188 Market-rent comparables. As already stated, the starting point for setting a fair rent today is the market rent: *Curtis v London RAC*, 1998. Accordingly, where there are good market rent comparisons available (from assured and assured shorthold tenancies) these should be used in preference to comparables from the register: *Curtis*; *Spath Holme Ltd v Greater Manchester and Lancashire RAC*, 1995; *Northumberland & Durham Property Trust v London RAC*, 1998. (Note: comparables from the register remain an appropriate approach, however, when there is no such market.)

2. APPLICATION OF FAIR RENTS

5.189 A fair rent comes to apply to a tenancy in one of two ways. Either there is a rent already registered, or there is an application for a registration after the tenancy starts.

Existing registered rent

5.190 Maximum rent. If there has been a registration before the tenancy starts, then the amount registered will be the maximum rent under a new protected tenancy, even if the tenancy agreement is for a higher figure (1977 Act s.44), until such time as there is a new registration (5.194). (If, however, the tenancy agreement is for a lower sum, that will—contractually—prevail.)

5.191 This is so, even where the nature of the letting has changed, e.g. from unfurnished to furnished, unless the change is to the structure of the premises such that it can no longer be called the same dwelling-house (*Rakhit v Carty*, 1990). The rent only applies, however, to exactly the same premises, i.e. not premises which have been enlarged by the addition of a room, nor even premises reduced in size by allowing them to let one less room (*Gluchowska v Tottenham BC*, 1954).

5.192 Cancellation of registration. In order to end the registration, application may in some circumstances be made to cancel it:

- at least two years after the last registration, at a time when the premises are unlet, by the person who would be the landlord if it were let; or

- pursuant to a rent agreement taking effect at least two years after the last registration, by the landlord and tenant jointly under a fixed-term tenancy on which there is at least one year to run, who agree on a higher rent which is approved by the rent officer (1977 Act s.73).

5.193 Recovery of excess. If a tenant has been paying more than the registered rent, then the excess is recoverable for up to two years after it was paid, either by deducting it from future rent owing, or by a normal civil action (1977 Act s.57).

5.194 New registration. Either landlord or tenant, or both jointly (1977 Act s.68), can apply for registration of a rent.

5.195 There cannot normally be an application for a new registration until two years has elapsed since the last, even if there is a new tenancy or, indeed, even if there is a new landlord (1977 Act s.67). Thus, two parties can find themselves bound by a registration secured by two completely different parties.

5.196 Early application. There are three exceptions to the two-year bar.

1. **Joint application.** Where a landlord and a tenant apply jointly for a new rent to be registered, this may be done in less than two years.

2. **Landlord's application.** A landlord may apply on his own, one year and nine months after the last registration, but the new rent cannot come into force until two years have elapsed.

3. **Change of circumstances.** There can also be an application before the expiry of two years, by either party, if there

have been such substantial changes in the terms of the tenancy of the condition of the premises or furniture, that, in all the circumstances, the rent last registered is no longer fair.

A change in the condition of the premises can be as a result of repairs carried out by the landlord, even where the landlord was obliged to carry them out under the terms of the tenancy agreement (11.22) or because he was required to do them by a local authority (12.35): *R. v West Sussex Registration Area Ex p. Haysport Properties Ltd*, 2001.

On such an application, the rent officer does not merely consider the changed circumstances and reduce or increase accordingly, but considers the whole rent anew (*London Housing and Commercial Properties v Cowan*, 1976).

This provision is therefore only likely to be of use to a landlord who has, for example, installed some facility, such as a hot water system, since the last registration. A tenant who applies because of some deterioration may well find that the amount by which the rent ought to be decreased on account of the deterioration is not as great as the amount by which the rent has increased, in respect of the rent of the tenancy, because of inflation.

On the other hand, on a landlord's application for a higher rent because of an improvement, a tenant should not hesitate to point out any deterioration or other new circumstances, e.g. reduced local amenities, which might prevent too great an increase.

5.197 Procedure. The party making the application completes the appropriate forms, which are available from the rent office and from most aid or advice agencies. The applicant is obliged to state what is the fair rent that he wishes to have registered. The forms will be sent to the other side, e.g. the landlord on a tenant's application, who will have an opportunity to comment and to put the case from his point of view.

5.198 If there are joint tenants or, indeed, joint landlords, then all must sign the application form or one must sign as agent for the others (*Turley v Panton*, 1975; *R. v Rent Officer for Camden LBC Ex p. Felix*, 1988).

5.199 Inspection and consultation. Although the rent officer is not obliged to do so, he will normally visit the premises. He will at that time hold a consultation, or else he may hold a consultation at a different time, and at his office.

5.200 He would not normally volunteer to hold a consultation if the rent has previously been registered, and there is no change other than the passage of time, but he must do so if either party asks him to.

5.201 The consultation is informal and it is not usual for parties to be represented, nor is legal aid available, although legal advice may be obtained beforehand. A lawyer may be of help if a question of jurisdiction arises, e.g. whether the tenancy is protected or not, or whether the time is correct for an application. A surveyor may be of more help if the only question is as to the amount of rent.

5.202 Some rent officers give their decision at the hearing, others do so later. In either case, the decision will be in writing.

5.203 Rent Assessment Committee. If either party is dissatisfied with the rent registration, he may appeal to the Rent Assessment Committee (1977 Act Sch.11). The Rent Assessment Committee is a tribunal, not a court, and legal aid is not available for proceedings before it, although legal advice may be obtained beforehand. Again, representation by a surveyor may be helpful.

5.204 This body has no power to decide an appeal on a point of law, e.g. as to jurisdiction (*London Housing and Commercial Properties v Cowan*, 1976). Such a challenge can only be taken to the Administrative Court or to the county court (1977, s.141).

5.205 Hearing de novo. When the Rent Assessment Committee hears an appeal, it does not start with the decision of the rent officer and decide whether he is right or wrong; rather, it starts all over again for itself.

5.206 It, too, will normally go to inspect the premises in question and will usually hold a consultation which will be slightly more formal than that before the rent officer, and will always be at its office, not at the premises.

5.207 Appeal from Rent Assessment Committee. There is no appeal from a Rent Assessment Committee decision, unless it can be shown to have acted wrongly in law, whether by the wrongful inclusion or exclusion of some consideration or otherwise. This would be made to the High Court. If asked to do so, the Rent Assessment Committee is bound to give its decision, and the reasons for it, in writing (Tribunals and Inquiries Act 1992).

5.208 Relevant date. The date when the registration is finally made, either by rent officer or Rent Assessment Committee, is known as the relevant date (1977 Act s.67(5)), and it affects the date when a new application can be made. The rent applies to the tenancy from the relevant date (1977 Act s.72).

5.209 Effecting an increase. The landlord cannot claim an increase unless it is either still within the contractual rent (1977 Act s.44) or else he has brought the contractual tenancy to an end, either by notice to quit or, in the case of a fixed-term tenancy, by expiry of time (1.126). He can also use a notice of increase (5.31) to claim the new rent, specifying a date no earlier than the date when the contractual tenancy could have been brought to an end; this has the effect of terminating a periodic tenancy (1977 Act ss.45, 49).

Initial applications

5.210 If there was no rent registration in force when the tenancy began, either party can apply at any time after the start of a tenancy although it will usually only be the tenant who will wish to do so in practice.

5.211 The procedure is the same as when there was an existing registration (5.197–5.209). Most usually, however, the application leads to a decrease, for which reason the notice of increase procedure will not be needed.

3. THE RENT LIMIT

5.212 Maximum rent. The rent limit is the term used to describe the maximum amount which a landlord can claim from the tenant. There is a number of different circumstances that must be considered.

- **Contractual period.** During the contractual period of the tenancy, the rent limit is either the registered rent or the contractual rent, whichever is the lower (1977 Act s.44).

  If there is no registered rent, then the limit is the contractual rent. Any increases up to the amount of the contractual limit can be imposed without notice of increase, but in order to exceed the contractual limit, the tenancy must be determined.

  Where there is no registered rent, the parties may agree to an increase, by means of a rent agreement (1977 Act s.51).

Such an agreement will, however, only be valid if it is in writing, and if at the head of the document there appears a statement in writing or print, no less conspicuous than that used elsewhere in the agreement, that the tenant is not obliged to enter into the agreement and that his security of tenure will not be affected if he refuses (1977 Act s.51(4)).

The statement must also advise the tenant of his right to apply to the rent officer at any time, then or even immediately after it has been signed, for registration of a fair rent.

An agreement which does not comply with these terms is invalid (1977 Act s.54) and the excess can be reclaimed by the tenant for up to one year after it was paid, as an ordinary civil debt or by deduction from the rent (1977 Act s.57).

- **Statutory period: pre-registration.** By the time the contractual tenancy comes to an end, there may still be no registered rent.

  In this case, the landlord is confined by the former contractual rent limit until such time as he applies for registration of a fair rent (1977 Act s.45).

  If the result of an application is an increase, then the landlord must first serve a notice of increase (1977 Act ss.45, 49).

  The landlord can, however, increase the rent without applying for registration on account of increases in rates (1977 Act s.46), or the costs of providing services or furniture (1977 Act s.47). The tenant may be able to challenge the amount claimed in the county court (1977 Act s.49).

- **Statutory period: post-registration.** Once a rent has been registered for the premises, then this becomes the rent limit and cannot be increased except by a new application and, where applicable, notice of increase (1977 Act s.45).

  It is, however, possible to pass on increases in the cost of providing services without a new application, provided that the rent officer has agreed that the service element should be entered on the register variable and has endorsed the landlord's proposed terms for calculating any future variations.

Further financial protection and assistance

5.213 Rent in advance. Whether contractual or statutory, and whether or not a rent is registered in respect of the premises, it is

FURTHER FINANCIAL PROTECTION AND ASSISTANCE

illegal for a landlord to demand rent further in advance than the beginning of the period for which it is paid, i.e. the first day of a week for which a weekly rent is paid, or the first day of a month for which a monthly rent is paid (1977 Act s.26). If the tenancy is yearly, then the landlord cannot charge the year's rent earlier than halfway through the year for which it is due.

5.214 A tenant can recover any money improperly demanded too far in advance, for up to two years after it was paid. This probably does not mean that the landlord is not entitled to the actual rent at the time when it would be lawful to ask for it; so this would probably only be of any use to a tenant who has been charged a considerable amount in advance, or by way of defence to an action for arrears, or part of them, based on rent improperly charged in advance, i.e. because it is, in law, not yet due and therefore not in arrears.

5.215 Premiums and deposits. It is illegal to charge a tenant a premium on the grant, continuance or renewal of a Rent Act protected tenancy (1977 Act s.119). A tenant who has paid one such premium can sue for its return (1977 Act s.125). Such a claim must be made within six years of the payment, in the same way as for the recovery of a normal civil debt (Limitation Act 1980).

5.216 It is also a criminal offence to require or to receive a premium. Such conduct should be reported to the Tenancy Relations Officer: see Chapter 8. There are two main exceptions where premiums may lawfully be charged (see also 1977 Act Sch.18 for other limited exceptions).

5.217 The first applies to tenancies where the landlord has no power to determine the tenancy at any time within 20 years, beginning on the date when it was granted, and the terms of the tenancy do not inhibit both the assignment and the underletting of the whole of the premises comprised in the tenancy (1977 Act s.127(2)). Such tenancies are wholly exempt from the illegal premium rules.

5.218 The second exception applies where a tenancy has ceased to fall outside the low rent exception (5.79) because of increases. Where:

- the tenancy was granted before July 16, 1980;
- a premium was lawfully required and paid on the grant of the tenancy;

- the tenancy was when it was granted, a tenancy at a low rent (5.79); and

- the terms of the tenancy do not inhibit both the assignment and the underletting of the whole of the premises comprising the tenancy,

the rules relating to premiums do not apply, and are deemed never to have applied (1977 Act s.127(3A), (3B)).

5.219 Premiums on change of tenant. A premium might be charged by a landlord, or by his agent, or by an outgoing tenant. An outgoing tenant might charge for an assignment, or else for arranging to surrender his own tenancy to the landlord, who contemporaneously consents to grant a new tenancy to the incoming tenant. In such a case, it may well be that there is no profit to the landlord. In all of these cases, however, the premium is an illegal payment (1977 Act s.120; *Farrell v Alexander*, 1976).

5.220 Premiums paid to or by another. It is a premium whether a person demands that the money is paid to himself, or to someone else, perhaps, for example, in discharge of a debt that the person demanding the premium owes to the other (*Elmdene Estates Ltd v White*, 1960). Another example would be that of the outgoing tenant who agrees to assign the tenancy or arrange for a new tenancy to be granted to the incoming tenant, if the incoming tenant will pay arrears of rent that he owes.

5.221 Premiums in cash or kind. The most obvious form that a premium will take is cash. But an illegal premium might also be demanded or paid other than in cash, for otherwise this protection too could be circumvented without difficulty, e.g. by demanding payments in kind, such as goods, or else by demanding excessive prices for fixtures, fittings or furniture.

5.222 Premiums for fittings and furniture. It is lawful to make it a condition of the grant of a tenancy, whether by assignment or from the landlord, that an incoming tenant purchase fittings, or even furniture (1977 Act s.123). Items such as fitted carpets may well be valueless to an outgoing tenant in his new home, and it is considered only fair that he should be able to insist, before the assignment or an arrangement for surrender and new grant, that the incoming tenant, as it were, takes them off his hands.

5.223 Only a fair price for fittings and furniture can be demanded, and the excess constitutes an illegal premium (1977 Act s.123). Anyone seeking to make an incoming tenant pay for furniture is obliged to provide an inventory of it and of the price sought for each item; failure to do so is a criminal offence (1977 Act s.124).

5.224 Premiums for fixtures, alterations and outgoings. The position is slightly different where "fixtures" are concerned. These are items such as fitted cupboards or double glazing which effectively become a part of the premises and are valueless when removed. No tenant is allowed to remove fixtures in any event; as they attach to the premises, they become, eventually, the property of the landlord.

5.225 An outgoing tenant is permitted to charge an incoming tenant the amount it cost him to install fixtures (1977 Act s.120). An outgoing tenant is also permitted to charge what it cost him to do any structural alterations to the premises, any amounts paid by way of outgoings on the premises, e.g. telephone rental, which are attributable to a period after he leaves, and any amount paid by the outgoing tenant to a former tenant which was payment for fixtures or alterations (1977 Act s.120).

5.226 Deposits. Landlords frequently require an incoming occupier to pay a deposit, either for furniture, for rent arrears or, for example, damage. Such a deposit will not, however, be illegal if:

- it is reasonable in relation to the purpose for which it is claimed; and

- it does not exceed one-sixth of the annual rent (1977 Act s.128, as amended by the 1980 Act s.79). By inference, a larger deposit will be likely to be considered a premium.

5.227 Miscellaneous provisions. Housing benefits are available for protected tenants as for assured and secure (3.256). The provisions governing the resale of utilities (4.169) are the same for protected tenants as for assured. (The provisions governing accommodation agency charges are now inapplicable, as the circumstances in which a new protected tenancy can arise will not involve such charges.)

CHAPTER SIX

Limited Security

Introduction

6.01 Limitations on security. Whenever Parliament has conferred security of tenure on a body of tenants, it has—of definition—also created a body of tenants without that security. In turn, that has given rise to the question of what—if any—security should be enjoyed by those outside full security. Those who are between full security and no security may be considered to enjoy limited security, and are the subject of this chapter.

6.02 Examples of limited security: historic cases. Some of these—both current and past—have already been identified (Chapter 5):

- Furnished tenants, tenants provided with attendance and board, are examples of tenants excluded from full Rent Act protection from its introduction (1915), although it was not until 1946 that they were given limited security.

- When, in 1974, furnished tenants were brought into full Rent Act security, the tenants of resident landlords were moved out and into limited security.

- In 1980, a new exception was created—the protected shorthold tenant—and given only a limited form of security.

6.03 Examples of limited security: current cases. In 1989, when the Housing Act 1988 brought in the assured tenant to replace Rent Act protection, it, too, excluded the tenants of resident landlords (but left them without any security at all—see Chapter 7), and carried with it the assured shorthold, again with limited security. In addition, it reduced the extent of protection available to the tenants of resident landlords still governed by the

Rent Acts. The Housing Act 1996, for the first time, created a general exclusion to secure tenancy, the introductory tenancy.

6.04 The assured shorthold tenancy has gone on to become the most prevalent form of tenancy in the private rented sector, and is also used occasionally by registered social landlords. The use of the introductory tenancy has slowly grown amongst local authorities (although probably less than 50 per cent of authorities have adopted such schemes).

6.05 The Anti-social Behaviour Act 2003 introduced a power for the court to make a demotion order against a secure or assured tenant. Under a demotion order, tenants of local authorities and housing action trusts become demoted tenants, while tenants of registered social landlords become demoted assured shorthold tenants.

6.06 First, we address those tenancies most commonly encountered today: assured shortholds (including demoted assured shortholds), introductory tenancies and demoted tenancies. We then return to that now-very-small group who have limited security as a result of the Rent Act.

Outline

6.07 **Assured shorthold tenancies.** The Housing Act 1988 created the assured shorthold tenant (4.57–4.64).

- Such tenancies have been capable of creation since January 15, 1989.
- When originally introduced, such tenancies had to be for a fixed term of at least six months, and the tenant had to be given notice that the tenancy was to be an assured shorthold.
- Since February 28, 1997, all new tenancies which otherwise qualify as assured are automatically assured shorthold unless either:
    — the landlord indicates through notice or the tenancy agreement that the tenancy is to be fully assured; or
    — in a number of specified circumstances, it follows an existing tenancy.
- Assured shorthold tenants can be evicted by notice served by the landlord after, either, the fixed term of a tenancy has

elapsed or, if a periodic tenancy, at least six months has elapsed since the grant of the tenancy.

- There is provision for reference of rents to a Rent Assessment Committee, additional to that enjoyed by an ordinary Housing Act assured tenant.

- From April 6, 2007, a deposit paid by an assured shorthold tenant must be held under the terms of a tenancy deposit scheme.

6.08 Introductory tenants

- The Housing Act 1996 introduced (Pt 5 Ch.1) the "introductory tenancy regime", an optional scheme for local authorities and housing action trusts (only), to permit them to "try out" tenants for, in effect, a probationary period, before allowing them to become fully secure.

- Such tenants can be evicted by the landlord without the need to prove a ground for possession.

- A decision to evict may, however, be challenged by judicial review.

- Introductory tenants have some, but not all, of the additional rights granted to secure tenants.

6.09 Demoted status

- The Anti-social Behaviour Act 2003 introduced a power for the court to make a demotion order against a secure or an assured tenant as a result of antisocial behaviour.

- If an order is made against a secure tenant of a local authority or housing action trust, he becomes a demoted tenant; tenants of registered social landlords (secure or assured) become demoted assured shorthold tenants.

- Such tenants are given a period to demonstrate that their behaviour has improved. If the landlord does not take possession proceedings during this period, demoted tenants regain security of tenure as secure tenants; demoted assured shorthold tenants become fully assured tenants.

- Demoted tenants can be evicted by the landlord without the need to prove a ground for possession, but the decision to evict can itself be challenged.

- Demoted assured shorthold tenants can be evicted in the same way as other assured shorthold tenants.

6.10 Restricted contracts

- The first class of occupiers with limited security are those who came within the jurisdiction of the Rent Tribunal, a body the duties of which have subsequently been transferred to the Rent Assessment Committee.

- The RAC has power, where certain types of letting have been granted, to register a reasonable rent for the letting, and in some cases (now very rare), to defer for up to six months at a time, a notice bringing the letting to an end.

- These occupiers have what are known as "restricted contracts", which can be either tenancies or licences.

- No new restricted contracts could be granted after the commencement of Pt 1 of the Housing Act 1988 ("1988 Act"; January 15, 1989), unless in pursuance of a contract made before that date (1988 Act s.36).

6.11 Protected shortholds

- The "protected shorthold tenant", is a Rent Act protected tenant (see Chapter 5) on whom a notice was served before the commencement of his tenancy that he would be subject to the recovery of possession under the mandatory "protected shorthold" ground introduced by the Housing Act 1980.

- Although ostensibly otherwise a Rent Act protected tenancy (Chapter 5), it is so easy for a landlord to get possession that it is idle to consider the tenant as enjoying Rent Act security of tenure.

- Because (subject to exceptions that are not relevant here (see 5.09), no new Rent Act protected tenancies could be granted on or after the commencement of Pt 1 of the 1988 Act (January 15, 1989), it follows that no new protected shorthold tenancies could be granted after that date.

Assured shorthold tenancies

6.12 Pre- and post-1996. To qualify as an assured shorthold tenancy before the commencement of the relevant provisions of the

Housing Act 1996 ("1996 Act"), required the service of a notice; since those provisions came into force, the opposite is true—with certain exceptions, all lettings which would have been fully assured are assured shortholds, unless a notice is served to the contrary. The conditions for the creation of an assured shorthold, pre- and post-1996 Act commencement, and the corresponding exceptions (to each), are described in Chapter 4, above.

6.13 Assured and assured shorthold. The assured shorthold tenant is in every other respect a fully assured tenant (Chapter 4). It follows that the provisions governing, for example, grounds for possession, or references of rent, are as applicable to an assured shorthold, save so far as adapted. It is, in substance, only the adaptations which fall to be described in this chapter.

1. SECURITY

6.14 Mandatory ground for possession. The assured shorthold tenancy works by the addition of a mandatory (4.88) ground for possession, so that the landlord still enjoys all the usual grounds (Chapter 4). A challenge to the mandatory quality of the right to possession, based on Art.8 of the European Convention on Human Rights (right to respect for the home) was rejected in *Poplar HARCA v Donoghue*, 2001. The decision of Parliament to restrict the jurisdiction of the court when ordering possession was a policy decision to which the courts had to defer.

6.15 Pre-1996 Act. In the case of a pre-1996 assured shorthold, the landlord could only claim possession during the initial fixed term in the same way and in the same circumstances as under a fully assured tenancy (4.84), i.e. if there were grounds for terminating the letting early, but, once it is over, a court is obliged to make an order for possession provided the requisite notice of seeking possession has been served.

6.16 There are two kinds of notice. One notice is served before the initial fixed term comes to an end, or on its last day; such a notice merely has to be in writing, and for a minimum of two months. If no notice is served during the fixed term, however, the landlord's notice must fulfil additional criteria: it must still be in writing and of at least two months, but:

- it must end on the last day of a period of the tenancy (*McDonald v Fernandez*, 2003);

- that date must be no earlier than the tenancy could otherwise have been brought to an end by notice to quit (1.116–1.117); and

- the notice must state that possession is required under these provisions (1988 Act s.21).

6.17 Post-1996 Act. Following the 1996 Act changes, an assured shorthold need not be for a fixed term but may be. If fixed term, it can only be brought to an end in the same way and in the same circumstances as under a fully assured tenancy (4.84). Whether fixed term or periodic, however, no order on the shorthold ground may be made so as to take effect any earlier than six months after the shorthold was granted (or, if one shorthold of the same or substantially the same premises with the same landlord and tenant has followed another, after the original shorthold was granted) (1988 Act s.21(5)).

2. POSSESSION PROCEEDINGS

6.18 Accelerated procedure. Part 55 of the Civil Procedure Rules 1998 provides an accelerated possession procedure enabling landlords to recover premises let under an assured shorthold tenancy without a hearing. The procedure cannot be used if the landlord is making any other claim in the proceedings, e.g. for arrears of rent.

6.19 If the tenant wishes to dispute the claim for possession, he must complete the form of reply within 14 days of service of the application. On consideration of the application and the reply (if any), the judge may order possession without a hearing. If the judge is not satisfied that the claim was served, or that the claimant landlord is entitled to possession, he may fix a day for a hearing and give case management direction.

6.20 A hearing day must be fixed if the documents filed by the claimant might arguably disclose a defect in his claim, or where, on its face, the defendant's reply raises an issue which, if true, would constitute an arguable defence to the claim for possession: *Manel v Memon*, 2001.

3. RENT

6.21 Additional protection. Assured shorthold tenants are subject to the normal provisions governing rents which are applicable to Housing Act assured tenants generally, with the following qualification; that the tenant may refer the rent to the Rent Assessment Committee (1988 Act s.22) even though the landlord is not seeking an increase (4.145).

6.22   In the case of a pre-1996 Act assured shorthold, this power is only available once, and it is not available if the initial fixed-term tenancy has already expired, i.e. if the tenancy has become periodic. After that, only a request for an increase can trigger the reference.

6.23   In the case of a post-1996 Act assured shorthold, the power is only available during the first six months from the commencement of the original (6.17) tenancy, and otherwise it is likewise reliant on a request for an increase from the landlord.

6.24   Comparison with other rents.   A determination to fix a rent under this additional power arises only if the rent under the tenancy is significantly higher than rents under other assured tenancies (whether or not shorthold). But merely because the rent is referred does not mean that the Rent Assessment Committee are bound to make a determination: they can only make a determination if satisfied that there are sufficient other assured tenancies with which to make a comparison (and that the rent payable is significantly higher than other Housing Act assured tenancies). If they refuse to make a determination, the tenant may accordingly reapply in the future, if it seems that other rents are now available with which to make a comparison, or much lower.

6.25   Procedure.   Rent for this purpose excludes any service charges or rates (4.152). A reference may be withdrawn by written agreement between the landlord and the tenant (4.155).

6.26   If the Rent Assessment Committee does proceed to a determination, they will decide from when it is to take effect, although that cannot be earlier than the date of the application to them. Any excess rent over the determination is irrecoverable from the tenant (1988 Act s.22(4)(b)).

6.27   Once the Committee has determined a rent, the landlord cannot serve a notice seeking an increase (4.141) for a year after the determination takes effect (1988 Act s.22(4)(c)).

6.28   The Secretary of State has power to disapply this additional means of referring a rent to the Rent Assessment Committee (1988 Act s.23).

4. WRITTEN STATEMENT OF TERMS

6.29 Post-1996 Act. If a post-1996 Act assured shorthold tenant asks him in writing to do so, the landlord must provide him with a written statement of any term of the tenancy which is not (already) evidenced in writing and which governs:

- the date on which the tenancy began (or if a statutory periodic tenancy (4.73), or an assured shorthold by succession, i.e. succession to a Rent Act protected shorthold (6.139), the date on which it came into being);

- the rent and dates for payment;

- any rent review clause; and

- the length of a fixed-term shorthold (1988 Act s.20A(1), (2)).

5. TENANCY DEPOSIT SCHEMES

6.30 Deposits. Most landlords require assured shorthold tenants to pay a deposit at the commencement of the tenancy to cover any damage which may occur to the premises. Many tenants have found that their landlords have refused to refund their deposits at the end of their tenancies.

6.31 From April 7, 2007, deposits paid in respect of new assured shortholds must be dealt with under a tenancy deposit scheme (Housing Act 2004 ss.212–215; Housing (Tenancy Deposit Schemes) Order 2007 (SI 2007/796)).

6.32 There are two types of scheme: "custodial scheme" and "insurance scheme".

6.33 Custodial scheme. Under a custodial scheme, the landlord pays the deposit to the scheme administrator, who holds it until the end of the tenancy. At the end of the tenancy, unless the parties reach an agreement within 14 days, either party may apply to the administrator for the issue to be determined by alternative dispute resolution.

6.34 Insurance scheme. Under an insurance scheme, the landlord retains the deposit during the tenancy. At the end of the tenancy, if the tenant disputes the amount that the landlord intends to keep, the landlord must pay that amount to the administrator pending alternative dispute resolution. If the land-lord opts for the insurance scheme, the administrator is obliged to pay the tenant the amount that he is entitled to recover whether or not the landlord pays the amount into the scheme. It is for this reason that the administrator requires insurance.

6.35 Once the landlord has complied with such a request, he need not comply again unless the term has subsequently been varied (1988 Act s.20A(3)). The statement is not, however, to be treated as conclusive evidence of the terms (1988 Act s.20A(5)).

6.36 Non-compliance. Non-compliance with a request within 28 days of its receipt is liable on summary conviction to a fine (1988 Act s.20A(4)).

Introductory tenants

1. INTRODUCTORY TENANCY REGIME

6.37 Optional regime. The introductory tenancy regime is optional: it has no effect at all unless a local housing authority, or a housing action trust, decide to operate it (1996 Act s.124(1)). If at any time the landlord decides to cease operating the regime (without prejudice to its reintroduction: 1996 Act s.124(5)), an introductory tenancy ceases to be such, and becomes secure (1996 Act s.125(5)(c)).

6.38 Who may be an introductory tenant? Only a periodic tenant can be introductory; only someone who would otherwise be a secure tenant can be introductory, so that someone who would be excluded from full security (3.32–3.39) will likewise be excluded from being an introductory tenant (s.124(2)); indeed, if during the life of the tenancy, the tenant (or, if joint tenants, all of them) ceased to occupy as an only or principal home—which would cause the loss of security—so also would it cause the loss of status as an introductory tenant (6.46).

6.39 Introductory tenancy has no application to fixed-term tenancies.

6.40 Exclusions. If, immediately before the tenancy is granted, the tenant (or, if joint tenants, one or more of them) was a secure tenant of any premises (of any landlord, whether or not the same) (1996 Act s.124(2)(a)), or a fully assured tenant of a registered social landlord (but not a mere assured shorthold tenant), again of any premises (1996 Act s.124(2)(b)), the tenancy cannot be introductory.

6.41 The regime also does not apply to those whose tenancies are granted pursuant to a contract entered into before the decision was made to adopt the regime (1996 Act s.124(3)).

6.42 Licensees. As with secure tenancy (3.19), the introductory tenancy regime is applicable to licences, other than those granted as a temporary expedient to people who entered the property, or other land, as a trespasser (1996 Act s.126).

6.43 Period of introductory tenancy. The intention is that introductory tenants will become secure tenants unless the tenancy (or licence) is determined while the regime still applies to the tenant—"the trial period" (1996 Act s.125(1)).

6.44 The trial period lasts one year starting with the date when the tenancy was entered into or, if later, the date on which the tenant was first entitled to take possession under it (1996 Act s.125(2)). Where there are two (or more) introductory tenancies in immediate succession, or where the tenant formerly held an assured shorthold from a registered social landlord—in neither case necessarily of the same premises—the earlier period (or periods) counts (or count) towards the trial period (1996 Act s.125(3)). (Where there are joint tenants, one or more of whom has an earlier period to be taken into account, the earliest starting date is to be applied: 1996 Act s.125(4).)

6.45 Extension. The landlord can extend the trial period for a further six months (1996 Act s.125A, added by the Housing Act 2004). Before doing so, at least eight weeks before the original expiry date, the landlord must serve a notice of extension on the tenant. That notice must give reasons for the landlord's decision to extend, and notifies the tenant of his right to a review, which must be requested within 14 days. The extension becomes effective if the tenant fails to request a review or if the decision is confirmed on review. A challenge to a review decision can only be made on the limited grounds for judicial review (10.182).

6.46 Cessation of introductory tenancy. Unless terminated, or the introductory tenancy regime is abandoned, the tenancy becomes secure at the end of the trial period, unless before that time something has happened that means that the tenancy would not otherwise be secure, e.g. cessation of occupation as an only or principal home, or someone other than a local authority or housing action trust becomes the landlord, or the introductory tenancy ceases because of succession (1996 Act s.125(5)).

6.47 Once a tenancy ceases to be introductory, it cannot become introductory again (1996 Act s.125(6)).

6.48 A tenancy will not become secure, however, if proceedings for possession have been commenced and are not finally resolved (1996 Act s.125(7)).

6.49 Succession. The succession provisions are similar to those applicable to secure tenancies (3.40–3.54), and the succession will be to an introductory tenancy (1996 Act ss.131–133).

6.50 If there is no one entitled to succeed under the statutory provisions (1996 Act s.133(3)), then once the tenancy has vested pursuant to the provisions applicable to the devolution of property on death, it will cease to be introductory.

6.51 This is not so, however, if it is vested by an order of a court using powers under one of a number of family statutes, governing both partners and children, in which case the tenancy may remain introductory, notwithstanding the absence of a qualifying successor, e.g. if it is vested by the court in a child who had not been residing with the tenant, or a former spouse (likewise not residing with the deceased tenant). In the interregnum, it will therefore remain introductory.

2. POSSESSION PROCEEDINGS

6.52 Terminating the tenancy. Like the secure tenancy (3.65), an introductory tenancy can only be brought to an end by obtaining an order of the court, in which case the tenancy comes to an end on the date when the tenant must give up possession pursuant to the order (1996 Act s.127).

6.53 The court cannot make an order for possession unless there has first been served a notice of proceedings ("NOP"), which states that the court is to be asked to make an order, sets out the reasons for the decision to apply for it, and specifies a date after which the proceedings may be begun, being a date no earlier than when the tenancy could be brought to an end by a notice to quit (1.113) given on the same date as the NOP (1996 Act s.128(1)–(4)).

6.54 The proceedings cannot be begun before that date (1996 Act s.128(5)). The notice must inform the tenant:

- of the right to seek an internal review of the decision, and the time within which the review may be sought (1996 Act s.128(6)); and

- that if the tenant needs help or advice about the notice, and what to do about it, that he should take it immediately to a Citizens Advice Bureau, housing aid centre, law centre or solicitor (1.124) (1996 Act s.128(7)).

6.55 Reasons. While there are no "grounds for possession" (3.82–3.146), the landlord has to give its "reasons" for the decision to seek an order (1996 Act s.128(3)). This means that the reasons must be "good" reasons, in the sense that all public authorities (which includes both local authorities and housing action trusts) must reach decisions which accord with the principles of public law (10.182–10.194), in the sense that they cannot be absurd, irrational or whimsical, or reached in bad faith, nor can they disregard relevant considerations or take into account irrelevant matters.

6.56 Powers must also be used for the purposes for which they have been conferred. Much, therefore, may turn on how the courts view the purpose of the introductory regime. On a narrow approach, they may consider that it is purely related to issues of conduct (for the provisions appear in the 1996 Act Pt 5, which is headed "Conduct of Tenants"); in that case, the reasons will likewise have to relate to conduct. On a broader approach, the courts may consider that—although this Part of the Act is from where the powers derive—there is no reason why authorities should not use their regimes in order, for example, to give themselves some flexibility in relation to the use of their stock. In that case, wider questions of policy may be admissible, to which tenant conduct may be irrelevant. Reasons will, however, and in either event, have to be intelligible.

6.57 Review. The tenant is entitled to apply for an internal review of the decision to seek an order, but the application must be made within 14 days of the date on which the NOP is served (1996 Act s.129(1)).

6.58 The landlord is bound to carry out a review which has been properly asked for (1996 Act s.129(2)).

6.59 The Secretary of State has power to decide the procedure to be followed on a review (s.129(3), (4)). The current regulations (the Introductory Tenants (Review) Regulations 1987 (SI 1997/72)), require that any review is carried out by a person who was not involved in the decision to apply for possession and, if made by an officer, that the officer is senior to the officer who made the original decision.

6.60 There are also detailed provisions about the right to make representations, depending on whether or not a hearing is held. If there is a hearing, the tenant has a right to attend with the assistance of representation. The tenant also has the right to call witnesses, and may put questions to any person who gives evidence.

6.61 Notification. The landlord has to notify the tenant of the outcome of the review and, if it is to uphold the decision to evict, of its reasons (1996 Act s.129(5)). The review must be completed, and the tenant notified of the outcome, before the date when proceedings for possession may be begun (6.53) (1996 Act s.129(6)).

6.62 Challenge. If the review upholds the decision to evict, the tenant may challenge that decision by an application to the High Court for judicial review: *Manchester CC v Cochrane*, 1999. (See paras 10.182–10.194 below for a discussion of the basis on which the High Court could quash the decision of the landlord.)

6.63 The county court may adjourn possession proceedings to allow the challenge to be made. In order for the county court to make an informed decision as to whether to allow an adjournment, the landlord should provide an affidavit spelling out how the procedure operated in the individual case, dealing with the degree of independence of the tribunal from persons who took the original decision, the way the hearing was conducted, and the reason for taking the decision to continue the proceedings: *R. v Bracknell Forest BC Ex p. McLellan*, 2001.

6.64 ECHR compliance. The review by the authority of its own decision does not provide an impartial and independent tribunal to determine a tenant's civil rights in accordance with Art.6 of the European Convention on Human Rights. The availability of a challenge through judicial review (6.62), however, is sufficient to ensure compatibility with Art.6: *McLellan*.

6.65 Proceedings and status as introductory tenant. Proceedings might not be completed before either an introductory tenancy would otherwise become secure because of the expiry of the trial period (6.44) or circumstances arise such that the tenancy ceases to be secure, so that the tenancy would also cease to be an introductory tenant (6.46) (1996 Act s.130(1)).

6.66 In either case, the tenancy remains an introductory tenancy until the proceedings are finally determined by a court, withdrawn or abandoned (including on appeal), and the date arrives when the tenant has to give up possession pursuant to the court order (6.52) (1996 Act s.130(2), (5)).

6.67 If no order is made, the normal rules will continue to apply to determine whether the tenancy is still introductory. If the tenancy would have ceased to be introductory because of a change of landlord, or the introductory tenancy regime is abandoned, or on succession (6.46, 6.49), then the tenancy will cease to be introductory notwithstanding the proceedings, but the landlord may continue with the proceedings as if it was still introductory (1996 Act s.130(3)). If no order is then made, the tenant may become secure, or assured (but not introductory), and will indeed in substance have been declared to have been secure or assured pending the outcome.

3. OTHER RIGHTS

6.68 Assignment. An introductory tenancy is incapable of assignment (1996 Act s.134(1)), unless it is in pursuance of a court order made under one of a number of family statutes, governing both partners and children, or else it is to a person who would be qualified to succeed to the introductory tenancy (6.49) (1996 Act s.134(2)).

6.69 If the introductory tenancy has ceased to be introductory for want of occupation as an only or principal home, the same provisions apply (1996 Act s.134(3)).

6.70 Rights to repair. The Secretary of State has power to apply the "right to repair" (3.213) to introductory tenants, and has amended the regulations to do so.

6.71 Consultation and information. There are similar provisions governing introductory tenancies to those governing secure tenancies in respect of:

- consultation on housing management (3.219); and
- the publication and provision of information about the terms of tenancies (3.223) (1996 Act ss.136, 137).

6.72 Right to buy. Introductory tenants do not have the right to buy. Where proceedings have been brought on the ground of change of landlord, abandonment of introductory regime or succession (6.65), and the tenant ceases to be an introductory tenant pending their outcome, that tenancy may prove to have been secure (6.67). Pending the outcome, however, a tenant claiming to have become secure cannot exercise the right to buy (3.171) (1996 Act s.130(4)), although in the event of a successful defence, the intervening time will count towards qualification and discount (3.172).

Demoted status

1. DEMOTION

6.73 Demotion. An introductory tenancy is a trial period at the start of a tenancy which must be completed before security of tenure is obtained. A demotion order takes security of tenure away from existing secure or assured tenants for a period, before allowing them to regain protection.

6.74 Replacement of tenancy. A demotion order does not convert the existing tenancy into another tenancy. Instead it terminates the existing tenancy and replaces it with either a demoted tenancy or a demoted assured shorthold tenancy.

6.75 Effect of order. On the making of a demotion order, secure tenants of local authorities or housing action trusts become demoted tenants (1985 Act s.82A(8)(a)). By contrast, an order against a tenant of a registered social landlord (whether secure or assured) causes the tenant to become a demoted assured shorthold tenant (1985 Act s.82A(8)(b); 1988 Act s.6A(11)).

6.76 Framework. Demoted tenants are governed by the provisions in the 1985 Act s.82A and the 1996 Act ss.143A–143P. Demoted assured shorthold tenants are governed by the 1988 Act s.20B.

6.77 Demotion period. In each case, the intention is that the tenant will regain security of tenure unless the tenancy is determined during the demotion period. That period lasts one year starting with the date on which the demotion order takes effect (1996 Act s.143B(1); 1988 Act s.20B(2)). In contrast to the trial period for introductory tenants (6.45), the period cannot be extended.

2. DEMOTED TENANTS

(i) *Demoted tenancy regime*

6.78 New tenancy. A demoted tenancy is a weekly periodic tenancy, irrespective of the periods of the prior secure tenancy or even if the secure tenancy was a fixed-term tenancy (1985 Act s.82A(6)). The parties to the tenancy and the rent are the same as under the secure tenancy (1985 Act s.82A(5)). Rent arrears (or credit) outstanding under the secure tenancy transfers to the new tenancy (1985 Act s.82A(3)). The landlord may serve a statement of any other terms which are to govern the demoted tenancy (1985 Act s.82A(7)).

6.79 Cessation of demoted tenancy. Unless terminated, a demoted tenancy becomes secure at the end of the demotion period, unless before that time something has happened that means that the tenancy would not otherwise be secure, e.g. cessation of occupation as an only or principal home, or someone other than a local authority or housing action trust becomes the landlord, or the demoted tenancy ceases because of succession (1996 Act s.143B).

6.80 A tenancy will not become secure, however, if proceedings for possession have been commenced and are not finally resolved (1996 Act s.143B(3)).

6.81 Succession. The succession provisions are similar to those applicable to secure tenancies (3.40–3.54); the succession will be to a demoted tenancy (1996 Act ss.143H).

6.82 If there is no one entitled to succeed under the statutory provisions, then once the tenancy has vested pursuant to the provisions applicable to the devolution of property on death, it will cease to be demoted (1996 Act s.143B(2)(c)).

6.83 This is not so, however, if it is vested by an order of a court using powers under one of a number of family statutes, governing both partners and children, in which case the tenancy may remain demoted, notwithstanding the absence of a qualifying successor, e.g. if it is vested by the court in a child who had not been residing with the tenant, or a former spouse (likewise not residing with the deceased tenant). In the interregnum, it will therefore remain demoted (1996 Act s.143J).

(ii) *Possession proceedings*

6.84 Terminating the tenancy. Like the secure tenancy (3.65), a demoted tenancy can only be brought to an end by obtaining an order of the court, in which case the tenancy comes to an end on the date when the tenant must give up possession (1996 Act s.143D).

6.85 The scheme for possession proceedings against a demoted tenant is similar to that for introductory tenants. The court cannot make an order for possession unless there has first been served a notice of proceedings ("NOP"), which states that the court is to be asked to make an order, sets out the reasons for the decision to apply for it and specifies a date after which the proceedings may be begun, being a date no earlier than when the tenancy could be brought to an end by a notice to quit (1.113) given on the same date as the NOP (1996 Act s.143E).

6.86 The proceedings cannot be begun before that date (1996 Act s.143E(4)). The notice must inform the tenant:

- of the right to seek an internal review of the decision and the time within which the review may be sought (1996 Act s.143E(2)(e)); and

- that if the tenant needs help or advice about the notice, and what to do about it, that he should take it immediately to a Citizens Advice Bureau, housing aid centre, law centre or solicitor (1996 Act s.143E(5)).

6.87 Reasons. Similar considerations arise in relation to the reasons given for eviction as arise in relation to the decision to evict an introductory tenant (6.55–6.56).

6.88 Review. The tenant is entitled to apply for an internal review of the decision to seek an order; the application must be made within 14 days of the date on which the NOP is served (1996 Act s.143F(1)).

6.89 The landlord is bound to carry out a review which has been properly asked for (1996 Act s.143F(2)).

6.90 The procedure to be followed on a review is governed by either the Demoted Tenancies (Review of Decisions) (England) Regulations 2004 (SI 2004/1679) or the Demoted Tenancies (Review of Decisions) (Wales) Regulations 2005 (SI 2005/1228). The requirements mirror those for introductory tenancies (6.59–6.60).

6.91 Notification. The landlord has to notify the tenant of the outcome of the review and, if it is to uphold the decision to evict, of its reasons (1996 Act s.143F(5)). The review must be completed, and the tenant notified of the outcome, before the date when proceedings for possession may be begun (6.85) (1996 Act s.143F(6)).

6.92 Challenge. If the review upholds the decision to evict, it appears that the tenant may challenge that decision in the county court, as the county court is given a wide jurisdiction in relation to demoted tenancies (1996 Act s.143N) (*cf.* the position for introductory tenancies: 6.62).

6.93 Proceedings and status as demoted tenant. Proceedings might not be completed before a demoted tenancy would otherwise become secure because of the expiry of the demotion period. In that case, the demoted tenancy is continued until the proceedings are finally determined by a court, or withdrawn or abandoned (including on appeal) (1996 Act s.143G(1), (4)).

6.94 On the other hand, if the demotion period expires before proceedings are completed, but circumstances have arisen which mean that the tenancy cannot become secure, e.g. because the tenant no longer occupies the property as his only or principal home (3.32), the tenancy becomes a tenancy without security and the landlord may continue the possession proceedings (1996 Act s.143G(1), (2)).

6.95 If no order is made, the normal rules will continue to apply to determine whether the tenancy is still demoted. If the tenancy would have ceased to be demoted because of a change of landlord, or on succession, then the tenancy will cease to be demoted notwithstanding the proceedings, but the landlord may continue with the proceedings as if it was still demoted (1996 Act s.143G(2)).

(iii) *Other rights*

6.96 Assignment. A demoted tenancy is incapable of assignment (1996 Act s.143K(1)) unless it is in pursuance of a court order made under one of a number of family statutes, governing both partners and children (Chapter 9), or else it is to a person who would be qualified to succeed to the tenancy (6.81) (1996 Act s.143K(2)).

6.97 Rights to repair. The Secretary of State has power to apply the "right to repair" (3.213) to demoted tenants but has yet to do so.

6.98 Information. There are similar provisions governing demoted tenancies to those governing secure tenancies in respect of the publication and provision of information about terms of tenancies (3.223) (1996 Act s.143M).

3. DEMOTED ASSURED SHORTHOLD TENANTS

6.99 Assured shorthold. A demoted assured shorthold tenancy is merely a form of assured shorthold. The rights of such a tenant are the same as any other post-1996 assured shorthold tenant, and possession may be obtained against him in the same way (6.14–6.20).

6.100 Possession. Accordingly, to obtain a possession order against a demoted assured shorthold tenant, all a registered social landlord has to do is serve a notice in the correct form. In contrast to the position for demoted tenants (6.88–6.92), there is no requirement for the landlord to give reasons for eviction or to conduct a review if requested by the tenant.

6.101 It is possible that a tenant could seek to challenge a decision to evict him by way of judicial review. The difficulty is that registered social landlords have traditionally not been considered to be subject to judicial review, but see Chapter 7 on the position under the Human Rights Act 1998.

6.102 Cessation. Unless terminated, a demoted assured shorthold tenancy becomes a fully assured tenancy at the end of the demotion period (6.77) unless before that time something has happened that means that the tenancy would not otherwise be assured, e.g. cessation of occupation as an only or principal home (1988 Act s.20B(2)).

6.103 A tenancy will not become assured, however, if the landlord serves a notice requiring possession (6.16) (1988 Act s.20B(3)). In that case the tenancy remains a shorthold tenancy pending the conclusion of the proceedings.

Restricted contracts

6.104 Tenants with resident landlords. The largest class of occupiers with restricted contracts are tenants who have resident landlords (5.43–5.59). In addition, those who are provided with sufficient attendances to take them out of full Rent Act protection (5.71–5.75) or board, provided it is not substantial (5.63), have restricted contracts. Hostel-dwellers will frequently have restricted contracts, as will those in long-stay hotels. The class does not normally cover lettings from landlords who are in some way publicly accountable, e.g. local authorities, nor family/friendly arrangements, nor those where no long-stay is involved.

1. DEFINITION

6.105 Categorising restricted contracts. There are two ways in which restricted contracts are defined: by general definition and by specific definition. Some lettings, however, are specifically excluded from the jurisdiction.

6.106 General definition. Restricted contracts are generally defined in the Rent Act 1977 s.19. Restricted contracts are those "contracts . . . whereby one person grants to another person, in consideration of a rent which includes payment for the use of furniture or for services, the right to occupy a dwelling as a residence".

6.107 In every case, it is the relationship between the occupier and the person who granted the right of occupation which is relevant; an occupier might be the restricted occupier of a protected tenant, or of a secure tenant, or of an owner-occupier or, indeed, even of a wholly unprotected tenant.

6.108 Tenancy and licence. The use of the term "contracts" has been interpreted to include both tenancies and licences:

Luganda v Service Hotels Ltd, 1969. The arrangement must, however, be contractual, i.e. it has to be intended to be binding on the parties.

6.109 Services. "Services" includes attendances (5.71–5.75) and also the provision of heating or lighting, the supply of hot water and any other privilege or facility connected with the occupancy of a dwelling, other than a privilege or facility necessary for the purposes of access to the premises let, the supply of cold water or sanitary accommodation (1977 Act s.85). Furniture means any amount of furniture.

6.110 Exclusive occupation. The key element of a restricted contract is that of exclusive occupation. A hostel-dweller who is given a room to share with another will not have exclusive occupation, unless the occupiers approached the hostel together and took the room jointly.

6.111 Any tenant will of definition have exclusive occupation (1.103).

6.112 A hostel-dweller with his own room will usually have exclusive occupation sufficient to amount to a restricted contract (*R. v South Middlesex Rent Tribunal Ex p. Beswick*, 1976).

6.113 In every case, it will be a question of fact whether or not an occupier has exclusive occupation. It will not be missing just because, for example, a landlord retains a key to the room, or because one of the landlord's employees comes in to clean.

6.114 There will still be enough exclusive occupation for these purposes if, in addition to the exclusive use of at least one room, there is shared use of other rooms (1977 Act s.19), even if those shared rooms constitute "living accommodation" (3.23).

6.115 Specific definition. Even if a tenant does not qualify under the general definition, above, the tenants of resident landlords who are excluded from full Rent Act protection for that reason have restricted contracts, even if no furniture or services are provided (1977 Act s.20).

6.116 Those who are excluded from full protection because they share living accommodation with their landlords (5.66–5.68) are also included regardless of the provision of furniture or services (1977 Act s.21).

6.117 Specific exclusion. There are certain conditions which exclude an occupier from the definition of restricted contract, whether or not he qualifies under the general definition, or by specific inclusion (1977 Act s.19):

- **Rateable values**: the rateable value of the (occupier's part of the) premises exceeds £1,500 (Greater London) or £750 (elsewhere). This is so unlikely to be the case that it may be assumed not to apply unless the landlord shows the contrary.

- **Regulated tenancy**: the letting creates a regulated tenancy (5.24). This provision is inserted to ensure that there is no overlap between full Rent Act protection and Rent Tribunal restriction (*Baldock v Murray*, 1980).

- **Public landlords**: the landlord under the letting is the Crown, a government department or a local authority. If Crown property is under the management of the Crown Estate Commissioners, however, it is not so excluded.

- **Quasi-public landlords**: the landlord under the tenancy is a registered housing association, housing trust, the Housing Corporation, or a housing co-operative. Note that this only excludes the tenants of such landlords, and does not prevent their licensees from using the powers of the Rent Tribunal, if they otherwise qualify.

- **Board**: under the terms of the letting, the occupier is provided with board and the value to the occupier of the board forms a substantial proportion of the whole rent paid. This is a similar application of the test applicable to whether or not premises were let furnished in law before August 14, 1974, and whether or not sufficient attendances are provided to keep a tenancy out of protection (5.71–5.75). Board may be hard to value and is almost certainly worth more than the mere cost of the food. What constitutes board has already been considered (5.77). If any board is provided, a tenancy cannot be Rent Act protected, but if the value of the board forms an insubstantial proportion of the rent then it will be restricted. Otherwise, it will be wholly outside of both protection and restriction.

- **Holiday lettings**: if the letting is for the purposes of a holiday (4.38) the Rent Tribunal will not have jurisdiction over it.

2. RENT RESTRICTION

6.118 Reasonable rents. In respect of all restricted contracts, the Rent Tribunal can fix a reasonable rent (1977 Act s.78), which is to say, a rent which it considers reasonable in all the circumstances. There are no guidelines analogous to those to which the rent officer must pay heed, but, under different legislation, it has been said that it would not be reasonable to make a tenant pay for general shortages in the availability of accommodation, i.e. scarcity value: *John Kay Ltd v Kay*, 1952.

6.119 Rent jurisdiction. In comparison with the systems of rent regulation considered in Chapter 5, Rent Tribunal powers over rents are easy to describe. An application may be made in respect of any letting within its jurisdiction, so long as the letting lasts, and the Tribunal can reduce, confirm or increase the existing rent.

6.120 It can do this in respect of a periodic letting, or a fixed-term letting, and irrespective of any contractually agreed rent. The Rent Tribunal rent, if one exists in respect of the letting, forms the only rent limit which binds the landlord (1977 Act s.81), other, of course, than the actual terms of the agreement, e.g. for a fixed term at a specified rent. The likelihood of such an application now being made is so rare that we do not consider the procedure any further.

3. SECURITY PROVISIONS

6.121 Lettings pre- and post-November 28, 1980. The security provisions governing restricted contracts are completely different in relation to contracts starting before November 28, 1980 (the date when the relevant parts of the Housing Act 1980 came into force), and in relation to contracts starting on or after that date.

6.122 Pre-1980 Act security. Even if rent is not really a problem, security of tenure is obtained by application to the Rent Tribunal for consideration of the rent, plus security. The Tribunal has no powers at all unless the application is made also for a rent registration.

6.123 An occupier can only apply for security of tenure (together with the rent to be considered) if a notice bringing the right of occupation to an end has been given and has not yet expired. This means that a fixed-term agreement cannot be referred to the Tribunal for security of tenure. It can, however, before the time runs out, be referred for consideration of rent.

6.124 Suspension and deferral of notice to quit. The existence of a pre-1980 restricted contract is now so unlikely that we only set out the provisions here in outline.

6.125 Where the landlord has served a valid notice to quit, and the rent has been referred to the tribunal, the notice is automatically suspended (1977 Act s.104).

6.126 If a notice has been served before application, then the Tribunal will not only decide what rent is payable under the letting, but also when the notice should take effect (1977 Act s.104).

6.127 The Rent Tribunal can defer the notice for up to six months at a time. Before the six months run out, there is nothing to stop an occupier applying for more time. The Tribunal may order no security at all, or a period shorter than six months. Deferral is automatic once the rent has been registered (1977 Act s.103).

6.128 The landlord is entitled to apply during the period of deferral for a reduction in security, which will be granted if there has been misconduct, e.g. non-compliance with the contract, by the tenant (1977 Act s.106).

6.129 Post-1980 Act security. The position relating to these contracts is very different. Rent Tribunal jurisdiction over security was entirely abolished (1977 Act s.102A).

6.130 In its place, the county court has a more limited power; to allow suspension of an order for possession to a maximum of three months from the date of its order (1977 Act s.106A).

6.131 If the court grants less than three months initially, it can on a later application grant further suspension, to a maximum of three months from the date of the original order. These powers may be exercised not only for the benefit of the tenant or licensee, but also for the benefit of his spouse or ex-spouse (1977 Act s.106A(5), (6)).

6.132 The court's power may be exercised on terms or conditions, which must include terms as to payment of rent and of any arrears, unless the court considers that to do this would cause exceptional hardship or would otherwise be unreasonable.

6.133 The power is not limited to a former periodic restricted contract (6.123).

6.134 Although the obligation to take legal proceedings before evicting most licensees is less clear cut than former tenants (see Chapter 8), court proceedings must always be taken before evicting a former restricted licensee whose licence is a post-1980 Act contract (Protection from Eviction Act 1977 s.3(2A), added by the 1980 Act s.69). If it were not for this amendment, then the court's powers replacing the former security jurisdiction of the Rent Tribunal might well not have availed restricted licensees at all.

4. FURTHER PROVISIONS

6.135 Premiums and deposits. The prohibitions against premiums and excessive deposits described above (5.215–5.226) only applied to restricted contracts if there was an effective rent registration with the Rent Tribunal, i.e. one which applies to the letting in question (1977 Act s.122). If there was not, then there were no prohibitions on premiums. But if a rent registered with the Tribunal did apply to the letting, then all the remarks made under this heading in Chapter 5 will apply in the same way.

6.136 Change of terms. If the rent under a restricted contract is varied after the commencement of Pt 1 of the 1988 Act (January 15, 1989), then a new contract is deemed to come into existence at the time of the variation, and the contract will cease to be a restricted contract.

6.137 The only exceptions to this are if the variation is one resulting from an application to the Rent Tribunal, or if the variation is by agreement, but only in order to alter the rent to match one that is registered by the Rent Tribunal (1988 Act s.36).

6.138 If other terms of the contract are varied, then it is a question of fact in each case whether it is a sufficiently substantial variation to amount to a new contract (which will not be a restricted contract if after January 15, 1989), or only a minor variation which leaves the old contract in existence.

Protected shorthold tenancies

6.139 The protected shorthold tenancy was introduced by the Housing Act 1980, and abolished by the 1988 Act (when it was replaced by the assured shorthold).

1. NOTICE

6.140 Valid prior notice. A valid notice must have been given by the landlord to the tenant before the tenancy was granted, that the tenancy was to be a shorthold tenancy (1980 Act s.52(1)(b); 6.143(3)). The notice must be in the prescribed form of notice. A notice given after the tenancy has begun will not suffice.

6.141 On proceedings for possession under the shorthold ground, a court can, however, waive the requirement for notice if it considers that it is just and equitable to do so (1980 Act s.55(2)). This would be an extremely severe decision; in effect, the court would be retrospectively deeming the tenancy to have been a shorthold. The court should only use this power when the omission to serve notice was known to the tenant, perhaps known to be an oversight or accident of which the tenant now seeks to take advantage in a way that the court considers unmeritorious, or the notice was in very slightly the wrong form.

6.142 In *RJ Dunnell Property Investments Ltd v Thorpe*, 1991, where the tenancy agreement had stated that the letting was a protected shorthold but no notice had in fact been served, a decision to dispense with notice was upheld by the Court of Appeal. It should not be used, however, to take away from a tenant full security where the tenant had reason to believe that was what he enjoyed.

2. CONDITIONS

6.143 The protected shorthold tenancy (the Housing Act 1980— "1980 Act"—s.51), is a tenancy which is in all other respects a fully Rent Act protected tenancy (5.39–5.91), granted after November 28, 1980 (when the provisions were brought into force), which fulfilled the following conditions:

1. **Fixed term.** The tenancy had to be fixed term as distinct from periodic (1.102), granted for a minimum of one year, and a maximum of five (1980 Act s.52(1)).

   A tenancy granted on one date, but expressed to have commenced on an earlier date, would only be likely to be considered to fulfil the minimum/maximum time limits if they were fulfilled from the date when the tenancy was actually granted, rather than from any such earlier date (*Roberts v Church Commissioners for England*, 1971; *Brikom Investments Ltd v Seaford*, 1981).

2. **No break clause**. There had to be no provision in the agreement for bringing the tenancy to an end by the landlord, other than by way of forfeiture (1.131–1.146) for non-payment of rent or breach of some other term of the tenancy (1980 Act s.52(1)(a)).

Thus, a "break clause" allowing the landlord to give notice in the middle of, or any other time during, the term would defeat the shorthold.

A clause which allowed a landlord to forfeit if the tenant went bankrupt was construed as creating an obligation on the part of the tenant not to go bankrupt, with the effect that the tenancy was still shorthold (*Paterson v Aggio*, 1987).

3. **Prior notice**. Before the tenancy was granted, the landlord had given the tenant a valid shorthold notice (1980 Act s.52(1)(b)).

4. **Registered rent**. In some cases, either there must have been a registered rent (5.199–5.211) at the commencement of the tenancy, or the landlord must have secured a certificate of fair rent (now no longer available) by the time the tenancy was granted (1980 Act s.52(1)(c)). This, too, is considered further below (6.152–6.154).

5. **Previous Rent Act protected or statutory tenant**. The tenancy was not granted to a person who, immediately before the grant, was a Rent Act protected or statutory (**5.24**) tenant of the same premises (1980 Act s.52(2)). This is designed to prevent landlords persuading existing tenants to sign shorthold agreements. However, it only protects the tenant if the new tenancy was of exactly the same premises as the pre-existing tenancy (*cf.* 5.59). Thus, another flat in the same building would not keep the tenant out of shorthold, nor even a new agreement in respect of, for example, the same premises less or plus one room (*Gluchowska v Tottenham BC*, 1954).

6.144 Notice by tenant. Although the landlord could not reserve the right to give notice during the life of the shorthold (6.143(2)), the shorthold tenant is absolutely entitled to give notice, even if the written agreement prohibits him from doing so (1980 Act s.53(1)).

6.145 Furthermore, any clause purporting to penalise the tenant for giving notice under the provision, e.g. imposing additional rent, is wholly void and of no effect (1980 Act s.53(2)).

6.146 The notice may be given at any time during the fixed term: if the fixed term was for more than two years, the notice must be of three months; if for two years or less, it need only be of one month; in either event, it must be in writing (1980 Act s.53(1)).

6.147 Continuation of protected shortholds. A protected shorthold tenancy is only technically a shorthold during the initial fixed-term tenancy (1980 Act s.52(5)). This is only technical, because the power of the landlord to recover possession under the shorthold ground continues indefinitely (6.159; *Gent v De La Mare*, 1987) and references to "shorthold tenants" include those whose shorthold has ended, but who remain vulnerable to the shorthold ground. The shorthold tenant is also subject to the usual grounds for possession (5.119–5.171).

6.148 Limited assignability. A protected shorthold tenancy cannot be assigned (1.228) other than by order of the court under the Matrimonial Causes Act 1973 s.24 (9.06), at any time during the shorthold (6.147), or afterwards, i.e. so long as the tenant remains subject to the possibility (6.147) of use of the shorthold ground (1980 Act s.54(2)).

6.149 It is unclear whether the Family Law Act 1996 (9.42–9.45) could be used to order a transfer of tenancy between spouses, civil partners or cohabitants, though this seems likely on balance as there is no express prohibition against it.

6.150 Sub-letting. While there is no restriction on sub-letting, a sub-tenant to whom some part of the premises, or even the whole of the premises, has been let at any time while the tenant is still subject to the possibility (6.147) of use of the shorthold ground cannot avail himself of the Rent Act 1977 s.137 (1.173; 1980 Act s.54(1)), and so will only become the landlord's tenant directly if the circumstances would put him in that position at common law, i.e. if the tenant surrenders (1.191).

6.151 Succession. If there is a succession to a Rent Act protected tenancy (5.33) which is a protected shorthold, the succession takes effect as an assured shorthold (above) (1988 Act s.39(7)).

3. RENT

6.152 Need for registered rent. Under the Act, there must, at the time the tenancy was granted, either already have been a registered rent, or a certificate of fair rent, in relation to the premises (1980 Act s.52(2)(c); 6.143(4)). Registration of fair rents has already been considered (5.174–5.211).

6.153 The certificate of fair rent was repealed with the introduction of the Housing Act 1988. The certificate of fair rent was usually used by a landlord intending to let out premises on a fully Rent Act protected tenancy after the execution of works, and who wanted to know what was likely to be his return on the property. The same procedure used to be available to a landlord intending to let out on shorthold, even though no works were to be carried out by him beforehand.

6.154 If the landlord let out the premises when there was only a certificate of fair rent:

* prior to full registration, no more rent should have been charged than stated in the certificate; and

* the landlord had to apply for full registration within 28 days of the beginning of the tenancy (1980 Act s.52(1)(c)).

6.155 Waiver of need for registered rent. The Secretary of State reserved powers under the Act to waive the requirement for a registered rent or a certificate of fair rent (1980 Act s.52(4)). He used this power in 1981 to waive the requirement outside London (SI 1981/1578) and from 1987, throughout the whole of the country (SI 1987/265).

6.156 In any event, the court may still order possession on the shorthold ground (6.159–6.168) even when there has been a failure to comply with the registered rent requirement, if it is just and equitable to do so (1980 Act s.55(2)).

6.157 Again (*cf.* 6.141), this power is only likely to be used when there has been a technical defect, or an application pursued a matter of days late. It is highly unlikely to be used if a very high rent has been charged but where the failure was an honest mistake, and the rent set was fully acceptable to both parties, it may be (*RJ Dunnell Property Investments Ltd v Thorpe*, 1991).

6.158 Where a rent was already the subject of a certificate or registered, the tenant could still apply for registration himself (5.210–5.211) and if the rent officer registers a rent lower than that stated in a certificate, it is the lower rent that will be payable from registration (5.212).

4. THE SHORTHOLD GROUND

6.159 Mandatory ground for possession. The shorthold ground remains available for use as long as the original shorthold tenant remains the tenant of the premises (1980 Act s.54(3)).

6.160 The ground itself is to be found, by way of amendment, in the Rent Act 1977 Sch.15 Case 19 as an added mandatory ground for possession, although it was originally contained in the 1980 Act s.55(1).

6.161 The landlord must show not only that the preliminary conditions were fulfilled (6.143), save in so far as he hopes to rely on the court's discretion (6.141, 6.156), but also that since the technical end of the shorthold tenancy, i.e. the termination of the original fixed period (6.147), there has been no further grant of a tenancy of the premises to anyone other than the original shorthold tenancy. In addition, he must comply with the "warning" notice provisions (*Ridehalgh v Horsefield*, 1992).

6.162 Warning notices. The purpose of the warning notice provisions is to ensure that the tenant is not constantly subject to the likelihood of proceedings. Accordingly, before applying for possession under Case 19, the landlord must serve the appropriate notice. These notice provisions do not, however, need to be fulfilled once the tenancy has become statutory (5.24) if grounds for possession (5.119–5.171) other than the mandatory ground (6.159) are used instead.

6.163 The landlord can only commence proceedings within three months after the expiry of the notice (1977 Act Sch.15 Case 19(b)).

6.164 The notice must be in writing and must state that proceedings may be brought under Case 19 after it expires. The notice must give a minimum of three months, but it can be for an unlimited length, i.e. before it expires. It may be served during the last three months of the fixed term, or else during the same three months of any succeeding year, and no earlier than three months after the expiry of the last notice.

6.165 Warning provisions exemplified. These provisions are difficult to untangle. They are best approached by way of illustration. A fixed term was granted on April 1, 1988 to expire on March

31, 1990. A warning notice may be served at any time between the beginning of January and the end of March during 1990 or any subsequent year in which the ground remains available to the landlord. It must give the tenant at least three months: if served on January 1, therefore, proceedings could commence on April 1; if not served until March 1, however, they could not commence before June 1. If the landlord gave longer than three months, the proceedings could not be commenced before the time allowed expires.

6.166 Commencement of proceedings. Once the notice expires, the landlord must bring his proceedings within three months, or else the notice lapses. He cannot serve a further notice during these three months. Thus, if the notice was for three months, and was served on January 1, proceedings must be commenced between April 1 and June 30, and during that time no further notice can be served. Accordingly, July 1 would be the earliest date when a new notice could be served, but as the notice can only be served during the January–March "season", he cannot serve a further notice until January 1 next. If, however, he gives nine months, from January 1, he can commence his proceedings at any time between October 1 and December 30. If he fails to do so, he can serve a new notice immediately after December 30, as: (a) he will be back in the notice season and (b) three months will have passed since the notice lapsed.

6.167 Eviction season. It follows that while it is true that a tenant cannot be subject at any given moment to proceedings for possession under Case 19, the landlord has a generous discretion to select his eviction (as opposed to notice) season, and may in practice, by careful choice of the length of notice, keep the tenant in the position where proceedings are always looming, or to be anticipated.

6.168 These notice provisions do not, however, dispense with the normal requirement to bring the tenancy to an end at common law, by notice to quit (1.113) or forfeiture (1.131–1.146).

5. FURTHER PROVISIONS

6.169 Premiums and deposits. The premium and deposit provisions applicable to Rent Act protected tenants are also applicable to protected shorthold tenancies in the same way.

Further protection and assistance

6.170 Miscellaneous provisions

- Accommodation agency charges;
- Resale of utilities; and
- Housing benefit.

6.171 These are all applicable to assured shorthold tenants, those with restricted contracts and protected shorthold tenants, as they are to Housing Act assured or fully Rent Act protected tenants (4.159–4.166). Only the latter is likely to be relevant to Housing Act introductory tenants and demoted tenants (3.265).

CHAPTER SEVEN

Occupation Without Security

Introduction

7.01 Residual classes of occupation. This chapter examines the remaining classes of occupation, being those without any security at all. There are five such classes:

1. trespassers;

2. unrestricted licensees;

3. non-secure public tenants;

4. non-secure/assured social tenants;

5. unrestricted tenants.

Outline

7.02 Trespassers

- There is a special, speedy eviction procedure available against trespassers.

- Interim possession orders may also be obtained, breach of which creates a criminal offence.

- It is an offence to use violence to evict a trespasser.

- Trespassers may themselves commit offences in some circumstances, particularly if required to leave by a displaced residential occupier or a protected intended occupier, and they fail to do so.

7.03 Unrestricted licensees

- Most licensees do not enjoy any security of tenure.

- Unless it is an "excluded licence", a periodic license must be brought to an end by the service of a notice complying with the Protection from Eviction Act 1977.

- A court order is generally required to evict a licensee.

- The special procedures for eviction may be used against former unrestricted licensees.

7.04 Non-secure public tenants

- Some tenants of public landlords may fall outside security of tenure all together.

- Before eviction, any tenancy must be properly terminated and, save in the case of an "excluded tenant", a minimum of four weeks' notice to quit given to a periodic tenant.

- A court order is generally required to evict a non-secure tenant.

- A decision to evict a non-secure tenant by a local authority can be challenged on administrative law grounds, or the law which leaves him without security may be challengeable as being not compatible with the Human Rights Act 1998.

- There are special provisions relating to notices of increase of rent for non-secure, local authority tenants.

7.05 Non-secure/assured social tenants

- Before eviction, any tenancy must be properly terminated and, unless "excluded", a minimum of four weeks' notice to quit given to periodic tenants.

- A court order is generally required to evict such tenants.

- It is possible that a decision to evict a non-assured tenant of a registered social landlord may be challengeable under the Human Rights Act in the same way as an eviction by a local authority.

7.06 Unrestricted tenants

- These are tenants of private sector landlords who are not protected by the Rent Act 1977 or the Housing Act 1988.

- Before eviction, any tenancy must be properly terminated, and, unless "excluded", a minimum of four weeks' notice to quit given to periodic tenants.

- A court order is generally required to evict an unrestricted tenant.

Trespassers

1. EVICTION

7.07 Least security. Unless they have been in occupation for long enough to claim a right by adverse possession (1.35), trespassers have no rights of occupation and, because they pay no rent, are subject to no rent control. They have the least security of all. Court proceedings can be taken against them at any time, without any warning, and special, speedy procedures can, and in all probability will, be used: CPR Pt 55.

7.08 Proceedings for possession. These procedures do not even require the landlord to identify the occupiers. A landlord can issue proceedings against a named person on his own, or against persons unknown, or against both a named person and persons unknown. A claim is issued, stating the landlord's interest in the property, that the property in question has been occupied without his consent and, if the claim is also against persons unknown, that the landlord does not know the names of some or all of the people on the property.

7.09 Orders for possession. The claim is served by personal service, save in the case of persons unknown, where it can be served by fixing the summons to the door of the premises. Once it has been served, there need only be a delay of five days, in the case of residential premises (two otherwise), before a court hearing.

7.10 If the court finds that the occupiers are, indeed, trespassers, then it is obliged to make an immediate order for possession (*McPhail v Persons Unknown*, 1973; *Boyland & Son Limited v Rand*, 2006) not even subject to the normal 14–day delay to which, for example, a final order against a secure, or indeed any other tenant, will normally be subject (3.151).

7.11 Eviction. Landlords will still normally need to effect eviction by using court bailiffs, which may provide some slight delay of, perhaps, a week or 10 days.

7.12 When bailiffs attend on an eviction, they must turn out of the premises all those people found there, whether or not they were parties to the proceedings, or even if they moved into the premises between the date of the court order and the actual eviction, unless an occupier can claim to have some separate right of occupation, e.g. a tenant who is on the premises (*R. v Wandsworth County Court Ex p. Wandsworth London BC*, 1975).

7.13 Negotiated suspension. Although the court is obliged to make the immediate order, it is possible that the landlord will consent to a suspension of, for example, two or four weeks. They may agree to this before the actual hearing. If there is any prospect of a dispute, representatives of the landlord are likely to be amenable to granting such a delay by agreement, to avoid the need for the hearing. Even if there is no prospect of dispute, more responsible landlords, such as public and registered social landlords, will usually be willing to agree to some time.

7.14 Damages. Although the court can order costs against an occupier during the course of proceedings brought under one of these speedy procedures, there is no provision for awarding any monetary compensation by way of damages to the landlord. If a landlord wants to seek such damages, he must use normal possession proceedings and claim damages for use and occupation.

7.15 Interim possession. The interim possession order provides an even quicker remedy, allowing for a hearing only three days from the application to court. An application for an interim possession order may only be made against persons who have entered the premises without the applicant's consent (CPR Pt 55.21).

7.16 An application for such an order must be made on the prescribed form, and the applicant must give specific undertakings, in particular as to damages and putting the defendant back into possession if it turns out the interim possession order was wrongly granted. The court hearing date may be set at any time after three days from the making of the application. For the hearing to go ahead, there must be evidence that the order has been served on the defendant.

7.17 Order and breach. An interim possession order requires the defendant to vacate the premises within 24 hours. The order must also fix a return date (for a full hearing) not less than seven days after the date on which the interim order was made, and the order expires on this return date.

7.18 Eviction takes place through the police, rather than the court bailiffs. Failure to leave is a criminal offence, as is returning within 12 months to the premises to which the order applies, or knowingly or recklessly giving false information in order to obtain or resist such an order: Criminal Justice and Public Order Act 1994 ss.76, 75.

2. CRIMINAL OFFENCES

7.19 Criminal offences. The only protection that a trespasser has against eviction is such as is provided by the Criminal Law Act 1977, which created certain offences in connection with squatting, and repealed the earlier Forcible Entry Acts. The Act also, however, created offences which a trespasser may commit in connection with squatting.

7.20 Anyone who commits a criminal offence under the Criminal Law Act 1977 ("CLA 1977") in the course of evicting a trespasser who is using premises as a residence is likely also to commit an offence under the Protection from Eviction Act 1977 ("PEA 1977"): see Chapter 8.

7.21 The offence which serves to protect trespassers is that of:

- violent eviction.

The offences a trespasser must be careful not to commit are those of:

- trespass with an offensive weapon;
- trespass on diplomatic or consular premises;
- resisting or obstructing an officer of a court in the course of an eviction;
- refusing to leave premises when requested.

(i) *Violent eviction*

7.22 Violent entry. Any person, whether or not the landlord, who uses or threatens violence against either people or property in order to gain entry into premises, commits an offence if, but only if, the person seeking entry knows that there is someone present on the premises at the time of the attempted entry, and that that person is opposed to the entry (CLA 1977 s.6).

7.23 The offence is not committed if the person seeking entry has lawful authority to do so, i.e. a court bailiff. It does not constitute lawful authority that the person trying to get in has some greater interest, e.g. licence, tenancy or ownership of the property.

7.24 Displaced residential occupier. There is an important exception to this offence. The offence is not committed by a person otherwise offending against its provisions if he, or someone on whose behalf he, is acting, is a "displaced residential occupier" of the premises.

7.25 A displaced residential occupier is any person, other than another trespasser, who was using the premises or part of them as a residence immediately before the trespasser entered (CLA 1977 s.12). This exception is designed to permit the owner-occupier, or tenant, who goes away on holiday and finds on his return that the premises have been "squatted", to evict the trespassers without any need to take court proceedings and without fear of committing an offence. In practice, such incidents of squatting in people's homes have been very rare, as it is no part of the ethos of the squatter to make another homeless.

7.26 A displaced residential occupier must also take great care when using this privilege for he may still commit any of the ordinary, criminal offences of assault, actual or grievous bodily harm, etc.

7.27 Protected intending occupier. A second exception is made for "protected intending occupiers". There are three categories of protected intending occupier:

1. A person is a protected intending occupier if he either has a freehold or a leasehold interest in the property, and requires the premises for his own occupation (CLA 1977 s.12A). The leasehold interest must have not less than two years to run at the relevant time.

2. A private tenant (whose tenancy may be less than two years) or a licensee with a licence granted by a freeholder or leaseholder (whose lease has more than two years to run) may be a protected intending occupier if he requires the accommodation for his own occupation.

3. A person is also a protected intending occupier if he has been given permission to occupy the premises as a residence

by any of the public or other social landlords described below (7.55, 7.71).

7.28 In each case, the protected intended occupier must produce a statement which proves his status as a protected intending occupier. In the first and second cases, the statement has to specify the interest which the would-be occupier has, must state the requirement for use of the premises as a residence for himself, and must have been signed either in the presence of a justice of the peace or commissioner of oaths who has also signed the statement as a witness. In the third case, the statement must specify that the would-be occupier has been authorised to occupy the premises and that the landlord is one of the bodies referred to.

(ii)   Trespass with an offensive weapon

7.29   Offensive weapon.   It is a criminal offence for a person on the premises as a trespasser, having entered as such, to have with him any weapon of offence, i.e. anything which has been made or adapted for causing injury to another (CLA 1977 s.8). This, too, raises the spectre of "violent squatting" which has been virtually unknown in the recent history of the squatting movement.

7.30   Because such a weapon can either be made or adapted for causing violence, a person can, in theory, be charged with causing violence on the basis of possession of virtually any common household implement, e.g. a kitchen knife or screwdriver. But for a person to have committed this offence, he must not only be a trespasser, but must have entered as such. This refers to the common law rule that a former licensee and, strictly, even a former tenant, remaining on premises after the end of the licence or tenancy, becomes a trespasser (1.79). Such people are not trespassers for the purposes of this provision.

(iii)   Trespass on diplomatic or consular premises

7.31   Diplomatic premises.   This provision was designed to deal with "political squatting" (*Kamara v DPP*, 1974) and makes it an offence for a trespasser to enter diplomatic or consular buildings, unless he can show that he does not believe them to be diplomatic or consular premises (CLA 1977 s.9).

(iv)   Resisting or obstructing an officer of the court in the course of an eviction

7.32   Resisting official eviction.   It is an offence to resist or intentionally obstruct any person who is an officer of a court executing a possession order issued by a county court or the High Court (CLA 1977 s.10). This offence is only committed by someone in premises in circumstances that are also defined in the Act.

7.33 Briefly, the Act is intended to catch anyone resisting or intentionally obstructing an officer who is executing a possession order made under one of the speedy procedures contained in CPR Pt 55. It is so worded, however, that it applies to resistance or intentional obstruction of an officer executing any order which could have been brought under those procedures but which have in fact been brought under normal proceedings, e.g. because the owner wishes to claim damages for use and occupation.

7.34 The orders can be used against any trespasser, which includes a former licensee and has been held to include illegal sub-tenants (*Moore Properties (Ilford) Ltd v McKeon*, 1976; 1.179–1.183). The orders do not catch illegal tenants of mortgagors (*London Goldhawk Building Society v Eminer*, 1977; 1.226).

(v) *Refusing to leave premises when requested*

7.35 Refusal to leave. This was the major new offence introduced by the Act (CLA 1977 s.7). It makes it an offence for any trespasser, who enters as a trespasser, to fail to leave premises if asked to do so by a displaced residential occupier or by a person who is, within the terms of the Act, a protected intending occupier.

7.36 Displaced residential occupier and protected intending occupier have been described above (7.24, 7.27). In either case, the displaced residential occupier or the protected intending occupier must have been kept out of occupation by reason of the trespass and, obviously, there can be no offence of failing to leave when requested until a request has been made. The request does not need itself to be in writing but protected intending occupiers have to produce the required statement (7.28).

7.37 Defences. It is clear that a protected intending occupier could be a licensee, e.g. for short-life use, of one of the public or other social landlords; as it is necessary for a protected intending occupier to specify that the premises are to be used as a residence, it can only be used in connection with premises fit for use, i.e. not in connection with premises yet to be renewed or redeveloped.

7.38 It is a defence for the trespasser to prove that he did not believe that the person asking him to leave was either a displaced residential occupier or a protected intending occupier, or that the premises in question are or form part of premises used mainly for a non-residential purpose and that he was only on that part. It is also a defence to prove that a protected intending occupier did not produce the required statement (7.28).

Unrestricted licensees

7.39 Resort to common law. Most licensees do not enjoy any statutory protection at all and must therefore rely upon their common law rights of occupation. The exceptions are: a licensee within public sector security (3.19); a licensee whose licence pre-dates the commencement of the Housing Act 1988 ("1988"), and who has a restricted contract (6.104), and certain licensees who are service occupiers (1.161) who may either fall within the Housing Act 1988 (4.53) or the Rent (Agriculture) Act 1976 (5.15).

7.40 Service tenants and occupiers who work in agriculture but who are not protected by either the 1988 or 1976 Acts may also enjoy a degree more protection against eviction than others, as the county court enjoys power to suspend the operation of a possession order against them for up to six months in certain circumstances (PEA 1977 s.4, as amended by the 1988 Act).

7.41 Notice requirement. At common law, no licensee can be evicted until the licence has been brought to an end (1.81–1.86). A bare licence (1.81) can be brought to an end by reasonable notice, and a contractual licence by either reasonable notice or the contractually agreed period (and form), whichever is the longer (1.85).

7.42 A fixed-term contractual licensee requires no notice and the licence terminates on the expiry of the term (1.84). An example of such an arrangement might be a letting for short-life use which is for a specific period only.

7.43 If notice has to be given to determine a licence, then, since the commencement of Pt 1 of the 1988 Act (January 15, 1989), such notice has to be in writing, of a minimum of four weeks, and contain such information as may be prescribed (PEA 1977 s.5(1A), added by the 1988 Act s.32; 1.124), even if the licence began before the commencement of the 1988 Act. This is not so, however, if the licence is an "excluded licence" (s.5(1B)): excluded licences (and tenancies) are described in Chapter 8 (8.20), below.

7.44 Licensees and rent protection. Only those contractual licensees whose licences pre-date the commencement of Pt 1 of the 1988 Act (January 15, 1989), and fall within Rent Tribunal jurisdiction (Chapter 6) enjoy any protection over the levels of rent they have to pay.

7.45 Strictly, a licensee's rent cannot be increased without terminating the existing licence in the normal way and offering a new one. Most licensees, however, will consent to a mutual variation of the rent terms unless they are actually prepared to leave because, lacking any legislative protection, they are in no bargaining position.

7.46 Status of former licensee. Once the licence has terminated, the former licensee is in strict law a trespasser. Indeed, both the former bare licensee and the former contractual licensee are in exactly the same position as a trespasser (7.07–7.14), save that they are not liable to be convicted for certain of the offences described (7.30).

7.47 Court proceedings have to be taken to evict a former licensee, however, unless the licence is an "excluded licence" (PEA 1977 s.3(2B), (2C), added by the 1988 Act s.30), even if the licence was granted before the commencement of the 1988 Act.

7.48 This will not apply to hotel accommodation, as it is not occupied "as a residence" and therefore does not have the protection of the Act: *Mohamed v Manek*, 1995. Nor does it apply to accommodation provided as a temporary measure to a homeless person pending inquiries into his application for assistance (10.97) or following a decision that he is intentionally homeless (10.101) (*Manek*; *Desnousse v Newham LBC*, 2006).

7.49 It is also necessary to take legal proceedings to evict a former service occupier, who enjoys a special privilege of remaining in occupation until a court order is made, provided that he enjoyed exclusive occupation of the premises which he held with his job (PEA 1977 ss.3 and 8).

7.50 Use of speedy procedures. Proceedings may be brought against any former licensee under the speedy procedures provided by CPR Pt 55.

7.51 These proceedings should not, however, be used where there is a triable issue (*Cooper v Varzdari*, 1986), e.g. that the licence is a sham arrangement concealing a tenancy (*Crancour Ltd v Da Silvaesa*, 1986) or that the occupier is a tenant holding over (*Henderson v Law*, 1984).

7.52 Any licence must have been determined before the issue of these proceedings (*GLC v Jenkins*, 1975), though where normal possession proceedings are used, the landlord need only show determination of the licence by the date of the hearing.

7.53 In all cases, it is in any event practicable and advisable for the landlord to take court proceedings to evict a former licensee, because there is a risk that if he does not do so, he will commit a criminal offence, e.g. under CLA 1977, or of common law assault, etc. If a landlord commits a criminal offence in evicting a former licensee, then he will also commit an offence under PEA 1977 (Chapter 8).

7.54 Offences. Former licensees are not subject to proceedings for being on premises with an offensive weapon (7.29), nor are they required by law to leave when asked to go by a displaced residential occupier or a protected intending occupier (7.35–7.38). They can, however, commit the offence of resisting or intentionally obstructing an officer of the court in the execution of an order of the court for possession, because they are liable to the speedy procedures under CPR Pt 55, even if those proceedings are not actually used against them, e.g. because the landlord was claiming damages for use and occupation during or continuing after the licence and therefore chose to use normal possession proceedings (7.14), or because the proceedings are inappropriate on account of a dispute (7.51).

Non-secure public tenants

7.55 Public landlords. Those who are described as public tenants are the tenants of the Crown, a government department, or a local authority.

7.56 Where the tenancy began before the commencement of the 1988 Act Pt 1 (January 15, 1989), a tenant of the Crown, in property under the management of the Crown Estates Commissioners, is Rent Act protected (5.87); later lettings, however, are within Housing Act assured protection (Chapter 4).

7.57 Most tenants of local authorities are now secure tenants (3.17–3.38), and some may be introductory tenants (6.37–6.51).

7.58 In this section, we are concerned with tenants who are not secure or introductory (or protected or assured).

7.59 All former tenants are entitled to remain in occupation until such time as a court order is obtained against them (PEA 1977 s.3), save for those who qualify as "excluded tenants" (for the definition of which, see 8.21); it would be illegal eviction to regain possession in any other way: see Chapter 8.

7.60 Eviction. It is, of course, illegal to evict a tenant before the expiry of the tenancy. The rules relating to determination or expiry of a tenancy have been described above (1.113–1.146). Notices to quit must normally be in writing, contain prescribed information and be of a minimum period of four weeks, and are also subject to the other common law rules described: if the tenancy commenced on or after January 15, 1989, when Pt 1 of the 1988 Act, came into force, however, the requirement for a minimum period and for writing, and for prescribed information, has been waived for "excluded tenants" (as to the definition of which, see 8.21), so that only compliance with common law is required.

7.61 No rent protection. There is no rent control for the public tenant. In order to increase the rent, the landlord must normally bring the tenancy to an end in the usual way and, of course, in the case of a fixed-term tenancy, he will not be able to do that simply in order to raise the rent.

7.62 A fixed-term tenant could consent to an increase during the period, but it is fairly likely to be unenforceable should he subsequently change his mind, because, in effect, the landlord will have given nothing in exchange for the unplanned increase.

7.63 A periodic tenant could likewise consent to an increase without compelling the landlord to serve notice to quit and offer a new tenancy, but this might be enforceable because of the ease with which the landlord could otherwise bring the tenancy to an end, i.e. there could be said to be some consideration from the landlord, by way of failure to serve notice to quit. For this reason, many public periodic tenants would be inclined to consent to an increase.

7.64 Local authority notices of increase. Local authorities are under an obligation to keep rents in their areas under review. They have a discretion to charge such rents as they consider reasonable.

These matters have been considered in Chapter 3 (3.225). They apply as much to their tenants without any security as to those with.

7.65 Local authority tenancies are almost invariably periodic. Local authorities have a particular privilege, now to be found in the Housing Act 1985 s.25, to raise rents without serving a notice to quit. They may, instead, serve a notice of increase.

7.66 A notice of increase cannot take effect earlier than the authority could otherwise have brought the tenancy to an end by notice to quit, i.e. not less than four weeks, and the notice must warn the tenant of his right to leave rather than pay the increase. In addition, the notice must tell the tenant what he must do in order to bring the tenancy to an end if he chooses to leave, and by what date the tenant must serve his own notice to quit to the local authority, if he—as he rarely will in practice be able to do (especially if he may wish to apply as homeless: see Chapter 10)—chooses this course of action.

7.67 Reasonable use of powers. As regards security, although we are considering tenants without security of tenure as such, local authorities are obliged by common law to act within their powers. Powers are so defined at law as to preclude authorities acting in an unreasonable fashion, and to require authorities to act reasonably.

7.68 Where eviction is concerned, this means that a local authority could not serve a notice to quit, say, whimsically. Before making a decision to evict, the authority must take into account all proper and relevant considerations, and must exclude from consideration anything which it would be improper to take into account. For example, a corrupt decision will always be outside their powers, as will a decision borne of malice. These principles are sometimes called the principles of administrative law (see further 10.182–10.194).

7.69 Human rights. The Human Rights Act 1998 requires all public authorities to act in a way that is compatible with the Convention rights. An eviction may violate a person's right to respect for the home under Art.8(1) of the European Convention on Human Rights. Any interference with that right must be justified and proportionate (Art.8(2).

7.70 The relevance of Art.8 to local authority possession proceedings was considered in *Kay v Lambeth LBC*, 2006. The following propositions emerge from that case and from *Doherty v Birmingham CC*, 2006.

- Eviction in accordance with domestic law can be incompatible with Art.8 but only in exceptional circumstances.
- In bringing an action, an authority do not have to plead justification for their actions. It is for the defendant to raise any issues under Art.8.
- Where a landlord enforces its right to possession under domestic law, there are only two possible defences:

  — a challenge on the ground that the law under which the possession order is made is itself incompatible with Art.8; and
  — a serious argument that the decision to evict can be challenged on conventional administrative law grounds (7.68):

- Where the defendant has a serious argument based on administrative law grounds, he may raise it in the county court, even though such challenges must normally be made by way of judicial review.

Non-secure/assured social tenants

7.71 Other social landlords. Non-secure and non-assured social tenants are the tenants of registered social landlords (Housing Act 1996 Pt 1), or of the Housing Corporation, or of housing co-operatives, who for one reason or another do not qualify as Housing Act secure (3.17–3.38) or Housing Act assured (4.14–4.22) tenants.

7.72 Rents. Very little remains to be said of this class that cannot be achieved by cross-reference. If Housing Act secure, i.e. if preceding the commencement of the 1988 Act Pt I (January 15, 1989), their rents are governed by the fair rent system, subject to minor variations (3.228–3.233). Landlords may increase rents without having to serve a notice to quit (Rent Act 1977 s.93). Otherwise, tenants are subject to no rent control.

7.73 Eviction. Such tenants cannot be evicted without the tenancy being determined (1.113–1.146). The same principles of notice and requirements for a court order under the Protection from Eviction Act 1977 apply as to non-secure public tenants (7.59 and 7.60).

7.74 It has been held that housing associations are not normally subject, as are local authorities (7.67), to the principles of administrative law (*Peabody Housing Association v Green*, 1978). In view of developments generated by the Human Rights Act 1998, however, this has been held no longer to be absolutely true, where, for example, a housing association has been created to take over the stock of a local authority (*Donoghue v Poplar HARCA*, 2001); in such circumstances, they may be considered subject to that Act, and, as such, to the same considerations as local authorities so far as the Act goes (but not so far as concerns conventional grounds for judicial review) (above, 7.68).

Unrestricted tenants

7.75 Minimal rights. This class will include the pre-Housing Act 1988 tenant who is provided with substantial board, and the tenant occupying premises of very high rateable value. Unrestricted tenants enjoy the protection of their contracts against both eviction and rent increase but are in a weak bargaining position when it comes to increases, as the landlord can easily terminate the tenancy, e.g. if it is a periodic tenancy. Unless an "excluded tenancy" (as to the definition of which, see 8.21, below), the notice to quit must be in writing, contain the prescribed information, be of a minimum of four weeks, and must otherwise comply with the common law (1.113–1.118). Unrestricted tenants benefit from no system of rent protection.

Further financial protection and assistance

7.76 Miscellaneous provisions. As trespassers do not pay for their occupation of premises, there is no financial protection available to them. All of the other classes described in this chapter are subject to protection in respect of:

- accommodation agency charges (4.165–4.169);

- resale of utilities (4.170); and

- housing benefit (3.256).

7.77 There are no restrictions on the charging of premiums which apply to these classes of occupation.

CHAPTER EIGHT

Harassment, Illegal Eviction and Other Antisocial Behaviour

Introduction

8.01 In Chapters 1, 4, 5 and 7, we considered some of the ways used by landlords who seek to evade the effects of protective legislation. Some landlords, however, still resort to force or other crude tactics in order to get rid of their occupiers when they want to do so, without taking proceedings in court. To counter this, there are criminal offences of harassment and illegal eviction, now to be found in the Protection from Eviction Act 1977.

8.02 In practice, however, individual occupiers may be able to get much more help from the civil courts than the criminal law. Thus, there are only limited circumstances in which the magistrates' courts can make an order for compensation, and they will rarely order damages for suffering or inconvenience. Similarly, the magistrates' court has no power to make an order compelling a landlord to re-admit an evicted occupier, either immediately—which is when it will be most needed—or at all. Strictly, it cannot even order a landlord to cease harassing an occupier, although it can bind a landlord over to keep the peace, or could discharge a landlord without punishment, conditional on no further offences being committed.

8.03 The position is different in the civil courts (primarily the county courts), where remedies are pursued between the parties. These courts have power to order a landlord to re-admit an evicted occupier, and they can exercise this power so quickly that an occupier may be able to get back in the same day as the eviction, or, at least, the same day as he has sought advice. They can also make orders restraining further harassment or eviction. At the end of a case, civil courts can make permanent orders which remain in force indefinitely, and breach of which would be contempt of court. They can also order the landlord to pay the occupier damages for actual loss suffered, for distress, shock, suffering, and for the wrong that has been done him.

8.04 The phenomenon of harassment is, however, by no means limited to those suffering at the hands of their landlords. In recent years there has been an increasing concern with harassment and antisocial behaviour committed by neighbours and others, which may severely disrupt people's lives. This has been met by legislation (the Housing Act 1996, as amended by the Antisocial Behaviour Act 2003) which has strengthened the powers of social landlords to evict those guilty of antisocial behaviour (see 3.103 and 4.122, above) and which also provides for social landlords to obtain injunctions.

8.05 Another response has been less specifically related to housing law, but nonetheless provides important remedies which we consider here. First, the Protection from Harassment Act 1997 ("1997 Act") created both criminal offences of harassment and the right to seek an injunction to prevent it. Secondly, the Crime and Disorder Act 1998 ("1998 Act") permits local authorities, social landlords and the police to obtain antisocial behaviour orders against perpetrators of antisocial behaviour. Thirdly, under the Antisocial Behaviour Act 2003, the police may close premises which have been used for the production, supply or use of Class A drugs.

Outline

8.06 Criminal proceedings

- The Protection from Eviction Act 1977 creates offences of unlawful eviction and harassment.

- They are committed against "residential occupiers", i.e. someone occupying premises as a residence, whether under a contract or by virtue of any enactment or rule of law.

- Some of the offences may be committed by anyone, others only by landlords.

- Cases are generally heard in the magistrates' court.

- Local authorities have powers to prosecute these cases.

8.07 Civil proceedings

- Two civil remedies are available: injunctions and damages.

- Injunctions may be sought in interim proceedings, sometimes without giving notice to the defendant.

- Damages may be general, aggravated or exemplary.

- A cause of action is necessary if civil action is to be taken. The most common cause is breach of the landlord's covenant to afford the tenant quiet enjoyment of the premises; others include trespass and nuisance.

- The Housing Act 1988 ss.27 and 28 provide a separate cause of action, with damages based on the financial benefit to the landlord of obtaining vacant possession.

8.08 Protection from Harassment Act 1997

- The Protection from Harassment Act 1997 creates four offences in connection with harassment.

- In addition, the magistrates' court may impose a restraining order on someone convicted of an offence under the Act.

- Injunctions under the Act may be sought by the individual victim.

8.09 Antisocial behaviour injunctions

- Local authorities, registered social landlords and other social landlords may obtain injunctions restraining antisocial behaviour.

- An injunction may be made against a tenant of the landlord or any other person whose antisocial behaviour affects the landlord's housing management functions.

8.10 Antisocial behaviour orders (ASBOs)

- Either the police or a local authority may apply for an ASBO in the magistrates' court.

- The court may make such an order where a person (aged 10 or over) has acted in a manner that causes, or is likely to cause, harassment, alarm or distress to one or more persons not within his own household, if the order is necessary to protect persons in the area from further such behaviour.

- The order may prohibit a person from doing anything described in the order.

- Breach of an ASBO is a criminal offence.

8.11 Closure orders

- The police may serve a closure notice on premises which they have cause to believe have been used for the production, supply or use of Class A drugs.

- Within 48 hours of the closure notice, the police can apply for a closure order.

- Remaining in or entering premises subject to a closure notice is a criminal offence.

Criminal proceedings

8.12 Principal definitions. The definitions of the criminal offences of illegal eviction and harassment are contained in the Protection from Eviction Act 1977 ("PEA 1977") s.1, as amended by the Housing Act 1988:

"(2) If any person unlawfully deprives the residential occupier of any premises of his occupation of the premises or any part thereof, or attempts to do so, he shall be guilty of an offence unless he proves that he believed, and had reasonable cause to believe, that the residential occupier had ceased to reside in the premises.

(3) If any person with intent to cause the residential occupier of any premises—

  (a) to give up occupation of the premises or any part thereof; or

  (b) to refrain from exercising any right or pursuing any remedy in respect of the premises or part thereof;

does acts likely to interfere with the peace or comfort of the residential occupier or members of his household, or persistently withdraws or withholds services reasonably required for the occupation of the premises as a residence, he shall be guilty of an offence.

(3A) The landlord of a residential occupier or an agent of the landlord shall be guilty of an offence if—

  (a) he does acts likely to interfere with the peace or comfort of the residential occupier or members of his household, or

(b) subject to subsection (3B) below, he persistently withdraws or withholds services reasonably required for the occupation of the premises in question as a residence,

and (in either case) he knows, or has reasonable cause to believe, that that conduct is likely to cause the residential occupier to give up the occupation of the whole or part of the premises or to refrain from exercising any right or pursuing any remedy in respect of the whole or part of the premises.

(3B) A person shall not be guilty of an offence under subsection (3A) if he proves that he had reasonable grounds for doing the acts or withdrawing or withholding the services in question."

1. RESIDENTIAL OCCUPIER

8.13 Application of Act. The Act applies to "residential occupiers". The term is also defined in s.1 of the Act:

"(1) In this section 'residential occupier', in relation to any premises, means a person occupying the premises as a residence, whether under a contract or by virtue of any enactment or rule of law giving him the right to remain in occupation or restricting the right of any other person to recover possession of the premises."

8.14 Occupation as a residence. Occupation as a residence is a question of fact and common sense, not law. It is not necessary to show, for example, that the occupier had sufficient residence to sustain a claim to statutory tenancy (5.95–5.111). Obviously, someone who merely visits a friend is not residing in premises, not even if he stays overnight or, perhaps for a few nights. The same is no doubt true of a short-term hotel guest. But once a person begins to use premises to live in, in any normal sense of the expression, then the premises are being occupied as a residence.

8.15 A person can have two residences, e.g. a student who lives away from home during the term-time will normally be considered resident both at home and at college. A person does not stop residing in premises just because, for example, he goes away for a holiday, or for some other reason is temporarily absent. The residence will continue during such breaks as if the occupier was actually present.

8.16 Residential occupation by status. All tenants (including long leaseholders) and licensees (including service tenants and occupiers) whose tenancies and licences have not been brought to an end are residential occupiers because they are occupying under contract. It does not matter if the person harassing or evicting is not a party to the contract; what is in question is whether or not the occupier is a residential occupier.

8.17   Secure, assured and introductory tenants occupy both under contract and by virtue of statute (Chapters 3, 4), as do secure and introductory licensees.

8.18   Rent Act protected tenants whose contractual tenancies have been brought to an end and who occupy as statutory tenants (see Chapter 5) do so "by virtue of an enactment", and remain so protected until evicted by the bailiff (*Haniff v Robinson*, 1992).

8.19   Unless the tenancy was entered into on or after the commencement date of Pt 1 of the 1988 Act (January 15, 1989) and qualifies as an "excluded tenancy", all other former tenants (together with those lawfully living with them, even if the former tenant has himself departed) are residential occupiers because there is an enactment (PEA 1977 s.3) "restricting the right of any other person to recover possession of the premises".

8.20   Excluded tenancy.   If the tenancy was entered into on or after January 15, 1989, however, s.3 is disapplied, i.e. the former tenant will not be within s.3 and, the tenancy having ended, there will be no restriction on the right of the landlord to recover possession. It follows that neither eviction without court order, nor harassment, are illegal as against such a former excluded tenant.

8.21   The following are excluded tenancies:

- The tenant shares any accommodation (other than storage space, passages, corridors or other means of access, i.e. a bathroom or lavatory is accommodation for this purpose, *cf.* above, 3.25) with the landlord, who was himself in occupation of another part of the premises as an only or principal home (3.32) both before the tenancy was granted and at the time it comes to an end.

- The tenant shares any accommodation (other than storage space, passages, corridors or other means of access, so that again a bathroom or lavatory is included) with a member of the family of the landlord, who was in occupation of another part of the premises as an only or principal home (3.32) both before the tenancy was granted and at the time it comes to an end, and immediately before the tenancy was granted and at the time it comes to an end, the landlord occupies, as his only or principal home (3.32), premises in the same building (not being a purpose-built block of flats: 4.48).

- The tenancy was granted as a temporary expedient to someone who originally entered premises as a trespasser, i.e. a former squatter who is granted a tenancy for a period of time (*cf.* 3.21).

- The tenancy was a holiday letting (4.38) or was granted other than for money or money's worth, i.e. was not a commercial arrangement.

- The tenancy was granted in order to provide accommodation under Pt 6 of the Immigration and Asylum Act 1999.

8.22 Former licensees. Section 3 also protects former licensees who have occupied under restricted contracts commencing on or after November 28, 1980 (see Chapter 6), former service occupiers who were granted some exclusive occupation of their accommodation under the employment arrangement (PEA 1977 s.8), and all other former licensees other than those with "excluded licences".

8.23 This has the same meaning as "excluded tenancy", in each case including anyone lawfully living with such a licensee at the end of the occupancy.

8.24 Hostels. In addition, a licence of part of a hostel is also excluded if it is provided by one of a specified number of public bodies, including local authorities, registered social landlords, development corporations, housing action trusts and charitable housing trusts.

8.25 Homeless persons. In a judicial extension to these provisions, it has been held that accommodation provided by way of licence (1.47) as a temporary measure to a homeless person pending inquiries into his application for assistance (10.97) or following a decision that he is intentionally homeless (10.101) is not—normally—"occupied as a dwelling under a licence" because of the transience of the occupation (*Mohamed v Manek and Kensington and Chelsea RLBC*, 1995; *Desnousse v Newham LBC*, 2006). Such licence arrangements do not, therefore, have the protection of the PEA 1977. It has, however, been suggested (although not yet decided) that if the letting is by way of tenancy, it may be that tenancies of such accommodation are protected (*Desnousse*).

8.26 Spouses and cohabitees. In addition, there are enactments restricting the right of another person to recover possession of premises which serve to protect deserted spouses and, in some cases, even trespassers. The Family Law Act 1996 (Chapter 9) prohibits an owner or tenant-spouse/cohabitee from evicting a non-owner or non-tenant-spouse/cohabitee from the matrimonial home without an order of a court. Such an order will normally be made during the course of domestic proceedings, and this subject is considered in the next chapter. Because, however, there is an enactment which restricts the right of some other person to recover possession, meaning the owner/tenant-spouse/cohabitee, the deserted partner qualifies as a residential occupier for the purposes of the PEA 1977, even if it is not the other partner who is attempting to recover possession.

8.27 Trespassers. The criminal offence of violent entry for the purposes of eviction of a trespasser has been described in Chapter 7. In so far as a trespasser is protected from eviction by that provision, so also will he be protected from eviction under this Act.

8.28 Advisability of proceedings. The definition of residential occupier is, therefore, very wide indeed. It is possible to evict certain occupiers, e.g. trespassers, and some former licensees and tenants, without taking court proceedings, so long as the Criminal Law Act 1977 is not broken, so long as no other criminal offence is committed, so long as the licence or tenancy is already at an end (*R. v Blankley*, 1979), and so on. This list of reservations should deter any landlord from seeking to recover possession without taking court proceedings, for the risk of committing an offence when doing so will otherwise be very high. It is for this reason that landlords are invariably advised—and well-advised—by lawyers to take court proceedings before evicting an occupier.

2. ACTS OF HARASSMENT

8.29 Intention and knowledge. The difference between s.1(3) and s.1(3A) is that the former creates an offence when the landlord does the specified acts with the intention of causing the occupier to quit or to refrain from exercising a right, while the latter creates an offence when the landlord does those acts knowing or having reasonable cause to believe that the consequence is likely to be to cause the occupier to quit or refrain from exercising a right.

8.30 The most common intention is that of wanting the occupier to give up possession of the premises or part of them, e.g. one room, and that is also the most common consequence. Harassment also occurs with the other objective in mind, e.g. to try and deter an occupier from applying to the rent officer or Rent Assessment Committee, or to deter him from complaining to an environmental health officer (see Chapter 13) about the condition of the property.

8.31 Services, peace and comfort. The criminal action can also be committed in different ways: by persistently withholding or withdrawing services, such as gas and electricity, reasonably required for the occupation of the premises as a residence; or, by doing an act (*R. v Polycarpou*, 1983) or acts, which are likely to interfere with the peace or comfort of the residential occupier or members of his household.

8.32 "Persistently" means more than just once or twice. Withholding or withdrawal of services can be justified under s.1(3B) if the landlord proves there were reasonable grounds for it, e.g. that services were dangerous to use. Mere non-payment of rent or other charges by the occupier is not sufficient justification, for the landlord has other remedies for this, i.e. to seek an order for possession.

8.33 Other conduct. The breadth of the definition allows the law to catch odd actions which may not be obvious acts of harassment, such as hanging around a sensitive and perhaps elderly occupier, or coming into the premises so frequently that the occupier ceases to feel secure in his home.

8.34 The act in question does not need also to be a civil wrong, so that a criminal offence may be committed by an act with the appropriate intention, even if it does not conflict with an occupier's other rights, e.g. refusing to supply a spare key when the occupier has lost his (*R. v Yuthiwattana*, 1984), or deliberately disconnecting the door bell and preventing use of a particular bathroom and lavatory (*R. v Burke*, 1990).

3. ACTS OF EVICTION

8.35 Definition. There are three points to note in connection with the definition of eviction:

1. eviction can be from the whole or part of the premises in question;

2. an offence is committed either by a successful eviction or by an attempted eviction; and,

3. the defence which is available to an accused requires him to show that he believed and had reasonable cause to believe that the residential occupier had ceased to reside in the premises.

8.36   The requirement of reasonable cause means that a subjective but unreasonable belief will not be a defence.

8.37   Eviction or harassment.   Eviction means more than intending to lock the occupier out for only a short time, e.g. overnight; such an action is more likely to be one of harassment (*R. v Yuthiwattana*, 1984).

8.38   Homelessness and eviction.   An occupier who is illegally evicted will be homeless, and will qualify for assistance under Pt 7 of the Housing Act 1996 (see Chapter 10), although how much will depend on priority need (10.31–10.46).

4.   THE ACCUSED

8.39   Under s.1(2) and (3), anyone can be charged with either illegal eviction or harassment, not only a landlord or his friends or agents. It may, however, be difficult to establish the necessary intention for harassment unless the act is done by someone with connections to the landlord. On the face of it, no one else is likely to have the incentive to try and make the occupier get out.

8.40   Where s.1(3A) is alleged, the perpetrator must be or be acting on behalf of the landlord. In addition, the acts must have been committed with the knowledge—actual or deemed—that it will cause the occupier to quit or to refrain from exercising a right or remedy.

8.41   For this purpose, however, the definition of "landlord" is extended (PEA 1977 s.1(3C)) to include anyone who would have a right to occupation of the premises but for the occupier's protection, or a superior landlord from whom the immediate landlord derives his right.

8.42   A prospective future occupier could qualify in this way (*Jones v Miah*, 1992). If the harassment or eviction is performed on behalf of a limited company, then a director or any officer of the company will also be guilty of an offence if he consented to or connived at the harassment, or it happened because of his negligence (PEA 1977 s.1(6)).

5. CRIMINAL PROCEEDINGS

8.43 Magistrates' court. Criminal proceedings are initiated in the magistrates' court. The landlord may elect trial in the Crown Court, but most cases are tried in the magistrates' court.

8.44 Local authorities have power to prosecute offences under the Act (PEA 1977 s.6), and almost all prosecutions are brought by them, usually through a tenancy relations officers employed to deal with private sector disputes.

8.45 Role of police. The police are not liable for a failure to prevent an offence being committed under the PEA 1977, even where the tenant has requested them to attend (and prevent) an unlawful eviction. It has been held that they cannot be expected to inform themselves about landlord and tenant law before attending such a call: *Cowan v Chief Constable of Avon & Somerset Constabulary*, 2001.

8.46 Role of tenancy relations officer. In the event of any act of harassment or eviction, the tenancy relations officer ("TRO") should be contacted without delay. If it is urgent, he will normally call straight round to the premises and try to sort the problem out face to face with the landlord and the occupier. Some TROs have radio-linked cars. In addition or, if the matter is not urgent, in the alternative, he may write to the landlord, warning him of the possible offences and penalties and inviting comment.

8.47 The TRO does not usually make prosecution the goal of his job. The officers tend to work by way of conciliation, reinforced by the possibility of prosecution, although the degree of emphasis will vary between officers and/or authorities.

8.48 A TRO cannot normally decide on his own initiative to prosecute: the prosecution will be handled by the local authority's legal service (internal or external).

8.49 Private prosecution. If the TRO will not prosecute, then it is still open to the individual occupier who has been harassed or illegally evicted to do so. Legal aid will not be available for a prosecution, although publicly funded legal advice can be sought beforehand. Unsurprisingly, not many occupiers are prepared to shoulder the responsibility of a private prosecution unassisted, and run the risk of having to pay the landlord's costs if he is acquitted.

8.50 Penalties. The court can impose a fine or up to six months' imprisonment, or both. If the landlord elects trial in the Crown Court, then he could be fined up to an unlimited amount, or sent to prison for up to two years, or both.

8.51 Compensation. Either sort of court has power to award compensation for "personal injury, loss or damage resulting from [an] offence" (Powers of Criminal Courts (Sentencing) Act 2000 s.130). The power is only used in relation to ascertainable loss, such as damaged property, time off work through injury, cost of overnight accommodation or eating out, etc. It is not used for shock, distress, inconvenience or discomfort. Nor, in the case of illegal eviction, will the power be used for loss of the home itself, as this does not have an easily identified value. Awards are limited to £5,000 (s.131). Any documentary evidence of loss sustained by the occupier, such as bills, should be brought to court.

Civil proceedings

8.52 County courts. Civil proceedings are brought in either the county court, usually for the area in which the incident happens, or in the High Court. Most cases of harassment and illegal eviction will be brought in the county courts, as a case which includes a claim for damages may not be started in the High Court unless the value of the claim is more than £15,000 (CPR Pt 7; CPR PD 7A para.2.1). If the claim includes a claim for damages for personal injury, the claim may not be started in the High Court unless the value of the claim is more than £50,000 (CPR Pt 7; CPR PD 7A para.2.2).

8.53 Remedies. The county court has the jurisdiction to make any order which the High Court can, e.g. an injunction (County Courts Act 1984 s.38).

8.54 The civil remedies which may be awarded by either sort of court are:

(i) injunctions; and

(ii) damages.

1. INJUNCTIONS

8.55 Injunctions. An injunction is an order of the court. It will always identify the person, or persons, who is or are to be bound by it. Failure to comply with the terms of an injunction is a contempt of court. Contempt can be punished by either a fine or imprisonment. It is uncommon for civil courts to send a landlord who is in breach of an injunction to prison, unless he persists in his refusal to obey it.

8.56 Final injunctions. Injunctions are either final or interim. A final injunction is awarded at the end of a trial when the factual disputes between the parties have been resolved.

8.57 Interim injunctions. The trial may not, however, take place for some months after the commencement of proceedings, and the prospect of a final injunction is of little assistance to the victim of an ongoing campaign of harassment or other antisocial behaviour, or someone locked out of his home who is sleeping rough or staying with friends.

8.58 In such circumstances, the victim may apply for an interim injunction, which may be granted at any time from the commencement of proceedings in order to maintain the status quo pending the trial. In extremely urgent cases, an injunction may even be awarded on an undertaking to go through the formal process of issuing proceedings within a specified time afterwards.

8.59 Without-notice orders. Likewise, a matter can be so urgent that it cannot even be left for the few days necessary to give the other side an opportunity to attend court. In cases of such urgency, the court will grant a "without-notice" interim order, i.e. one that is based upon the unchallenged evidence of the occupier only.

8.60 The matter must be serious, e.g. eviction or disconnection of utilities, before a court will make an order on a without-notice hearing.

8.61 No delay. The courts will only use their powers to make a without-notice order if there has been little or no delay before they are asked to do so. A without-notice order should always be sought immediately.

8.62 On-notice hearing. If an order is granted without notice, it will usually be for only a few days or a week, until a further hearing—on notice—at which the court can hear the other side of the case and decide whether or not the order should be continued until a full trial of the matter.

8.63 An on-notice hearing may also be suitable if a matter is not serious enough to merit a without-notice order, but the matter cannot be left until the full trial.

8.64 Balance of convenience. When a judge is deciding whether or not to grant an interim injunction, he does not decide the full merits of the case. He only decides what order should be made, pending the full trial, on what was formerly called a balance of "convenience" (*American Cyanamid Co Ltd v Ethicon*, 1975) but which is now more properly called a "balance of justice" between the parties (*Francome v Mirror Group Newspapers*, 1984).

8.65 Unless the premises have already been reoccupied by someone else, or by the landlord himself, the balance of justice in a case of illegal eviction will almost always be in the occupier's favour, although it may be subject to an undertaking by the occupier to pay rent pending the trial. The balance of justice will also almost invariably be with the occupier where harassment is in issue.

8.66 Premises re-let. If the premises have been re-let, however, the court will not usually grant an interim injunction requiring the landlord to re-admit the evicted occupier. As between the landlord and the new occupier, there is a valid agreement. Between the evicted occupier and the new occupier, however, if the eviction was unlawful, it is the evicted occupier who has the right to possession. If the evicted occupier wishes to be re-admitted to the property, he may ask the court to join the new occupier as a party to the proceedings, and claim possession against him. The possession claim cannot be decided until the court has decided whether the eviction was unlawful, which will usually require a trial, so possession is unlikely to be ordered at the hearing of a claim for an interim injunction (*Love v Herrity*, 1990).

8.67 Strength of claim. Although the issue is one of balance of justice, the strength of a case may still affect the decision of the court. If the occupier's case is a strong one, on the face of it, then even if the landlord is in occupation, the court will be reluctant to allow him to benefit from what appears to be both the commission of a criminal offence and a very serious breach of the civil law, by allowing him to remain in occupation until trial.

2. DAMAGES

8.68 Types of damages. Damages are not awarded until the end of the case. There are several different sorts of damages:

- A person claims special damages for specific sums of money, e.g. damage to furniture, cost of eating out or overnight accommodation, lost property, etc. These are the same sorts of damages which may be awarded in the magistrates' courts as compensation.

- General damages are unquantified sums which are claimed in respect of, for example, suffering, shock, distress, physical injury, inconvenience, the lost right of occupation itself or any other harm to which a specific value cannot be attached, e.g. additional electricity costs because gas is cut off.

- Aggravated damages are awarded to compensate for injury to proper feelings of dignity and pride, and for aggravation generally (*Ramdath v Daley*, 1993), e.g. where the manner of that which is being sued for was especially mean, unpleasant, brutal, etc.

- Exemplary damages are awarded where it would appear that the landlord has, for example, evicted a tenant, calculating to himself that any profit made, e.g. from sale of the property with vacant possession, will be more than any damages awarded against him. In other words, that he can make a profit, even out of doing something wrong.

8.69 Exemplary damages. In *Cassell & Co Ltd v Broome*, 1972, the House of Lords considered when exemplary damages might be awarded. Lord Hailsham L.C. said:

"How, it may be asked, about the late Mr. Rachman, who is alleged to have used hired bullies to intimidate statutory tenants by violence or threats of violence into giving up vacant possession of their residences and so placing a valuable asset in the hands of the landlord? My answer must be that if this is not a cynical calculation of profit and cold-blooded disregard of a plaintiff's rights, I do not know what is."

8.70   In the case of *Drane v Evangelou*, 1977, Lawton L.J. said that to deprive a tenant of a roof over his head was one of the worst torts (wrongs) that could be committed. It brought the law into disrespect. He also expressed his surprise that the landlord had not been prosecuted under what is now s.1 of the PEA 1977. Lord Denning M.R. applied the words of an earlier case:

> "Exemplary damages can properly be awarded whenever it is necessary to teach a wrongdoer that tort does not pay."

8.71   Exemplary damages cannot, however, be claimed where there is only a claim based on breach of contract (see further below).

3.   CAUSE OF ACTION

8.72   Need for cause of action.   Neither the county court nor the High Court can make any order at all, however, until an action has been commenced (or an undertaking to commence it has been accepted; see above, 8.54). Public funding will generally be available for a civil action based on harassment or illegal eviction

8.73   In order to commence an action in a civil court, it is necessary to show that the plaintiff has a "cause of action". A court does not have power to make an order because, for example, someone does not like the colour of his neighbour's hair, or because someone jumps in front of someone else in a bus queue, or because another person calls someone a silly idiot. On the other hand, there will be a cause of action if a neighbour plays music so loudly or at antisocial hours that he disturbs someone else's enjoyment of his own home, or if the queue-jumper used so much force that he assaulted someone, or if what was said was of a defamatory character.

8.74   Causes of action classified.   All of the causes of action referred to at the end of the last paragraph are "torts", or civil wrongs. A tort is an action which the law recognises that it is wrongful for one person, who is the person complained about, to do to the person complaining. There are several torts which may be used in connection with harassment and illegal eviction.

8.75   In addition, there is always a cause of action when one party breaks a contract with another, whether completely or in a material particular. Breach of contract will also often be appropriate to cases of harassment and illegal eviction.

(i) *Breach of contract*

8.76 Tenancies and licences. Both tenancy and licence are contracts. A licensee may sue for breach of contract or breach of a term of the contract (*Smith v Nottinghamshire CC*, 1981). A term of a contract may actually be stated, or it may be implied, although only where it is a term which is necessary for the contract to be effective. In the case of a residential licence, this will usually mean such terms as are necessary for the property to be capable of use as a residence, although standards may vary depending on the type of licence, e.g. a hostel licence normally implies a "full" or "high" standard of occupancy, but a licence to share property scheduled for demolition or refurbishment, i.e. what is called short-life use, would probably be at the opposite end of the spectrum.

8.77 Quiet enjoyment. In addition, into every tenancy (but not a licence) there is implied, unless it is actually spelled out in the agreement, a promise by the landlord that the tenant will have the "quiet enjoyment" of the premises so long as the tenancy lasts.

8.78 In *Kenny v Preen*, 1962, it was said that the promise was broken by an act which was an invasion of the right of the tenant to remain in possession undisturbed. Clearly, this includes an actual or threatened eviction, and almost every act of harassment. In *McCall v Abelesz*, 1975, disconnection of utilities was described as both a breach of implied term, and as an interference with quiet enjoyment. Any conduct by a landlord which interferes with the tenant's freedom of action in exercising his rights as tenant will be an interference with the covenant for quiet enjoyment.

8.79 Excessive noise. Excessive noise made by the landlord is capable of amounting to breach of the covenant: *Southwark LBC v Tanner*, 2001. In *Tanner*, however, the disturbance arose from tenants being able to hear their neighbours due to poor sound insulation. There was no breach of the covenant for quiet enjoyment because the landlord had not caused the noise (other than by letting the flats, as it was obvious and intended that it would).

8.80 Derogation from grant. In addition, some actions by a landlord in common parts, or in neighbouring property under his control, could amount to derogation from his grant of the tenancy to the tenant (see further, 11.35). This is also an action in contract.

(ii) *Housing Act 1988 sections 27 and 28*

8.81 Breach of Housing Act 1988 section 27. In *McCall v Abelesz*, 1975, it was held that, even though a landlord had committed an act or offence of illegal eviction or harassment, the occupier did not necessarily have a civil remedy, i.e. a right to sue.

8.82 Accordingly, s.27 of the 1988 Act affords an express right to sue where either illegal eviction within the PEA 1977 s.1(2) has taken place, or such harassment within s.1(3), (3A) (8.12) has been committed (after June 9, 1988), that it leads to the occupier's departure. This right is conferred on all residential occupiers, as defined (8.13–8.26), and carries an express right to damages.

8.83 The action can be brought against the landlord (but not someone acting as his agent: *Sampson v Wilson*, 1995), or anyone else who, but for the occupier's right to occupy, would be entitled to occupy, or any superior landlord from whom that person derives his right.

8.84 The action is an action in tort (8.74) and is additional to any other rights, save that damages for loss of occupation are not to be awarded twice over. A landlord can defend the action by showing that he believed, and had reasonable cause to believe, that the residential occupier had already quit, or—in the case of a departure based on withholding of services—that there were reasonable grounds for withholding services (*Wandsworth LBC v Osei-Bonsu*, 1999).

8.85 Damages may be reduced if either the court considers that the occupier's conduct provoked the eviction or harassment, or (where eviction is concerned) that the landlord has offered to reinstate the occupier, before the proceedings under the 1988 Act were begun, and the offer was unreasonably refused. (There can be unreasonable refusal even if the occupier had found somewhere else before the offer.) The offer of reinstatement must be genuine, and merely handing the tenant a key to a lock which does not work, and inviting her to resume occupation of a room which has been totally wrecked, will not suffice (*Tagro v Cafane*, 1991).

8.86 Amount of damages. There are detailed provisions (1988 Act s.28) governing the amount of damages for breach of this "statutory tort", designed to deprive the landlord of the financial benefit of vacant possession. No damages at all are payable if, before the action is commenced, or at any time before it is finally over, the occupier is actually reinstated.

8.87 Where the evicting landlord holds only an intermediate interest, that is the interest which must be valued for the purpose of preventing him from securing a profit (*Jones & Lee v Miah*, 1992). The nature of the interest of the tenant, and the fact of other occupiers, should be taken into account, so that where the tenancy which has been lost is an assured shorthold in a house still occupied by other tenants, the award is likely to be quite low (*Melville v Bruton*, 1996).

(iii) *Other torts*

8.88 Trespass to land. If there is a tenancy, the tenant has possession of the premises to the exclusion of all others including the landlord. A landlord can, therefore, trespass on the premises of his own tenant.

8.89 There is some legal authority for the proposition that the sort of exclusive occupation which most licensees have is enough possession for the purposes of trespass. This is because it is possession in fact, rather than legally defined possession, which matters.

8.90 A person is a trespasser whenever he enters the land or premises of another without permission. It is also a trespass to place anything on someone else's property without permission. In one case it was held to be a trespass to drive a nail into someone else's wall, which, by analogy, would apply to a landlord who nails up a door or blocks up a lock. A person is also a trespasser if he has permission to be on someone's premises for one purpose but uses it for another. For example, a landlord calling around to collect the rent or inspect for repairs will become a trespasser if he uses the occasion to abuse, threaten or harass the occupier.

8.91 A person given permission to enter must leave once he is asked to do so and, once a reasonable time has been given for the exit, becomes a trespasser. Reasonable time here, as with residential licence (1.85), is reasonable in all the circumstances and, where a person is just visiting, will be a matter of however long it would normally take to get to the door.

8.92 Trespass is a tort, and anyone who trespasses can be sued for it. A landlord is liable for the torts of his agents, if they were committed with his approval or on his behalf. An evicted or harassed occupier can sue the landlord and, if the landlord got someone else to do the job for him, that person as well.

8.93 Assault. Harassment and eviction will often be accompanied by assaults. An assault is not necessarily a directly physical act. It may be no more than some gesture which suggests that the person to whom it is made is about to be attacked physically. Threatening words on their own are not an assault, and it is difficult to prove unless there has been some sort of physical attack, although this might be with a weapon, piece of furniture, or merely by shoving an occupier around. An assault is a tort and the remarks in the last paragraph will, therefore, apply in the same way to assault.

8.94 Nuisance. Like trespass, this is a cause of action which can be used by someone in possession of land, which certainly includes a tenant and may include a licensee. It includes a "tolerated trespasser" (1.44): *Pemberton v Southwark LBC*, 2001. It is, however, only the person with the interest in the land who can sue, not other family members: *Hunter v Canary Wharf*, 1997.

8.95 A nuisance is anything which interferes with the reasonable use and enjoyment of property, e.g. noise, smells, even hanging about outside someone's home. Most acts of harassment will constitute a nuisance, although this may not be so if the act is negative, e.g. a withdrawal of services. Nuisance is also a tort.

8.96 Trespass to goods. Any direct interference with another person's belongings is a trespass to goods. If belongings are actually removed, this may also be conversion. Conversion is the act of dealing with someone else's property in any manner that is inconsistent with the right of the other person to possession of it. Trespass to goods and conversion are torts.

Protection from Harassment Act 1997

8.97 Criminal offences. The 1997 Act generally prohibits harassment; breach of which is actionable in both the civil and criminal courts. It creates four criminal offences:

1. harassment;
2. putting another person in fear of violence;

3. breach of a restraining order; and

4. breach of an injunction.

8.98 The Act gives a criminal court the power to make a restraining order, which has similar effect to an injunction.

8.99 Harassment. The 1997 Act s.1(1) prohibits a person from:

". . . pursuing a course of conduct—
    (a) which amounts to harassment of another; and
    (b) which he or she knows or ought to know amounts to harassment of the other."

8.100 It is an offence to pursue a course of conduct in breach of the prohibition against harassment (1997 Act s.2).

8.101 There is no exhaustive definition of harassment for this purpose. It includes, but is not limited to, alarming or causing distress to a person (1997 Act s.7(2)). It is a matter for the court to determine on the facts of the particular case whether the conduct complained about "amounts to harassment", in the everyday sense of the word. The prosecution must also prove that the defendant was aware that the conduct amounted to harassment or, if not, that he "ought to have known".

8.102 Conduct is not defined, but includes speech. To amount to a "course of conduct" there must be conduct on more than one occasion (1997 Act s.7(4)).

8.103 Putting another person in fear of violence. Section 4(1) makes it an offence to pursue a course of conduct (8.102) which:

"causes another to fear, on at least two occasions, that violence will be used against him . . . if he knows or ought to know that his course of conduct will cause the other so to fear on each occasion".

8.104 Restraining orders. The court may impose a "restraining order" on a defendant to protect the victim (or any other specified person) from further conduct which may amount to harassment or causing a fear of violence (1997 Act s.5).

8.105 The power is available where a court is sentencing or otherwise dealing with a defendant convicted of an offence under ss.2 (8.100) or 4 (8.103). The order must describe the prohibited conduct and the order may be for a specified period or until a further order is made.

8.106   Breach of a restraining order. It is an offence for a person to do anything prohibited under a restraining order, without reasonable excuse (1997 Act s.5(7)).

8.107   Breach of an injunction. Where proceedings are taken under the 1997 Act in a civil court, it may grant an injunction to prevent further harassment. If it does so, then it is a criminal offence for the defendant, without reasonable excuse, to do anything which he is prohibited from doing by the injunction (1997 Act s.5(6)). This offence cannot be pursued, however, if the defendant has already been punished for contempt of court for breach of the injunction.

8.108   Obtaining an injunction. PHA 1997 s.3 specifically provides a civil claim for actual or apprehended harassment, as defined in the 1997 Act s.1 (8.99), allowing the victim to seek an injunction and damages.

8.109   Damages. It is expressly provided that damages may be awarded for any anxiety caused by the harassment, as well as any financial loss (1997 Act s.3(1)).

Antisocial behaviour injunctions

8.110   Policies on antisocial behaviour. It is not only landlords who may be guilty of harassing tenants. During the mid-nineties there was an upsurge of concern about antisocial activity on—in particular, local authority—estates, particularly intimidation of residents by gangs, usually of youths, often involving the use and sale of drugs, and other criminal activity.

8.111 In the absence of sufficient support from the criminal justice system, a number of local authorities used their powers as such, or as landlord or landowner, to seek injunctive relief from the civil courts.

8.112 The success of such action by local authorities led to the introduction of a statutory basis for injunctive relief under Pt 5 of the Housing Act 1996 ("1996 Act"). These provisions were amended by the Antisocial Behaviour Act 2003 to strengthen the powers available and to allow other social landlords, in particular registered social landlords, to apply for antisocial behaviour injunctions.

8.113 Relevant landlords. An application for an injunction under the 1996 Act may be made by a relevant landlord, i.e. a local authority (3.08), a housing action trust (3.11), a registered social landlord (3.12) and a charitable housing trust.

8.114 Injunctions. There are three types of injunction:

1. an antisocial behaviour injunction (1996 Act s.153A);

2. an injunction against unlawful use of premises (1996 Act s.153B); and

3. an injunction against breach of tenancy agreement (1996 Act s.153D)

8.115 Antisocial behaviour injunction. A landlord can seek an injunction either from the county court or from the High Court against any person who is engaging in, has engaged in, or is threatening to engage in, conduct capable of causing a nuisance or annoyance to any person. The conduct complained of must directly or indirectly relate to or affect the housing management functions of the authority (1996 Act s.153A(1), (2) and (3)).

8.116 Affected persons. For an injunction to be made, the conduct complained of must be capable of causing a nuisance or annoyance to tenants or licensees of housing owned or managed by the landlord, or to members of their households, or to any other person who has a right to reside in accommodation in the neighbourhood, e.g. tenants of other landlords or owner-occupiers, or to persons engaged in lawful activity in the neighbourhood, e.g. a postman or milkman, or to the landlord's employees or contractors (1996 Act s.153A(4)).

8.117 Location of conduct. The antisocial behaviour need not take place in the neighbourhood concerned: a landlord can seek an injunction to prevent harassment of one of its tenants when away from his home.

8.118 Unlawful use. A landlord may apply for an injunction to prevent the use of—or the threat of the use of—housing accommodation which it owns or manages from being used for an unlawful purpose, e.g. drug-dealing (1996 Act s.153B).

8.119   Breach of tenancy agreement.   In contrast with the previous two forms of injunction, this is only available against tenants or licensees (1996 Act s.153D(5)). The grounds for applying for an injunction are that the tenant is engaging in or threatening to engage in conduct that is capable of causing a nuisance or annoyance to any person, or that he is allowing, inciting or encouraging someone else to engage in such conduct (1996 Act s.153D(1)).

8.120   Exclusion zone.   An injunction under any of these provisions can prevent a person entering specified premises or a particular area (1996 Act ss.153C(2) and 153D(3)). This even means that a tenant can be excluded from his own home (1996 Act s.153E(2); *Moat Housing Association v Harris*, 2005). To order such an exclusion zone, however, either the conduct must include the use or threatened use of violence or there must be a significant risk of harm to someone. In the case of an injunction to restrain breach of tenancy agreement, the risk of harm can be to any person (1996 Act s.153D(2)). Otherwise, the risk of harm must be to one of the persons described at 8.116. Harm includes serious ill-treatment or abuse, whether physical or not (1996 Act s.153E(12)).

8.121   Power of arrest.   A power of arrest may be attached to any terms of an injunction (1996 Act ss.153C(1), (3) and 153D(3)). A power of arrest allows a police officer to arrest, without warrant, any person whom he suspects is in breach of the order (1996 Act s.155(1)). A person arrested must be produced to the court within 24 hours. If the matter is not dealt with by imposing a sentence for contempt of court, e.g. imprisonment or a fine, the court can remand the defendant in custody or on bail. Remand in custody cannot be for more than eight days, unless the court adjourns the case for a medical report on the defendant (1996 Act s.156), in which case it can remand for up to three weeks at a time.

8.122   Conditions.   The conditions for attaching a power of arrest are the same as those which apply to ordering an exclusion zone (8.120).

8.123   Duration.   An injunction may be made for a specified period or else be expressed to last until it is varied or discharged (1996 Act s.153E(2)). The power of arrest may last for a shorter period (1996 Act s.157(1)).

8.124   Without notice orders.   Though normally the person must be given notice of the application for an injunction, the court may make an order without notice, e.g. where there is concern for the safety of victims or a fear that residents of estates will not co-operate and give evidence until an injunction is in place. To make a without-notice order, the court must consider that it is just and convenient to do so (1996 Act s.153E(4)).

8.125 Before including an exclusion zone in the order or attaching a power of arrest, the court must consider that the conduct includes the use or threatened use of violence; there must be a significant risk of harm to those whom the order seeks to protect (*Moat*).

8.126 If the court uses this power, it must as soon as is reasonably practicable afford the person against whom it is made an opportunity to be heard (1996 Act s.153E(6)).

8.127 Discharge or variation. The person against whom an order is made, or who is subject to a power of arrest under the terms of an order, may apply for the order, or the power of arrest, to be discharged or varied (1996 Act s.157(3), (4)).

8.128 Children. An injunction cannot usually be made against a child, as the means of enforcing it are imprisonment, fine or sequestration of assets, and only a fine or sequestration are available against a child (*Wookey v Wookey*, 1991). An injunction can be obtained against a teenager in work, however, if the landlord provides evidence of his income (*G v Harrow LBC*, 2004). If this is not possible, the landlord may consider obtaining an antisocial behaviour order against the child (8.129)

Antisocial behaviour orders

8.129 Acting in an antisocial manner. An antisocial behaviour order ("ASBO") may be sought against a person aged 10 or over who has acted in an antisocial manner, i.e. in a manner "that causes or is likely to cause harassment, alarm or distress to one or more persons not of the same household as himself", if the order is necessary to protect persons from further such behaviour by the individual (Crime and Disorder Act 1998 ("1998 Act") s.1(1)).

8.130 Use of the phrase "likely to cause" enables someone other than the victim of the behaviour to give evidence, particularly professional witnesses who can provide evidence to a court where victims feel unable to come forward for fear of reprisals or intimidation.

8.131 Who can apply for an ASBO. An application for an ASBO can only be made by a relevant authority, which is one of the following (1998 Act s.1):

- any council for the local government area; in a two-tier area, either the district or the county council;

- any chief police officer, any part of whose area lies within the local government area in question;

- the chief constable of the transport police;

- a registered social landlord if the antisocial behaviour affects residents in or visitors to premises which it owns or manages;

- a housing action trust if the antisocial behaviour affects residents in or visitors to premises which it owns or manages.

8.132 Consultation. An authority wishing to apply for an ASBO must first consult each of the other relevant authorities (1998 Act s.1E). The police must consult the council for the local government area and vice versa. A registered social landlord or housing action trust must consult both the council and the police.

8.133 Application. A free-standing application for an ASBO is made by complaint to the magistrates' court in whose area the alleged behaviour took place.

8.134 An application may be made, however, in the course of any other county court proceedings (1998 Act s.1B). Thus, a landlord bringing possession proceedings might include in those proceedings an application for an ASBO against a child of the tenant.

8.135 Civil proceedings. Proceedings for an application for an ASBO—as opposed to its enforcement for breach—are civil, not criminal (*Clingham v Kensington and Chelsea RLBC*, 2002). Accordingly, the civil rules of evidence apply (so that hearsay evidence is admissible) but the case needs to be proved to the criminal standard.

8.136 Criteria for making an ASBO. The court may make an ASBO if (1998 Act s.1(1) and (4)):

- the person has acted in an antisocial manner to one or more persons not of the same household as himself; and

- the order is necessary to protect persons from further such behaviour by the individual.

8.137 In deciding whether these conditions are satisfied, the court must disregard any act which the defendant shows was reasonable in the circumstances. What is reasonable is for the court to decide on the facts of the individual case.

8.138 Terms of ASBO. The ASBO may prohibit a person from doing anything described in the order. Accordingly, the terms must be negative in character, i.e. they must prohibit the person from doing something. The 1998 Act does not constrain the court as to the terms other than requiring that the prohibition(s) must be necessary to protect the public from further antisocial acts by the person. The court must specify a period for the duration of the ASBO, of a minimum of two years (1998 Act s.1(7)), but the order may be varied or discharged on application by either party.

8.139 Interim ASBO. Where an application for an ASBO has been made, the court can make an interim ASBO to last until the conclusion of the main application (1998 Act s.1D)). Such an order may be made where the court considers it just to do so (1998 Act s.1D(2)). The application may—with the permission of a justices clerk—be made without notice where it is necessary to do so (*R. (Manchester CC) v Manchester Magistrates' Court*, 2005). The order may be varied or discharged on application by either party.

8.140 Breach of ASBO. An ASBO (interim or final) is breached if, without reasonable excuse, the person subject to it does anything which he is prohibited from doing by it (1998 Act s.1(10)). Whether an excuse is reasonable is to be determined objectively. It is for the defendant to establish both the excuse and that it is reasonable. The standard of proof is the balance of probabilities. The existence of a reasonable excuse is a question of fact for the court to decide.

8.141 Criminal offence. Breach of an ASBO (interim or final) is a criminal offence, triable in the magistrates' court or the Crown Court. The maximum penalty that can be imposed on an adult by a magistrates' court is six months imprisonment and/or a fine not exceeding Level 5 on the standard scale (currently £5,000) and, in a Crown Court, five years' imprisonment or a fine or both.

8.142 Appeal. A person against whom an ASBO is made may appeal to the Crown Court, which is empowered to make such orders as are necessary to give effect to its decision on the appeal (1998 Act s.4(1)).

Closure orders

8.143 Class A drugs. Part 1 of the Antisocial Behaviour Act 2003 ("2003 Act") provides for closure orders (sometimes known as "crack-house orders") which allow premises used for the production, use or supply of Class A drugs to be closed down. Applications for closure orders can only be made by the police.

8.144 Closure notice. Before applying for a closure order, the police must consult the local authority for the area in which the premises are situated. Having done so, they must serve a closure notice on the premises warning of their intention to make an application, which must contain certain information (2003 Act s.1(4)). The notice must be fixed to the premises and must also be given to at least one person who appears to have responsibility for the premises.

8.145 Service of a closure notice must be authorised by an officer not below the rank of superintendent. To authorise service, he must have reasonable grounds for believing that the premises have been used in connection with the production, use or supply of Class A drugs within the past three months, and that the use of the premises is associated with disorder or serious nuisance to the public. He must also be satisfied that the local authority have been consulted and that reasonable steps have been taken to identify any person who lives in the premises or has control or responsibility for them (2003 Act s.1(2)).

8.146 Closure order. Within 48 hours of service of the closure notice, the police may apply for a closure order. The application is to the magistrates' court. The magistrates may make an order if satisfied that (2003 Act s.2(3)):

- the premises have been used in connection with the production, use or supply of Class A drugs;
- the use of the premises is associated with disorder or serious nuisance to the public; and
- an order is necessary to prevent the occurrence of disorder or serious nuisance.

8.147 The magistrates may adjourn the application for a maximum of 14 days to allow an occupier of the premises, or any other person with an interest in the premises, to show why the order should not be made (2003 Act s.2(6)).

8.148 Criminal offence. A person commits an offence if he remains on, or enters, premises in contravention of the order without reasonable excuse (2003 Act s.4). The offence is punishable by a maximum of six months' imprisonment and/or a fine.

8.149 Appeal. A person served with the closure notice or any other person with an interest in the premises may—within 21 days—appeal against the order to the Crown Court (2003 Act s.6).

CHAPTER NINE

Break-up of Relationship

Introduction

9.01 Housing law and relationship breakdown. In this chapter, we shall consider in outline only (see Introduction on p.viii) some of the law as it relates to housing in the event of the break-up of a relationship. This is in one sense an artificial study, because decisions cannot and will not be taken on the basis of housing law, or law itself, alone. There will be many other considerations to bring to bear, including that of the desirability of exercising particular rights and (always) the best interests of any children of the relationship. The law affecting domestic breakdown is substantial, and a study in its own right; the purpose of this chapter is merely to indicate some of the possibilities which it raises.

Outline

9.02 Relevant provisions. There is a number of relevant provisions which are considered briefly in this chapter:

- the Matrimonial Causes Act 1973, which contains broad powers to divide up matrimonial property on divorce, separation or nullity proceedings;

- the Civil Partnership Act 2004, which contains broad powers to divide up property on dissolution, separation or nullity proceedings;

- home rights under the Family Law Act 1996, which gives rights to spouses and civil partners to occupy the home during the currency of a marriage;

- occupation rights under the Family Law Act 1996, which gives the court power to regulate who may occupy the home in the case of spouses, ex-spouses, civil partners, former civil partners and cohabitees; the extent of the powers depend on whether the applicant has a legal right to occupy the home or not;

- non-molestation orders under the Family Law Act 1996, which provide protection against violence and other molestation;

- transferring tenancies under the Family Law Act 1996, giving the court power to transfer tenancies between spouses, former spouses, civil partners, former civil partners and cohabitees;

- the Matrimonial and Family Proceedings Act 1984, which deals with divorce or legal separation in another country;

- the Children Act 1989, which regulates the residence of children on relationship breakdown.

9.03 Further considerations

- Matrimonial and family proceedings have to be brought in a properly accredited court.

- When women are fleeing violence, they may apply as homeless, and it is important to consider the provisions of the Housing Act 1996 Pt 7.

- When re-housing, landlords must comply with the Sex Discrimination Act 1975.

9.04 Cumulative provisions. None of these Acts or laws is mutually exclusive: it will be common for provisions contained in more than one Act to apply in the same case. In addition, the courts have a fairly broad discretion to make such orders as are considered appropriate at any stage in proceedings; interim orders are commonplace. It is also necessary to consider the common law position, and the rights of any spouse or cohabitee under trust law (set out at 1.23–1.29, above).

Relevant provisions

1. MATRIMONIAL CAUSES ACT 1973

9.05 Division of property. It is this Act which contains the broad powers which a court has to divide up matrimonial property when a marriage is in the course of breaking up or has broken up. These powers are only exercisable between married partners. They can be exercised during the course of divorce, separation or nullity proceedings.

9.06 The court has power to apportion property between the parties and, if necessary, to order that property, including a home, be transferred from the name of one party to that of another or be sold (Matrimonial Causes Act 1973 ("MCA 1973") ss.24 and 24A). Note that the Family Law Act 1996 contains amendments to these provisions, which amendments are not, however, yet in force.

9.07 Former position. At one time, a wife who did not work and who had not contributed financially to the value of the property was not entitled as of right to any share in the property when the marriage broke up. She had to rely on common law provisions, if there was any direct financial contribution (1.27). She might, of course, have been entitled to maintenance, and there may have been a settlement which took the form of a transfer of ownership of the matrimonial home. Alternatively, property might be transferred into her name, but for the benefit of children of the marriage, in which case she would become the trustee of it herself, but only the trustee, which could have serious implications when children reached the age of majority.

9.08 Relevant considerations. Over the years, however, the courts came to recognise that the contribution of the non-earning spouse could not be measured purely in terms of direct financial contribution. A husband's earning power is enhanced by the provision of domestic services by the wife who remains at home, including but not exclusively, those involved in care of the children. Similarly, the courts came to recognise that a woman should not live with and be dependent upon her husband for a period of time and suddenly be discarded by him without any further provision for her accommodation or support.

9.09 Use of section 24. Accordingly, s.24 may be used to divide up matrimonial property, including the matrimonial home, in proportions which do not necessarily reflect the limited financial or quasi-financial considerations to which the common law will be limited.

9.10 These rights are mainly of interest only to owner-occupiers, even though a court can order the transfer of a tenancy under these provisions (*Hale v Hale*, 1975; *Newlon Housing Trust v Alsulaimen*, 1998) regardless of whether the tenancy is protected or not. But it seems likely that this will only be possible if there is no provision in the tenancy agreement prohibiting assignment. The powers could not be used in connection with a licence, however, as a licence does not constitute "property" which a court can transfer.

9.11 Section 24A. While s.24 permits adjustment of property rights, e.g. transfer between the parties, s.24A permits the court to order sale of the home, so that the proceeds may be divided between the parties.

9.12 Criteria for making an order. When deciding whether or not to make an order for adjustment or sale, the MCA 1973 s.25 sets out a number of matters to which the court must have regard. These include the income, earning capacity and other financial resources each party has or is likely to have in the forseeable future, the financial needs, obligations and responsibilities each party is taking on, the age of the parties and duration of the marriage, any physical or mental disability, and the conduct of the parties (whatever its nature), but only if it is such that in the opinion of the court it would be inequitable to disregard it.

9.13 Dealing with the home. Section 37(2) prevents one spouse trying to dispose of or otherwise deal with the assets once the other spouse has commenced proceedings. Section 37(2)(b) relates to "dispositions" of property, and it has been held that the service of a notice to quit by one joint tenant (1.204, above) is not a disposition for the purposes of the MCA 1973: *Newlon Housing Trust v Alsulaimen*, 1998. It has been suggested, however, without being decided, that s.37(2)(a), which provides a broader power to prevent "dealing" with the property and/or the inherent powers of the court, may be used to prohibit the service of a notice by a spouse (*Bater v Greenwich LBC*, 1999).

2. CIVIL PARTNERSHIP ACT 2004

9.14 Division of property. The court has similar powers to divide up property when a civil partnership is in the course of breaking up or has broken up (Civil Partnership Act 2004 ("CPA 2004") Sch.5). These powers may be exercised during the course of dissolution, separation or nullity proceedings.

9.15 As under the MCA 1973, the court has power to apportion property between the parties and, if necessary, to order that a home be transferred from the name of one civil partner to the other (CPA 2004 Sch.5 Pt 2) or be sold (CPA 2004 Sch.5 Pt 3). When deciding whether or not to make an order for adjustment or sale, the court must have regard to the same factors as are relevant under the MCA 1973 (CPA 2004 Sch.5, Pt 5; see 9.12). Likewise, there are provisions preventing a civil partner disposing or otherwise dealing with assets once the other civil partner has commenced proceedings (CPA 2004 Sch.5 Pt 14 para.13).

3. HOME RIGHTS UNDER THE FAMILY LAW ACT 1996

9.16 Home rights. The Family Law Act 1996 ("FLA 1996") introduced the concept of "matrimonial homes rights". These rights are now called "home rights", reflecting the fact that they are now also enjoyed by civil partners. The rights arise where one spouse or civil partner has the right to occupy a dwelling-house by virtue of ownership of the property, tenancy or a contractual licence, and the other does not.

9.17 In those circumstances, the spouse or civil partner who does not have legal rights over the property is given the right not to be excluded by the other from occupation of the home without an order of the court (FLA 1996 s.30(1), (2)).

9.18 Such an order will normally be made in the course of matrimonial or dissolution proceedings dealing with a number of considerations, but it could be made on application under this Act alone. The court also has power to make an order permitting a spouse or civil partner who has been wrongfully evicted or excluded from the home to re-enter. The court can make the order in respect of part only of the premises, e.g. excluding a husband from the residential part of the premises but allowing him to carry on his business in another part.

9.19 Effect of terminating tenancy. These rights under s.30 do not prevent a tenant from otherwise validly terminating his tenancy. Thus, if the spouse who is the tenant validly surrenders that tenancy (*Sanctuary Housing Association v Campbell*, 1999) or serves a notice to quit (*Harrow LBC v Johnstone*, 1997), there are no rights which can be protected under this provision.

9.20 Acceptance of payments. Where the person with home rights (9.16) takes over mortgage or rent payments under these provisions, the landlord or mortgage company is obliged to accept them as though they were made by the owner-occupier, tenant or licensee (FLA 1996 s.30(3), (4) and (5)).

9.21 Registrable right of occupation. A person who has home rights (9.16) over an owner-occupied home is entitled to register these rights as a charge on the dwelling (FLA 1996 s.31). The effect of this is that, if the house is sold, the purchaser buys it subject to the right of occupation, and is deemed to have known that the person was and can remain in occupation. This is to prevent, for example, a husband selling the home over the head of a wife, before a court has an opportunity to make any order for transfer.

4. OCCUPATION RIGHTS UNDER THE FAMILY LAW ACT 1996

9.22 Spouses, cohabitees and associated persons. While basic matrimonial homes rights have been dealt with above, the FLA 1996 also makes provision for occupation rights to be enforced where the parties are already divorced or where they are merely cohabiting, and indeed even if they are only "associated persons".

9.23 Associated person. A person is associated with another if:

- they are or have been married to each other;
- they are or have been civil partners of each other;
- they are cohabitants or former cohabitants (see 9.24);
- they live or have lived in the same household, otherwise than merely by reason of one of them being the other's employee, tenant, lodger or boarder (this would include, for example, carers);
- they are relatives;
- they have agreed to marry one another;
- they have entered into a civil partnership agreement;
- they are both parents of, or have or had parental responsibility for, the same child;
- they are both parties to other family proceedings (FLA 1996 s.62).

9.24 For these purposes, cohabitants are a couple who, although neither married to each other nor civil partners, are living together as husband and wife or as if they were civil partners (FLA 1996 s.62(1)).

9.25 Termination by tenant. FLA distinguishes between those applicants with legal rights of occupation and those with no such rights. The same point made above (9.19) in relation to matrimonial homes rights not preventing a tenant from validly terminating the tenancy also apply to occupation rights.

9.26 Applicants with legal rights. Where an applicant has a legal right to occupy the home (as an owner, tenant or contractual licensee), or is entitled to occupy under home rights (9.16), he may apply for an occupation order in relation to a dwelling-house which was or is his home or was intended to be his home, e.g. where a home has been bought for renovation but not moved into against an ex-spouse, former civil partner, current or former cohabitee or another associated person (above, 9.23).

9.27 The court has power to make one of the following orders (FLA s.33):

1. enforcing the applicant's entitlement to remain in occupation;

2. requiring the associated person to permit the applicant to enter and remain in the home;

3. regulating the occupation by either or both parties;

4. limiting the legal right to occupy of the associated person;

5. requiring the associated person to leave the home; and

6. excluding the associated person from a defined area around the home.

9.28 Criteria. In deciding whether to make an order under s.33, the court must have regard to all the circumstances including:

• the housing needs and housing resources of each of the parties and of any relevant child;

• the financial resources of the parties;

- the likely effect of any decision on the health, safety or well-being of the parties or any relevant child; and

- the conduct of the parties towards each other.

9.29 Former spouses and civil partners. Where the former spouse or civil partner does not have legal rights but is in occupation of the home, he or she may apply for an order for a specified period excluding the other former spouse or civil partner from the home, or giving him or her the right not to be evicted or excluded from the home. If not in occupation, the applicant may be given the right to enter and occupy. In either case, any of the orders set out at 9.27(3)–(6) may also be granted.

9.30 The criteria to be applied in making an order where the applicant is a former spouse are as set out in 9.28 above, with the addition of:

- the length of time since the parties ceased to live together;

- the length of time since the marriage or civil partnership was dissolved or annulled;

- the existence of any pending proceedings which will adjust the legal rights in the home, e.g. under the MCA 1973 or CPA 2004.

9.31 In the unlikely event of neither party having any legal rights to occupy the home, e.g. where a mortgage company has obtained a possession order but is allowing a period of grace, a short-term order excluding one former spouse or civil partner and allowing the other into possession may be made under the FLA 1996 s.37.

9.32 Cohabitants. Where one cohabitant has legal rights to occupy the home, and the other does not, the party with no rights may apply to the court for any of the orders set out at 9.27(3)–(6) (FLA 1996 s.36). Former cohabitants may also apply.

9.33 The criteria to be used in deciding whether to make an order are the same as those set out at 9.28, above, together with the following:

1. the nature of the parties' relationship (including the level of commitment involved in it);

2. the length of time during which they have cohabited;

3. whether there are or have been any children who are children of both parties or for whom both parties have or have had parental responsibility;

4. the length of time which has elapsed since the parties ceased to live together;

5. any pending legal proceedings in relation to the home, e.g. under the Children Act 1989; 9.48.

9.34 As with former spouses or civil partners, where neither has any legal occupation rights (9.31), short-term orders may be made (FLA 1996 s.38).

9.35 Additional orders. When making an occupation order (other than in cases where neither party has any legal occupation rights), the court may also require one party to repair and maintain the home and pay the rent or mortgage, or other outgoings (FLA 1996 s.40).

9.36 The court may also order the party who is given occupation to make payments to the other party, where that person would otherwise be legally entitled to occupy the home. Orders may also be made in relation to furniture (FLA 1996 s.40).

5. NON-MOLESTATION ORDERS UNDER THE FAMILY LAW ACT 1996

9.37 Earlier provisions. Statutory powers to protect against molestation were originally introduced in the 1970s. Two Acts—the Domestic Violence and Matrimonial Proceedings Act 1976 and the Domestic Proceedings and Magistrates Courts Act 1978—created two separate jurisdictions, the former in the county court and the latter in the magistrates' court. One of the purposes of the Family Law Act 1996 was to unify this jurisdiction. The FLA 1996 also significantly widens the availability of molestation orders through the concept of "associated persons", who may apply for such an order.

9.38 Content of orders. A non-molestation order is one which prohibits a respondent from molesting another person with whom he is associated (9.23) and/or from molesting a relevant child (FLA 1996 s.42(1)).

9.39 Applications. An application for a molestation order may be made by a person associated with the respondent or in the course of other family proceedings (FLA 1996 s.42(2)). An order can be made without notice where the court considers it just and convenient to do so (FLA 1996 s.45).

9.40 Molestation. Molestation is not defined by the Act, nor was it in earlier legislation. It is a wider term than violence, and can include pestering and harassment. In *Horner v Horner*, 1982, it was held that handing the claimant menacing letters and intercepting her on her way to work amounted to molestation. In *Johnson v Walton*, 1990, sending partially nude photographs of the claimant to a national newspaper, to cause her harm, was also molestation.

9.41 Power of arrest. The court has an additional power; to "back" the injunction for arrest. This means that a police officer can arrest, without warrant, any person whom he suspects is in breach of an order under the Act. The person must be brought back before the judge within 24 hours. This power can, however, only be used where there has been actual violence or the threat of violence (FLA 1996 s.47).

6. TRANSFER OF TENANCY UNDER THE FAMILY LAW ACT 1996

9.42 Transfer of tenancy. The court has power to order the transfer of tenancies under the FLA 1996 s.53 and Sch.7, between spouses, former spouses, civil partners, former civil partners, cohabitants and former cohabitants (9.24).

9.43 The tenancy must have been the home of the parties concerned. The tenancies which may be transferred are protected or statutory tenancies under the Rent Act 1977, statutory tenancies under the Rent (Agriculture) Act 1976, secure tenancies under the Housing Act 1985, assured and assured agricultural occupancies within the Housing Act 1988, and introductory tenancies within the Housing Act 1996.

9.44 Criteria. In deciding whether to make a transfer, the court must consider the circumstances in which the tenancy was granted, and the criteria set out at 9.27(1)–(3) above. Where cohabitants are involved the courts must also consider those at 9.33(1)–(4).

9.45 Statutory tenancies. Although transfer may take place after divorce, or dissolution or the cohabitation, the law is unclear as to whether a transfer order can effectively be made after decree absolute if the tenancy is statutory and the tenant-spouse is no longer in occupation. From the one case which has touched upon this point (*Lewis v Lewis*, 1985), it would seem that it cannot. For this reason it is essential to seek the order before decree absolute. The same powers apply to Housing Act secure and Housing Act assured tenancies, but there are similar difficulties if a divorce is already final or the cohabitant tenant has moved out, since it will cease to be secure/assured if the tenant is not occupying it as his only or principal home (3.32, 4.22).

7. MATRIMONIAL AND FAMILY PROCEEDINGS ACT 1984

9.46 Relationship to foreign orders. This Act is intended to deal with divorce or legal separation in another country but which is entitled to be recognised as valid in this, where one of the parties is domiciled or has been habitually resident in this, or either or both of the parties had at the date of application under the Act an interest in a dwelling-house in this country which has at some time during the marriage been a matrimonial home (ss.12 and 15).

9.47 The Act permits applications for financial relief, of various kinds, including (1984 Act s.17) a property adjustment order under ss.24 of the 1973 Act (9.05), sale under s.24A of that Act, and (1984 Act s.22) transfer of tenancy under the 1996 Act (9.42).

8. CHILDREN ACT 1989

9.48 Orders. Under the Children Act 1989 there is a number of specific orders—"contact order", "prohibited steps order", "residence order" and "specific issue order"—which may be sought in proceedings under any of the above Acts, or under the inherent jurisdiction of the High Court in relation to children, some of which orders e.g. "an order settling the arrangements to be made as to the person with whom a child is to live", i.e. a residence order, will concern housing.

9.49 If such an order is sought during proceedings under these Acts, the general principles of the Children Act 1989 s.11 will be applied, and ancillary powers will be available, e.g. a family assistance order under s.16. In general terms, the Act does not substantively alter the description in the foregoing paragraphs of this chapter, nor is it possible here to describe its terms in any detail.

Further considerations

1. WHICH COURT?

9.50 Accredited courts. All matrimonial proceedings have to be brought in a properly accredited court. The High Court has power to conduct matrimonial proceedings which means that, in London, the Family Division of the High Court will hear the case, and—in other cities where the High Court sits—the case will be brought in the Divorce Registry.

9.51 Some county courts, however, also have power to hear matrimonial disputes, provided that they have been listed as a divorce county court. Under the Family Law Act, the court is defined as "the High Court, a county court or a magistrates' court" (FLA 1996 s.57(1)). For cases involving transfer of tenancies (9.44), the court excludes the magistrates' court.

9.52 The Lord Chancellor has power to specify by order the level of court at which proceedings may or must be commenced.

2. RE-HOUSING

9.53 Homelessness. A person who leaves the domestic home because of violence or the fear of violence is considered to be homeless for the purposes of Pt 7 of the Housing Act 1996.

9.54 In deciding whether it was reasonable for the applicant to continue to occupy the home for the purposes of deciding homelessness or intentional homelessness, authorities may not take into account the fact that the applicant could have taken proceedings under the provisions considered in this chapter, unless they are in fact proceedings which have commenced or which are going to commence (*Bond v Leicester CC*, 2001; 10.24).

9.55 Discrimination. A woman who is not re-housed by the local authority may have difficulties finding anywhere else to live. She should bear in mind the provisions of the Sex Discrimination Act 1975 which make it unlawful for those concerned in the management, sale or rental of property to treat a woman any less favourably than they would treat a man, e.g. by refusing to grant a mortgage to a woman, or adding some term such as a demand for a guarantor for rent or mortgage payments.

9.56 Exemptions. This Act does not apply to resident landlords or buildings so small that they are either subdivided into no more than three separate units of accommodation, or can only accommodate a maximum of six people within them. A housing association set up to cater for the needs of one sex only, e.g. single mothers, female ex-prisoners, male ex-mental patients, etc. is also exempt from the Act.

9.57 Court. Unlawful discrimination can be the subject of a normal county court action.

CHAPTER TEN

Homelessness and Allocations

Introduction

10.01 Homelessness. Since 1977, local authorities have been under a duty to secure that accommodation is made available for many of those who are homeless. The provisions, first contained in the Housing (Homeless Persons) Act 1977, were later consolidated into Pt 3 of the Housing Act 1985 ("1985 Act"). Major changes were made by Pt 7 of the Housing Act 1996 ("1996 Act") and further amendments by the Homelessness Act 2002.

10.02 Allocations. In large part because of the extent to which housing the homeless was affecting the allocation of housing stock, Pt 6 of the 1996 Act also introduced a new regime governing the allocation of housing, which was also amended by the Homelessness Act 2002. Because of this link between the two Parts, they are both considered in this chapter.

Outline

10.03 Homelessness duties

- Part 7 places an obligation on local housing authorities to secure that suitable accommodation is made available for a person who is homeless, in priority need of accommodation and who did not become homeless intentionally, subject to the requirements of Pt 6 as to allocation of their own accommodation.

- The obligation is the peak housing duty under Pt 7, but permanent housing will normally only be made available once the applicant is allocated accommodation under Pt 6.

- The obligation is subject to local connection provisions which permit one authority, in some circumstances, to pass the responsibility for complying with the legislation to another authority (ss.193(2) and 198(1)).

● Subject to exceptions set out in regulations, persons from abroad are excluded from assistance if they are subject to immigration control. Regulations also provide that some persons from abroad are excluded from assistance even though they are not subject to immigration control.

● Since April 2000, asylum seekers have likewise been excluded from assistance, but they may be provided with accommodation under a scheme operated by the National Asylum Support Service.

● There are also obligations in respect of those who are not yet homeless, those who do not have a priority need, those who have a priority need but become homeless intentionally, and those who may be the responsibility of another authority while the position is resolved.

10.04 Additional homeless duties

● Authorities have duties to make enquiries, to notify applicants of their decisions and the reasons for them, and to protect the property of the homeless.

● Where there is no duty under Pt 7, duties to accommodate or assist may arise under other legislation such as the Children Act 1989 and the National Assistance Act 1948.

● There are ancillary provisions governing obtaining accommodation by deception, and funding voluntary agencies.

● There are provisions for the internal review of decisions and an appeal to the county court on a point of law.

● The Homelessness Act 2002 introduced a new strategic duty requiring authorities to formulate a homelessness strategy.

10.05 Allocation duties

● Local authorities no longer need to maintain a housing register governing the allocation of housing, whether their own or by way of nomination to another landlord's stock, but they must maintain a scheme to ensure that housing is preferentially (although not exclusively) allocated to those statutorily defined as being most in need of it.

- The allocation scheme must include a statement of the authority's policy on offering applicants a choice of housing accommodation or an opportunity to express their preferences as to the housing to be allocated.

- Certain persons from abroad are excluded from allocation, as are those whom an authority decide to treat as ineligible on the ground of antisocial behaviour, although there are provisions enabling the latter class to reapply if the applicant considers that he should no longer be excluded on this ground.

10.06 Additional allocation duties

- Authorities have to make advice and information about allocations freely available.

- The allocation scheme has to be framed so as to afford applicants the information that will allow them to assess how their applications are likely to be treated, whether accommodation is likely to be made available under it and, if so, when it is likely to become available.

- Applicants have to be notified of decisions, and there is provision for internal review, although not for appeal to the county court (on a point of law or otherwise).

- Before adopting a scheme, or making major changes to it, authorities must consult with registered social landlords with whom they have nomination arrangements.

- There are ancillary provisions governing false statements.

Homelessness

10.07 Key concepts. The approach adopted here is to deal first of all with the key concepts contained in Pt 7, before matching them to the duties which Pt 7 imposes, considering separately and under their own headings the ancillary provisions and those governing review and appeal.

10.08 Definitions. The key definitions are:

- authorities;

- eligibility for assistance;

- homelessness;

- priority need;
- intentional homelessness; and
- local connection.

10.09 Duties. The duties which have to be considered are:

- preliminary duties;
- principal duties; and
- local connection provisions.

10.10 Other matters. The other matters which must be considered are:

- duties under other Acts;
- protection of property;
- homelessness strategies;
- advice, information and voluntary organisations;
- Code of Guidance;
- review and appeal;
- criminal offences; and
- co-operation between authorities.

1. AUTHORITIES

10.11 Three classes. Part 7 refers (1996 Act s.217) to three classes of authority: local housing authorities, relevant authorities and social services authorities.

10.12 Local housing authority. In a two-tier area of local government, "local housing authority" means the district council; otherwise, the local housing authority will be the unitary authority, the London Borough Council or the Common Council of the City of London, or (in Wales) the (unitary) county or county borough council (1985 Act s.1, as amended).

10.13 Contracting out. Some of the functions of the local housing authority may, however, be contracted out: see Local Authorities (Contracting out of Allocation of Housing and Homelessness Functions) Order 1996 (SI 1996/3205).

10.14 Relevant authorities. "Relevant authority" means, in England and Wales, a local housing authority and a social services authority (1996 Act s.217).

10.15 Social services authority. In a two-tier area of local government, "social services authority" means the county council; otherwise, it means the unitary authority, London Borough Council or the Common Council of the City of London, and (in Wales) the (unitary) county or county borough council (1996 Act s.217 and Local Authority Social Services Act 1970 s.1, as amended).

2. ELIGIBILITY FOR ASSISTANCE

10.16 Persons from abroad. "Persons from abroad" are ineligible for assistance if they are subject to immigration control under the Asylum and Immigration Act 1996, unless requalified by regulations (s.185)(1), (2)). The regulations govern requalification based on issues of immigration status. Examples of those who are subject to immigration control but who are nevertheless eligible for assistance include refugees and those who have been granted exceptional leave to remain: Allocation of Housing and Homelessness (Eligibility) Regulations 2006 (SI 2006/1294) reg.5 or Homelessness (Wales) Regulations 2006 (SI 2006/2646) reg.5.

10.17 In addition, the regulations provide that certain persons from abroad who are not subject to immigration control are ineligible for assistance: reg.6 of SI 2006/1294 or reg.4 of SI 2006/2646. The primary effect of the provisions is to exclude from assistance EU citizens unless they are exercising their rights under the EU Treaty, e.g. to work in the UK.

10.18 Information. In order to reach a decision on eligibility, a local housing authority may seek such information as they require from the Secretary of State, who is bound to provide it (and— whether or not the original request for information was in writing—to provide it in writing if the authority in writing ask for it so to be provided) (s.187(1) and (2)).

10.19 The Secretary of State is under an additional duty to notify the authority in writing if it subsequently appears to him that any application, decision or other change of circumstance has affected the status of a person about whom he had previously provided information (s.187(3)).

10.20 Asylum seekers. Since April 3, 2000, all new asylum seekers have been ineligible for assistance under the homelessness provisions. Instead, they may obtain assistance from the National Asylum Support Service ("NASS") under the Asylum Act 1999 Pt 6. No support can be provided if the claim for asylum was not made as soon as reasonably practicable after the asylum seeker arrived in the UK, unless it is necessary to provide assistance in order to prevent a breach of a person's rights under the European Convention on Human Rights, e.g. the prohibition on degrading treatment in Art.3 (National Immigration and Asylum Act 2002 s.55; *R. (Limbuela) v Secretary of State for the Home Department*, 2004).

3. HOMELESSNESS

10.21 No rights in accommodation. A person is homeless for the purposes of Pt 7 if he has no accommodation in the UK or elsewhere, and a person is deemed to lack accommodation if there is no accommodation:

- which he is entitled to occupy by virtue of an interest in it, e.g. ownership, tenancy; or
- which he is entitled to occupy by virtue of an order of a court, e.g. in the course of domestic proceedings (see Chapter 9); or
- which he has an express or implied licence to occupy, e.g. service occupants, members of the family; or
- which he is occupying as a residence by virtue of any enactment or rule of law giving him the right to remain in occupation or restricting the right of any other person to recover possession of it (1996 Act s.175(1)).

10.22 Available accommodation. Accommodation is only available for an applicant's occupation if it is available for him, together with any other person who normally resides with him as a member of his family, and any other person who might reasonably be expected to reside with him (1996 Act s.176). Persons from abroad, disqualified for assistance in their own right, will also fall to be disregarded when considering availability (10.16–10.17), even though this provision has been held to be discriminatory under Art.14 of the European Convention on Human Rights (*R. (Morris) v Westminster CC*, 2006). Accessibility to accommodation, e.g. whether the applicant can travel to it, is a relevant factor in determining whether it is available (*Begum (Nipa) v Tower Hamlets LBC*, 1999).

10.23 Accommodation reasonable to continue to occupy.
Accommodation is disregarded if it is not accommodation which it
would be reasonable to continue to occupy (1996 Act s.175(3)), e.g.
if it is in such bad condition that no one could be expected to stay
in it. When deciding whether or not it would be reasonable for a
person to remain in occupation, an authority to which application
has been made can take into account the general housing circumstances prevailing in their area (1996 Act s.177(2)), i.e. whether
others are living in accommodation just as bad. The meaning of
the term "reasonable to continue to occupy" is considered below,
in relation to intentional homelessness (10.66), as the purpose of
this part of the definition is in substance to secure that if an
applicant could quit accommodation without being considered
homeless intentionally, he ought to be treated as, in effect, already
homeless.

10.24 Violence. It is also not reasonable to continue to occupy
accommodation if it is probable that to do so will lead to violence
(domestic or otherwise) against the applicant, or against someone
who normally resides with the applicant as a member of his family,
or against anyone else who might reasonably be expected to reside
with the applicant (s.177(1)). Violence means actual physical
violence from another person (*Danesh v Kensington & Chelsea
RLBC*, 2006) or threats of violence from another person which are
likely to be carried out (s.177(1A)). In deciding whether it is
reasonable for an applicant to continue to occupy under s.177(1),
the only question the authority may ask is whether it is probable
that continued occupation of the accommodation will lead to
violence against that person; that is purely a question of fact
devoid of value judgments about what an applicant should or
should not do, e.g. whether he should take out an injunction
against the perpetrator: *Bond v Leicester CC*, 2001.

10.25 Domestic violence. Violence is domestic if it is from a
person who is associated with the victim (s.177(1A)).

10.26 Associated persons. Persons are associated if:

- they are or have been married to each other;
- they are cohabitants or former cohabitants (meaning a man
  and a woman who are living together without being married
  to one another);
- they live or have lived in the same household;
- they are relatives, meaning:

— parent, step-parent, child, step-child, grandparent or grandchild of a person or of that person's spouse or former spouse; or

— sibling, aunt or uncle, niece or nephew of a person or that person's spouse or former spouse, whether of full or half-blood, or by affinity;

• they have or had formerly agreed to marry;
• in relation to a child, each of the persons is a parent of the child, or has or has had parental responsibility (within the meaning of the Children Act 1989) for the child; and
• in relation to a child who has been adopted (or subsequently freed from adoption), if one person is a natural parent or the natural parent of a natural parent, and the other is the child, or is a person who has become a parent by adoption, or who has applied for an adoption order, or with whom the child was at any time placed for adoption (s.178).

10.27   Additional categories of homelessness. In addition, a person is homeless if he has accommodation which he is entitled to occupy, and which is available for his occupation, and which it is reasonable to continue to occupy, but:

• he cannot secure entry to it; or

• the accommodation consists of a movable structure, vehicle or vessel, designed or adapted for living in, and there is no place where he is entitled or permitted both to place it and to reside in it, i.e. houseboat, caravan (1996 Act s.175(2)).

10.28   Threatened with homelessness. A person is threatened with homelessness if it is likely that he will become homeless within 28 days (1996 Act s.175(4)).

10.29   Meaning of accommodation. Under the equivalent provisions of the 1985 Act, it was held that the only gloss which can be put on the word "accommodation" is that which the statute imports, i.e. availability (10.22) and reasonableness to continue to occupy (10.23). Other than that, it simply means "a place which can fairly be described as accommodation", *per* Lord Hoffman in *R. v Brent LBC Ex p. Awua*, 1996. (Note, however, that although a person may not be homeless because of this lowlevel test, he may still be threatened with homelessness.)

10.30   Homelessness and temporary accommodation. Before *Awua*, a number of cases which are still likely to be followed had also considered the meaning of accommodation. Thus, in *R. v Ealing LBC Ex p. Sidhu*, 1982 (not considered in *Awua*), the local authority held that a woman temporarily housed in a women's refuge was not homeless because she had a licence to occupy a room in the hostel. The court rejected this argument. Likewise, the court rejected the argument that a man who usually slept in a night shelter on a day-to-day basis but who could be turned away if the shelter was full at the time of his arrival, was not homeless: *R. v Waveney DC Ex p. Bowers*, 1982 (approved in *Awua*).

4. PRIORITY NEED

10.31 Statutory definition. A person has a priority need for accommodation under Pt 7 if:

- he has dependent children who are residing with him, or who might reasonably be expected to reside with him; or

- he, or anyone who resides or might reasonably be expected to reside with him, is vulnerable as a result of old age, mental illness or handicap or physical disability or other special reason; or

- she is a pregnant woman, or the applicant resides or might reasonably be expected to reside with a pregnant woman; or

- he is homeless or threatened with homelessness as a result of an emergency such as flood, fire or other disaster (1996 Act s.189).

10.32 Further classes. The Secretary of State may specify further classes of person as having a priority need for accommodation, or may amend or repeal any of the present classes (s.189(2)).

10.33 England. In England, the following additional classes have been specified in the Homelessness (Priority Need for Accommodation) (England) Order 2002 (SI 2002/2051):

1. all 16 and 17 year olds, provided they are not a relevant child (as defined by the Children Act 1989 s.23A) or owed a duty under the Children Act 1989 s.20;

2. any person who is aged 18 to 20 who at any time while 16 or 17 was, but is no longer, looked after, accommodated or fostered but not a relevant student (as defined by the Children Act 1989 s.24B(3));

3. those aged 21 or over who are vulnerable because they have previously been looked after, accommodated or fostered;

4. those who are vulnerable as a result of service in Her Majesty's regular armed forces;

5. those who are vulnerable as a result of having served a custodial sentence, having been committed for contempt of court or having been remanded in custody;

6. those who are vulnerable because they have had to cease to occupy accommodation because of violence or threats of violence which are likely to be carried out.

10.34 Wales. In Wales, this power has been exercised in the Homeless Persons (Priority Need) (Wales) Order (SI 2001/607) to specify:

- all those who are aged 18 or over, and under 21, if at any time while they were a child they were looked after, accommodated or fostered, or they are at particular risk of sexual or financial exploitation;

- all 16 and 17 year olds;

- those without dependent children who have been subject to domestic violence, who are at risk of such violence or who would be if they returned home;

- those who formerly served in the regular armed forces and have been homeless since leaving;

- former prisoners who have been homeless since leaving custody, provided they have a local connection (10.69) with the local housing authority.

10.35 Dependent children. Dependent children are usually treated as those still in full-time education or training, or otherwise up to the age of 16: *R. v Kensington and Chelsea RLBC Ex p. Amarfio*, 1995. Even where a 16 or 17 year old is financially independent, however, it is possible that he is dependent in other ways (*Amarfio*).

10.36 Residence. The issue is solely one of fact: are dependent children residing, or are there dependent children who ought reasonably be expected to reside, with the applicant? In *R. v Hillingdon LBC Ex p. Islam*, 1981 in the High Court, the authority suggested that priority need only arise if children both are residing, and might reasonably be expected to reside, with the applicant. But, as the court held, Pt 3 (now Pt 7) says "or".

10.37 Split families. It is not a requirement that the child is wholly dependent on—or wholly and exclusively residing with—the applicant; in a genuine case of split custody, an applicant may be in priority need even though the child is with him only for part of the week: *R. v Lambeth LBC Ex p. Vagliviello*, 1990. In *R. v Port Talbot BC Ex p. McCarthy*, 1990, however, it was held that where a father was granted staying access to his children, under an order of joint custody, but the mother had care and control of the children, the children were not necessarily to be treated as residing with their father. Again, where children were residing with their mother, even though they were dependent on their father and a joint residence order had been made under the Children Act 1989 s.8, it did not necessarily follow that the children were reasonably to be expected to reside with both parents (*R. v Oxford CC Ex p. Doyle*, 1997).

10.38 Custody. In *Sidhu* (10.30), the authority argued that until the applicant had what they called a "final" or "full" custody order, in the course of pending divorce proceedings, she need not be considered in priority need. The court held that custody was irrelevant to priority need, for a custody order can be varied at any time until the child reaches 18, or one parent may have custody, while another has care and control.

10.39 Children in priority need. A dependent child is not entitled to apply under the Act in his own right, and will not qualify as vulnerable (10.40) simply because of youth or any disability. Dependent children are expected to be provided for by those on whom they are dependent: *R. v Oldham LBC Ex p. G*, 1993.

10.40 Vulnerability. Vulnerability means "less able to fend for oneself so that injury or detriment will result where a less vulnerable man will be able to cope without harmful effects" (*R. v Waveney DC Ex p. Bowers*, 1983; *R. v Camden LBC Ex p. Pereira*, 1998; *Osmani v Camden LBC*, 2004). Authorities must compare an applicant's ability to fend for himself with that of an "ordinary homeless person"; and in doing so, they must apply the test on the basis that the applicant has become or will become street homeless rather than considering the applicant's ability to fend for himself while still housed (*Osmani*).

10.41 Assessing vulnerability. In *R. v Kensington & Chelsea RLBC, Hammersmith & Fulham LBC, Westminster CC, and Islington LBC Ex p. Kihara*, 1996, the Court of Appeal said that whether someone is vulnerable—for one of the stated reasons (10.31, 10.33)—should preferably be approached as a composite question rather than in two separate stages, i.e. it should not be approached by asking first whether there is vulnerability at all and, secondly and separately, whether that vulnerability (if any) is attributable to any of those factors.

10.42 Mental illness and handicap. A distinction may be drawn between mental illness, i.e. psychotic and "mere" mental handicap, although subnormality will not necessarily amount to vulnerability in every case (*R. v Bath CC Ex p. Sangermano*, 1984). Nor will every case of epilepsy render a person vulnerable (*R. v Reigate and Banstead BC Ex p. Di Domenico*, 1987).

10.43 Medical assessment. An authority are entitled to obtain their own medical advice as to an applicant's medical condition (*Hall v Wandsworth LBC*, 2004). If that advice raises new issues or calls the applicant's medical evidence into question, the applicant should be allowed an opportunity to comment on it. If the advice is merely intended to assist the authority in assessing the applicant's medical evidence, however, the authority do not have to disclose their advice before making a decision on the application (*Hall*). The authority must reach their own decision, however, and must not merely "rubber-stamp" a medical opinion on the applicant's medical condition, unless that condition is decisive on the question (vulnerability) that they are considering, e.g. where the existence of a medical condition is the only relevant issue (*R. v Lambeth LBC Ex p. Carroll*, 1987 and *R. v Wandsworth LBC Ex p. Banbury*, 1986).

10.44 Mental capacity. Where vulnerable, an applicant must have the capacity to understand and respond to the offer of accommodation, and to undertake its responsibilities. If incapable of doing so, he may not apply at all, notwithstanding his vulnerability (*R. v Tower Hamlets LBC Ex p. Begum*, 1993).

10.45 Other special reason. In *Kihara* (above), the Court of Appeal rejected an argument that "other special reason" was limited to the applicant's mental or physical characteristics. The category is free-standing, unrestricted by any notion of physical or mental weakness other than that which is inherent in the word "vulnerable". The word "special" imports a requirement that the housing difficulties faced by an applicant are of an unusual degree of gravity, enough to differentiate him from other homeless persons; it does not include financial impecuniosity by itself: an absence of means does not mark out one case from the generality of cases to a sufficient degree to render it "special".

10.46 Emergency. A person who has been unlawfully evicted from his home is not in priority need due to an emergency. If not actual flood or fire, the emergency must be of a similar nature which—while not needing to be a natural disaster—must encompass some physical damage to the home: *R. v Bristol CC Ex p. Bradic*, 1995 (see also *Noble v South Herefordshire DC*, 1983).

5. INTENTIONAL HOMELESSNESS

10.47 Principal definition. A person becomes homeless intentionally if he deliberately does anything or fails to do anything in consequence of which he ceases to occupy accommodation which is available for his occupation and which it would have been reasonable for him to continue to occupy (1996 Act s.191(1)).

10.48 Threatened with homelessness. Becoming threatened with homelessness intentionally is similarly defined (1996 Act s.196(1)). There is no distinction in principle between the two concepts (*Dyson v Kerrier DC*, 1980). (All future references to intentional homelessness may accordingly, and save where an express distinction is drawn, be taken to refer also to becoming threatened with homelessness intentionally.)

10.49 Different elements. The principal definition (10.47) of intentional homelessness incorporates a number of elements:

- something must be done deliberately, or there must be a deliberate failure to act;
- the act or omission must have a consequence;
- the consequence must be that accommodation ceases or will cease to be occupied;
- that accommodation must be, or have been, "accommodation available for [the] occupation" of the homeless person (see 10.22, above); and
- it must have been reasonable to continue in occupation of that accommodation (see 10.66, below).

10.50   Good faith.   An act or omission in good faith, on the part of a person who was unaware of any relevant fact, e.g. the availability of financial assistance towards rent, etc., the right to remain in occupation after notice to quit or expiry of tenancy, is not to be treated as deliberate for these purposes (1996 Act ss.191(2), 196(2)). Good faith in these circumstances can encompass honest blundering and carelessness, e.g. in a business deal, and should be contrasted with dishonesty (where there can be no question of good faith): *R. v Hammersmith & Fulham LBC Ex p. Lusi*, 1991. Whether an act is in good faith, and whether it is done in ignorance of relevant facts, are two questions which the authority must therefore consider separately (*O'Connor v Kensington & Chelsea RLBC*, 2004).

10.51   Whose conduct?   One preliminary question is "whose conduct is to be taken into account, when an application is by or on behalf of more than one person." In *R. v North Devon DC Ex p. Lewis*, 1980, a woman lived with a man by whom she had a child but to whom she was not married. He quit his job and in consequence lost his tied accommodation. When he applied as homeless, he was held to have become homeless intentionally. The woman then applied in her own right. The authority said two things: (a) that they did not have to consider her application, because she was governed by the decision on his application; and (b) that she had in any event acquiesced in his decision to quit his job, so that she, by association, had committed an act of intentionality in her own right. The court rejected the authority's first argument but upheld the second on the facts of the case. It would not, however, have been appropriate for her to be deemed to have acquiesced if she had done all she could to prevent his conduct, but he had gone ahead notwithstanding, e.g. a woman who has done all she can to prevent her husband spending the rent money on drink or otherwise.

10.52   Lewis applied.   In *R. v West Dorset DC Ex p. Phillips*, 1984, *Lewis* was applied so as to compel an authority to house a woman who turned on her husband during their homelessness interview and attacked him for spending money on drink. In *R. v Mole Valley DC Ex p. Burton*, 1988, the authority failed to consider that a wife had acted in good faith when she had believed her husband's assurances that they would be re-housed if he quit his job and accordingly lost his tied accommodation, for which reason their decision could not be upheld. In *R. v East Northamptonshire DC Ex p. Spruce*, 1988, it was said that a spouse's mere knowledge of, for example, rent or mortgages arrears would not be enough to amount to acquiescence, for he or she might have learned so late that the arrears were too big to do anything about.

10.53 Lewis not applied. In other cases, attempts to apply the *Lewis* principle have failed. In *R. v Nottingham CC Ex p. Cain*, 1995, in particular, the Court of Appeal held that an authority were entitled to infer that the applicant had known of her partner's conduct in withholding the rent, even though there was no direct evidence that she had done so. (The intentionality of parents cannot be circumvented by a child's application, as a dependent child is not in priority need in his own right: *R. v Oldham LBC Ex p. G*; *R. v Bexley LBC Ex p. B*, 1993; 10.39).

10.54 Deliberate act or omission. The definition does not require that the applicant deliberately became homeless so much as that he deliberately did (or failed to do) something as a result of which he became homeless. The word "deliberate" only governs the act or omission: *Devenport v Salford CC*, 1983. The link between the act and the homelessness must be judged objectively: *Robinson v Torbay BC*, 1982.

10.55 In consequence. The homelessness must be "in consequence of" the deliberate act or omission. This is a question of "cause and effect" (*Dyson v Kerrier DC*, 1980; *Din v Wandsworth LBC*, 1983). The principal issue which has arisen in practice is the attribution of present homelessness to past act or omission. That is to say there is commonly a past act which has or could have been the subject of a finding of intentionality, and the argument then becomes whether or not that act or omission is the cause of the present homelessness.

10.56 Cause and effect. A causal link may continue to subsist following the act of intentionality even though the applicant ceases to be homeless in the interim, e.g. because he finds some temporary accommodation from which he is subsequently evicted: *R. v Brent LBC Ex p. Awua*, 1996. The authority has to look back to the original cause of the homelessness and determine whether it was intentional (*Din*).

10.57 Prison. Commission of a criminal offence may be considered deliberate conduct, and lead to a finding of intentionality where it can properly be regarded as having caused the homelessness, e.g. where subsequent imprisonment leads to repossession of the home, i.e. for want of ability to pay rent. The test is whether the loss of accommodation could reasonably have been regarded at the time as a likely consequence of the commission of the offence (*R. v Hounslow LBC Ex p. R*, 1997; *Stewart v Lambeth LBC*, 2002)

10.58 Loss of tied accommodation. It will not always be appropriate to treat someone who has quit or been dismissed from his job and thus lost tied accommodation as intentionally homeless. There must be a sufficient link, or proximity, between the act which caused the loss of job, and the loss of accommodation (*R. v Thanet DC Ex p. Reeve*, 1981). A direct act, e.g. theft from an employer, which could reasonably be foreseen to lead to loss of job and accommodation, may well amount to intentional homelessness; loss of job through, for example, a period of incompetence, should, however, not do so.

10.59 Assessing loss of tied accommodation. The fact that someone appears voluntarily to have quit employment does not necessarily mean that he has become homeless intentionally: he may have been forced into it, so that his resignation was constructively dismissal (*R. v Thurrock BC Ex p. Williams*, 1982).

10.60 Burden in intentionality. If there is any doubt about whether or not someone has done a sufficiently direct act to qualify as intentionally homelessness, it should be resolved in the applicant's favour (*Williams*). In every case, it is for the authority to satisfy themselves that a person became homeless intentionally, not for an applicant to satisfy the authority that he did not do so (*Lewis*; *Williams*).

10.61 Grounds for possession. Rent arrears, non-payment of mortgage instalments, and nuisance and annoyance causing eviction (3.103–3.106, 4.122, 5.147–5.149) can qualify as acts of intentional homelessness, although in each case there must be sufficient proximity, or foreseeability, between act and loss of home. In each case, too, ignorance of ways of avoiding loss of the home will be a defence.

10.62 Arrears and resources. In *R. v LB Hillingdon Ex p. Tinn*, 1988, which only secondarily concerned this issue, it was said by the court that it could not be reasonable to continue to occupy accommodation if an applicant could not pay the rent or mortgage without depriving himself of the ordinary necessities of life, such as food, clothing, heat and transport. Authorities must therefore consider whether the applicant has adequate resources when deciding whether failure to pay the rent amounts to a deliberate act: *R. v Wandsworth LBC Ex p. Hawthorne*, 1994. In *R. v Leeds CC Ex p. Adamiec*, 1991, however, a sale before the commencement of possession proceedings by a building society was upheld as intentional, even though it was likely that, in the long run, the applicant would not have been able to afford to continue living in the house. See now the regulations relating to affordability which authorities must consider: the Homelessness (Suitability of Accommodation) Order 1996 (SI 1996/3204).

10.63 Breaking the chain of causation. Where an applicant has done a deliberate act which has caused homelessness, the question becomes how the chain of causation may be broken. It will be broken by a period of "settled accommodation" (*Din; Awua*). It may also be broken by other events, e.g. separation from husband or reduction in housing benefit payments, provided that the event is unconnected with the temporary nature of the accommodation (*R. v Camden LBC Ex p. Fahia*, 1997, in the Court of Appeal).

10.64 Settled accommodation. There is no judicial or other definition of settled accommodation but accommodation which is indefinite at its outset should qualify, although an intention that it should be indefinite will not always be sufficient where the accommodation is of a precarious nature (*R. v Merton LBC Ex p. Ruffle*, 1988). An assured shorthold may be settled depending on the circumstances of the case, e.g. whether the applicant knew that the tenancy was only for a fixed term of six months and would not be renewed (*Knight v Vale Royal BC*, 2004).

10.65 Available accommodation. Accommodation is only available for a person's accommodation if it is available for himself and for anyone with whom he might reasonably be expected to reside (1996 Act s.176).

10.66 Reasonable to continue to occupy. When considering whether or not it was reasonable for the applicant to remain in occupation of his former accommodation, the authority are entitled to have regard to the general circumstances prevailing in relation to housing in their own area (1996 Act s.177(2)), i.e. they may consider others who are putting up with bad housing conditions. This permits authorities to claim that applicants should have remained in what objectively may be considered appalling conditions. It means in practice that people can rarely safely quit their current accommodation on account of its physical condition without a real likelihood of a finding of intentionality.

10.67 Range of questions. In *R. v Hammersmith and Fulham LBC Ex p. Duro Rama*, 1983, it was said that "reasonable to continue to occupy" involves a range of questions, not confined to the condition of the housing formerly occupied, and in *R. v Tower Hamlets LBC Ex p. Monaf*, 1988, that it calls for a "balancing exercise" between the reasons for leaving accommodation and coming to the area where application has been made, and housing conditions in that area. In *R. v B Hillingdon LBC Ex p. H*, 1988, political and racial harassment was considered relevant to the question of reasonable to continue to occupy. When applicable, the specific provisions relating to violence will make it not reasonable to continue to occupy accommodation (10.23).

10.68 Collusive arrangements. There is one "added" definition of intentional homelessness. A person becomes homeless intentionally, or threatened with homelessness intentionally, if he enters into an arrangement under which he is required to cease to occupy accommodation which it would have been reasonable for him to continue to occupy, the purpose of which arrangement is to enable him to qualify for assistance under Pt 7, and there is no other, or independent, good reason for the actual or threatened homelessness (1996 Act ss.191(3), 196(3)).

6. LOCAL CONNECTION

10.69 Statutory definition. A person has a local connection with an area:

- because he is, or in the past was, normally resident in it and that residence was of choice; or

  — because he was employed in it; or
  — because of family associations; or
  — for any special circumstance (1996 Act s.199(1)).

10.70 Residence of choice. Residence is not "of choice" if:

- it is in consequence of service in the armed forces; or

- it is in consequence of detention under an Act of Parliament, e.g. imprisonment or compulsory in-patient (1996 Act s.199(3), (4)).

10.71 Employment. Employment does not count if it is employment in the armed forces (1996 Act s.199(2)).

10.72 Temporary accommodation. An applicant housed in temporary accommodation by an authority (under, for example, s.188; 10.97, below) will still be normally resident in that accommodation (*Mohamed v Hammersmith & Fulham LBC*, 2001).

10.73 Former asylum-seekers. A former asylum-seeker has a local connection with an area in England or Wales in which he was provided with accommodation under the Immigration and Asylum Act 1999 (10.20) unless:

- he was subsequently provided with accommodation under the 1999 Act in another authority's district; or

- the accommodation was in an accommodation centre provided by NASS (1996 Act s.199(6), (7), added by the Asylum and Immigration (Treatment of Claimants etc.) Act 2004).

10.74 Relation between local connection and grounds. The overriding term is "local connection", which must be attributable to one of the specified "grounds"; merely demonstrating that there is, for example, employment or family connection, without a finding sufficient to amount to a "local connection" will not be enough (*Re Betts*, 1983).

10.75 Timing of decision. Whether an applicant has a local connection or not is established as at the date of the decision, not the date of the application (*Mohamed v Hammersmith & Fulham LBC*, 2001). Furthermore, where the applicant seeks an internal review of the decision (see 10.168, below), it is the facts at the date of the decision which must be considered (*Mohamed*).

10.76 Conditions. The local connection provisions allow one housing authority to shift the burden of making accommodation available to another housing authority. The provisions apply when the authority are satisfied that the applicant is homeless (note: not merely threatened with homelessness), in priority need, and not homeless intentionally, and either:

- the applicant was—within the previous five years—placed in accommodation in their area by another authority, in pursuance of Pt 7 functions (1996 Act s.198(4)); Homelessness

Regulations 1996 (SI 1996/2754) reg.6; see also 10.122 for
the notification requirements imposed on the other authority at the time of the placement); or

● the authority consider that all of the following conditions
  applies:

  — neither the applicant nor anyone who might reasonably
    be expected to reside with him has a local connection
    with their area; and
  — the applicant or a person who might reasonably be
    expected to reside with him does have a local connec-
    tion with the area of another housing authority; and
  — neither the applicant nor any person who might reason-
    ably be expected to reside with him will run the risk of
    domestic violence in the area of the other authority
    (1996 Act s.198(1), (2)).

10.77 Further condition. In addition, a local connection referral may not be made where the applicant or any person who might
reasonably be expected to reside with him has suffered non-
domestic violence in the area of the other authority, and it is
probable that the return of the victim to that area will lead to
further violence of a similar kind against him (s.198(2A)).

10.78 Violence and domestic violence. These are defined in
the same terms as when determining whether or not it is reasonable to remain in occupation (s.198(3); 10.23–10.24).

10.79 Passing responsibility. The housing duty passes to the
other authority if the conditions are satisfied (1996 Act s.200(4)).
The other authority's obligation is to house under the 1996 Act
s.193 (10.107).

10.80 Retaining responsibility. The housing duty under s.193
remains with the notifying authority if the conditions are not
satisfied (1996 Act s.200(3)).

10.81 No local connection. If an applicant has no local connection with anywhere in England, Scotland or Wales, the local
connection provisions do not apply, and the burden of housing
will remain with the authority to which application is made (*R. v
Hillingdon LBC Ex p. Streeting*, 1980).

10.82 Interim accommodation and notification. Pending resolution of the question "which authority will have final responsibility", the authority to which the application is made will

provide temporary accommodation (1996 Act s.200(1)). Once the question has been decided, it is they who must notify the applicant of the decision and of the reasons for it, as well as of his right to request a review (and the time within which it must be requested; 10.170) (1996 Act s.200(2)). Notification is effected in the same way as under the 1996 Act s.184(6) (1996 Act s.200(6); 10.96). The temporary housing duty ceases when the notification is given, even if a review is requested, although the authority still have a discretion to continue to provide it pending review (1996 Act s.200(5)).

10.83 Arbitration. These provisions are clearly a breeding ground for differences of opinion between authorities. Part 7 provides elaborate machinery for the determination of disputes between them either by agreement or, if necessary, by reference to an independent arbitrator (1996 Act s.198(5)). An arbitration decision can nonetheless be the subject of internal review, and thence appeal on a point of law to the county court (10.168 *et seq.*) (1996 Act ss.198(5) and 202(1)(d), (e)).

10.84 "Merry-go-round". Decisions of the authority to which the application has been made on the issues of homelessness, priority need and intentionality are binding on an authority to whom they subsequently refer the application. This remains true even if the applicant had formerly applied to one authority, been found homeless intentionally, and moved on to apply to another authority; the second authority can still reach a decision, different from that of the first authority, that the applicant did not become homeless intentionally, and then invoke the local connection provisions to refer the applicant back (*R. v Slough BC Ex p. Ealing LBC*, 1980). This produces what has been described as a "merry-go-round", for the first authority will be bound by the decision of the second, notwithstanding that it contradicts their own, earlier decision. The proposition illustrates how views may differ as to whether or not someone has become homeless intentionally. There is nothing to stop an applicant applying to authority after authority in the hope of a favourable decision.

10.85 Enquiries by second authority. Where there has been no intervening change of circumstances, however, the authority to which the later application has been made must treat the application carefully and must give the authority which had made the earlier decision, and to which the applicant will be returned, an opportunity of discussing the case and, above all, of discussing any discrepancies in the explanations offered for the homelessness by the applicant (*R. v Tower Hamlets LBC Ex p. Camden LBC*, 1988). Before deciding to refer, the second authority must take into account the general housing circumstances in the area to which they are referring the application (*R. v Newham LBC Ex p. Tower Hamlets LBC*, 1990).

10.86 No change of mind. An authority who find that an applicant is unintentionally homeless and who then refer the applicant to another authority cannot change their mind on intentionality simply because the referral is unsuccessful and the applicant comes back to them (*R. v Beverley DC Ex p. McPhee*, 1978).

10.87 Local authority agreement. As a first stage, authorities will try to reach agreement as to who should house the applicant (1996 Act s.198(5)). In default of agreement, disputes are to be resolved in accordance with arrangements made by the Secretary of State by order. The current arrangements are to be found in the Homelessness (Decision on Referrals) Order 1998 (SI 1998/1578) and the agreement reached between the relevant association of local authorities (the Local Authority Agreement). The terms of this document do not bind anyone, not even an authority who are party to it: it is a voluntary guideline, for administrative purposes only, and if an authority chooses to depart from it in a particular case, they are free to do so; indeed, it will be irrelevant to any court or arbitration proceedings which may arise under the 1998 Order (*R. v Mr Referee McCall Ex p. Eastbourne BC*, 1981).

7. PRELIMINARY DUTIES

10.88 Applications. The preliminary duties described below arise where a person applies to a housing authority for accommodation, or for assistance in obtaining it, and the authority have reason to believe that he may be homeless or threatened with homelessness (1996 Act s.184(1)). There is no provision for any particular form of application, or even that the application should be in writing (*R. v Chiltern DC Ex p. Roberts*, 1990).

10.89 Illegal immigrants. While certain immigrants are precluded from assistance (10.16–10.17), illegal immigrants are precluded from applying altogether (*Tower Hamlets LBC v Secretary of State for the Environment*, 1993).

10.90 Mental capacity. As noted above (10.44), the applicant must have sufficient capacity to understand and respond to the offer of accommodation, and to undertake its responsibilities: *R. v Bexley LBC Ex p. B*; *R. v Oldham MBC Ex p. G*; *R. v Tower Hamlets LBC Ex p. Begum*, 1993.

10.91 Three preliminary duties. The three main preliminary duties are: to make enquiries, to notify the applicant of the decision, and, in the case of an eligible homeless person in priority need, to accommodate pending the outcome of enquiries and notification. These duties are immediate; the authority cannot avoid them by keeping their offices shut for prolonged periods—in the major cities, they may be expected to maintain a 24-hour service, i.e. an emergency, out-of-hours service as well as a normal office service (*R. v Camden LBC Ex p. Gillan*, 1988). Nor can an authority postpone a decision in the hope of a change of circumstances that will reduce their duty (*R. v Ealing LBC Ex p. Sidhu*, 1982).

10.92 Mediation. Where an applicant is a young person who has been required to leave the family home, many authorities operate a mediation service intended to achieve reconciliation between the family members. Authorities cannot, however, delay making a decision pending mediation, as mediation forms no part of enquiries—they are different exercises (*Robinson v Hammersmith & Fulham LBC*, 2006).

10.93 Enquiries. Where the authority have reason to believe there is actual or threatened homelessness, then they must make enquiries:

- such as are necessary to satisfy them whether the applicant is eligible for assistance (10.16–10.17); and

- if so, whether any, and what, duties are owed to him under Pt 7 (1996 Act s.184(1)).

10.94 Local connection enquiries. The authority may also make further enquiries as to whether there is a local connection with the district of another authority (1996 Act s.184(2)).

10.95 Notification. It follows that if the authority are not satisfied as to homelessness, they need not proceed to make any further enquiries. If they do make enquiries, then the authority must, on their completion, notify the applicant of their decision, and "so far as any issue is decided against [the applicant's] interests" inform him of the reasons for the decision (1996 Act s.184(3)). If the decision is to notify another authority under the local connection provisions (10.75), the applicant must likewise be notified of this decision and its reasons (1996 Act s.184)). Notification must also inform the applicant of the right to request a review (within 21 days) (1996 Act s.184(5); 10.168).

10.96 In writing. A notification must be in writing. If the applicant does not receive the notification, he will, however, be treated as having done so if the notice is made available at the authority's office for a reasonable period, for collection by him or on his behalf (1996 Act s.184(6)). The burden is therefore on the applicant who does not receive the decision to go to the authority's office and ask for it.

10.97 Accommodation pending enquiries. Enquiries may take some time. If the authority have reason to believe that the applicant may be homeless and eligible for assistance, and in priority need, then—pending their decision—they are obliged to secure that accommodation is made available (1996 Act s.188(1)). This is so whether or not the applicant may have a local connection with another authority (1996 Act s.188(2)).

10.98 Accommodation for whom. The accommodation must be made available for the applicant and for any other family member who normally resides with him, or anyone else who might reasonably be expected to reside with him (1996 Act ss.176, 188(1)).

10.99 Cessation of interim accommodation duty. The duty ceases on notification of decision, even if the applicant requests a review, but the authority have a discretion to continue to house pending the review (1996 Act s.188(2), (3)).

8.   LESS THAN THE FULL HOUSING DUTY

10.100 Types of duties. Duties towards the homeless depend on the findings of the authority as to priority need and intentionality.

10.101 Priority need but homeless intentionally. If the authority are satisfied that an applicant is homeless, and in priority need of accommodation, but they are also satisfied that he became homeless intentionally, they have two duties:

1. to secure that temporary accommodation is made available for such period as they consider will give him a reasonable opportunity to secure his own accommodation (s.190(2)(a)); and

2. to assess the applicant's housing needs and provide him (or secure that he is provided) with advice and assistance (s.190(2)(b), (4)).

10.102 Reasonable opportunity. What constitutes a reasonable opportunity for securing accommodation depends on the applicant's circumstances; authorities cannot take into account the extent of their resources and other demands on them when determining this issue (*R. (Conville) v Richmond upon Thames LBC*, 2006).

10.103 Advice and assistance. The advice and assistance must include information about the likely availability in the authority's area of types of accommodation appropriate to the applicant's housing needs, including as to the location and sources of such types of accommodation (s.190(5)).

10.104 Local authority accommodation. If the authority provide their own accommodation, it will not be secure unless and until the authority notify the applicant otherwise (1985 Act Sch.1 para.4), which they may not do otherwise than in accordance with the allocation provisions considered below.

10.105 Private accommodation. If the authority secure accommodation through a landlord whose tenants are not secure, then this temporary accommodation will likewise not be within any statutory protection at all, albeit only for a year from when the authority first gave notification of their decision (above, 10.95), or—if there is a review (or an appeal)—from its final determination, and again unless the tenant is previously notified by the landlord that it is to be regarded either as an assured shorthold or a fully assured tenancy (s.209(2)).

10.106 Priority need but threatened with homelessness intentionally. If the authority are satisfied that the applicant is threatened with homelessness intentionally, eligible for assistance and in priority need, then the advice and appropriate assistance duty (above, 10.101(2)) arises (s.195(5)(b), (6), (7)), on the basis that, once the homelessness itself occurs, an application will entitle the applicant to a period of temporary accommodation (10.101(1)).

10.107 No priority need. If the authority are satisfied that the applicant is homeless—whether intentionally (s.190(3)) or unintentionally (s.192)—or threatened with homelessness (intentionally or not) (s.195(5)(a)), and eligible for assistance, but they are also satisfied that he is not in priority need, they owe an identical advice and appropriate assistance obligation (10.101(2)) to the applicant.

10.108 Additional powers. In addition, if the authority are satisfied that the applicant is unintentionally homeless but not in priority need, they still have a power to secure that accommodation is made available for occupation by the applicant (s.192(3), as added by the Homelessness Act 2002 s.5), even if no duty. Likewise, an applicant not in priority need who is unintentionally threatened with homelessness may benefit from reasonable steps taken by the authority to secure that accommodation does not cease to be available for his occupation (s.195(6)).

10.109 Priority need and unintentionally threatened with homelessness. If the authority decide that the applicant is threatened with homelessness and eligible for assistance, and has a priority need, but did not become threatened with homelessness intentionally, their duty is to take reasonable steps to secure that accommodation does not cease to be available for his occupation (s.195(1) and (2)), i.e. either to help him remain in his current accommodation (s.195(2)), or else to have other accommodation waiting for him once homelessness occurs.

10.110 No limits on obtaining possession. This duty cannot be used to prevent the authority themselves obtaining vacant possession of any accommodation (s.195(3)), i.e. the fact that the authority have this duty cannot be raised as a defence in any action by the authority against one of their own tenants. If the authority provide their own accommodation when the homelessness itself occurs, then s.193 applies in the same way as it applies to those who apply when already homeless (10.112) (s.195(4)).

10.111 Other Acts. Other statutory provisions may be available to afford housing, when there is no duty, or no full duty, under the 1996 Act (see below 10.127 *et seq.*).

9. FULL HOUSING DUTY

10.112 Full duties. If the authority are satisfied that the applicant is homeless, eligible for assistance, in priority need and not intentionally homeless, then their duty is (subject to the possibility of referral to another authority, 10.69 *et seq.*) to secure that accommodation is made available for his occupation (and, therefore, for any other family member who normally resides with, or anyone else who might reasonably be expected to reside with, the applicant: 10.22) (s.193(2)).

10.113 Provision of allocation policy statement. In addition, the authority must give the applicant a copy of the statement included in their allocation policy (10.214) on offering choice to people allocated housing accommodation under Pt 6 (s.193(3A)).

10.114 Securing accommodation. The duty to secure that accommodation is made available for the applicant's occupation can be discharged by:

- making available suitable accommodation held by the authority under the Housing Act 1985 Pt 2, or under any other powers; or

- securing that the applicant obtains suitable accommodation from some other person; or

- giving the applicant such advice and assistance as will secure that he obtains suitable accommodation from some other person (s.206(1)).

10.115 Suitability. Suitability is governed by the 1996 Act s.210, which states that, when determining whether accommodation is suitable, the authority must have regard to Pts 9 and 10 of the Housing Act 1985 (slum clearance and overcrowding) and Pts 1 to 4 of the Housing Act 2004 (hazardous housing, houses in multiple occupation and selective licensing of accommodation) (see Chapters 12 and 14).

10.116 Personal circumstances. In determining suitability, the authority must also take into account the particular circumstances of the applicant and his family, e.g. medical evidence (*R. v Brent LBC Ex p. Omar*, 1991). Accommodation must be adequate as regards size for the family's needs as well as appropriately having regard to such other factors as nature of area and employment prospects (*R. v Wyre BC Ex p. Parr*, 1982).

10.117 Affordability. Regulations have been made to govern consideration by authorities of affordability: Homelessness (Suitability of Accommodation) Order 1996 (SI 1996/3204). The Order requires the authority to take into account:

- the financial resources available to the applicant;
- the costs of accommodation;
- payments being made under a court order to a spouse or former spouse;
- any payments made to support children whether under a court order or under the Child Support Act 1991; and
- the applicant's other reasonable living expenses.

10.118 Suitability: Wales. In Wales, the Homelessness (Suitability of Accommodation) (Wales) Order 2006 (SI 2006/650) requires Welsh authorities to take into account the following additional matters when considering suitability of accommodation for a person in priority need:

- the specific health needs of the person;
- the proximity and accessibility of social services;
- the proximity and accessibility of the support of the family or other support services; and
- any disability of the person.

10.119 Bed and breakfast accommodation: England. In England, the use of bed and breakfast accommodation is restricted by the Homelessness (Suitability of Accommodation) (England) Order 2003 (SI 2003/3326). Bed and breakfast accommodation is not suitable for families or pregnant women, unless there is no other accommodation available and then only for a period not exceeding six weeks (or for periods not exceeding six weeks in total). Accommodation owned or managed by an authority, registered social landlord or voluntary organisation is exempt from this prohibition, i.e. does not class as a B&B.

10.120 Bed and breakfast accommodation: Wales. In addition, in Wales, bed and breakfast accommodation provided by a Welsh authority is not to be regarded as suitable for any applicant unless it meets a specified "basic standard": Homelessness (Suitability of Accommodation) (Wales) Order 2006 (SI 2006/650). The Order also makes detailed provision for restricting the use of any bed and breakfast accommodation for pregnant women and minors. Further limitations on the use of such accommodation in relation to any person in priority need are to come into effect from April 7, 2008.

10.121 Accommodation in own area. So far as reasonably practicable, authorities are bound to secure accommodation within their own area (s.208(1)).

10.122 Out-of-area accommodation. If the authority nonetheless place an applicant in another area, they must give notice to the local housing authority with responsibility for that area, stating:

- the name of the applicant;
- the number and description of other members of his family normally residing with him, or of anyone else who might reasonably be expected to reside with him;
- the address;
- the date on which the accommodation was made available to the applicant; and
- what Pt 7 function the authority were discharging when securing the accommodation for him (s.208(2) and (3));

The notice must be given in writing within two weeks from when the accommodation was made available (s.208(4)).

10.123 Security. Where an authority provide their own accommodation in discharge of the full duty, it cannot be a secure tenancy, but continues to be provided under Pt 7, hence the expression "Pt 7" accommodation, in contrast to accommodation allocated under Pt 6 (10.203), which—if owned by the authority— is normally held by them under Pt 2 of the Housing Act 1985 (see 3.09).

10.124 Charges. Authorities have a general power to make reasonable charges for the provision of their own accommodation under Pt 2 of the 1985 Act (s.24). Part 7 likewise entitles them to make charges to a homeless person for accommodation which they provide, or for or towards accommodation which they arrange for some other person to provide, under Pt 7 (s.206(2)). This applies to both accommodation under s.193 and accommodation provided under any of the temporary duties (10.97, 10.101).

10.125 Continuation of duty. The duty continues to be owed to an applicant until it is brought to an end by any of the circumstances set out in s.193 (s.193(3)).

10.126 Cessation of duty. The duty comes to end in any of the following circumstances:

1. if the applicant refuses an offer under Pt 7, which the authority are satisfied is suitable for him (10.115), and the authority have informed the applicant that if he does not accept the offer, they will regard themselves as having discharged the duty (s.193(5)).

   This is directed towards the Pt 7 offer, i.e. the accommodation that the application will occupy until allocated a permanent home; it is in this sense "temporary", although that is misleading, because it can be a matter of years (even a decade or more) before such a "final" offer is made.

   In this context, an authority may discharge their duty by securing an assured shorthold tenancy from a private sector landlord (*Griffiths v St Helens BC*, 2006). In offering the tenancy, they should explain to the applicant that if the landlord lawfully exercises his right to recover possession after the end of the fixed term (and there has been no intervening event bringing the duty to an end under one of the following sub-paragraphs), they will still be obliged to secure that accommodation is available for him. (*Cf.* a "final" offer of a qualifying assured shorthold tenancy, at (8), below.)

2. If the applicant ceases to be eligible for assistance (s.193(6)(a)) (10.16);

3. If the applicant becomes homeless intentionally (10.47) from the Pt 7 accommodation (s.193(6)(b)).

4. If the applicant accepts an allocation under Pt 6 (s.193(6)(c)).

5. If the applicant accepts an offer of an assured tenancy (other than an assured shorthold tenancy) from a private landlord, i.e. one whose tenants are not secure (s.193(6)(cc)).

6. If the applicant voluntarily ceases to occupy the Pt 7 accommodation as his only or principal home (s.193(6)(d); see 3.32).

7. If the applicant, having been informed of the possible consequences of refusal, and of his right to request a review of the suitability of accommodation refused, refuses a written final offer of a Pt 6 allocation, and the authority are satisfied that the accommodation was suitable for him (10.115), and that it was reasonable for him to accept it (s.193(7), (7A), (7F)).

   For this purpose, an applicant may reasonably be considered to accept an offer even though he is currently under a contractual or other obligation in respect of his existing accommodation, if (but only if) he can bring that other obligation to an end before he is obliged to take up the offer (s.193(8)), i.e. the offer must run from no earlier than the first date when the obligation can be brought to an end, e.g. a four-week period for notice to quit.

8. If the applicant accepts a qualifying offer of an assured shorthold tenancy from a private landlord (s.193(7B)).
    An offer is only a qualifying offer if:

    (a) it is made with the approval of the authority, in pursuance of arrangements made by the authority with the landlord with a view to bringing the duty towards the applicant to an end;
    (b) the offer is of a fixed-term tenancy; and
    (c) it is accompanied by a statement in writing which states the term of the tenancy being offered and explains in ordinary language that there is no obligation on the applicant to accept it, but that if it is accepted the authority will cease to be under a duty to the applicant (s.193(7D).

Acceptance of a qualifying offer is only effective if the applicant acknowledges in writing that he has understood the authority's statement (s.193(7E)).

An authority may not make a qualifying offer unless they are satisfied that the accommodation is suitable for the applicant and that it is reasonable for him to accept the offer (s.193(7F)).

For this purpose, an applicant may reasonably be considered to accept an offer even though he is under a contractual or other obligation in respect of his existing accommodation, if (but only if) he can bring that other obligation to an end before he is obliged to take up the offer (s.193(8)): see last sub-paragraph.

10.   DUTIES UNDER OTHER ACTS

10.127   Social service legislation. As well as discharging their duty under Pt 7 itself, authorities may also choose to discharge their duties towards the homeless under other statutory provisions, such as through housing in an old person's home under the National Assistance Act 1948 Pt 3, or else, in the case of a minor, by using powers under the Children Act 1989, Pt 3. A duty may arise under Pt 3 of the Children Act, even though no duty—or, in practice, no full housing duty—exists under Pt 7.

10.128 Social service authorities. Duties under these Acts are imposed on social service authorities (10.15).

10.129 Part 3 of the Children Act 1989. The 1989 has two relevant sections which must be considered: ss.17 and 20.

10.130 Section 17. Section 17 provides:

"(1) It shall be the general duty of every local authority . . .

    (a) to safeguard and promote the welfare of children within their area who are in need; and

    (b) so far as is consistent with that duty, to promote the upbringing of such children by their families by providing a range and level of services appropriate to those children's needs."

10.131 Social service power. Although this section does not positively require authorities to provide accommodation, it does comprise a further—"safety net"—power permitting authorities to assist a family, including with the provision of accommodation (*R. (W) v Lambeth LBC*, 2002, following *AG Ex rel. Tilley v Wandsworth LBC*, 1981 and *R. v Tower Hamlets LBC Ex p. Monaf*, 1988.)

10.132 Section 20. Section 20 of the Children Act 1989 provides:

"(1) Every local authority shall provide accommodation for any child in need within their area who appears to them to require accommodation as a result of—

    . . .

    (c) . . . the person who has been caring for him being prevented (whether or not permanently, and for whatever reason) from providing him with suitable accommodation or care . . .

    . . .

    (3) Every local authority shall provide accommodation for any child in need within their area who has reached the age of sixteen and whose welfare the authority consider is likely to

be seriously prejudiced if they do not provide him with accommodation."

10.133 Social service duty. The effect of the section is to impose a duty on social services authorities to house children in the circumstances set out in subs.(1) and to house young people in the circumstances set out in subs.(3). The duty is exclusive to the child and does not confer a duty (or even a power) on the authority to accommodate a child's family: *R. (G) v Barnet LBC*, 2001.

10.134 Co-operation. Where not themselves also the housing authority, as they will be in unitary authorities and London borough councils (10.12), social service authorities (10.15) may request assistance discharging their duties under the 1989 Act (1989 Act s.27(1)). An authority whose help is requested "shall comply with the request if it is compatible with their own statutory or other duties and obligations and does not unduly prejudice the discharge of any of their functions" (1989 Act s.27(2)).

10.135 Part 7 v Part 3. In *Smith v Northavon DC*, 1994, the housing authority found the applicant to be intentionally homeless and sought to evict him from his temporary accommodation. The applicant applied to the social services authority for assistance. The social services authority considered that the applicant's children would be in need when the eviction took place and therefore requested the housing authority to provide accommodation. The housing authority declined. The House of Lords refused to quash their decision. The request of the social services authority did not give the applicant any priority over other homeless persons or waiting-list applicants for housing. In the event of the housing authority being unable to provide assistance, the social services authority remained under a responsibility to protect the applicant's children.

10.136 Referrals to social services. The Homelessness Act 2002 makes specific provision for applicants with children who are not owed a full Pt 7 duty to be referred to social services. Where a local authority have reason to believe that an applicant with whom children reside or normally reside may be ineligible for assistance (10.16), may be homeless intentionally (10.47), or may be threatened with homelessness intentionally (10.48), they must make arrangements for ensuring that the applicant is invited to consent to the referral of his case to the social services authority (or department in the case of a unitary authority) and, if consent is given, must make the social services authority/department aware of the facts of the case and the subsequent decision in relation to it (s.213A(1), (2)). (The decision is necessarily later because this duty arises when the housing authority first have reason to believe that the applicant may be disqualified from full assistance for one or other relevant reason, even though they are not yet satisfied as to their final decision.)

10.137 Social service response. Following a referral, the social services authority/department may request the housing authority to provide them/it with advice and assistance in the exercise of their functions under Pt 3 of the Children Act 1989, and the housing authority must provide them with such advice and assistance as is reasonable in all the circumstances (s.213A (5), (6)).

10.138 National Assistance Act 1948. The National Assistance Act 1948 s.21(1) (as amended) provides that:

> "a local authority may with the approval of the Secretary of State, and to such extent as he may direct shall, make arrangements for providing—
>
> (a) residential accommodation for persons aged eighteen or over who by reason of age, illness, disability or any other circumstances are in need of care and attention which is not otherwise available to them."

10.139 Assessment of need. Once an applicant has sought assistance from a local authority under s.21, the authority must assess his needs: see National Health Service and Community Care Act 1990 s.47.

10.140 Immigrants and asylum seekers. Section 21(1A) of the 1948 Act (added by the Immigration and Asylum Act 1999) provides:

> "A person to whom section 115 of the Immigration and Asylum Act 1999 (exclusion from benefits) applies may not be provided with residential accommodation under subsection (1)(a) if his need for care and attention has arisen solely—
>
> (a) because he is destitute; or
> (b) because of the physical effects or anticipated physical effects of his being destitute."

10.141 The effect of this provision is to exclude those who are subject to immigration control (unless reincluded by regulations:

10.16) from making an application under s.21 of the 1948 Act, where their need for care and attention arises solely from destitution. Their needs are, instead, intended to be met under the Asylum and Immigration Act 1999, through the National Asylum Support Service. Local authorities have no power to provide any accommodation for non-asylum-seeking immigrants whose need is based solely on destitution, and who do not have children.

10.142 In the case of asylum seekers whose need for care and attention does not arise because of destitution but because, for example, of disability, responsibility for meeting their care needs remains with the local authority (*R. (Westminster CC) v Secretary of State for the Home Department*, 2001).

10.143 Provision of accommodation. Once the local authority have assessed an applicant's needs as satisfying the criteria in s.21, they must provide accommodation on a continuing basis so long as the need of the applicant remains as originally assessed (*R. v Kensington & Chelsea RLBC Ex p. Kujtim*, 1999). Residential accommodation may include "ordinary" housing accommodation (*Khana v Southwark LBC*, 2001). A duty to supply such accommodation will arise where a person needs care and attention, including housing accommodation, that is not otherwise available. The need for care and attention remains, however, a precondition of such a duty.

10.144 Discharge of duty. The duty under s.21 is not, however, absolute, and may be brought to an end by an applicant's unreasonable behaviour (*Kujtim*, above) or by the unreasonable refusal of an offer of accommodation (*Khana*, above).

10.145 Local Government Act 2000. A final safety net may also be available under the Local Government Act 2002 s.2, which provides that:

> "Every local authority are to have power to do anything which they consider is likely to achieve any one or more of the following objects—
>> (a) the promotion or improvement of the economic well-being of their area,
>> (b) the promotion or improvement of the social well-being of their area, and
>> (c) the promotion or improvement of the environmental well-being of their area."

10.146 Safety net. In *R. (J) v Enfield LBC*, 2002, which was decided prior to the decision in *W*, above (10.130), it was held that in order to ensure that there was no breach of an applicant's right to respect for family right under the ECHR Art.8, s.2 could be used in order to provide financial assistance and, if no other power was available, that the authority would have to use it in order to assist. In *Morris* (10.22), it was argued that—given that s.185(4) had been declared to be incompatible with Art.8 of the European Convention on Human Rights—the authority were under a duty to provide assistance to the applicant under alternative powers, including s.2. That argument was rejected. Although the authority had power to provide accommodation under s.2, they were not under a duty to do so.

11. PROTECTION OF PROPERTY

10.147 Duty to protect property. If an authority are or have been under a (temporary or permanent) duty under the 1996 Act ss.188 (10.97), 190, 193, 195 (10.100–10.126) or 200 (10.81), they may also be under a duty to take reasonable steps to prevent the loss of an applicant's property, or to prevent or mitigate damage to it (1996 Act s.211(2)). The applicant's personal property, for these purposes, includes that of any person reasonably to be expected to reside with him (1996 Act s.211(5)).

10.148 When the duty arises. This duty arises if the authority have reason to believe:

- that there is a danger of loss of or damage to property because of the applicant's inability to protect or deal with it; and

- that no other suitable arrangements have been or are being made (1996 Act s.211(1)).

10.149 Power to protect property. If the authority have not been under one of the identified duties (10.147) but have reason to believe there is such a danger, they nonetheless have power to protect property (1996 Act s.211(3)).

10.150 Terms and charges. The authority may, however, refuse to take action under these provisions other than on such conditions as they consider appropriate, including for reasonable charges and the disposal of property (1996 Act s.211(4)).

10.151 Relocation of property. If the applicant asks the authority to move the property to a nominated location, the authority may (if they consider that the request is reasonable) discharge their responsibilities under these provisions by doing so, and treat their responsibilities as being at an end (1996 Act s.212(2)).

10.152 Powers of entry. In connection with these provisions, the authority have power, at all reasonable times, to enter any premises which are or were the usual or last usual place of residence of the applicant, and to deal with his property in any way that is reasonably necessary, including by way of storage (1996 Act s.212(1)).

10.153 Termination. Duties and powers end when the authority consider that there is no longer any danger of loss or damage, by reason of the applicant's inability to protect or deal with his personal property, although if the authority have provided storage, they have a discretion to continue to do so (1996 Act s.212(3)).

10.154 Notification. Where the authority's responsibilities end, they must notify the applicant, and of the reasons for it (1996 Act s.212(4)). Notification may be given by delivery, or by leaving it or sending it to the applicant's last known address (1996 Act s.212(5)).

12. HOMELESSNESS STRATEGIES

10.155 Duty to review and publish strategy. The Homelessness Act 2002 ("2002 Act") imposed a new duty on local housing authorities to carry out a homelessness review (10.157) in their area and formulate and publish a homelessness strategy (10.159) based on the results of that review (2002 Act s.1(1)). The first strategy must be published within 12 months of s.1 coming into force, and thereafter a new one must be published at least every five years (2002 Act s.1(3), (4)).

10.156 Authorities. Where they are different from the housing authority (10.12), the social services authority (10.15) must give assistance in the review and in the formulation of the strategy (2002 Act s.1(2)). The strategy must be taken into account by both the local housing authority and the social services authority in the exercise of their functions (2002 Act s.1(5), (6)).

10.157 Review. For these purposes a homelessness review means a review of:

- the level, and likely future levels of homelessness in the authority's area;

- the activities which are carried out in the area to:
  - prevent homelessness in the authority's area;
  - secure that accommodation is or will be available for people in the area who are or may become homeless; and
  - provide support for people in the area who are or may become homeless or who have been homeless and need support to prevent it happening again; and

- the resources available to the authority, the social services authority, other public authorities, voluntary organisations and other persons for such activities (2002 Act s.2(1), (2)).

10.158 Information about review. On completion of the review, the authority must arrange for the results to be available for inspection at their principal office, at all reasonable hours, without charge, and provide (on payment of a reasonable charge, if required) a copy of the results (2002 Act s.2(3)).

10.159 Strategy. A homelessness strategy means one formulated for:

- preventing homelessness in the authority's area;

- securing that sufficient accommodation is and will be available for people in the area who are or may become homeless; and,

- securing that there is satisfactory provision of support for people in the area who are or who may become homeless or who have become homeless and need support to prevent them becoming homeless again (2002 Act s.3(1)).

10.160 Content of strategy. The strategy may include specific objectives to be pursued as well as specific action planned to be taken in the course of the exercise of the authority's housing functions and also of the functions of the social services authority for the district (2002 Act s.3(2)).

10.161 Other action. The strategy may also include specific action which the authority expects to be taken by any other public authority or by any voluntary organisation or other person who can contribute to the objectives of the strategy, although only with the approval of the body or person concerned (2002 Act s.3(3), (4)).

10.162 Partnership. The authority must consider how far the objectives of the strategy can be met by joint action between themselves, the social service authority or any other body or persons (2002 Act s.3(5)).

10.163 Review and modification. The strategy must be kept under review and may be modified (2002 Act s.3(6)). Before adopting or modifying the strategy, the authority must consult such public or local authorities, voluntary organisations or other persons as they consider appropriate (2002 Act s.3(7), (8)). Any modification must be published.

10.164 Information about strategy. A copy of the strategy must be available at the authority's principal office for inspection at all reasonable hours, free of charge, and provided to members of the public on request, on payment (if required) of a reasonable charge (2002 Act s.3(8)).

13. ADVICE, INFORMATION AND VOLUNTARY ORGANISATIONS

10.165 Voluntary organisations. Provision is made in Pt 7 for giving grants, loans, premises or goods in kind to voluntary organisations concerned with the homeless (1996 Act s.180). The assistance may be given on terms and subject to conditions and undertakings as to the use of the assistance (1996 Act s.181).

10.166 Advice and information. In addition, authorities have an obligation to ensure that advice and assistance about homelessness and its prevention are available to any person in their areas, free of charge (1996 Act s.179(1)). This duty can be discharged by providing assistance (grant or loan, use of premises, furniture or other goods, or making staff available) through another person (not necessarily a voluntary organisation, although on the same terms and conditions as would apply to a voluntary organisation): 1996 Act s.181(1)) (1996 Act s.179(2), (3)).

14. CODE OF GUIDANCE

10.167 The Code. In the exercise of their functions under Pt 7, authorities are bound to have regard to such guidance as may from time to time be given by the Secretary of State (1996 Act s.182). This is not the same as saying that they are bound to comply with its contents in the same way as they are bound to comply with Pt 7 itself (*De Falco v Crawley BC*, 1979). It is, rather, something they are bound to take into account. In practice, if an authority deviate from the provisions of the Code, they may find themselves obliged to explain their reasons for doing so in any challenge.

15. REVIEW AND APPEAL

10.168 Right to internal review. Applicants have a statutory right to request an internal review of any of the following decisions:

- as to eligibility for assistance (10.16);

- as to the duty (if any) owed (10.100–10.126);

- to notify another authority (10.94);

- whether the conditions for referral are met (10.76);

- what duty is owed following a local connection referral (10.79); or

- any decision as to suitability of accommodation offered in discharge of duty, including a Pt 6 offer (10.115).

10.169 Request for review. The right of review does not, however, entitle the applicant to a review of an earlier review (1996 Act s.202(2)). This does not prevent an authority from further reconsidering a decision if they are minded to do so (*R. v Westminster CC Ex p. Ellioua*, 1998), although if an applicant wishes still to challenge the decision after a further review, he must do so by way of appeal to the county court on the original decision (*Demetri v Westminster CC*, 2000).

10.170 Time limits for request. A request for a review must be made within 21 days of notification of the decision (10.95), or such longer period as the authority may in writing allow (1996 Act s.202(3)).

10.171 Review procedure. The Secretary of State has power to regulate the review procedure, including requiring the review to be conducted by a person of "appropriate seniority . . . not involved in the original decision", and the "circumstances in which the applicant is entitled to an oral hearing, and whether and by whom [the applicant] may be represented at such a hearing" (1996 Act s.203(2)). The Allocation of Housing and Homelessness (Review Procedures) Regulations 1999 (SI 1999/71) require that an officer of the authority conducting a review should not have been involved in the original decision and should be senior to the original decision-maker.

10.172 In carrying out the review, the reviewer must usually have regard not only to the information available at the time of the original decision but also to that obtained thereafter and to matters occurring after the initial decision: *Mohamed v Hammersmith & Fulham LBC*, 2001. This is not the case, however, if the original decision by the authority was unlawful. In *Robinson v Hammersmith & Fulham LBC*, 2006, the authority decided that the applicant was not in priority need, notwithstanding that she was only 17 years old at the time. By the time of the review, she was 18 and no longer in priority need (see 10.33(1)). The authority therefore sought to uphold their original decision. The Court of Appeal held that the reviewing officer should have decided that the original decision was unlawful and had denied the applicant the rights to which she was entitled; to be given those rights and on review, she should therefore have been found to be in priority need.

10.173 Time limit for review. The review must generally be carried out within eight weeks, although a longer period is permitted in the case of local connection reviews: see Review Procedure Regulations reg.9. The parties may agree a longer period between themselves.

10.174 Notification. The authority have to notify the applicant of the outcome of the review and, if it is adverse to his interests, or confirms a local connection referral of the reasons for it (1996 Act s.203(4)). In any event, they must notify the applicant of the right to appeal to the county court on a point of law (1996 Act s.203(5)). If either of these requirements is not fulfilled, the notification is treated as not having been given (1996 Act s.203(6)). Otherwise, notification is given in the same way as under the 1996 Act s.184 (1996 Act s.203(8); 10.91).

10.175 Accommodation pending review. Pending the outcome of the review, the authority may—but do not have to—provide accommodation for the applicant (s.188(3)). As there is no provision for appeal against a decision not to house pending review, a challenge can only be made by judicial review: *R. v Camden LBC Ex p. Mohammed*, 1997.

10.176 Appeal to the county court. Appeal lies to the county court if the applicant is either dissatisfied with the outcome of the review or if he has not been notified of the outcome within any time that may be prescribed (1996 Act s.204(1)). Exercise of the right to a review is therefore an essential precondition of appeal. Appeal lies only on a point of law, whether it arises from the original decision or the decision on review (1996 Act s.204(1)).

10.177 Time for appeal. The appeal must be brought within 21 days of notification, or of when the applicant ought to have been notified of the outcome (s.204(2)). The court may give permission for appeal out of time where there is good reason for the applicant being unable to bring the appeal within the 21–day limit (s.204(2A)).

10.178 Accommodation pending appeal. Pending an appeal (and any further appeal), the authority may continue to provide accommodation (1996 Act s.204(4), added by the Homelessness Act 2002). If the authority refuse to do so, the applicant may appeal that decision to the county court (s.204A).

10.179 Powers of court on interim accommodation appeal. The court may order accommodation to be made available pending the outcome of the appeal (or such earlier time as it may specify) (s.204A(4)(a), (b)). In considering whether or not to do so, the court must apply the principles that would be applied by the High Court on an application for judicial review (s.204A(4)). As applied to interim accommodation pending appeal, this requires the authority to carry out a balancing exercise, to which the following will always be relevant (although other factors may also need to be considered): the merits of the applicant's case that the authority's decision is wrong; the extent to which the original decision appears to be contrary to the merits or to involve a fine degree of judgment; whether new material needs to be considered; whether there is a new argument which would change the original decision; and applicant's personal circumstances (*R. v Camden LBC Ex p. Mohammed*, 1997). If the court quashes the authority's refusal, it may order the authority to exercise the power to accommodate pending appeal in the applicant's case for such period as it specifies (s.204A(5)). Such an order may, however, only be made if the court is satisfied that failure to exercise the accommodation power in accordance with its order would substantially prejudice the applicant's ability to pursue his substantive appeal (s.204A(6)(a)).

10.180 Powers of court on appeal against decision. The court may make such an order as it thinks fit, confirming, quashing or varying the decision (1996 Act s.204(3)).

10.181 Basis of appeal. The right of appeal is on a point of law, as distinct from an appeal on the facts. Point of law includes issues of jurisdiction or vires. The distinction between a point of law and a question of fact is not always straightforward, in so far as a conclusion of fact for which there is no, or insufficient, evidence may in itself comprise an error of law. Furthermore, even a straightforward error or mistake of fact may itself serve to vitiate a decision as a matter of law. For practical purposes, the grounds of intervention will be the same, therefore, as have been available on judicial review hitherto (*Begum v Tower Hamlets LBC*, 1999), both under Pt 3 of the 1985 Act, and indeed on issues of allocation, and as will remain available where there is no appeal.

10.182 General principles. The general principles are those of administrative law, which have been largely developed in the course of proceedings for judicial review, and which now comprise both a growth area of legal activity and case law, and of legal literature. What these principles import is that a straightforward difference of opinion or judgment between an authority and an applicant as to what decision should have been reached will not suffice to justify the intervention of the courts. If Parliament has entrusted a decision to a local authority, it is that authority's view of what is reasonable which must prevail, rather than that of a court (*Associated Provincial Picture Houses Ltd v Wednesbury Corp*, 1948).

10.183 Judgment of the authority. It follows that it is not sufficient merely to know what rights and duties are set out in Pt 7, or of knowing what the Code of Guidance under either the 1996 Act s.169 (10.230) or s.182 (10.167) suggests is appropriate in a particular case. The principal Pt 7 duties only arise when the authority have "reason to believe", "consider" or are "satisfied" that a certain state of affairs exists: see the 1996 Act ss.183, 184, 188, 190, 193, 195, 197, 198 and 211. An applicant's rights therefore only arise and can only be enforced once the authority's satisfaction, belief or view has been established (*Cocks v Thanet DC*, 1983) and it is, accordingly, essential to distinguish between the actual—undisputed, or indisputable—facts of a particular case, and whether the authority are "satisfied", have "reason to believe" or are "of the opinion" that those facts exist.

10.184   Intervention.   At first glance, one might think that this subjective assessment of rights and duties would mean that an authority's decision could never be challenged at all:

"The section is framed in a 'subjective' form . . . This form of section is quite well-known and at first sight might seem to exclude judicial review"

per Lord Wilberforce, *Secretary of State for Education and Science v Tameside MBC*, 1977. It is here, however, that the principles that have evolved come into play.

10.185   Ultra vires.   What the principles invariably involve is that authorities should always approach their decisions in a lawful manner. If it can be shown that a public body such as a local authority have approached their decision unlawfully, the decision will be void and the courts will not give effect to it. A decision improperly reached is ultra vires, i.e. outside the authority's powers, and without effect in law, whether it is because on the face of the statute there was no power to reach a decision or engage in an act at all, or because the statute has been misconstrued, or because the authority have misapplied the statute in another sense, e.g. by failing to use the powers to implement the purpose of the statute, or by reaching a decision under the statute by reference to something which is irrelevant—or in ignorance of something which is relevant—to the way the power under the statute is intended to be operated.

10.186   Proper decision-making.   At the heart of the case law is the proposition that Parliament intends that bodies such as local authorities should always act properly, in the sense of reasonably and lawfully. That is not to say that they would always arrive at "the" reasonable decision: one person's view of what is reasonable will often quite properly differ from that of another, and again, Parliament has entrusted decision-making under Pt 7 to authorities, not to the courts.

10.187   Puhlhofer.   The House of Lords, in *R. v Hillingdon LBC Ex p. Puhlhofer*, 1986 stressed that in cases where the wording of an obligation is subjectively qualified (in the *Tameside* sense: 10.183), it is the local authority and not the court who Parliament intended to be the judge of fact:

"I am troubled at the prolific use of judicial review for the purpose of challenging the performance by local authorities of their functions under the Act of 1977. Parliament intended the local authority to be the judge of fact. The Act abounds with the formula when, or if, the housing authority are satisfied as to this, or that, or have reason to believe this, or that. Although the action or inaction of a local authority is clearly susceptible to judicial review where they have misconstrued the Act, or abused their powers or otherwise acted perversely, I think that great restraint should be exercised in giving leave to proceed by judicial review. The plight of the homeless is a desperate one, and the plight of the applicants in the present case commands the deepest sympathy. But it is not, in my opinion, appropriate that the remedy of judicial review, which is a discretionary remedy, should be made use of to monitor the actions of local authorities under the Act save in the exceptional case. The ground upon which the courts will review the exercise of an administrative discretion is abuse of power—e.g. bad faith, a mistake in construing the limits of the power, a procedural irregularity, or unreasonableness in the *Wednesbury* sense— unreasonableness verging on an absurdity . . . Where the existence or non-existence of a fact is left to the judgment and discretion of a public body and that fact involves a broad spectrum ranging from the obvious to the debatable to the just conceivable, it is the duty of the court to leave the decision of that fact to the public body to whom Parliament has entrusted the decision-making power save in a case where it is obvious that the public body, consciously or unconsciously, are acting perversely."

10.188 Classification. The principles of administrative law may be expressed, and classified, in a number of different ways. In *Council of Civil Service Unions v Minister for the Civil Service*, 1985, Lord Diplock re-classified them under three headings: "illegality", "irrationality" and "procedural impropriety":

"By 'illegality' as a ground of judicial review I mean that the decision-maker must understand correctly the law that regulates his decision-making power and must give effect to it. Whether he has or not is *par excellence* a justiciable question to be decided, in the event of dispute, by those persons, the judges, by whom the judicial power of the state is exercisable.

By 'irrationality' I mean what can by now be succinctly referred to as 'Wednesbury unreasonableness' . . . It applies to a decision which is so outrageous in its defiance of logic or of accepted moral standards that no sensible person who had applied his mind to the question to be decided could have arrived at it. Whether a decision falls within this category is a question that judges by their training and experience should be well equipped to answer, or else there would be something badly wrong with our judicial system . . . 'Irrationality' by now can stand upon its own feet as an accepted ground on which a decision may be attacked by judicial review. I have described the third head as 'procedural impropriety' rather than failure to observe basic rules of natural justice or failure to act with procedural fairness towards the person who will be affected by the decision. This is because susceptibility to judicial review under this head covers also failure by an administrative tribunal to observe procedural rules that are expressly laid down in the legislative instrument by which its jurisdiction is conferred, even where such failure does not involve any denial of natural justice."

10.189 Human Rights Act 1998 and proportionality. The Human Rights Act 1998 is relevant in two ways: (a) it imports the specific articles of the European Convention on Human Rights into domestic law; and (b) it has influenced the development of the principles of administrative law. In particular, after the 1998 Act, the courts have shown a willingness to subject administrative decision-making to greater scrutiny where a case involves interference with a person's fundamental rights. Indeed, it has even been suggested that in such cases, the court should ask—applying an objective test—whether the decision-maker could reasonably have concluded that the interference with the right was necessary, i.e. whether the justification for the interference is proportionate.

10.190 In *Runa Begum v Tower Hamlets LBC*, 2002, however, it was held that this higher standard of scrutiny did not apply when considering the findings of fact made by an authority on the review of a homelessness decision because such a decision was administrative in nature and did not engage convention rights. Nevertheless, the principles of administrative law are developing (*R. (Prolife Alliance) v British Broadcasting Corporation*, 2003) and the more traditional, restrictive approach may no longer suffice.

10.191   Practical classification.   In practice, the principles tend to overlap with one another. They may be considered under one or more of the following:

- A statutory authority must take into account all the relevant factors before making their decision, and must disregard the irrelevant: *Wednesbury*. See also *Bristol DC v Clark*, 1975.

- The decision must be based on the facts; a decision totally at variance with the facts or for which there is no factual basis cannot be sustained:

  "If a judgment requires, before it can be made, the existence of some facts, then although the evaluation of those facts is for the Secretary of State alone, the courts must enquire whether those facts exist, and have been taken into account, whether the judgment has been made on a proper self-direction as to those facts, whether the judgment has not been made on other facts which ought not to have been taken into account" (*Tameside*).

- The authority must not act in bad faith or dishonestly: *Wednesbury*.

- The authority must direct themselves properly in law, so that a decision based on a misunderstanding or misapplication of the law will not have been reached properly: *Wednesbury*. This is the point in *Wednesbury* that is restated as "illegality" in *Council of Civil Service Unions* (10.188). Thus, in *Re Islam*, 1983, the authority's misunderstanding of the test to be applied when determining whether someone was intentionally homeless (10.46) rendered the decision unlawful.

- The authority must act so as to promote, and not to defeat, the objects or policy of the Act in question. Powers conferred for public purposes must be used in a way that Parliament can be presumed to have intended (*Padfield v Minister of Agriculture, Fisheries & Food*, 1968).

- The decision must not be one to which no reasonable authority could have come: this is conclusive evidence that the decision is improper (or irrational): *Wednesbury*.

- The authority must reach their own decision on each individual case; they must not fetter their discretion by approaching a decision with a predetermined policy as to how they will deal with any case falling within a particular class.

The leading case on this is probably still *British Oxygen Co Ltd v Minister of Technology*, 1971. While a public authority can adopt a policy or limiting rule in order to guide the future exercise of their discretion if they think good administration requires it, they must consider its application individually in every case where it is sought to make an exception (*Stringer v Minister of Housing and Local Government*, 1970). *British Oxygen* was adopted and applied by the House of Lords in *Betts* (10.74). A blanket policy of requiring all applicants who were joint tenants of an authority to serve notice to quit (thereby terminating the tenancy: 1.113) before they could be accepted as homeless due to domestic violence was held to be unlawful (*R. (Hammia) v Wandsworth LBC*, 2005).

- It is the authority who are entrusted with the decision-making power and must make the decision. The authority cannot avoid their duties by adopting the decision of another body: *Lavender & Sons v Minister of Housing and Local Government*, 1970).

A distinction must be drawn, however, between adoption of the decision of another body and the proper use of resources when reaching a decision. The authority may employ staff (Local Government Act 1972 s.112), and have implied power to employ contractors or agents, and to enter into contracts with them (*Crédit Suisse v Allerdale BC*, 1997. There is now an express power to contract: see s.1 of the Local Government (Contracts) Act 1997.) These resources can all be used when reaching a decision. What cannot be abdicated is responsibility for the essential elements of a decision which are to determine what is to be done or what is to happen. See, also, the express power to contract out functions (10.13).

- The authority's decision must be reached properly. Under the Local Government Act 2000, local authorities now function in what may be described as two parts: an executive (of one of three kinds: mayor and cabinet, leader and cabinet or mayor and council executive: see Local Government Act 2000 s.11), and the full authority.

Decisions not conferred on the authority by statute, statutory instrument or (where the power is left to the authority to decide) conferred by the authority on themselves under "local choice" (2000 Act s.13(3)(b)), must be taken by the executive (2000 Act s.13(2), (10)). Decisions on allocations and homelessness are—by this route—matters for the executive (2000 Act s.13 and SI 2000/2853).

Decisions to be taken by the executive may be dealt with in any way that the 2000 Act permits, which includes delegation to an individual member of the executive, or to a committee or sub-committee of the executive, or to an officer (or, in some circumstances, an area committee not of the executive but of the authority themselves) (2000 Act ss.14–16 and 18). For the first time, therefore, individual decisions can properly be taken by an individual councillor, although this is not only unlikely but, it must be said, undesirable, and it is probable that they will continue to be delegated to officers.

Decisions which the authority are to take themselves cannot, however, be delegated to an individual member, only to a committee, sub-committee or officer of the authority (Local Government Act 1972 s.101).

- In all cases, an authority must act fairly, or in accordance with natural justice (*Ridge v Baldwin*, 1964). The extent of this duty will depend upon circumstances, and the nature of the decision. Even if a statute or other instrument contains its own procedural requirements to ensure fairness, including to give reasons for decisions, the courts may—if they consider that the circumstances of an individual case (or, presumably, class of case) call for it—impose yet further requirements to ensure that a matter has been decided fairly and/or give reasons (*Wiseman v Borneman*, 1971). This requirement means that, if relevant to the decision, an applicant must know what is being said against him (*Board of Education v Rice*, 1911).

The requirement of fairness will also mean that an authority must respect any legitimate expectations which an applicant may enjoy. Conventionally, the expression refers to a legitimate procedural expectation, i.e. as to how a matter is to be handled, such as an assurance that no decision will be taken at all on an aspect of a matter until there has been a further opportunity to comment, or until the authority have managed to contact someone, or that it will only be taken by an officer of a particular level of seniority, or by a panel (member or officer) (*Schmidt v Secretary of State for Home Affairs*, 1969; *R. v Devon CC Ex p. Baker*, 1995), provided always that to do so would not interfere or conflict with the authority's statutory duty (*R. v AG of Hong Kong Ex p. Ng Yuen Shiu*, 1983).

Less frequently it has been held to encompass a legitimate substantive expectation, i.e. of a particular outcome of a decision-making process, as opposed to its procedure, where there has been a clear and unambiguous statement, devoid of qualification, on which it was reasonable to rely (*R. v IRC Ex p. MFK Underwriting*, 1990).

The court has to determine the nature of the legitimate expectation which has been engendered, and whether it would be an abuse of power for the court to frustrate it or whether there is a sufficient overriding interest to justify a departure from what had been promised (*R. v North and East Devon Health Authority Ex p. Coughlan*, 2001).

In *R. v Newham LBC Ex p. Bibi and Al-Nashed*, 2001, the local authority had promised a "permanent" home to homeless applicants. A legitimate expectation had arisen, which was sufficient to justify derogation from the authority's housing allocation scheme, and which required the authority to provide reasons if the expectation was not to be fulfilled.

10.192 Human Rights Act 1998. As public authorities within the meaning of the Human Rights Act 1998 s.6, local housing authorities must act in a way which is compatible with the European Convention on Human Rights ("ECHR"). Two Articles of the ECHR are particularly relevant in homelessness cases.

10.193 Article 6. First, Art.6 provides that in the determination of his civil rights, everyone is entitled to a fair and public hearing within a reasonable time by an independent and impartial tribunal. This is particularly relevant to review and appeal processes. In *Runa Begum v Tower Hamlets LBC*, 2002, it was held that homelessness rights comprised civil rights. Although an officer of an authority conducting an internal review (10.168) could not be said to provide an independent and impartial tribunal, the county court appeal process (10.176) was nonetheless held to be a sufficient safeguard to ensure compliance with Art.6. The different stages could be considered cumulatively to decide whether Art.6 had been complied with.

10.194 Article 8. By Art.8 of the ECHR: "Everyone has the right to respect for his private and family life, his home and his correspondence." This does not amount, however, to a right to

housing to be provided by the state (*Chapman v UK*, 2001). Given
this interpretation of Art.8, it is highly unlikely that any claim for
breach of Art.8 will succeed where an authority have properly
applied the provisions of Pt 7 and reached the conclusion that
there is no substantive duty to house an applicant, as the provisions of Pt 7 are themselves compliant with ECHR (and, indeed,
go further than any duties under Art.8).

16. CRIMINAL OFFENCES

10.195 False statements. It is a criminal offence knowingly or
recklessly to make a statement which is false in a material
particular, or knowingly to withhold information which an authority have reasonably required in connection with the exercise of
their functions under Pt 7, with intent to induce an authority to
believe that the person making the statement, or any other person,
is entitled to accommodation or assistance (or accommodation or
assistance of a particular kind) (1996 Act s.214(1)). The offence is
punishable on summary conviction by a fine of up to level five on
the standard scale (1996 Act s.214(4)), i.e. £5,000).

10.196 Change of circumstances. An applicant has a duty to
notify an authority as soon as possible of any material change of
facts material to his case which occurs before he receives the
notification of the authority's decision on his application (1996 Act
s.214(2)). The authority are under a corresponding obligation to
explain to an applicant, in ordinary language, the nature of this
duty, and the effect of the statutory defence to a charge of non-
compliance (1996 Act s.214(2)).

10.197 Defence. The statutory defence to a charge of non-
compliance is that no such explanation was given, or that although
such an explanation was given there is some other reasonable
excuse for non-compliance (1996 Act s.214(3)).

10.198 Penalty. In the absence of such a defence, it is a
criminal offence to fail to comply with the duty to notify of
material changes, punishable on summary conviction at up to level
five on the standard scale.

17. CO-OPERATION BETWEEN AUTHORITIES

10.199 Requests for assistance. In the discharge of their functions under Pt 7, a local housing authority (10.12) may request

assistance from another local housing authority, a new town corporation, a registered social landlord or a housing action trust, or a Scottish local authority, development corporation, registered housing association or Scottish Homes (1996 Act s.213(1)(a), (2)). They may also ask a social services authority (in England, Wales or Scotland) (10.15) to exercise any of their functions on their behalf (1996 Act s.213(1)(b)). The other authority (or body, etc.) must co-operate with the housing authority, by rendering such assistance as is reasonable in the circumstances (1996 Act s.213(1)).

10.200 Assistance. Although an authority may request assistance under s.213, they may not delegate their substantive duty to inquire under s.184 except as expressly permitted (under the regulations permitting contracting out: 10.13): *R. v West Dorset DC Ex p. Gerrard*, 1994. Even prior to those express provisions, however, in *R. v Hertsmere BC Ex p. Woolgar*, 1995, it was held that so long as the key decision-making function was preserved by the authority, the inquiries themselves could be carried out by another body on their behalf.

10.201 Discretion. Whether or not to seek assistance is a matter for the authority, and the court will be slow to interfere with the exercise of such a discretion (*R. v Wirral MBC Ex p. Bell*, 1994).

Allocation duties

10.202 Homelessness Act 2002. Allocation of housing by local housing authorities is regulated by the Housing Act 1996 Pt 6, as extensively amended by the Homelessness Act 2002.

1. DEFINITION OF ALLOCATION

10.203 Meaning of allocation. When allocating housing, local housing authorities are obliged to comply with the provisions of Pt 6 (1996 Act s.159(1)). For these purposes, allocation has the following meanings:

- Selecting a secure (3.17) or introductory (6.30) tenant for their own accommodation. This includes notifying an existing tenant or licensee that his tenancy is to be secure (1996 Act s.159(3)), e.g. under 1985 Act Sch.1 paras 2 (employment-related accommodation), 5 (temporary accommodation for people taking up employment), or 10 (student accommodation), each of which has been amended (Sch.16) to substitute a requirement for notice for the previous conditions which related to the expiry of time (3.39).

- Nominating a person to be a secure or introductory tenant of another. Nomination includes formal and informal such arrangements (1996 Act s.159(4)).

- Nominating (in the same sense: 1996 Act, s.159(4)) a person to be an assured tenant (4.15) of a registered social landlord (3.12) (1996 Act s.159(2)).

10.204 Excluded allocations. Allocations to existing secure or introductory tenants are excluded, unless the allocation involves a transfer of housing accommodation for that tenant, and the transfer is made on his application (s.159(5)). In effect, therefore, management transfers initiated by the authority, to which the tenant accedes (or which are ordered by the court: see above 3.124 *et seq.*), do not count as allocations to which Pt 6 applies.

10.205 Additional exclusions. In addition, there is a number of other cases which are not treated as allocation:

- succession and devolution on death, or assignment to a potential successor (3.40);
- assignment by way of exchange (3.205);
- vesting under a number of family or domestic law provisions (Chapter 9); and
- other cases as may be prescribed by regulations (1996 Act s.160).

2. ELIGIBILITY

10.206 Eligibility. Any person may be allocated housing, provided that he is not ineligible under s.160A (s.160A(1), (2)). An allocation may not be made to two or more persons jointly if even one of them is ineligible (s.160A(1)(c)).

10.207 Persons from abroad. Persons subject to immigration control under the Asylum and Immigration Act 1996 are ineligible unless reincluded by regulations (s.160A(3)). The Secretary of State may not include in regulations any person who is excluded from entitlement to housing benefit by the Immigration and

Asylum Act 1999 s.115 (s.160A(4)). The Secretary of State may prescribe other persons from abroad who are ineligible, either in relation to local housing authorities generally or any particular local housing authority (s.160A(5)). Detailed provision has been made in England by regs 3 and 4 of the Allocation and Homelessness (Eligibility) (England) Regulations 2006 (SI 2006/1294) and in Wales by the Allocation of Housing (Wales) Regulations 2003 (SI 2003/239). These provisions do not affect the eligibility of someone who is already a secure or introductory tenant or an assured tenant of housing accommodation allocated to him by a local housing authority (s.160A(6)).

10.208 Unacceptable behaviour. A local authority may decide that an applicant is to be treated as ineligible, if they are satisfied that:

- the applicant or a member of his household has been guilty of unacceptable behaviour serious enough to make him unsuitable to be a tenant of the authority; and

- by reason of the circumstances at the time his application is considered is unsuitable to be a tenant of the authority by reason of that behaviour (s.160A(7)).

10.209 Definition. Unacceptable behaviour is that which would (if the applicant was a secure tenant of the authority) entitle the authority to a possession order under s.84 of the Housing Act 1985 on any of Grounds 1–7 of Sch.2 to that Act (see 3.84–3.120), or behaviour by a member of the applicant's household which would (if he were a person residing with a secure tenant of the authority) entitle the authority to such a possession order (s.160A(8)).

10.210 Reapplication. An applicant who is treated as ineligible because of unacceptable behaviour may (if he considers that he should no longer be so treated) make a fresh application (s.160A(11)).

10.211 Notification. If the authority decide that the applicant is ineligible for an allocation, they must notify him of that decision and the grounds for it (s.160A(9)). Notification must be given in writing, and, if not received by the applicant, shall be treated as having been given if made available at the authority's office for a reasonable period for collection by him or on his behalf (s.160A(10)), i.e. if unreceived, the burden is on the applicant to go to the authority's offices and ask for it.

10.212 Applications: advice and assistance. Authorities must ensure that there is free advice and information available in their area about the right to make an application for an allocation of housing (s.166(1)(a)). Authorities must also ensure that any necessary assistance in making an application is available free of charge to those who are likely to have difficulty in doing so without assistance (s.166(1)(b)). Authorities must ensure that applicants are aware of their right to request information about the likely availability of accommodation (10.225) (s.166(2)).

10.213 Consideration of applications. Every application for an allocation of housing made in accordance with the procedural requirements of the authority's allocation scheme must be considered by the authority (s.166(3)). The fact that a person is an applicant for an allocation may not, without the applicant's consent, be divulged by the authority to any member of the public (s.166(4)).

3. ALLOCATION SCHEMES

10.214 Allocation schemes. The authority have to maintain an allocation "scheme" governing both priorities and procedures (including all aspects of the allocation procedure, including by whom decisions may be made) (s.167(1)).

10–215 Choice policy. The allocation scheme must include a statement of the authority's policy on offering people who are to be allocated housing:

- a choice of housing accommodation; or

- the opportunity to express preference about the housing accommodation to be allocated to them (s.167(1A)).

10.216 Preference. The scheme must be framed to ensure that a reasonable preference is given to the following:

- persons who are homeless (10.20, above);

- persons who are owed a duty by a local housing authority under s.190(2) (10.101), 193(2) (10.112), or 195(2) (10.107) (or under s.65(2) or 68(2) of the Housing Act 1985) or who are occupying accommodation secured by any such authority under s.192(3) (10.108);

- persons occupying insanitary or overcrowded housing or otherwise living in unsatisfactory housing conditions;

- persons who need to move on medical or welfare grounds; and

- persons who need to move to a particular locality in the authority's area, where failure to meet that need would cause hardship to themselves or to others (s.167(2)).

10.217 Reasonable preference. To afford a reasonable preference means that the criteria must be an "important factor in making a decision about the allocation of housing" (*R. v Lambeth LBC Ex p. Ashley*, 1996), and that "positive favour should be shown to applications which satisfy any of the relevant criteria" (*R. v Wolverhampton MBC Ex p. Watters*, 1997). More recently, to afford reasonable preference has been described as providing those who fall within the relevant categories with a "reasonable head start" over other applicants (*R. (A) v Lambeth LBC*, 2002). "Reasonable preference does, however, imply a power to choose between different applicants on 'reasonable grounds' . . . it is not unreasonable to prefer good tenants to bad tenants" (*R. v Newham LBC Ex p. Miah*, 1995 at 288). Preference does not imply prospects of success, which depend of many factors, of which the most significant is the fact that demand for housing greatly exceeds supply: it is quite possible for a scheme to give reasonable preference to a person and for that person never to be allocated housing; indeed, as it is the scheme which must afford the reasonable preference, assessed in itself rather than according to its outcome, it is even possible for someone with no preference to be allocated accommodation ahead of someone with a preference (*Lin v Barnet LBC*, 2007).

10.218 Quotas. The requirement to give a reasonable preference to the specified groups does not prevent an authority allocating a quota of all vacancies to one particular group, e.g. the homeless (*R. v Islington LBC Ex p. Reilly and Mannix*, 1998; *R. v Westminster LBC Ex p. Al-Khorshan*, 2000). Where a separate quota is kept for a group, that list may not, however, be run in simple date order, but must reflect the different priorities of applicants within the group (*Al-Khorshan*).

10.219 Composite assessments. Any allocation scheme must be able to take into account multiple categories of need so as to reach a composite assessment of the needs of the applicant; the categories of need can be cumulative and are not to be treated separately (*Reilly and Mannix*). This principle is not affected by the fact that applicants have a measure of choice in the allocation of accommodation (10.215; *R. (A) v Lambeth LBC*, 2002).

10.220 Additional preference. The scheme may be framed so as to give additional preference to those within these categories who have an urgent housing need (s.167(2)). Additional preference means giving those applicants "additional weight" or "an extra head start", but it does not require an allocation to be made to applicants entitled to it ahead of all others, (*R. (A) v Lambeth LBC*, 2002).

10.221 Determining priorities. The scheme may also include provision for determining priorities between those in the reasonable preference categories, taking into account:

- the financial resources available to a person to meet housing costs;

- any behaviour of a person (or a member of his household) which affects his suitability to be a tenant;

- any local connection (10.69) which exists between a person and the authority's area (s.167(2A)).

10.222 Unacceptable behaviour. The scheme does not have to provide for any preference to an applicant where the authority are satisfied that:

- he, or a member of his household, has been guilty of unacceptable behaviour (10.208) serious enough to make him unsuitable to be a tenant of the authority; and

- in the circumstances at the time his case is considered, he deserves by reason of that behaviour not to be treated as a member of one of the groups to whom a reasonable preference is to be given (s.167(2C), (2D)).

10.223 Regulations. The Secretary of State has power to add to, amend or repeal any part of the list of those to whom a reasonable preference is to be accorded (s.167(3)). He also has power to specify factors which are not to be taken into account when allocating housing (s.167(4)).

10.224 Other allocations. Subject to the reasonable preference categories, the scheme may contain provision about the allocation of particular accommodation to a person who makes a specific application for it and to persons of a particular description, whether or not they are within the reasonable preference categories (s.167(2E)).

10.225 Procedure. The scheme must be framed so as to give an applicant the right to request general information that will enable him to assess:

- how his application is likely to be treated under the scheme (including whether he is likely to be regarded as in one of the reasonable preference categories); and

- whether accommodation appropriate to his needs is likely to be made available to him and, if so, how long it is likely to be before such accommodation becomes available for allocation to him (s.167(4A)(a)).

10.226 Notification. The scheme must be framed so that an applicant is notified:

- in writing of any decision that he is a person being given no preference because of a decision as to behaviour under s.167(2C) (10.208); and

- of the right to request the authority to inform him about the facts of his case which are likely to be, or have been, taken into account in considering whether to allocate housing accommodation to him (s.167(4A)(b), (c)).

10.227 Review. The scheme must include the right for applicants to request a review of a decision as to whether they are to be given no preference under s.167(2C) (10.222), about the facts of their case or that they are considered ineligible under s.160A (10.206) (s.167(4A)(d)). There are, however, no regulations governing the conduct of reviews (as there are in relation to homelessness decisions: 10.171), nor is there any appeal to the county court (again, as in relation to homelessness: 10.176). It follows that any challenge can only be by way of judicial review, according to the same principles as discussed in relation to homelessness (10.182–10.194).

10.228 Regulations. The Secretary of State may require that the procedures are framed in accordance with such principles as he may prescribe (s.167(5)).

10.229 Changing the scheme. Priorities and procedures are otherwise in the discretion of the authority (s.167(6)). Before adopting or making any major policy change to a scheme, the authority must send a copy of it in draft to every registered social landlord with which they have nomination arrangements, and afford them a reasonable opportunity to comment (s.167(7)).

10.230 Code of Guidance. As under Pt 7 (10.167), there is provision for the Secretary of State to issue guidance to which authorities must have regard (s.169).

10.231 Co-operation. When an authority ask a registered social landlord to offer accommodation to people with priority under the authority's allocation scheme, such landlords are bound to co-operate to such extent as is reasonable in the circumstances (s.170).

10.232 Information. An authority must publish a summary of their scheme, and provide a copy of it free of charge to any member of the public who asks for it (s.168(1)). The full scheme must be made available for inspection at the authority's principal office, and a copy must be made available to any member of the public who asks for it, on payment of a reasonable fee (s.168(2)).

10.233 Changes. When the authority make a major policy alteration to their scheme, they have to take such steps as they consider reasonable to bring the effect of the alteration to the attention of those likely to be affected by it (s.168(3)).

4. CRIMINAL OFFENCES

10.234 Criminal offences. It is a criminal offence knowingly or recklessly to make a statement—in connection with the exercise by an authority of their functions under Pt 6—which is false in a material particular, or knowingly to withhold information which an authority have reasonably required in connection with the exercise of their functions under Pt 6 (1996 Act s.171(1)).

10.235 Penalty. The offence is punishable on summary conviction by a fine of up to level five on the standard scale (1996 Act s.171(2)), i.e. £5,000.

CHAPTER ELEVEN

Disrepair

Introduction

11.01 Civil proceedings. In this chapter, we consider civil proceedings for disrepair, primarily from the viewpoint of the occupier who suffers its effects. Redress by way of complaint to a justice of the peace under s.4 of the Housing Act 2004; that a house is hazardous is considered in Chapter 12 (12.162). Proceedings by way of a summons for statutory nuisance, under s.82 of the Environmental Protection Act 1990, are considered in Chapter 13 (13.27–13.42).

11.02 Repair and improvement. In practice, there is a considerable overlap between what is or is perceived to be an issue of disrepair and what is considered to be improvement. Although the overlap between the two concepts or activities is considered in this chapter, improvement powers—and financial assistance for their exercise—are themselves considered in Chapter 12.

11.03 Cumulative remedies. It should be remembered that these other proceedings and possibilities remain available, however, and that they, as well as other remedies considered in the following three chapters, are additional to those considered in this.

11.04 Contract and tort. In this chapter, therefore, we are concerned with remedies in contract and tort. Contract will assist when there is a specific agreement, whether express or implied; tort is the body of law governing relations between individuals where there is no contractual relationship, or where the contractual relationship does not itself cover the harm alleged to have been suffered.

Outline

11.05 Contract

- The starting-point is the written agreement governing the occupation in question, if any, but contractual terms may be implied by common law or statute, which may add to or even override written terms.

- Landlords are generally not in breach of any obligation to repair until they have notice of the disrepair.

- The Unfair Contract Terms Act 1977 and EC regulations may impose a requirement that any contractual terms are reasonable.

- Common law implies a number of terms into tenancies: that a furnished tenancy is fit for habitation at the start of the letting, that the landlord will keep any common parts in a reasonable condition, and that the tenant will use the premises in a "tenant-like manner".

- The Landlord and Tenant Act 1985 s.8 imposes an obligation on landlords to keep premises fit for human habitation; the obligation only applies, however, to tenancies at a very low rent, and is therefore rarely applicable today.

- The most important statutory obligation is that implied by the Landlord and Tenant Act 1985 s.11, which requires landlords of dwellings let on short leases, i.e. fixed terms of less than seven years and periodic tenancies, to keep in repair the structure and exterior of the dwelling, and the water, gas, electrical and heating installations.

- An obligation to repair a dwelling is not an obligation to improve it, although there may be an overlap.

- There are also special provisions applicable to repairs when a long leaseholder becomes a statutory tenant.

- There is a number of contractual remedies for disrepair.

- Both the landlord and tenant may seek damages for breach of any repairing covenant.

- In certain circumstances, the tenant may "set off" any repairing costs against his rent.

- A court may order specific performance of a repairing covenant or an injunction requiring works to be carried out.

- A receiver or manager of the property may be appointed by the court.

- In cases where the tenant under a long lease is in breach of a repairing covenant, the landlord may seek to forfeit the lease.

11.06   Tort

- A number of torts—arising at common law or by statute—may be committed in cases of disrepair or unacceptable housing conditions.

- Certain relationships will give rise to a legal duty of care, so that a failure to take reasonable care may lead to a claim in negligence. These relationships include: the landlord in relation to the users of common parts of premises, builders in relation to occupiers of a house, developers and other professionals involved in building in relation to future occupiers, and surveyors in relation to purchasers of a house.

- Failure to comply with the Building Regulations could give rise to an action in tort.

- The Defective Premises Act 1972 s.3 imposes a liability on anyone who carries out construction, repair, maintenance or demolition or any other work in relation to premises in respect of persons who might reasonably be expected to be affected by any resulting defects in the premises.

- Section 1 of the 1972 Act imposes a duty of care on anyone doing any work for or in connection with the provision of a dwelling by erection, conversion or enlargement, to ensure that the dwelling when completed is fit for human habitation.

- The Occupiers Liability Act 1975 s.2 imposes a duty on "occupiers" of property to ensure that the premises are reasonably safe for any visitors.

- Liability is imposed on landlords by the Defective Premises Act 1972 s.4 where the landlord is under an obligation to repair. The obligation is to take reasonable care to ensure that any persons who might be affected by a defect are reasonably safe from personal injury or damage to their property.

- In some circumstances, landlords may be liable in nuisance, and tenants liable for waste, i.e. an act causing deterioration to the premises.

- The main remedies in tort are damages and injunctions.

11.07 Limitation

- There is generally a six-year time limit on bringing claims in contract or tort.

- Where damages for personal injury are being claimed, the limit is three years.

- Where a defect is "latent" and does not become obvious until later, more time may be available.

Contract

11.08 Contractual and statutory provisions. The starting point will always be what—if anything—is set out in any written agreement that may exist. In the main, it is landlords who draw up letting agreements and consequently the object of the agreement will be to impose upon the tenant the most extensive obligations that the law permits, while limiting the landlord's own obligations.

11.09 In a number of cases, however, the law will intervene. These circumstances are considered in context but it should be noted that in short leases and periodic tenancies any such attempts by a landlord are likely to contravene the provisions of s.11 of the Landlord and Tenant Act 1985 (11.47–11.79), that other leases, at low rents, may have to comply with the provisions of s.8 of the Landlord and Tenant Act 1985 (11.43–11.46), and that relief may be obtainable under the provisions of the Unfair Contract Terms Act 1977 or regulations (11.15–11.21). Further, remedies in tort may be available where there are none in contract.

11.10 Notice of disrepair. There is one principle that is common to almost all of the provisions to be considered under this heading. That is, that a landlord's obligation to repair does not arise until he has had actual notice of conditions such as to put him, if not on actual notice of what is in disrepair, then at least on sufficient notice to cause him to inspect and find out. The only exception to this is the case of an express repairing covenant which does not state that the tenant has to give notice (*Minchburn v Peck*, 1987).

11.11   Cases. The leading cases on the need for notice usefully illustrate its operation. In *O'Brien v Robinson*, 1973, works had been executed to a ceiling several years before it fell down. There had been no further complaint or warning, by tenant or otherwise, to the landlord before it came down, and the landlord was, accordingly, held not to be in breach of the obligation to repair. In *Sheldon v West Bromwich Corp*, 1973, however, a plumber employed by the defendant corporation inspected a water tank. The tank was corroded although it was not yet weeping. Subsequently, it burst. It was held that the condition of the water tank at the time of the inspection, even without the weeping (which would be a sure and final sign of corrosion calling for repair) was sufficient to put the corporation on notice that something needed to be done.

11.12   In *McGreal v Wake*, 1984, a repairs notice was served on the landlord by the local authority. When the landlord did not carry out the works, the local authority carried them out in default (see Chapter 12). For the period from after the landlord had a reasonable opportunity to comply with the notice, until the authority completed the works, the landlord was held to be in breach of his obligation to repair.

11.13   From these and other cases (see also *Dinefwr BC v Jones*, 1987; *Hall v Howard*, 1988) emerge the following propositions:

- **Actual notice.** Notice need not come from the tenant. It is sufficient that the landlord has actually had notice, e.g. by way of a notice under one of the many provisions considered in the next three chapters.

- **On notice.** Notice must be sufficient to warn the landlord that there may be a problem. It is not necessary for the tenant actually to identify causes, or to specify defects in such detail to serve as a schedule of (necessary) works.

- **Unequivocal notice.** Notice must, however, be unequivocal. Where a tenant gave notice of disrepair, saying that he would subsequently provide the landlord with the details, the landlord was entitled to await the further information (*Al-Hassani v Merrigan*, 1987).

11.14   Notice and common parts. The rule that notice has to be given does not apply in relation to any part of the premises still in the landlord's control (*British Telecommunications Plc v Sun Life Assurance Society Plc*, 1996). In *Passley v Wandsworth LBC*, 1996, the landlord authority were held responsible for burst pipes, even though they had no notice of any defect, because the pipes were located in a roof space above a top floor flat which was a part of the property which was not within the flat but rather was within a part of the property under the landlord's control.

1. UNFAIR CONTRACT TERMS ACT 1977

11.15 Application. Although this Act does not apply to the creation or termination of an interest in land (Unfair Contract Terms Act 1977 s.1 and Sch.1), it may apply to other terms in a tenancy, and applies generally to licences. It follows that it may affect the operation of a repairing obligation imposed on an occupier (which is not already excluded by another statutory provision, e.g. Landlord and Tenant Act 1985 s.11). The Act only applies to "consumers" dealing with a person, on his written standard terms of business (Unfair Contract Terms Act 1977 s.3), and so is unlikely to apply, e.g. in the case of a resident landlord (4.44–4.51; 5.43–5.59).

11.16 Requirements. Under the provisions of this Act, a landlord may neither limit his own liability for breach of contract, nor claim to be entitled to offer either no service at all or a service substantially different from that which might reasonably be expected of him, save to the extent that is reasonable (Unfair Contract Terms Act 1977 s.3). In this context, no service or a substantially different service than that expected, may be the provisions most relevant to repairing obligation, i.e. if the landlord seeks to abdicate responsibility altogether or seeks to limit his responsibility unreasonably.

11.17 Reasonableness. For these purposes, reasonableness means that the term in question is or is not one that is fair and reasonable to include in the contract:

- having regard to the circumstances actually known to the parties when the contract was made, or which ought to have been so known; and
- having particular regard to:
  - the relative bargaining positions of the parties;
  - alternative possibilities, i.e. alternative accommodation here, open to the consumer; and
  - trade or custom (Unfair Contract Terms Act 1977 s.11).

11.18   EC regulations.   In addition to the 1977 Act, contracts are also governed by the Unfair Terms in Consumer Contracts Regulations 1999 (SI 1999/2083), which directly implement European Council Directive 93/13 (and which do not exclude the creation or termination of interests in land).

11.19   The regulations import a requirement of good faith into contracts between a "seller or supplier" and a "consumer". The requirement of good faith is almost an identical requirement to that of "reasonableness" under the Unfair Contract Terms Act 1977 (11.17).

11.20   The regulations list a variety of illustrations of unfair terms. In the context of disrepair, the most relevant will be any term "excluding or hindering the consumer's right to take legal action or exercise any other legal remedy", e.g. clauses which seek to limit the right of the tenant to set-off against arrears of rent (11.105).

11.21   Detailed guidance on unfair terms in relation to assured and assured shorthold tenancies is now available from the Office of Fair Trading, which offers a number of further examples of possible exclusions and limitations of liability which would be unfair.

2.   CONTRACTUAL TERMS

11.22   In the following paragraphs we shall consider:

- express terms which may be found in tenancy agreements;
- terms implied by law, which may be additional to those expressed in an agreement, or may provide a basic and minimum statement of liabilities when there is neither written nor verbal agreement between the parties; and
- terms implied by statute, which may override what has expressly been agreed or may operate where nothing express has been agreed.

(i)   *Express terms*

11.23   Content.   The express terms are exactly that: express and explicit. What they say is—subject to being overridden by statute (including the Unfair Contract Terms Act and Regulations, above,

11.15)—what they mean. While there is a number of common terms that have given rise over the centuries to a considerable body of law as to their interpretation (most of the relevant aspects of which have fed through to the interpretation of statutorily implied terms and are considered, so far as relevant, in that context), they are essentially idiosyncratic in the sense that the parties may seek to allocate responsibilities between themselves and/or expressly to address specific repairing items in any way they see fit.

11.24 Higher standards. Although most landlords seek to limit their repairing obligations to a minimum, this is not always the case. Some local authorities have expressly agreed to higher standards than those imposed by the Landlord and Tenant Act 1985 s.11 (11.47, below). In *Welsh v Greenwich LBC*, 2001, the authority covenanted to keep the premises in "good condition", which was held to include liability for severe condensation dampness that would not have fallen under a mere covenant to repair (11.66).

11.25 Reasonable steps. Another term concerned a covenant to "take all reasonable steps to keep the estate clean and tidy". It was held that this was not discharged by the mere appointment of outside contractors, however competent, without also putting in place an adequate system for the landlord to monitor the contractor's performance and effectiveness (*Long v Southwark LBC*, 2002).

(ii) *Terms implied by law*

11.26 Fitness for human habitation. There is no general term implied into contracts for the letting of residential accommodation, either that a dwelling is fit for human habitation at the start of the tenancy, or that it will be so kept by the landlord during the tenancy (*Hart v Windsor*, 1844). It is, however, implied that a furnished lettings will at the start of the tenancy be fit for human habitation (*Smith v Marrable*, 1843).

11.27 Fitness for these purposes means fitness at common law, not fitness for human habitation as defined in the Landlord and Tenant Act 1985 (11.43). What is meant by fitness, therefore, must be considered as a matter of common law, although statute may on occasion afford a helpful guide to contemporary standards—it is clear that what one generation means by fitness is not the same as another.

11.28 Licences. It would seem that today a similar covenant will normally be implied into a licence of furnished accommodation (*Smith v Nottinghamshire CC*, 1981), although there could be cases where it would not be consistent with the nature of the licence to do so.

11.29 Weekly tenancies. Nor, in the absence of any express agreement as to repair, will the courts necessarily assume that under a weekly or monthly periodic tenancy, the landlord will take responsibility for "major" repairs, even though the courts readily accept that it is unlikely to have been intended that the tenant will do so instead, for want of any sufficient interest in the property to merit substantial expenditure (*Mint v Good*, 1950; *Sleafer v Lambeth LBC*, 1959).

11.30 Under a weekly, or probably other short periodic tenancy, the landlord will, however, have a right to do repairs, and correspondingly to enter to view the state of the property, but whether or not it is implied at law that he is obliged so to do will depend on whether anything was written or said, or otherwise on the court's view as to what was intended.

11.31 In *Barrett v Lounova*, 1988, where the tenant was liable for internal repairs but nothing had been agreed or said about structural or external repairs, the court concluded that it must have been intended that the landlord would have liability, in order to make the agreement work effectively, i.e. to give it business efficacy, because the tenant could not otherwise comply with his obligations.

11.32 In practice, this issue rarely arises today, because *lacunae* in responsibility are cured by the provisions of s.11 of the Landlord and Tenant Act 1985, although there remains in existence a number of tenancies which predate its predecessor (Housing Act 1961 s.32), and to which, accordingly, its provisions do not apply, as in *Barrett*.

11.33 Licences. In the case of a licence, it will not only be the case that the landlord will usually be assumed to undertake liability to keep the property in repair (*Smith v Nottinghamshire CC*, 1981), but it may be considered inconsistent with the nature of licence for the licensee to be under any significant repairing obligation (*Addiscombe Garden Estates v Crabbe*, 1958). There could, however, be exceptions if some particular aspect of the licence so suggested.

11.34 Common parts. A clear distinction must be drawn between the premises which are the subject of the tenancy and other parts of a house or building which are not included in the letting. These parts, e.g. stairs, roof, halls, corridors, foundations and—in some houses—bathrooms and toilets, are kept in the landlord's possession and control and are consequently his responsibility. He is wholly responsible for their upkeep (*Cockburn v Smith*, 1924). He must keep them reasonably safe (*Dunster v Hollis*, 1918). Where they form the means of access to a house, flat or room, and in the absence of any express agreement to the contrary, he is to keep them in a reasonable condition (*Liverpool CC v Irwin*, 1977; *King v South Northamptonshire DC*, 1991), probably in a condition reasonably approximating that in which they were at the commencement of the letting. (It is thought that this obligation is related to, or derived from, that considered in the next paragraph.)

11.35 Non-derogation from grant. Where a tenant occupies property which adjoins that occupied by the landlord (whether actually so occupied or as a matter of law, e.g. common parts), it is implied that the landlord will not use his retained property so as to "derogate from the grant" of the tenancy, i.e. in such a way as to interfere with the tenant's use of the property for the purpose for which it was let.

11.36 Quiet enjoyment. This covenant has been considered above (8.77). It is not usually considered in relation to disrepair. As, however, a covenant by the landlord that the tenant will be able quietly to enjoy the premises which are the subject of the tenancy is implied into every letting, it may be a useful catch-all where, for example, repairs take an undue time to complete or are executed with such disregard for the tenant's convenience that it may be said unreasonably and unnecessarily to interfere with his use of the premises. There is no reason why disrepair should not also be considered breach of the covenant for quiet enjoyment (*Gordon v Selico Co*, 1986).

11.37 The covenant can only be used, however, in relation to a complaint about conditions arising after the grant of the tenancy. The tenant takes the premises in the physical conditions which he finds them and subject to the uses contemplated for those premises. Thus, everyday noise from neighbouring flats arising because of a lack of soundproofing does not amount to a breach of the covenant (*Southwark LBC v Mills*, 1999).

11.38 Estoppel and rent registration. In some circumstances, even where one party has no direct or express legal rights against another, the law will stop the other party denying an obligation. This is known as "estoppel".

11.39 One circumstance related to repairs, and which relies heavily upon estoppel, was at one time quite common, although is of decreasing contemporary relevance.

11.40 It is noted below (11.49) that the provisions of s.11 of the Landlord and Tenant Act 1985, apply only to tenancies granted after October 24, 1961. Where a tenancy commenced before that date, therefore, there might have been no repairing obligations implied into the tenancy at all (as in *Barrett v Lounova*, 1988; above, 11.31, 11.32). Over time, however, there may have been applications for registration of a fair rent (5.189–5.211) in the course of which it is possible—perhaps even likely—that the rent officer will have assumed, or even been informed, either that s.11 applies or that the landlord is in any event responsible for major and structural repairs, and will have assessed the rent on this basis.

11.41 As the tenant will therefore be paying—and the landlord receiving—a higher rent than if the tenant were responsible for the major repairs, or than if no one had any such responsibility, the landlord will be "estopped" from denying the liability (*Brikom Investments v Seaford*, 1981), although he can subsequently apply for a variation in the registration. The estoppel will not, therefore, guarantee future responsibility. In an appropriate case, estoppel may override even the express terms of an agreement.

11.42 Use in a tenant-like manner. The tenant is under an obligation to use premises in a "tenant-like manner". That is to say, he:

> "must take proper care of the place. He must, if he is going away for the winter, turn off the water and empty the boiler. He must clean the chimneys, when necessary, and also the windows. He must mend the electric light when it fuses. He must unstop the sink when it is blocked by his waste. In short, he must do the little jobs about the place which a reasonable tenant would do. In addition, he must, of course, not damage the house, wilfully or negligently; and he must see that his family and guests do not damage it; if they do, he must repair it. But apart from such things, if the house falls into disrepair through fair wear and tear or lapse of time, or for any reason not caused by him, then the tenant is not liable to repair it". (*Warren v Keen*, 1953, *per* Denning L.J.).

(iii) *Terms implied by statute*

Landlord and Tenant Act 1985 section 8

11.43 Fit for human habitation. Contrary to the normal rule (11.26)—that there is no covenant that premises are fit for human habitation at the commencement of a tenancy or that they will so be kept throughout the tenancy—statute implies such a term into tenancies at a very low rent (Landlord and Tenant Act 1985 s.8). For these purposes, a property is unfit if it is not reasonably suitable for occupation because it is defective in respect of one or more of the following: repair, stability, freedom from damp, internal arrangement, natural lighting, ventilation, water supply, drainage and sanitary conveniences, facilities for preparation of food and for the disposal of waste water.

11.44 As discussed above (11.10–11.13), there will be no obligation until the landlord has had notice of the disrepair (*Morgan v Liverpool Corp*, 1927), and the term has no application where the premises cannot be rendered fit for human habitation at a reasonable expense (*Buswell v Goodwin*, 1970). The term will, however, carry over into a statutory tenancy (11.81). The term carries with it a right on the part of the landlord, on not less than 24 hours' notice in writing, to enter to view the state and condition of the premises.

11.45 Rent limits. The covenant is, however, implied only into tenancies at such low rents that the covenant is today rarely encountered in practice. The rent levels are as follows:

- Where the contract was made before July 31, 1923, the rent at the beginning of the tenancy must not have been more than £40 per annum in the administrative county of London, nor more than £26 per annum in a borough of an urban district outside London, nor elsewhere more than £16 per annum.

- In relation to contracts made on or after that date, but before July 6, 1957, the rent at the commencement of the tenancy must not have been more than £40 per annum in the administrative county of London, nor more than £26 elsewhere.

- In relation to contracts made on or after that date, the rent at the commencement must not have been more than £80 in what was until April 1, 1965 the administrative county of London and thereafter Greater London, or £52 per annum elsewhere.

11.46   Short and long leases.   The covenant is implied into both short lettings and, unless excluded, into longer leases. In relation to a lease for not less than three years, the covenant will not take effect if the lease contains a term that the tenant put the property into a condition reasonably fit for human habitation, and the lease cannot be brought to an end by the landlord or by the tenant, other, perhaps, than by forfeiture (1.131–1.146) within the first three years.

Landlord and Tenant Act 1985 section 11

11.47   Principal repairing covenant.   This is the principal repairing covenant now implied into most lettings of residential accommodation. It does not apply if the letting is for a term of seven years or more (Landlord and Tenant Act 1985 s.12), which means seven years from the commencement of occupation, either under the tenancy or under a binding agreement for a tenancy (*Brikom Investments v Seaford*, 1981).

11.48   The Act allows the parties to apply to the county court for an order excluding or modifying the operation of s.11, but in the absence of any such order the Act overrides the express terms of any agreement, and any contract purporting to exclude the provisions of s.11—or to penalise the tenant because the landlord has to comply with them—is void and of no effect.

11.49   Old tenancies.   The section applies only to tenancies granted after commencement of the Housing Act 1961, when the provision was introduced (October 24, 1961).

11.50   Periodic tenancy.   A periodic tenancy is not for seven years or more, even though it may last or have lasted that long or longer, so that the covenant accordingly applies to it.

11.51   The implied covenant.   The term is that:

"In any lease of a dwelling-house, being a lease to which this section applies, there shall be implied a covenant by the lessor—

(a) to keep in repair the structure and exterior of the dwelling-house (including drains, gutters and external pipes); and

    (b) to keep in repair and proper working order the installa-
        tions in the dwelling-house—

        (i) for the supply of water, gas and electricity, and for
            sanitation (including basins, sinks, baths and sani-
            tary conveniences but not, except as aforesaid, fix-
            tures, fittings and appliances for making use of the
            supply of water, gas or electricity), and
        (ii) for space heating or heating water."

11.52 The covenant carries with it a right on the part of the landlord, on giving not less than 24 hours' notice in writing, to enter to view the state of the premises (Landlord and Tenant Act 1985 s.11(6)).

11.53 The obligation extends to essential means of access to the premises (*Brown v Liverpool Corp*, 1969).

11.54 Part of house or building. The provision applies as much to part of a house or building—even as little as a single room—as to a house (Landlord and Tenant Act 1985 s.16).

11.55 Where only a part of house or building is involved, then the covenant extends to an obligation to keep the structure and exterior of the house or building in repair, and to keep in repair and proper working order an installation (for the same purposes) which serves the part of the house which is the subject of the tenancy, provided it forms part of a building in which the landlord has an interest or the installation itself is owned by the landlord or is under his control (Landlord and Tenant Act 1985 s.11(1A), added by the Housing Act 1988 s.116; *Niazi Services Ltd v Van der Loo*, 2004).

11.56 This will not be so, however, unless the disrepair actually affects the tenant's enjoyment of his property or of the common parts (Landlord and Tenant Act 1985 s.11(1B)).

11.57 These provisions extending s.11 beyond the premises which are the subject of the tenancy relate only to tenancies granted on or after November 15, 1988 (unless pursuant to a contract for a tenancy which predates November 15, 1988).

11.58 Limits of covenant. The provisions do not, however, go so far as to require the landlord to do works for which the tenant is liable under the duty to use premises in a tenant-like manner (11.42), nor do they require him to rebuild or reinstate the premises in the case of destruction or damage by fire, tempest, flood or other inevitable accident, nor to keep in repair or maintain such of the tenant's own belongings as he is entitled to remove from the property (Landlord and Tenant Act 1985 s.11(2)).

11.59 It is a defence to an action based on failure to repair a building in which the premises are situated, or installations outside the premises but which service them, that the landlord was unable to obtain sufficient rights to do the works (Landlord and Tenant Act 1985 s.11(3A)), e.g. under the Access to Neighbouring Land Act 1992 (11.168).

11.60 Unless the defect arises in a part of the premises which is not let to the tenant, there will only be a breach of the covenant if the landlord has had notice of disrepair (11.10–11.14), but the covenant will carry over into any statutory tenancy (11.81).

11.61 Standard of repair. The main problem arising under this provision is that of the standard of repair it imposes. The Act itself provides that regard shall be had to the age, character and prospective life of the property, and the locality in which it is situated (Landlord and Tenant Act 1985 s.11(3)). This may mean that patch repairs are adequate even where a higher standard of repair would be desirable (*Trustees of Hungerford Charity v Beazeley*, 1993).

11.62 It is not a defence to an allegation that installations are not in proper working order to show that they suffer from a design defect (*Liverpool CC v Irwin*, 1976) and a change in the nature of the supply may require the landlord to modify the installations to ensure that they continue to function (*O'Connor v Old Etonian Housing Association Ltd*, 2002). Indeed, although the covenant requires only that the landlord keep the premises in repair to the extent set out, this is interpreted as meaning that the landlord must also put them in repair, for that which is not in repair at the commencement of the tenancy can hardly be kept in repair (*Saner v Bilton*, 1878).

11.63 Exterior. A dividing wall between two terraced houses will be part of the exterior of each (*Green v Eales*, 1841), and the walls of a flat—whether to the outside or the inside of the building—and the ceiling and floor, will all be part of the exterior for the purpose of the covenant (*Campden Hill Towers v Gardner*, 1976).

11.64 Windows. Windows are part of the exterior (*Quick v Taff Ely BC*, 1985; *Ball v Plummer*, 1979; *Boswell v Crucible Steel*, 1925; *Irvine v Moran*, 1990). That is not to say that the landlord is liable for a breakage by the tenant, for that would be the tenant's responsibility as part of his duty to use the premises in a tenant-like manner (11.42), but it does mean that breakage by someone else, or because, for example, the frame broke or warped, would be the liability of the landlord.

11.65 Structure. Structure is perhaps a more difficult concept. A house is a complex whole, and anything which touches upon that complex unit may properly be deemed to be part of the structure (*Pearlman v Keepers and Governors of Harrow School*, 1978). The roof of a block of flats or a house converted into flats may be part of the structure of the top floor flat, but then again it may not, depending on, for example, whether there is a roof space or an attic (*Douglas-Scott v Scorgie*, 1984).

11.66 Disrepair to structure. Disrepair must be to the structure or exterior, not merely resulting from it. Thus, dampness caused by a leak or defective brickwork will mean that the structure or exterior is in disrepair, but where the construction of the structure and exterior results in dampness from ordinary use of the premises, i.e. "condensation dampness", without actual disrepair, this will not class as disrepair within this implied covenant (*Quick v Taff Ely BC*, 1985).

11.67 Thus, in *Stent v Monmouth DC*, 1987, it was held that if a door "merely" fails to keep out water, there will be no disrepair to the structure, although if the water ingress damages the door itself, there will be.

11.68 In *Staves v Leeds CC*, 1990, condensation dampness meant that the physical condition of the plaster required renewal. It was conceded that the plaster was part of the structure and it therefore followed that there was disrepair.

11.69 In *Irvine v Moran*, 1990, however, it was held that internal wall plaster was not part of the structure of a dwelling-house since it was more in the nature of a decorative finish than an essential material element of the house.

11.70 Repair. It is "repair" which the covenant requires. For many years, it was believed that the proper way to define the word repair in a repairing covenant was by distinguishing it from such other terms as "improvement", "renewal" or "replacement", i.e. if the works needed to cure the problem amounted to improvement, renewal or replacement, they would not comprise a repair. For this reason, it was commonly believed that an inherent defect could not be cured within a repairing obligation, because that would comprise an improvement.

11.71 The key test was—and to this extent remains—whether the works executed would result in the delivery up of something different in quality to that which was originally let. Thus, for example, it was thought that a repairing obligation could not be used to require a landlord to introduce a damp-proof course (*Pembery v Lamdin*, 1940), or to provide underpinning (*Sotheby v Grundy*, 1947).

11.72 Extent of works. More recently it has been held, however, that these older cases turned on their own facts rather than setting precedents as to what works are or are not within a covenant to repair: *Ravenseft Properties Ltd v Davstone (Holdings) Ltd*, 1978, a case involving the same block of flats as the subject of the action in *Campden Hill Towers v Gardner*, 1976.

11.73 In that case, the block had been constructed without expansion joints to retain a stone cladding once natural movement ("settling") commenced. Accordingly, the stone cladding threatened to fall away. The only proper way to rectify this, however, was by the introduction of the missing expansion joints. It was argued that such works to the structure, involving the introduction of a new method of construction and the curing of a construction defect, could not be within the covenant to repair. Having regard to the sort of works involved (which were not, in comparison to the whole block, that extensive), to the necessity for the joints, and to the cost of the works compared to the value of the block as a whole, it was held that the works could be compelled within the repairing obligation.

11.74 Contemplation of parties. In another case (*Smedley v Chumley and Hawkes*, 1981), a riverside restaurant was built on a pier, or raft. It was a recent construction, and there was inadequate underpinning. The restaurant threatened to sink into the river. The court asked itself what had been in the contemplation of the parties, and was influenced by the fact that these were modern premises, not an old and deteriorating property: it was held that underpinning could be compelled within a covenant to repair.

11.75 Principles in practice. How do these principles work in housing? In *Wainwright v Leeds CC*, 1984, the older authorities prevailed. In *Elmcroft Developments Ltd v Tankersley-Sawyer*, 1984, and most recently in *Quick v Taff Ely BC*, 1985, however, the Court of Appeal upheld the *Ravenseft* approach.

11.76 Accordingly:

- where a modern property is in issue, works can be required within s.11 of the Landlord and Tenant Act 1985, even though they comprise works to cure an inherent or constructional defect and which involve the introduction of a new construction method; and

- where an older house is in issue, the courts are—having regard both to contemporary values and to the comparatively small cost of such works as damp-proof coursing, and perhaps also influenced by the modern emphasis on retention in use of older housing stock—also now prepared to order whatever works are necessary to keep a house in a reasonable condition, provided they are not so extensive or expensive as to involve virtual reconstruction or such overall improvement as will turn the old house into a new dwelling.

11.77 Thus, in *Murray v Birmingham CC*, 1987, it was held that the covenant could (in principle) extend to the provision of a new roof, although in that case such extensive works were in fact not held necessary.

11.78 Three tests. In *McDougall v Easington DC*, 1989, the Court of Appeal considered whether a major rehabilitation programme requiring over £10,000 worth of works to each property, but only increasing their value from £10,000 to £18,000, amounted to their repair, and concluded that the works amounted to an improvement not within the repairing obligation.

11.79 The court identified three tests which could be applied separately or concurrently to decide whether works amounted to a repair within s.11 of the Landlord and Tenant Act 1985:

- **Whole or subsidiary structure**: whether the alterations went to the whole or substantially the whole of the structure or only to a subsidiary part;

- **Character**: whether the effect of the alterations was to produce a building of a wholly different character than that which had been let; and

- **Cost**: the cost of the works in relation to the previous value of the building and their effect on the value and life span of the building.

Other statutory provisions

11.80   Rent Act 1977; Housing Act 1988.   Though the Rent Act 1977 and the Housing Act 1988 are not directly concerned with repairs, they contain a number of provisions affecting the subject:

- **Continuation of covenants.** Both a Rent Act statutory tenancy (5.25) and a Housing Act assured statutory periodic tenancy (4.75) are on the same terms as the preceding contractual tenancy (1977 Act s.3(1); 1988 Act s.5), from which it follows that any express or implied repairing obligations will be continued (*McCarrick v Liverpool Corp*, 1947).

- **Access.** It is an implied term of all Rent Act protected tenancies (whether contractual or statutory: see Chapter 5), and of all Housing Act assured tenancies (Chapter 4), that the tenant will afford the landlord all reasonable facilities for access and the execution of any repairs which the landlord is entitled to carry out (1977 Act ss.3(2), 148; 1988 Act s.16).

- **Grant-aided works and court order.** Where a landlord wishes to carry out works which qualify for a grant under the Housing Grants, Construction and Regeneration Act 1996 (12.98), and a Rent Act protected tenant will not consent to their execution, the landlord may apply to the court for an order compelling the tenant's consent, which may be subject to terms, e.g. tenant's housing during works, and which will be granted or refused bearing in mind such alternative accommodation, the age and health of the tenant, and any disadvantages that might be expected to result to the tenant from such works (1977 Act s.116). There is no equivalent provision under the Housing Act 1988, although extensive works may constitute a ground for possession (4.98).

11.81   Landlord and Tenant Act 1954.   On termination of a long lease, a tenant at a low rent may become a statutory tenant under the Rent Act 1977 (2.11–2.15). Under the long lease, the tenant will usually have been responsible for repairs. It would be inconsistent with the nature of a statutory tenancy for the tenant to retain such an obligation, but on the other hand it might be considered unfair were the landlord suddenly to find himself having to rectify breaches of the tenant's covenant, i.e. the tenant's failure to repair during the lease.

11.82 To this end, amongst the provisions governing "conversion" of the long leaseholder to the status of statutory tenant, is to be found provision for the execution of "initial repairs" (Landlord and Tenant Act 1954 s.7). The notice proposing the statutory tenancy (2.14) must itself propose:

- what initial repairs are to be carried out; and

- what balance of repairing obligation is to pertain during the statutory tenancy.

11.83 There are no equivalent provisions where the termination of the long tenancy falls to be dealt with under the Local Government and Housing Act 1989 Sch.10 (2.16–2.20).

11.84 Initial repairs. These matters are to be agreed between landlord and tenant at least two months before the statutory tenancy comes into existence, or otherwise application must be made to the county court for a determination (Landlord and Tenant Act 1954 s.7). The purpose of the provision is to ensure that the property is in an acceptable state for the commencement of the statutory tenancy, for which purpose it is assumed that the state will be the same as if the tenant had fulfilled all his contractual obligations.

11.85 The burden of initial repairs will then commonly fall on the tenant. Unless the tenant is willing to have them carried out himself, however, the court cannot order him to do so; instead, the landlord is ordered to execute the works, and the tenant to pay for them.

11.86 The works are required to be to a maximum standard of "good repair", or such higher standard of works as the landlord indicates he is willing to attain (Landlord and Tenant Act 1954 s.9). The court may order payment for the initial repairs in instalments, or in a lump sum (Landlord and Tenant Act 1954 s.8).

11.87 Continuing repairs. The court can also determine the balance of obligations to follow the initial repairs, but cannot order the landlord to maintain the premises at a higher standard than at the completion of the initial repairs or, if there are no initial repairs, than the state of the premises at the date of the court's hearing (Landlord and Tenant Act 1954 s.9).

11.88 The court is under no obligation to make any order governing continuing repairing obligations (Landlord and Tenant Act 1954 s.8). It is, however, common to order or agree that the balance will be as under the Landlord and Tenant Act 1985 s.11 (11.47–11.79).

11.89 Leasehold Reform Act 1967. On the extension of a lease under this Act (2.22–2.25), there is a general provision for variation of the repairing terms of the original lease by consent or by court order (Leasehold Reform Act 1967 s.15).

3. CONTRACTUAL REMEDIES

11.90 Either landlord or tenant may wish to obtain a remedy against the other for breach of a repairing obligation. If the tenant breaks his obligations, the landlord may seek possession of the premises by way of an action for forfeiture and under the Rent Act 1977, the Housing Act 1985 and the Housing Act 1988. He may also seek damages. More commonly, it is the tenant who will be seeking redress against the landlord: here, possession will not be in issue, but the tenant will want an order for works to be executed and may also seek compensation for the period of disrepair.

11.91 The remedies which fall to be considered are therefore:

- damages for breach by landlord;
- damages for breach by tenant;
- set-off and counterclaim by tenant;
- specific performance/injunctions;
- receiving orders;
- forfeiture; and
- possession.

(i) *Damages for breach by landlord: unfitness*

11.92 If furnished premises are not fit for human habitation, the
tenant can quit and will not be liable for the rent. Unfortunately,
that is rarely an option available for most tenants, especially as this
could lead to a finding of intentional homelessness under Pt 7 of
the Housing Act 1996 (10.47–10.68). It would seem at the least
arguable that if premises are not fit at the commencement of the
tenancy, the breach by the landlord should today be treated as the
breach of any other repairing obligation, i.e. that the tenant can
remain in occupation, press for repairs to be executed (11.116) and
claim damages (11.93).

(ii) *Damages for breach by landlord: disrepair*

11.93 Where a landlord is in breach of a repairing covenant, the
tenant is entitled to damages which, so far as money can, will put
the tenant in the position in which he would have been but for the
breach of covenant (*Pembery v Lamdin*, 1940; *Calabar Properties Ltd
v Stitcher*, 1983).

11.94 Special damages. The tenant is entitled to special
damages for any losses such as the cost of alternative accommodation while the repairs are carried out, the value of damaged
belongings, or the costs of redecoration (*Calabar*).

11.95 General damages. The tenant will also usually be
entitled to an award of general damages to reflect any discomfort,
inconvenience and ill health suffered. Such an award may include
damages for the tenant's mental distress (*Personal Representatives of
Chiodi v De Marney*, 1988).

11.96 Prior to the decision in *Wallace v Manchester CC*, 1998, the
Court of Appeal had approved a number of approaches to the
assessment of general damages:

- an award for the diminution in the value of the property to
  the tenant calculated by reference to a proportion of the rent
  payable (*McCoy & Co v Clark*, 1982);

- global assessment of the discomfort and inconvenience
  suffered made without reference to the rent payable (*Personal Representatives of Chiodi v De Marney*, 1988); and

- a combination of an award for diminution in value calculated as a percentage of the rent payable and a separate sum

for discomfort and inconvenience (*Sturolson & Co v Mauroux*, 1988).

11.97 In *Wallace*, the Court of Appeal restated the principles for awarding general damages to a periodic tenant:

- For periods when the tenant remains in occupation of the property, the loss requiring compensation is the loss of comfort and convenience which results from the disrepair.

- Expert evidence is of no assistance in assessing this figure; the question is the monetary value of the discomfort and inconvenience suffered by the tenant, which is a question for the judge.

- Compensation for the distress and inconvenience may be ascertained in a number of different ways, including diminution in value assessed as a notional reduction in the rent; some judges may prefer to use that method alone, some may prefer a global award for discomfort and inconvenience, and others may prefer a combination of the two.

- The judge is not, however, bound to assess damages separately under heads of both diminution in value and discomfort and inconvenience; they are merely alternative ways of expressing the same concept.

- A judge who decides that he will assess the award on a global basis should cross-check his prospective award by reference to the rent payable for the period during which the landlord is in breach of covenant.

- The source of the money used to pay the rent is irrelevant to the amount of compensation so that it is irrelevant that the rent is paid by housing benefit.

11.98 Cross-check against rent. Where a court decides to award a tenant general damages at a level which exceeds the amount of the rent payable by the tenant during the relevant period, the court must give clear reasons for doing so, and the facts of the case—in particular, the landlord's conduct—must warrant such an award (*Shine v English Churches Housing Group*, 2004).

11.99 High-class accommodation. The quality of the accommodation is relevant to the amount of damages. A tenant who pays a high rent for high-class accommodation will be awarded damages reflecting the standards he is entitled to expect (*Niazi Services Ltd v Van der Loo*, 2004).

11.100 Long-leaseholders. A long-leaseholder is in a different position to a periodic tenant, as his property is not only a home but is also a significant investment. If he sells or sublets the property, he is entitled to damages reflecting the reduction in the purchase price, or the reduction in the rent obtained for the subletting (*Calabar*; *Wallace*). If he remains in the property or leaves because of the disrepair, he is entitled to damages reflecting a proportion of the market rent at which he could have let out the property (*Earle v Charamboulos*, 2006).

11.101 Reinstatement of premises. Finally, the tenant is entitled to require the premises to be reinstated, including by way of any internal redecoration necessitated by the landlord's works, and in the absence of such reinstatement or redecoration will be entitled to damages for having to do them himself (*McGreal v Wake*, 1984; *Bradley v Chorley BC*, 1985).

(iii) *Damages for breach by tenant*

11.102 Reversionary interest. The principles governing a breach of an obligation to repair on the part of a tenant are different. The amount which the landlord can recover is the amount by which his reversionary interest in the premises, i.e. the interest which he enjoys on account of his future repossession of the premises, has been depreciated (*Smith v Peat*, 1853; *Drummond v S & U Stores*, 1980; Landlord and Tenant Act 1927 s.18(1)).

11.103 If the landlord has already repossessed the premises, the damages represent the depreciation in the value of that of which he has recovered possession compared to what he ought to have got back (*Hanson v Newman*, 1934). If the landlord intends to demolish the premises, or redevelop the premises by carrying out works which are so extensive that works to remedy the disrepair would be valueless, he cannot obtain any damages (Landlord and Tenant Act 1927 s.18(1)).

11.104 If the tenant is to remain in occupation, e.g. as a statutory tenant on account of the Landlord and Tenant Act 1954 (2.11– 2.14), then it would seem that unless "initial repairs" (11.84–11.86) serve to eliminate any deterioration in the value of the landlord's reversion, the valuations of repaired and unrepaired property are based on the fact that a sitting tenant is, and will remain, in occupation (*Jeffs v West London Property Corp*, 1954).

(iv)   *Set-off and counterclaim by tenant*

11.105   One of the most common responses by tenants to repairs inactivity by the landlord is to withhold the rent.

11.106   What set-off covers.   "Set-off" is the main principle with which we are here concerned. It is now accepted that breach of a repairing covenant is so closely related to the obligation to pay rent that it is appropriate for a tenant to set-off his damages (11.93–11.100) against the rent.

11.107   In the earlier stages of its recent development, this privilege extended only to money actually expended by the tenant on arranging for his landlord's obligations to be executed in default, and was not technically a set-off, but an ancient common law entitlement achieving the same effect (*Lee-Parker v Izzet*, 1971).

11.108   Initially, it was thought this could only be done when the landlord had been given a warning, an opportunity to review estimates, and the money was to be taken out of future rent. Subsequently, it was held that the same principle could apply in relation to past rent withheld, i.e. rent arrears (*Asco Developments Ltd v Lowes*, 1978).

11.109   In the most recent development, it was held that not only could the tenant withhold money so expended, but he could also set-off his general damages, i.e. reduction in value of premises/loss of enjoyment, or his special damages, e.g. destroyed property (*British Anzani (Felixstowe) v International Marine Management (UK)*, 1978; *Televantos v McCulloch*, 1990).

11.110   Caution.   Nonetheless, a tenant should, if possible, withstand the temptation to resort to this way of trying to force the landlord to carry out repairs. It is much better to pay the rent, and then to claim damages, in the course of proceedings, calculated as described above (11.93–11.100). Otherwise, there is a risk that the tenant will lose the monetary claim and find himself in arrears.

11.111   It is true that, where there is a discretion, a court is unlikely to find it reasonable to make an order for possession if rent has been withheld because of a dispute over repairs (*Lal v*

Nakum, 1982, but *cf. Haringey LBC v Stewart*, 1991), even where in the end result the tenant fails to prove his case: nonetheless, there remains a risk.

11.112 Furthermore, in the case of a Housing Act assured tenant (Chapter 4), if the tenant fails to establish his entitlement to damages, he may even find himself subject to a mandatory ground for possession, i.e. with no room for the exercise of discretion by the judge (4.105).

11.113 There are probably only two circumstances in which set-off should be considered:

- when there is a clear breach, and the tenant, after giving his landlord ample warning of his intentions, causes the work to be carried out in default; and

- when arrears have already accrued by the time an adviser is in a position to assist.

11.114 Even so, in the first circumstance there will continue to be a danger that the tenant will be incorrect as to his rights (and the landlord's obligations), for which reason if withholding can be avoided, it should be. In the second circumstance, it will remain preferable to pay as much off the arrears as possible.

11.115 Unless the amount claimed by way of set-off is clearly substantially less than the amount owing to the landlord in rent, a counterclaim should in any event be added, with which to recoup the excess of damages over rent unpaid.

(v) *Specific performance and injunctions*

11.116 An order for specific performance is an order of the court requiring someone to fulfil a contractual obligation; an injunction is an order to do something, which may or may not arise under contract, i.e. it may also be used in relation to tort (11.133).

11.117 Although there has been contention in the past as to whether the county court has had power to grant an order for specific performance, there is now no practical difference between the two remedies: either may be sought in the county court (Landlord and Tenant Act 1985 s.17, governing specific performance; County Courts Act 1984 s.38, governing injunctions).

11.118 A landlord's want of financial ability to comply with an order is no defence to such an order (*Francis v Cowcliffe*, 1976).

11.119 Although it was formerly considered that neither class of order could be made against a tenant (*Hill v Barclay*, 1811; *Regional Properties v City of London Real Property*, 1980) a more recent case suggests that this is no longer the case (*Rainbow Estates Ltd v Tokenhold Ltd*, 1999).

11.120 Court procedure. Where the tenant does not claim an injunction and the value of a claim is less than £5,000, a matter will normally be dealt with in the county court on the small claims track. Where, however, there is a claim for an order requiring the landlord to carry out work, it will not be allocated to the small claims track, provided that the cost of the works is estimated to be more than £1,000 and the financial value of the remainder of the claim is more than £1,000 (CPR r.26.6(1)(b)).

(vi) *Receiving orders*

11.121 Where a landlord fails to carry out his obligations, the High Court has power (Supreme Court Act 1981 s.37)—where it considers it just and convenient to do so—to appoint a receiver to take over the whole or part of the management of a property, including the receipt of rents and/or the execution of works.

11.122 A court will not, however, appoint a receiver under this power where the landlord is a local authority carrying out their statutory housing duties, i.e. to provide and manage housing, because to do so would usurp Parliament's express conferral of those powers on the authority (*Parker v Camden LBC*, 1985).

11.123 Landlord and Tenant Act 1987 Part 2. This power has been codified into Pt 2 of the Landlord and Tenant Act 1987 and, where Pt 2 applies, it replaces earlier powers. Part 2 applies, however, only to a building where there are two or more flats, where at least 50 per cent of the floor area of the building (excluding its common parts) is occupied for residential purposes, and the landlord is neither a resident landlord (defined in similar terms as under the Housing Act 1988; see 4.43), nor an "exempt landlord", defined to include local authorities and a number of other public bodies (Landlord and Tenant Act 1987 s.21).

11.124 Action under Pt 2 requires a prior notice fulfilling statutory requirements to be found in s.22 of the Act, followed—if the landlord does not comply with the notice—by application to a leasehold valuation tribunal under s.23 for the appointment of a manager. (See now also the general power to seek the appointment of a manager even in cases of no default: 2.70.)

(vii) *Forfeiture*

11.125 Forfeiture is one of the means of bringing a tenancy to an end (1.131–1.146). There is no right to forfeit a tenancy unless such a right is expressly reserved in the agreement. The right is, however, commonly reserved in most written tenancy agreements, and is commonly drafted in such terms as to apply on breach of a tenant's repairing obligation.

11.126 Waiver. If the obligation in question is to put (but not also to keep) the premises in repair, a landlord who has known of a breach by the tenant, but has so conducted himself as to be considered to have waived the breach (*cf.* waiver of illegal sub-letting; 1.186), will also have waived his right to forfeit the tenancy (*Doe d. Morecraft v Meux*, 1825).

11.127 If, however, the obligation in question is also to keep the property in repair, both the obligation and the breach continue so long as the tenant fails to repair, and there is, accordingly, no waiver (*Doe d. Hemmings v Durnford*, 1832).

11.128 Remedying the breach. Before seeking to forfeit, the landlord must serve notice specifying his complaint and, if the breach is remediable, requiring remedy and demanding compensation (Law of Property Act 1925 s.146). The landlord must also allow sufficient time for remedy of a repairing breach.

11.129 Leasehold Property (Repairs) Act 1938. In relation to a long lease of which at least three years remain unexpired, the s.146 notice must also advise the tenant of his right to claim, by way of counter-notice, the protection of the Leasehold Property (Repairs) Act 1938, under the terms of which the landlord cannot proceed with an action for forfeiture based on disrepair other than with the leave of the court.

11.130 The court will not grant leave unless an immediate remedy is needed in order to prevent a substantial reduction in the value of the landlord's interest, or where remedy now would be cheap compared to remedy later, or in order to comply with any statute, or where the tenant is not in occupation and repair is needed for the protection of other occupiers, or where in all the circumstances the court considers it just and equitable to grant leave.

11.131 Relief. Where a landlord seeks to forfeit a tenancy, the tenant can usually apply to the court for relief from forfeiture, which will, however, almost invariably be on conditions, in this case meaning conditions requiring the tenant to rectify the breach, although not if the court considers that the extent of the obligation is unreasonable (Law of Property Act 1925 s.147): a Housing Act assured tenant (Chapter 4), however, cannot apply for relief (4.74).

(viii) *Possession*

11.132 Even if a tenancy is determined by forfeiture, or where— without forfeiture—proceedings against either a Rent Act protected or statutory (Rent Act 1977; see Chapter 5) tenant, or a Housing Act secure (Housing Act 1985; see Chapter 3, above) or Housing Act assured (Housing Act 1988; see Chapter 4) tenant are taken based on breach of the tenant's repairing obligation (3.97; 4.119; 5.144), it will still be necessary to prove that it is reasonable to make an order for possession.

Tort

1. INTRODUCTION

11.133 In this section, we briefly consider remedies for disrepair, or other unacceptable housing conditions, which arise independently of contract. They may be available to those with a contract, or those without.

2. CAUSES OF ACTION

11.134 The torts with which we are here concerned are:

- negligence;
- breach of the Building Regulations;
- defective premises;
- occupier's liability;
- nuisance; and

● waste, a tort peculiar to the relationship of landlord and tenant.

(i) Negligence

11.135 Duty of care. Action in negligence only arises when there is a legal duty of care. This means:

> "you must take reasonable care to avoid acts or omissions which you can reasonably foresee would be likely to injure your neighbour. Who, then, in law is my neighbour? The answer seems to be: persons who are so closely and directly affected by my act that I ought reasonably to have them in contemplation as being so affected when I am directing my mind to the acts or omissions which are called into question" (*Donoghue v Stevenson*, 1932, *per* Lord Atkin).

11.136 Duty to tenants and visitors. Thus, in addition to the landlord's contractual duty to make sure that common parts are kept reasonably safe (11.34), he also owes a duty of care to tenants or others who may visit premises to ensure that they are safeguarded against damage from any danger of which he knows, or ought to have known (*Cunard v Antifyre Ltd*, 1933).

11.137 Duty of builders. Anyone carrying out work on premises is under a general duty to use reasonable care for the safety of those whom he knows or ought to know might be affected by those works, or who are lawfully in the vicinity of those works (*AC Billings & Son v Riden*, 1958). A builder of a house, whether or not he is also the landlord, owes a duty of care in the construction of the building to potential occupiers of it, but the liability only extends to personal injury and not to economic loss, i.e. because, for example, it is worth less than was paid for it (*Murphy v Brentwood DC*, 1990) or cannot be used for the purpose for which it was acquired.

11.138 Developers. Developers (whether or not also the owner) of, for example, housing for sale, owe a duty of care to purchasers (*Sutherland v Maton (CR) & Son*, 1976; *Batty v Metropolitan Property Realisations*, 1978; *Rimmer v Liverpool CC*, 1985; *Targett v Torfaen BC*, 1991).

11.139 Building professionals. Architects, engineers, surveyors, and others involved in the construction of a dwelling owe a

similar duty to future occupiers to take reasonable care in the
execution of their functions (*Cedar Transport Group v First Wyvern
Property Trustees Co*, 1980). In the light of *Murphy*, any such
liability will be limited to damages for personal injury, and not
extend to economic loss (*Preston v Torfaen BC*, 1993).

11.140 Works by the landlord. A landlord may also be responsible in negligence for other works, e.g. for the manner of carrying
out his repairing obligations (*Sharpe v Manchester MDC*, 1977) or
for the quality of works done prior to the commencement of a
letting.

11.141 Whether the landlord has complied with his duty of care
will normally turn on whether, in selecting a particular design or
materials for the repair or maintenance, the landlord has acted "in
accordance with a practice accepted as proper by a reasonable body
of . . . men skilled in that particular art" (*Adams v Rhymney Valley
DC*, 2000). There is no negligence, however, in failing to carry out
works before a letting (*Arden v Pullen*, 1842; 11.26).

11.142 Home purchase. A further, and important, illustration
of negligence arises in the course of home purchase. Most people
buying their own homes will take advice from a surveyor and a
solicitor. The surveyor will report on the condition of the house: if
he does so negligently, he will be liable for the effects of his
default. A solicitor will have a number of legal functions to carry
out, including finding out information about the purchaser's title,
and whether the local authority have any plans, e.g. for clearance
(12.88–12.97), which may adversely affect the purchaser's intended
occupation. He, too, may be liable in negligence.

11.143 Report to building society. Where a purchaser failed to
have his own survey carried out, but instead relied on the fact that
a building society was willing to advance the mortgage, knowing
that the building society had themselves sought a survey, the
surveyor was held liable to the purchaser, even though the
purchaser never saw his report to the building society (*Yianni v
Evans (Edwin) & Sons*, 1981; see also *Smith v Bush*, 1987; *Harris v
Wyre Forest DC*, 1987; *Davies v Idris Parry*, 1988). The surveyor is
deemed to know that the consequences of his negligence would not
only affect the building society's decision on mortgage but also the
purchaser's decision as to whether or not to buy. In practice today,
many building societies (and banks) release such reports to the
borrower.

11.144 Local authorities. It should also be remembered that local authorities may commit negligence in the execution of their functions. Alternatively, they may be liable for breach of statutory duty, which is technically a separate tort, for failing properly to carry out their obligations under an Act of Parliament.

11.145 Thus, where an authority were obliged to inspect property in the course of construction to see whether there had been compliance with Building Regulations (see also 11.148), and were alleged to have done so negligently, action was available at the instigation of later occupiers (*Anns v Merton LBC*, 1977). Whether an authority can be liable in these circumstances has, however, subsequently been doubted, and it is clear that any liability is limited to damages for personal injury and do not extend to economic loss (*Murphy v Brentwood DC*, 1990).

11.146 Causation and consequence. The fact that there is a defect, however, is not enough to give rise to action: that defect must be caused by an act which a reasonable man would not have done, or an omission to do something which a reasonable man would have made sure was done (*Bolton v Stone*, 1951).

11.147 Further, the act or omission must cause the harm (or the likelihood of harm). There must be a line of causation between act or omission and harm, so that the latter is not too remote a consequence of the former. Another way of putting the same proposition is that it must have been reasonably foreseeable (which is not to say reasonably foreseen) that harm of the order which has resulted would result.

(ii) *Breach of the building regulations*

11.148 Building Act 1984 section 38. In a large number of cases where housing is constructed, improved or altered, or its use changed, it will be obligatory to comply with the Building Regulations. Under the Building Act 1984 s.38 (replacing the Health and Safety at Work Act 1974 s.71) anyone who is obliged to comply with the Regulations and who fails to do so will, save where the Regulations themselves otherwise specify, be liable to an action in tort at the instance of a person harmed by his failure. This section, however, has yet to be brought into force.

(iii) *Defective premises*

11.149 Defective Premises Act 1972 section 3. Anyone who carries out work of construction, repair, maintenance or demolition, or any other work in relation to premises, owes a duty of care to persons who might reasonably be expected to be affected by resulting defects in the state of the premises (Defective Premises Act 1972 s.3).

11.150 The duty of care persists through any subsequent sale or letting of the premises, and is co-extensive with the duty of care in negligence (11.135). It does not, however, apply to omissions to repair or execute other works which may be needed.

11.151 The duty applies only in relation to works carried out prior to a sale or letting which itself followed the commencement of the Act (January 1, 1974).

11.152 Defective Premises Act 1972 section 1. The same Act imposed a duty of care on anyone doing any work for or in connection with the provision of a dwelling by erection, conversion or enlargement (Defective Premises Act 1972 s.1).

11.153 The duty of care is to see that work is done in a workmanlike manner and with proper materials or—if the person involved is a professional, e.g. architect, engineer—that it is done in a professional manner, so as to ensure that the dwelling will be fit for habitation when completed.

11.154 The duty is owed to, among others, purchasers and tenants. The duty is also additional to the duty of care in negligence (11.135) but again applies only to work following the commencement of the Act (January 1, 1974).

11.155 Defective Premises Act 1972 section 4. Further, whenever a landlord is under an obligation to repair (however arising, i.e. implied by law (11.26–11.41); implied by statute (11.43–11.79); or express), he owes:

> "to all persons who might reasonably be expected to be affected by defects in the state of the premises a duty to take such care as is reasonable in all the circumstances to see that they are reasonably safe from personal injury or from damage to their property" (Defective Premises Act 1972 s.4).

11.156 The duty arises whenever the landlord knows of the defect, or even if he only ought to have known of it, so that it may be an appropriate cause of action if, for want of notice (11.10–11.13), action cannot be taken under a contractual obligation. The duty is owed both to tenants, and to the tenant's visitors. (Although there is no notice requirement, however, damages may be reduced on the basis on contributory negligence by a tenant who has failed to notify the landlord of the defect: *Sykes v Harry*, 2001.)

11.157 The duty only arises, however, in relation to "relevant defects". A relevant defect is one arising from or continuing because of an act or omission by the landlord which actually constitutes a breach of his repairing obligation, or which would have constituted a breach of his repairing obligation if he had had notice of it. In substance, this means any defect which is within the obligation to repair, of which the landlord knew, or ought to have known.

11.158 Even if repairing obligations are obscure, however, if the landlord has a right to repair (as distinct from a duty), he is treated for these purposes as if he were under a repairing obligation (Defective Premises Act 1972 s.4(4), and see *McCauley v Bristol CC*, 1991), so that in weekly tenancies (11.29), Rent Act protected and statutory tenancies, and Housing Act assured tenancies (11.80), and those to which the Landlord and Tenant Act 1985 ss.8 (11.44) and 11 (11.52) apply, there will be an obligation for the purposes of this provision, in relation to any class of works which the right of entry is designed to permit the landlord to execute. The Act does not create any obligation wider than the landlord's repairing obligation (*McNerney v Lambeth LBC*, 1988; *Alker v Collingwood Housing Association*, 2007).

(iv)   *Occupier's liability*

11.159   Occupier's Liability Act 1957 section 2. The occupier of premises is the person in possession and control of them. Thus, a tenant is an occupier, but only of the premises which are the subject of the letting. In a block of flats, the landlord is the occupier of the block, just as in a house let out in bedsitting-rooms or flats the landlord retains possession and control of the house itself.

11.160 An occupier owes a common duty to take such care as is reasonable in all the circumstances of the case to see that "visitors" to premises will be reasonably safe in using the premises for the purposes for which he was allowed in (Occupier's Liability Act 1957 s.2). The term "visitors" will include those on the premises with the express or implied permission of the occupier, e.g. a tenant or licensee of some part, or the tenant's or licensee's own visitors. The extent of the duty may vary with circumstances, including factors affecting the class of visitor e.g. the elderly and children. In some circumstances, there is even a duty of care to those not lawfully on the premises, i.e. trespassers: see the Occupier's Liability Act 1984.

(v) Nuisance

11.161 Act or state of affairs. The concept of nuisance has been considered earlier (8.94). It is mentioned here because, like breach of covenant for quiet enjoyment (11.36), a landlord's control of neighbouring property may in appropriate circumstances be such that it interferes with the tenant's reasonable use of the premises let. To constitute a nuisance, there must be some act or state of affairs in one set of premises, which adversely affects use and enjoyment of another. A claim in nuisance can only be brought by someone in possession of land, which certainly includes a tenant and may include a licensee. It includes a "tolerated trespasser" (**1.44**): *Pemberton v Southwark LBC*, 2001. It is, however, only the person with the interest in the land who can sue, not other family members: *Hunter v Canary Wharf*, 1997.

(vi) Waste

11.162 Alteration of nature of premises. Waste is a tort peculiar to the law of landlord and tenant. In some ways, it may be considered the equivalent in tort of action in contract for breach of the tenant's duty to use premises in a tenant-like manner (11.42). An act of waste is an act by the tenant which alters the nature of the premises let.

11.163 Normally, this will be an act of deterioration of the premises, e.g. cutting down a tree or knocking down an outhouse, or any other act of damage, including to the premises themselves. Technically, it can also be something which might otherwise be regarded as an improvement, e.g. an alteration. There will be no waste, however, if the landlord's consent to the act in question has been secured, and an act of waste will only give rise to a claim for possession (3.113; 4.122; 5.150) if it is also an act of deterioration.

3. REMEDIES IN TORT

11.164 Classes of damages. If one person commits a tort which causes harm to another, that other is to be put in the position he would have enjoyed had the tort not occurred. Thus, damages will be available on this principle, whether the claim is against landlord or tenant, for such harm as has ensued.

11.165 "Special damages" are those which are identifiable, such as loss of earnings, loss of property, including clothing, medical expenses, alternative accommodation, travelling expenses. In addition, there are "general damages", for pain and suffering, personal injury, and nervous shock, although not, as a general rule, for inconvenience or discomfort (*cf.* 11.95).

11.166 Two points to note. Two points on damages are of importance to occupiers of housing. First, there is no reduction in a claim for damages because the claim is against a public body, engaged in a socially useful task, such as the discharge of their housing functions (*Taylor v Liverpool Corp*, 1939). Secondly, where the claim is in relation to damage to a house, e.g. by an owner-occupier suing someone who has negligently advised on the purchase (11.142), damages will be the cost of repairs, assessed as at the date when, having regard to all the circumstances, the repairs could reasonably have been undertaken, rather than when the harm occurred: in this connection, the financial ability or inability of the person suing may be a factor in requiring the deferral (and so the increased cost) of repairs (*Perry v Sidney Phillips & Son*, 1982). In some cases, however, any claim will be limited to damages for personal injury and will not cover any loss of value in the house or cost of repairs (11.137; *Murphy v Brentwood DC*, 1990).

11.167 Injunction. In addition, and in principle, there is no reason why an injunction should not be sought, either to prevent harm arising from a tort, or to rectify it. Although the prospect of damage should not be too remote, it is not necessary to wait until a building is about to collapse, and assistance may be secured by way of injunction as soon as it is clear that if something is not done, the harm feared will indeed occur (*Anns v Merton LBC*, 1977; *Crump v Torfaen BC*, 1982).

11.168 Access to Neighbouring Land Act 1992. Where, in order to preserve the condition of land, works are required to neighbouring land, it is possible to obtain an order for access to that neighbouring land in order to carry out the required works (Access to Neighbouring Land Act 1992).

Limitation

11.169 Six years or three years. As a general rule, actions both in tort or contract must be brought within six years of the date on which the cause of action accrued, i.e. when the right to sue arose (Limitation Act 1980 ss.2, 5). If, however, the claim is for personal injuries, it must be brought within three years (Limitation Act 1980 s.11). The three years run from when the person injured knew of the injury, knew that it was serious enough to merit action, knew that it was attributable to the landlord's default, and knew who the landlord was (Limitation Act 1980 s.14). Time does not, however, start to run against a minor until he achieves his majority (18) (Limitation Act 1980 s.28).

11.170 An obligation to keep property in repair is a continuing breach, not a breach only at its outset, so that time can run from any point until the landlord rectifies the defect.

11.171 Latent damage. More problematic is from when times run if a defect is not obvious, perhaps for many years. In such a case, the limitation period will be the longer of the usual six-year period, accruing from the date when the damage came into existence, or three years from the date when the complainant discovers (or could have discovered) the damage (Limitation Act 1980 s.24A, added by the Latent Damage Act 1986). An overriding time limit (or "long-stop") of 15 years is applied, during which the complainant must bring the action (Limitation Act 1980 s.24B, added by the Latent Damage Act 1986). A successor in title, who buys in ignorance of the damage, may also benefit from the extended time limits (Latent Damage Act 1986 s.3).

CHAPTER TWELVE

Housing Acts: Disrepair and Improvement

Introduction

12.01 Housing Health and Safety Rating System. Local authorities have long had powers to ensure that buildings used for housing are only so used if they are of an acceptable standard. Formerly, the principal standard which related to housing conditions was that of fitness for human habitation, as most recently set out in the Housing Act 1985 ("1985 Act"). The Housing Act 2004 ("2004 Act") Pt 1 introduced the Housing Health and Safety Rating System ("HHSRS") which set new standards for housing conditions. Whereas action could only be taken under the fitness provisions in relation to a limited number of housing defects, e.g. structural instability, serious disrepair and lack of sanitation, HHSRS allows authorities to address a whole range of housing problems against which they could not previously take action.

12.02 Private sector. It is to be emphasised that this chapter is concerned with enforcement of standards in the private sector. The mechanism for enforcing HHSRS is by service of notices on those required to take action to remedy conditions. Local authorities cannot serve notices on themselves (*R. v Cardiff CC Ex p. Cross*, 1983). The provisions of this chapter do not, therefore, assist tenants of local authorities, although they may have other remedies for disrepair (considered in Chapter 11) or under the Environmental Protection Act 1990 (13.27).

12.03 Grants. Financial assistance for owners of land to carry out works—which may include those needed to respond to a notice under HHSRS provisions—may be available from authorities by way of grants under the Regulatory Reform (Housing Assistance)

(England and Wales) Order 2002 (SI 2002/1860), "the Regulatory Reform Order".

Outline

12.04   Preliminary matters

- Local authorities are defined for the purposes of the relevant legislation by the Housing Act 2004 s.261.
- They are under a duty to consider the housing conditions in their area at least once a year.

12.05   Housing Health and Safety Rating System

- The main thrust of the Housing Act 2004 Act Pt 1 is to ensure that houses which present a risk to the health and safety of their occupiers should either be rendered safe by works or closed to domestic use.
- An authority may take enforcement action if one of a number of hazards exists in a property.
- The severity of a hazard is determined by HHSRS, which provides for the numerical evaluation of a hazard.
- Hazards fall into two types: Category 1 and Category 2. An authority must take enforcement action against a Category 1 hazard and may take action against a Category 2 hazard.
- The main courses of action available to the authority are service of a hazard awareness notice or an improvement notice, or making a prohibition or demolition order.
- If there is an imminent risk of serious harm to the health and safety of the occupiers, the authority can take emergency remedial action themselves or make an emergency prohibition order.
- There are provisions for appealing any notice or order to the residential property tribunal; subject to this, any breach of the requirements of a notice or order is a criminal offence.
- In some circumstances, authorities can carry out works in default and recover the expenses of doing so.

12.06   Slum clearance

- Part 9 of the 1985 Act concerns the clearance of areas of hazardous housing by compulsory purchase and demolition.

12.07 Grants

- Grant assistance is available to land owners under the Regulatory Reform (Housing Assistance) (England and Wales) Order 2002 (SI 2002/1860), "the Regulatory Reform Order", which includes wide-ranging power for authorities to provide assistance for housing renewal.
- The order gives authorities the power to provide "assistance for housing renewal". Assistance may be provided for:
  - repair, improvement and adaptation of housing;
  - demolition of a dwelling and help with rebuilding costs;
  - provision of alternative accommodation, either where this supports improvement of living conditions and the authority propose to purchase the existing accommodation, or else where the provision of accommodation of alternative accommodation represents a better alternative than repair, improvement or adaptation;
  - assistance may be provided to persons directly or through a third party, and may be in any form, including grants and loans.

12.08 Renewal areas

- Local authorities may declare a renewal area when the requirements set out in Local Government and Housing Act 1989 Act are met.

- Prior to declaring the area, an authority must compile a report on the circumstances justifying the declaration.

- There are publicity requirements which must be met both before and after declaration of the area.

- Once an area has been declared, the authority have additional powers to acquire land in the area and to carry out works on land they own.

12.09 Displacement of occupiers

- Many of the provisions referred to will lead to the displacement of occupiers, permanently or temporarily.

- In the case of permanent displacement, occupiers will enjoy rights to re-housing and to compensation, both for tenants and for owner-occupiers.

12.10 Occupier action

- Occupiers may complain to local authorities about conditions.

- The 2004 Act specifically provides for complaint about hazardous housing to a magistrate and—if satisfied that the complaint is well-founded—the magistrate must forward it to the local authority, who must inspect the premises concerned.

Preliminary matters

12.11 Local authorities. For the purposes of these provisions, local authorities are:

(i) unitary authorities;

(ii) other district councils;

(iii) London Borough councils;

(iv) the Common Council of the City of London;

(v) Welsh county or county boroughs;

(vi) the sub-treasurer of the Inner Temple or the under-treasurer of the Middle Temple; and

(vii) the council of the Isles of Scilly (2004 Act s.261(1)).

12.12 Inspection duties. Under s.3(1) of the 2004 Act these authorities are obliged at least once a year to consider the housing conditions in their areas with a view to deciding what action they ought to take under the provisions to be considered in this chapter (and in Chapter 14). The Secretary of State may give the authority directions as to exercise of this duty, with which directions the authority are obliged to comply.

12.13 Powers of entry, offences and information sharing. To assist them in discharging their functions under the Act, authorities have a number of powers:

- the power to enter properties (2004 Act s.239);

- offences of obstruction of authorities in exercising any of their powers under the Act (2004 Act s.241);

- the power to use housing benefit and council tax records (2004 Act s.237).

HHSRS

1. PRELIMINARY DEFINITIONS

12.14 Residential premises. Duties under the 2004 Act Pt 1 arise in relation to "residential premises", which are (2004 Act s.1(4)):

- dwellings;

- houses in multiple occupation (HMOs);

- unoccupied HMO accommodation; and

- common parts of a building containing one or more flats.

12.15 Dwellings. A dwelling is a building or part of a building intended to be occupied as a separate dwelling (2004 Act s.1(5); 4.17).

12.16 HMO. HMO is defined in the same way as for the provisions which govern their use (additional to the general provisions governing housing conditions which also apply to them, as set out in this chapter) (14.25).

12.17 Unoccupied HMO accommodation. This is a building or part of a building constructed or adapted for use as an HMO (14.25) but which is currently not an HMO because it is either unoccupied or only occupied by a single household (14.26(2)).

12.18 Common parts. These include the structure and exterior of a building containing flats and any common facilities provided to the flats (2004 Act s.1(5)). A flat is a separate set of premises that which is constructed or adopted for use as a dwelling and which forms part of a building (2004 Act s.1(5)).

2. HAZARDS

12.19 Hazard. A hazard is any risk of harm to the health or safety of an actual (or potential) occupier of a dwelling or HMO which arises from a deficiency in the dwelling or HMO or in any building or land in the vicinity (2004 Act s.2(1)). "Health" includes mental health (2004 Act s.2(5)).

12.20 Hazards fall into two categories, depending on their severity: Category 1 and Category 2.

12.21   Prescribed hazards. Regulations—Housing Health and Safety Rating System (England) Regulations 2005 (SI 2005/3208) or Housing Health and Safety Rating System (Wales) Regulations 2006 (SI 2006/1702) ("HHSRS Regulations")—prescribe 29 hazards and circumstances giving rise to them. They are as follows:

1. damp and mould growth: exposure to house dust mites, damp, mould or fungal growths;

2. excess cold: exposure to low temperatures;

3. excess heat: exposure to high temperatures;

4. asbestos and MMF: exposure to asbestos fibres or manufactured mineral fibres;

5. biocides: exposure to chemicals used to treat timber and mould growth;

6. carbon monoxide and fuel combustion products: exposure to carbon monoxide, nitrogen dioxide or sulphur dioxide and smoke;

7. lead: the ingestion of lead;

8. radiation: exposure to radiation;

9. uncombusted fuel gas: exposure to uncombusted fuel gas;

10. volatile organic compounds: exposure to volatile organic compounds;

11. crowding and space: a lack of adequate space for living and sleeping;

12. entry by intruders: difficulties in keeping the dwelling or HMO secure against unauthorised entry;

13. lighting: a lack of adequate lighting;

14. noise: exposure to noise;

15. domestic hygiene, pests and refuse: poor design layout or construction such that the dwelling or HMO cannot readily be kept clean; exposure to pests; inadequate provision for the hygienic storage and disposal of household waste;

16. food safety: inadequate provision of facilities for the storage, preparation and cooking of food;

17. personal hygiene, sanitation and drainage: inadequate provision of facilities for maintaining good person hygiene and for sanitation and drainage;

18. water supply: inadequate supply of water free from contamination, for drinking and other domestic purposes;

19. falls associated with toilets, baths, showers and other washing facilities;

20. falling on any level surface or falling between surfaces where the change in level is less than 300 millimetres;

21. falling on stairs, steps or ramps where the change in level is 300 millimetres or more;

22. electrical hazards: exposure to electricity;

23. falling between levels: where the difference in levels is 300 millimetres or more;

24. fire: exposure to uncontrolled fire and associated smoke;

25. flames, hot surfaces, etc. contact with controlled fire or flames, hot objects, liquid or vapours;

26. collision and entrapment: collision with, or entrapment of body parts in, doors, windows or other architectural features;

27. explosions at the dwelling or HMO;

28. position, location and operability of amenities, fittings and equipment;

29. structural collapse and falling elements: the collapse of the whole or part of the dwelling or HMO.

12.22 Assessing severity. The HHSRS Regulations set out the method by which the seriousness of the hazard is to be calculated and, accordingly, into which category it falls. This requires three stages.

12.23 First, the authority must assess of the likelihood, during a period of 12 months beginning with the date of the assessment, of an occupier suffering any harm as a result of the hazard. The assessment must place the likelihood within the range of ratios set out in the regulations.

12.24 The second stage is to assess which of the four classes of harm a relevant occupier is most likely to suffer during the 12–month period. The classes of harm range from extreme harm, such as death in Class I, to moderate harm, such as slight concussion or a broken finger in Class IV. The likelihood of any of the classes harm occurring as a result of the hazard must be assessed in accordance with a formula set out in the regulations.

12.25 The third stage is to combine the figures obtained under the first two stages in accordance with a formula to produce a hazard-rating score. The score is then assigned to one of 10 bands (A–J), with A being the highest scores (5000 or more) and J the lowest (9 or less). A hazard falling within bands A, B, or C (1,000 and above) is a Category 1 hazard; a hazard within any other band is a Category 2 hazard.

3. OUTLINE OF ACTION

12.26 Duty or power. If a Category 1 hazard exists in a property, the authority are under a duty to take enforcement action (2004 Act s.5(1)); where there is a Category 2 hazard, they have power to take enforcement action (2004 Act s.6(1)).

12.27 There are six forms of enforcement action available:

1. hazard awareness notice;

2. improvement notice;

3. emergency remedial action (Category 1 only);

4. prohibition order;

5. emergency prohibition order (Category 1 only);

6. demolition order.

12.28 Choice of action. Where a Category 1 hazard exists, if there is only one course of action available, the authority must take it (2004 Act s.5(3)). Where more than one course of action is available, the authority must take the most appropriate action (2004 Act s.5(4)). Authorities must make the choice taking into account guidance given by the Secretary of State in Housing Health and Safety Rating System: Enforcement Guidance (2004 Act s.9). This is updated on a regular basis.

4. HAZARD AWARENESS NOTICE

12.29 Advisory only. A hazard awareness notice may be served in relation to either a Category 1 or Category 2 hazard. It advises the person served of the existence of the hazard which arises as a result of a deficiency on the premises (2004 Act ss.28(2) and 29(2)). It does not require any action on the part of the person served but warns him of the risk and advises what action may be appropriate.

12.30 Persons on whom served. The person on whom a hazard awareness notice is to be served depends on the nature of the property (2004 Act Sch.1):

- **Licensed dwellings and HMOs.** Where a dwelling or HMO is licensed under the 2004 Act Pts 2 or 3 (Chapter 14), the notice must be served on the licence-holder.

- **Dwellings and HMOs which are not flats.** In the case of all other HMOs and dwellings which are not flats, the notice must be served on the person having control (12.31) of the dwelling or HMO, or in the case of an HMO the person managing it (12.32).

- **Flats.** Where the premises are a flat, the notice must be served on the person who is an owner (12.33) of the flat who in the opinion of the authority ought to take the specified action. If the flat is also an HMO, the notice may be served on the person managing it (12.32).

- **Common parts.** Where a notice applies to the common parts serving flats, it must be served on the person who is an owner (12.33) of the premises who in the opinion of the authority ought to take the specified action.

12.31 Person having control. The person having control is defined in relation to a dwelling or HMO as the person in receipt of not less than two-thirds of the full net annual value of the premises (often referred to as the "rack rent"), whether on his own account or as agent or trustee for another, or who would be in receipt of the rack-rent were the premises let (1985 Act s.207). A rack-rent means "the full amount which a landlord can reasonably be expected to get from a tenant", having regard (where relevant) to rent restrictions (*Rawlance v Croydon Corp*, 1952).

12.32 Person managing. The person managing is the owner or lessee of the house who receives—directly or through an agent or trustee—rents or other payments from persons who are tenants of parts of the premises or who are lodgers. The manager remains so even if the rents or other payments are being paid to another person, who is not the owner or lessee, whether voluntarily or in pursuance of a court order. "Other payments" includes the collection of meter monies from gas and electricity meters used by tenants (*Jacques v Liverpool CC*, 1996).

12.33   Owner.   Owner means the freeholder or someone holding a lease of three years or more (2004 Act s.262(7)).

12.34   Copies of notice.   In addition, the authority must also serve a copy of the notice on every other person who, to their knowledge is a freeholder, mortgagee, lessee or occupier of the premises concerned (2004 Act Sch.1 para.5). They must be served within seven days of the service of the hazard awareness notice.

5.   IMPROVEMENT NOTICE

12.35   Preconditions.   An improvement notice may be served where a Category 1 or Category 2 hazard exists (2004 Act ss.11, 12).

12.36   On whom served.   The person on whom an improvement notice is to be served is the same as for a hazard awareness notice (12.30).

12.37   Requirements.   An improvement notice requires the person on whom it is served to carry out remedial action as specified in the notice. In relation to Category 1 hazards, the remedial action must ensure that the hazard in the premises ceases to be a Category 1 hazard. An improvement notice may relate to more than one category of hazard on the same premises or in the same property; a notice relating to a Category 2 hazard may be combined with that relating to a Category 1 hazard, where they both require remedial action.

12.38   Remedial action.   Remedial action is action which will remove or reduce the hazard (2004 Act s.11(8)). This will usually take the form of works but could also include the removal of hazardous waste from the premises.

12.39   In the case of premises containing flats, remedial action may be required in relation to the common parts or (any part of) the building containing the flats (this may include another flat), but only if the authority are satisfied that the deficiency from which the hazard arises is situated in the common parts of the building, and the action is necessary to protect the health or safety of any actual or potential occupiers of one or more of the flats in it (2004 Act ss.11(3), (4), 12(3)).

12.40 Contents. Although the 2004 Act allows for forms to be prescribed, neither the Secretary of State in England or the National Assembly in Wales has yet exercised this power. The 2004 Act sets out certain requirements in the 2004 Act s.13.

12.41 An improvement notice must specify:

- whether it is served in relation to a Category 1 or Category 2 hazard;

- the nature of the hazard and the residential premises on which the hazard exists, e.g. dwelling, HMO, etc.;

- the deficiency giving rise to the hazard;

- the premises in relation to which the remedial action is to be taken and the nature of the remedial action;

- the date when the remedial action is to be started, which is to be no earlier than 28 days after service of the notice;

- the period within which the remedial action is to be completed, or—if more than one action is required—the period within which each is to be completed; and

- that there is a right of appeal to the residential property tribunal and that there is a 21–day time limit for appealing.

12.42 Remedial action by authority. Unless there is an appeal, the notice becomes operative 21 days from service. If the person served agrees to them doing so, or neither appeals nor complies with the notice in the permitted time, the local authority may take the remedial action themselves and can recover the expenses of doing so (2004 Act Sch.3).

12.43 Criminal offence. Failure to comply with the notice without reasonable excuse is a criminal offence (2004 Act s.30(1)). Non-compliance means not commencing and completing within the time allowed (subject to the right to appeal: 12.48).

12.44 Suspension. An improvement notice may be suspended by the authority (2004 Act s.14) for a particular period of time, or until the occurrence of a particular event. Provision is made for termination of suspension where the nature of the occupancy of premises changes, e.g. where an occupier considered less vulnerable to the hazard is replaced by one who is more vulnerable. There may also be a suspension where the authority accept an undertaking from the person on whom the notice is served, e.g. where the landlord already intended to carry out works to the premises as a part of a programme of repairs and promises to do so. The suspension may be terminated if that undertaking is breached and the authority notify the person accordingly. The authority may review a suspended notice at any time and must do so at no greater intervals than every 12 months (2004 Act s.17).

12.45   Revocation and variation.   Revocation or variation of an improvement notice may occur either following an application made by the person on whom it was served or on the authority's own initiative (2004 Act s.16(8)). Decisions may be appealed to the residential property tribunal.

12.46   Revocation.   A notice must be revoked once the authority are satisfied it has been complied with (2004 Act s.16(1)). In addition, the authority may revoke a notice where they consider it appropriate to do so and (in the case of a Category 1 hazard) where they consider that there are special circumstances which justify revocation.

12.47   Procedure for variation or revocation.   Detailed provision is made for the procedure to be adopted by the authority either where they decide to vary or revoke a notice or where they refuse to vary or revoke a notice at the request of the person on whom it was served (2004 Act Sch.1).

12.48   Appeals.   A person served with an improvement notice may appeal to the residential property tribunal (2004 Act s.15 Sch.1 Pt 3). An appeal may be brought on any grounds, which may include that someone else should take the remedial action or that another form of enforcement action would be the best course of action to take. There is also a right of appeal against an authority's decision to revoke (or refuse to revoke) or to vary (or refuse to vary) a notice. An appeal against a notice must be lodged within 21 days of service. The time limit for any other appeal is 28 days. In each case, the tribunal has power to extend the time limit for "good reason".

6. EMERGENCY REMEDIAL ACTION

12.49 Preconditions. An authority may only take emergency remedial action in relation to a Category 1 hazard. Remedial action is any such action as may be required under an improvement notice, e.g. the carrying out of works (12.38). The authority must be satisfied that the hazard involves an imminent risk of serious harm to the health and safety of any of the occupiers of the premises concerned, or any other residential premises.

12.50 Procedure. Where an authority decide to take emergency remedial action, they may commence that action immediately and may recover its costs (2004 Act s.42(2)). Not later than seven days of the start of the action, they must serve a notice on the same persons as those on whom an improvement notice must be served (12.35). That notice must specify (2004 Act s.41(2)):

- the nature of the hazard and the residential premises on which the hazard exists, e.g. dwelling, HMO, etc.;

- the deficiency giving rise to the hazard;

- the premises in relation to which the remedial action has been (or is to be) taken and the nature of the remedial action;

- the power under which the remedial action has been (or is to be) taken;

- the date of the start or intended start of the remedial action; and

- that there is a right of appeal to the residential property tribunal and that there is a 28–day time limit for appealing.

7. PROHIBITION ORDER

12.51 Preconditions. An authority may make a prohibition order where a Category 1 or Category 2 hazard exists (2004 Act ss.21, 22). An order may relate to more than one category of hazard in the same building; a notice relating to a Category 2 hazard may be combined with that relating to a Category 1 hazard where they both impose prohibitions relating to the same premises (2004 Act s.21(5)).

12.52 Persons on whom served. The person on whom a prohibition order is to be served depends on the nature of the premises (2004 Act Sch.2).

- **Houses.** Where the property is a house which is not divided into flats, or an HMO which is not a flat, the order must be served on every person who is an owner (12.33), or on an occupier of the whole or part of the premises, or on anyone who is authorised to permit persons to occupy the property, e.g. a letting agent, or on a mortgagee.

- **Flats and common parts.** Where the premises consist of one or more flats, or common parts, the order must be served on every person who is an owner (12.33) or occupier of the whole or part of the building, or on anyone who is authorised to permit persons to occupy the whole or part of the premises, e.g. a letting agent, or on a mortgagee.

12.53 The order must be served within seven days of being made. In the case of occupiers, service can be effected by fixing the order on some conspicuous part of the premises.

12.54 Requirements. If the hazard exists in a house which is not divided into flats, or an HMO which is not a flat, the order may prohibit the use of the property. In the case of a hazard in a flat or flats, the order may prohibit use of the building containing the flat(s), or a part of the building, or any external common parts. If the hazard is in the common parts of a building containing one or more flats, the order may prohibit use of the building, any part of it or any external common parts (2004 Act ss.20(3), 21(3)).

12.55 The order may prohibit use for all purposes or permit limited approved purposes (2004 Act s.22(4)). Accordingly, the order may limit the number of occupiers or occupation by particular descriptions of persons, e.g. children or the elderly. The authority must not unreasonably withhold approval to a particular use (2004 Act s.22(7)); if they refuse approval, they must so notify the person who has applied for it (2004 Act s.22(8)).

12.56 A notice refusing approval must include reasons for the decision, and inform the recipient of his right to appeal to the residential property tribunal and of the 28–day time limit for appealing.

12.57 Contents. A prohibition order must specify the following (2004 Act s.22):

- whether it is served in relation to a Category 1 and/or Category 2 hazard;

- the nature of the hazard and the residential premises on which the hazard exists, e.g. dwelling, HMO, etc.;
- the deficiency giving rise to the hazard;
- the prohibitions imposed;
- the premises in relation to which the prohibitions are imposed;
- any remedial action which the authority consider would, if taken, result in their revoking the order; and
- that there is a right of appeal to the residential property tribunal and that there is 28–day time limit for appealing.

12.58 The order may prohibit use for all purposes or permit limited approved particular purposes (2004 Act s.22(4)). Accordingly, the order may limit the number of occupiers or occupation by particular descriptions of persons, e.g. children or the elderly. The authority must not unreasonably withhold approval to a particular use (2004 Act s.22(7)); if they refuse approval, they must so notify the person who has applied for it (2004 Act s.20(8)).

12.59 A notice refusing approval must include reasons for the decision, and inform the recipient of his right to appeal to the residential property tribunal and of the time limit for appealing.

12.60 Suspension. An authority may suspend a prohibition order, either for a particular period of time, or until the occurrence of a particular event (2004 Act s.23). Provision is made for termination of suspension where the nature of the occupancy of premises changes, e.g. where an occupier considered less vulnerable to the hazard is replaced by another who is more vulnerable. Suspension may also occur where the authority accept an undertaking from the person on whom the notice is served, e.g. a promise that a bedroom in which a hazard exists will in future only be used as storage space. The suspension may be terminated if that undertaking is breached and the authority give notice.

12.61 The authority may review a suspended order at any time and must do so at no greater intervals that 12 months (2004 Act s.26). Following a review, the authority's decision must be served on the same persons as are required to be served with the order itself.

12.62 Enforcement. Unless there is an appeal, the order becomes operative 28 days from service (2004 Act s.24). A person commits an offence if he uses the premises in contravention of the order or permits the premises so to be used (2004 Act s.32(1). The offence is punishable by a maximum fine of £5,000, and £20 for each day after conviction on which the order continues to be breached.

12.63   Loss of security. If possession is required to comply with the order, tenants in premises which are the subject of a prohibition order lose any Housing Act 1988 and Rent Act 1977 protection they may enjoy (2004 Act s.33), but they, as other occupiers, will gain rights to re-housing (12.142) and to compensation (12.155). The fact that statutory protection has been lifted does not, however, mean that the landlord can recover possession without terminating the contractual tenancy (*Aslan v Murphy*, 1989).

12.64   Owner compensation. Where a prohibition order prohibits the use of the whole of any premises for all purposes other than one approved by the authority, compensation is payable to every owner (12.33) of the premises (1985 Act s.584A).

12.65   Revocation and variation. Revocation or variation of a prohibition order may occur either on application by the person on whom it was served or on the authority's own initiative (2004 Act s.25(8)).

12.66   Revocation. An order must be revoked if the authority are satisfied that the hazard no longer exists on the premises (2004 Act s.25(1)). In addition, the authority may revoke an order where they consider it appropriate to do so and (in the case of a Category 1 hazard) where they consider that there are special circumstances which justify revocation (2004 Act s.25).

12.67 Where a notice deals with more than one hazard, the order can be revoked in relation to certain hazards, and varied in relation to the rest (2004 Act s.25(3)).

12.68   Variation. An order may be varied with the agreement of the person on whom it was served (2004 Act s.25(6)), and a person may request variation of an order, e.g. for an approved use of the property (12.55). By s.25(4)(b), the authority may unilaterally vary a suspended prohibition order so as to alter the time or events which bring the suspension to an end (2004 Act s.25(4)) and, thus, activate the order.

12.69   Procedure for variation or revocation. Detailed provision is made for the procedure to be adopted where an authority decide to vary or revoke a prohibition order (2004 Act Sch.2). Decisions may be appealed to the residential property tribunal.

12.70 Appeals. An owner (12.33), occupier, managing agent or mortgagee may appeal against the making of a prohibition order or any decision by the authority to revoke (or refuse to revoke) or vary (or refuse to vary) an order (2004 Act s.24 Sch.2 Pt 3). An appeal must be lodged within 28 days of the days of service of the order or of the authority's decision.

8. EMERGENCY PROHIBITION ORDER

12.71 Preconditions. An authority may only make an emergency prohibition order in relation to a Category 1 hazard. The authority must be satisfied that the hazard involves an imminent risk of serious harm to the health and safety of any of the occupiers of the premises concerned, or other residential premises.

12.72 Effect. A normal prohibition order comes into effect within 28 days (subject to appeal) (12.74). In contrast, an emergency order takes immediate effect. The prohibitions on use of the premises are the same as for other prohibition orders (12.55).

12.73 Service. An emergency prohibition order must be served on the same persons as a normal prohibition order (12.52). It must be served on the day that it is made or, if that is not possible, as soon as possible thereafter.

12.74 Content. An emergency prohibition order must specify:

- the nature of the hazard and the residential premises on which the hazard exists, e.g. dwelling, HMO, etc.;
- the deficiency giving rise to the hazard;
- the prohibitions imposed;
- the premises in relation to which the prohibitions are imposed;
- any remedial action which the authority consider would, if taken, result in their revoking the order; and
- that there is a right of appeal to the residential property tribunal and that there is a 28–day time limit for appealing.

12.75 The provisions relating to enforcement (12.62), revocation and variation (12.65–12.69), and compensation (12.64), in relation to normal orders also apply to emergency orders.

9. DEMOLITION ORDER

12.76 Preconditions. A demolition order can only be made in relation to a Category 1 hazard (1985 Act s.265(1)).

12.77 Effect of demolition order. Unless there is an appeal against a demolition order, it becomes operative 28 days after service (1985 Act s.268). The order must specify a time within which the building is to be vacated, which is to be not less than 28 days after the order becomes operative, and a time within which it is to be demolished, which is to be within six weeks of the premises being vacated or such longer period as the authority may specify (1985 Act s.267).

12.78 Service of order. Within seven days of the order being made, it must be served on any owner of the premises (12.33), any occupier, any person authorised to let the premises and every mortgagee (1985 Act s.268(1)).

12.79 Loss of security. Once a tenant is obliged to quit, he loses any Housing Act 1988 and Rent Act protection he enjoys (1985 Act s.270(3)), although he, and other occupiers, will be entitled to re-housing (12.142) and to compensation (12.155).

12.80 Enforcement. A person who knows of the demolition order and who enters into occupation of the property after it is made, or who permits someone else to enter, commits an offence, which is punishable by a maximum fine of £5,000 plus an additional £5 for every day on which occupation continues after conviction (1985 Act s.270(5)). Not only can the landlord seek possession of the premises from an occupier but so also can the local authority (1985 Act s.270(2)). The authority have power to cleanse the building of vermin before demolition, should it appear to be necessary (1985 Act s.273). If the owner does not proceed to demolish the building, the authority may themselves do so in default (1985 Act s.271), and recover their costs.

12.81 Substitution of prohibition order. If, after a demolition order has become operative but before the house is demolished, the house becomes a listed building under the Planning (Listed Buildings and Conservation Areas) Act 1990 s.1, the authority are to substitute a prohibition order (1985 Act s.304).

12.82 Deferral and revocation. An owner, or anyone else who appears to the authority to be in a position to put such a proposal into practice, may also cause demolition to be deferred, to allow an opportunity for the Category 1 hazard to be dealt with (1985 Act s.274). If the works are completed to the authority's satisfaction, the demolition order is then determined.

12.83 Purchase notice. In place of either demolition or prohibition order, the authority may serve a purchase notice if it appears to them that the premises are, or can be, rendered capable of providing accommodation which is adequate for the time being (1985 Act s.300). They cannot purchase premises which are a listed building (1985 Act s.300(7)).

12.84 Effect of purchase notice. The purchase notice becomes operative 28 days after service, unless there is an appeal, in which case it will become operative on the final determination of the appeal (1985 Act s.300(4)). If the owner will not agree to sell the house to the authority, the authority may, with government consent, purchase it compulsorily (1985 Act s.300(6)). Compensation will be available to owner-occupiers, tenants or other occupiers when they are actually moved (12.149), at which point they will also acquire rights to re-housing (12.142). During the intervening period, any Housing Act protection is lost (1988 Act s.1, Sch.1 para.12) as is any Rent Act protection (Rent Act 1977 ss.14, 19), but occupiers do not become secure tenants of the authority (1985 s.79 and Sch.1 paras 3–3.39(e)).

12.85 Use for time being. The standard to which a property that has been purchased is to be maintained for the time being is lower than that required by the HHSRS, and the provisions of s.8 of the Landlord and Tenant Act 1985 (11.43–11.46) are expressly stated not to apply (1985 Act s.302). The purpose of the power is to do no more than provide temporary accommodation: the power cannot be used to add to the authority's permanent housing stock (*Victoria Square Property Co Ltd v Southwark LBC*, 1977). The provisions of the Environmental Protection Act (Chapter 13) will, however, continue to apply, and the authority must prevent the property from becoming a statutory nuisance as long as it remains in use (*Salford CC v McNally*, 1975).

12.86 Appeals. A demolition order or purchase notice can be appealed to the residential property tribunal (1985 Act ss.269(3), 300(4)). The appeal must be lodged within 28 days of service of the appropriate notice; pending the appeal, the authority are to carry out no action in relation to the notice (1985 Act s.269). A tenant may not appeal if he is in occupation under a lease with less than three years to run, e.g. a periodic tenant (1985 Act s.269(2)), although in the rare circumstances when a challenge can be made on principles of administrative law (10.182), such a tenant may seek judicial review of the authority's decision (*R. v Maldon DC Ex p. Fisher*, 1986; *R. v Woking BC Ex p. Adam*, 1995).

12.87 It is a specific ground of appeal that an alternative course of action, e.g. improvement notice or prohibition order, would have been the best course of action (1985 Act s.269A). If the tribunal decides to allow the appeal on this basis, the authority may ask it to include in its decision a specific finding as to the best course of action, and the tribunal must do so.

Slum clearance

1. CLEARANCE AREAS

12.88 Decline of use. Clearance areas were once the principal means of dealing with large areas of poor housing. Today, improvement is more probable, although clearance has recently enjoyed a resurgence to deal with areas of uneconomic housing where the private market has collapsed and properties have been left vacant.

12.89 Outline. In outline, the clearance area provisions operate by:

- declaration of clearance area;
- compulsory purchase proceedings to enable the local authority to acquire property not already in their ownership; and
- demolition.

12.90 Provision is also made for temporary use pending demolition (12.97).

12.91 Pre-conditions. A declaration of a clearance area may be made in the following circumstances:

- **Health and safety.** The authority must be satisfied that:
  - each of the "residential buildings" in the area contains a Category 1 hazard and any other buildings in the area are dangerous or harmful to the health or safety of the inhabitants of the area; or

— both the residential buildings in the area, as a result of their bad arrangement or the narrowness or bad arrangement of their streets, and any other buildings, are dangerous to the health or safety of the occupiers; or

— each of the residential buildings in the area contains a Category 2 hazard and any other buildings in the area are dangerous to the health or safety of the occupiers.

- **Representations.** Before making a declaration, the authority must consult those with an interest in the buildings, and the occupiers of any residential buildings, and consider any representations in response.

- **Alternative accommodation.** The authority must be satisfied that they can provide or secure alternative accommodation for those displaced prior to demolition.

- **Resources.** The authority must be satisfied that they have sufficient resources to carry out the clearance programme (1985 Act s.289).

12.92 Compulsory purchase. The principal stage in the clearance procedure is compulsory purchase (1985 Act s.290). The authority are entitled not only to seek to purchase the houses and other buildings in the area but also any land (including houses and other buildings) surrounded by the area, or adjoining the area, which is necessary in order to acquire a cleared area of convenient shape, or in order satisfactorily to develop the area (1985 Act s.290(2)).

12.93 Own land. The authority may include in the proposals any land which they already own, which qualifies either under the principal criteria (12.91) or under the "added land" provisions referred to in 12.92 (1985 Act s.293).

12.94 Need for confirmation. Compulsory purchase will require central government approval, which will normally mean an inquiry into the proposals. At any time before the compulsory purchase order is confirmed, application can be made for the exclusion of land from the order on the ground that the owner will himself execute the demolition and that the authority do not, in those circumstances, actually need the land for the purpose of redevelopment of the area (1985 Act s.292).

12.95 Protection, rehousing and compensation. Tenants and other occupiers displaced by the programme will be entitled to re-housing (12.142) and to compensation (12.149). Tenants will lose any status as assured under the 1988 Act (1988 Act s.1 and Sch.1 para.12) once the authority become their landlord, as well as any Rent Act protection (1977 Act ss.14, 19), but do not become secure tenants of the authority (3.39(5) and 1985 Act s.79 and Sch.1 para.3).

12.96 Demolition. Once the order has been purchased, the authority's main obligation is to cause all the buildings to be vacated "as soon as may be". Thereafter, the authority must either demolish all the buildings within six weeks (or such period as they consider reasonable) and either sell or let the land for redevelopment or themselves redevelop, the land (1985 Act s.291).

12.97 "As soon as may be" is a vague phrase. Commonly, clearance area land is left untreated for many years. If satisfied that the houses are, or can be rendered, capable of providing accommodation "at a standard which is adequate for the time being", the authority may postpone demolition and retain the housing in use (*cf.* 12.85; 1985 Act s.301).

2. HOUSING ASSISTANCE

12.98 Adoption of policy. Before providing assistance under the regulatory reform order, an authority must have adopted a policy for the provision of assistance, of which they must have given public notice (Regulatory Reform Order art.4). The authority must ensure that a full copy of the policy is available for inspection free of charge at their principal office at all reasonable times, and that a summary document is available by post on payment of a reasonable charge. Any assistance must be provided in accordance with the policy.

12.99 Types of assistance. The purposes for which assistance may be provided are to be found in art.3 of the Regulatory Reform Order. For the purpose of improving living conditions in their area, local authorities may provide direct or indirect assistance to a person for the purposes of enabling him (art.3(1)):

- to acquire living accommodation (whether within or outside their area);

- to adapt or improve living accommodation (whether by alteration, conversion or enlargement);

- to repair living accommodation;

- to demolish building comprising of including living accommodation; or

- where buildings comprising or including living accommodation have been demolished, to construct buildings that comprise or include replacement living accommodation.

12.100 Living accommodation. For these purposes, "living accommodation" means a building or part of a building, or a caravan, boat or similar structure, occupied or available for occupation for residential purposes (art.2).

12.101 Types of assistance. Assistance may be provided in any form and may be subject to conditions, including as to repayment or making a contribution towards the assisted work (art.3(3), (4)). Examples of possible conditions, e.g. as to eligibility and payment, are provided in Annex B of the Guidance. Before imposing a condition as to repayment or contribution, the authority must have regard to the ability of the person to make the repayment or contribution.

12.102 The primary means of assistance will be grants or loans (see Guidance; Chapter 3), although other forms of assistance, e.g. discounted materials or access to tool hire schemes, may also be provided. Where a loan is given, the authority may take any form of security in respect of it (art.3(6)). Where the security is a charge on a property, the authority may at any time reduce the priority of the charge or secure its removal (art.3(7)).

12.103 Statements, advice and assistance. Before providing any assistance, the authority must provide the person with a statement in writing of any conditions attaching to the assistance, and satisfy themselves that the person has received appropriate advice or information about the extent and nature of any obligation (whether financial or otherwise) to which he will become subject as a consequence of the assistance (art.3(5)).

12.104 Consent of owner. By art.5 of the Regulatory Reform Order, assistance to adapt, improve, repair or demolish living accommodation may not be given unless the authority are satisfied that the owner of the living accommodation has consented to the works. The owner is the person entitled to receive a rent at an annual rate of not less than two-thirds of the net annual value (or who would be so entitled if the accommodation was let), who is not himself liable as tenant of the accommodation to pay such a rent to a superior landlord. Where the accommodation is a caravan, boat or similar structure, the owner is the person currently entitled to dispose of it.

12.105   Provision of information and evidence. The authority may require a person to whom assistance has been provided or who has applied for assistance to provide them, within a reasonable period, with such information as they may reasonably require (art.6). This may include information as to the person's financial circumstances. The Regulatory Reform Order does not lay down any procedures which authorities have to adopt, but guidance is provided in Annex B of the Guidance.

12.106   Central government contributions. Contributions towards expenditure incurred in providing housing assistance may be made by the Secretary of State in England, or the National Assembly in Wales (art.7).

3.   DISABLED FACILITIES GRANT

12.107   Nature of grant. A "disabled facilities grant" is available for the provision of facilities for a disabled person in a dwelling, a qualifying houseboat or park home, or in common parts of a building (1996 Act s.1).

12.108   Qualifying houseboat. A qualifying house boat is a boat or similar structure designed or adapted for use as a place of permanent habitation which has its only or main mooring with the area of a single local authority, which is moored in pursuance of a right to that mooring and which is a dwelling for council tax purposes (1996 Act s.58).

12.109   Qualifying park home. A qualifying park home is a caravan within the meaning of the Caravan Sites and Control of Development Act 1960 Pt 1, which is stationed on land forming part of a protected site within the meaning of the Mobile Homes Act 1983, which is occupied either under an agreement to which the 1983 Act applies or under a gratuitous licence, and which is a dwelling for council tax purposes (1996 Act s.58).

12.110   Purposes of grant. A disabled facilities grant may not be approved unless the authority are satisfied that the works are necessary and appropriate to meet the needs of the disabled occupant; and that it is reasonable and practicable to carry out the works having regard to the age or the condition of the building (1996 Act s.24(3)). Applications should be assessed in conjunction with the social services authority.

12.111 The grant is available if it is for one or more of the following purposes:

- facilitating access by the disabled occupant to and egress from the premises;

- making the dwelling, qualifying houseboat, park home (12.108, 12.109) or building safe for the disabled occupant or other persons residing with him;

- facilitating access by the disabled occupant to a room used or usable as the principal family room;

- facilitating access to, or providing, a room used or usable for sleeping;

- facilitating access to, or providing, a room in which there is a lavatory, bath, shower or wash-hand basin, or facilitating the use of such a facility;

- facilitating the preparation and cooking of food;

- improving any heating system in the dwelling to meet the needs of the disabled occupant, or, if there is no existing heating system or it is unsuitable, providing a suitable system;

- facilitating the use by the disabled occupant of a source of power, light or heat, by altering the position of access and control or providing additional means of control;

- facilitating access and movement by the disabled occupant around the dwelling in order to enable him to care for a person who is normally resident in the dwelling and who is in need of such care; and

- other purposes specified by the Secretary of State (1996 Act s.23(1)).

12.112 Constraints on commencement of works. Works for which it is intended to apply for a disabled facilities grant should generally not have been started before approval of application, unless there is good reason and provided the works have not been completed (1996 Act s.29).

12.113 Pre-conditions. An application for a disabled facilities grant must be in writing and include details of the works and at least two estimates for the costs of carrying out the works (1996 Act s.2). The applicant must be at least 18 years old (1996 Act s.3).

12.114 Required interest. The applicant must have the requisite interest in the property. He must either be an owner, i.e. the freeholder or under a leasehold interest of at least five years, or be a tenant (1996 Act s.19). In the case of a qualifying houseboat or park home, he may be an occupier of the houseboat or park home.

12.115 Future use. An application for a disabled facilities grant must be accompanied by either an owner's certificate stating that the applicant has or proposes to acquire an owner's interest (12.114) and intends that the disabled occupant will live in the property as his only or main residence for five years, or a tenant's certificate stating that the applicant is a tenant and has the same intention (1996 Act ss.21, 22).

12.116 In the case of a qualifying houseboat or park home (12.108, 12.109), an occupier's certificate is required stating that the disabled occupier intends to live in the houseboat or park home as his only or main residence for five years (1996 Act s.22A).

12.117 The authority may—in the case of any of these certificates—set a shorter period of intended residence, as the health of the disabled person or other relevant circumstance permits.

12.118 Approval. Authorities must, by notice in writing, approve or refuse a grant application as soon as reasonably practicable and in any event no later than six months after it has been made (1996 Act s.34).

12.119 An approval must include a statement of the works eligible for grant, the amount of expenses which in the authority's opinion are properly to be incurred on the eligible works, together with any preliminary or ancillary services or charges, e.g. the cost of having plans drawn up, and the amount of grant which will be paid.

12.120 Grant maxima. The amount of grant will be calculated applying the means testing provisions (12.95). Maximum amounts

(1996 Act s.33) have been set of £25,000 in England, and £30,000 in Wales (the Disabled Facilities and Home Repair Assistance (Maximum Amounts) Order 1996 (SI 1996/2888), as amended).

12.121 Means-testing. Where the application is by an owner-occupier or a tenant, the amount of grant is reduced in accordance with regulations which are similar to those applied to housing benefit calculations, and which ascertain an amount which the applicant could himself finance, by which the grant is accordingly to be reduced (1996 Act s.30).

12.122 Landlords' means test. The means-testing provisions applicable where the application is by a landlord letting or intending to let to a disabled occupier are somewhat less pre-scribed. In deciding the amount of grant, the authority should have regard to the extent to which the landlord is able to charge a higher rent for the premises because of the works and such other matters as may be directed pursuant to the statute (1996 Act s.31). Authorities may seek the advice of rent officers (1996 Act s.31(4)).

12.123 Payment of grant. Once approved, an authority may only refuse to pay the grant in one or more of seven circumstances:

1. where the applicant ceases to be a person entitled to the grant;

2. where the authority ascertain that the amount to be paid was determined on the basis of inaccurate or incomplete infor-mation and exceeds that to which the applicant was entitled;

3. where the applicant fails to complete the works satisfactorily within the time allowed (12.126);

4. where the cost of the eligible works and costs incurred on preliminary or ancillary service is less than the estimated expense;

5. where the authority ascertain that without their knowledge the works were not carried out by one of the contractors who submitted an estimate (1996 Act ss.42, 43);

6. where the works are not carried out to the satisfaction of the authority; and

7. where the applicant fails to provide an acceptable invoice, demand or receipt for payment for the works or for the preliminary or ancillary services and charges (1996 Act s.37).

12.124   In such circumstances there are provisions, where appropriate, for the recovery of grant already paid (1996 Act ss.42, 43).

12.125   Stage payments.   The authority may make the whole payment after completion of the works. Alternatively, they may make stage payments, as the work progresses, provided that no more than nine-tenths of the grant is paid before completion (1996 Act s.35). The authority may specify a delayed date for payment, up to 12 months after the date of application (1996 Act s.36). This is to enable authorities to stagger payments of the grant to fit their budgets. Grants may be paid directly to the contractor provided that the applicant was informed of this prior to approval of the grant (1996 Act s.39).

12.126   Conditions as to completion of works.   The authority may make it a condition of the grant that the works are carried out in accordance with their specifications, e.g. as to materials to be used. It is a mandatory condition of all grants that the works are finished within 12 months of approval, although the authority may extend this time at their discretion (1996 Act s.37). It is also a mandatory condition that the works are carried out by one of the two contractors from whom estimates were submitted with the application (12.113), unless the authority direct otherwise (1996 Act s.38). An approved contractor scheme may be centrally established, in which case it will be a condition that the contractor is a member of the scheme.

12.127   Compensation conditions.   With the consent of the Secretary of State, an authority may attach a condition that the applicant takes reasonable steps to pursue any relevant insurance or legal claim which relates to the premises, e.g. where a grant is being sought following fire damage and an insurance claim can be made (1996 Act s.51).

12.128   Other conditions.   Other conditions may be applied with the consent of the Secretary of State, e.g. as to nomination rights, insurance or maintenance (1996 Act s.52).

12.129   Voluntary repayment.   An owner or mortgagee entitled to exercise the power of sale can repay the grant voluntarily. On such a repayment, all grant conditions cease to have effect (1996 Act s.55).

Renewal areas

12.130 Area action. The provisions governing the declaration of and powers and duties in renewal areas are to be found in the Local Government and Housing Act 1989 Pt 7, as amended by the Regulatory Reform Order.

12.131 Declaration. The starting point for the declaration of a renewal area is a "report" requested by the local housing authority, which should contain a reasoned recommendation that the renewal area should be declared (1989 Act s.89).

12.132 The report may include any matters which the authority consider relevant, and in particular must include particulars of the following matters:

- **Living conditions**: the living conditions in the area concerned;

- **Improvement**: the ways in which conditions may be improved (whether by the declaration of a renewal area or otherwise);

- **Powers**: the powers available to the authority if the area is declared;

- **Proposals**: the authority's detailed proposals for the exercise of those powers during the period that the area will be a renewal area;

- **Costs**: the costs of the proposals;

- **Resources**: the financial resources available, or likely to be available, to the authority for implementing the proposal; and

- **Representations**: any representations (12.135) made to the authority in relation to the proposals.

12.133 Guidance. A renewal area may be declared if the authority are satisfied, on the basis of the report, that the living conditions in an area within their district which consists primarily of housing accommodation are unsatisfactory and can most effectively be dealt with by declaring a renewal area (1989 Act s.89(1)). In reaching this decision or a decision to extend (12.136), the authority must have regard to central government guidance issued (1989 Act s.89(5)), to be found in the Housing Renewal Guidance (Consultative Document) (ODPM, June 2002), Annex H.

12.134 The guidance recommends a method known as Neighbourhood Renewal Assessment, which "provides a thorough and systematic appraisal technique for considering alternative courses of action". It involves both an economic and a socio-environmental assessment of different options.

12.135 Prior publicity. Prior to declaration, the authority must take steps designed to secure that the proposals are brought to the attention of persons residing or owning property in the proposed area, and that those persons are informed of the name and address of the person to whom inquiries and representations concerning the proposals should be addressed (1989 Act s.89(6), (7)).

12.136 Duration and termination. It is for the authority to determine the length the renewal area is to last (1989 Act s.89(4)(a)). The authority may decide to extend the period (1989 Act s.89(4)(b)) or the authority may decide to bring the area to an end at an earlier date, or to exclude land from it (1989 Act s.95). Prior and subsequent to making such a resolution, the authority must fulfil requirements as to publicity and consideration of representations.

12.137 Duties and powers. As soon as possible after the declaration or any later extension, the authority must take steps designed to secure that their decision is brought to the attention of persons residing or owning property in the proposed area, and that those persons are informed of the name and address of the person to whom inquiries and representations concerning action to be taken should be addressed (1989 Act s.91). As well as the duty to publicise the declaration, the authority are under a continuing duty to bring to the attention of residents and property-owners information about the proposed and existing action in the area, and assistance available for the carrying out of works (1989 Act s.92).

12.138 Compulsory purchase powers. Local housing authorities may by agreement or, with the consent of the Secretary of State, compulsorily acquire land in a renewal area which comprises premises consisting of or including housing accommodation. The purchase must be for one of the following objectives (1989 Act s.93):

- improvement or repair of premises, either by the authority or by someone, e.g. a housing association, to whom they propose to dispose of them;

- proper and effective management and use of housing accommodation, again either by the authority themselves or by another; or

- the well-being of residents in the area.

12.139 The authority may also compulsorily acquire any land in the area in order to improve the amenities in the area, whether they intend to effect the improvement themselves or dispose of the land to someone else intending to do so (1989 Act s.93(4)).

12.140 Works. The authority have power to carry out works on any land they own in the area (whether acquired under their powers of acquisition outlined above, or not) (1989 Act s.93(5)). This power may be delegated to a housing association or other person.

12.141 Ancillary provisions. There are also special powers relating to extinguishing rights of ways over highways (1989 Act s.94) and powers of entry, together with correlative offences of obstruction, in order to survey and inspect (1989 Act s.97).

Re-housing and compensation

1. RE-HOUSING

12.142 Relationship to homelessness. The rights to be considered under this heading are entirely separate from, and are additional to, those provided under Pt 7 of the Housing Act 1996 (Chapter 10). Thus, for example, it is not necessary for a displaced occupant qualifying under these provisions to be able to show that he has a priority need for accommodation (10.31–10.46). Nor is re-housing under these provisions an allocation under Pt 6 (10.202) (Allocation of Housing Regulations (SI 1996/2753) reg.3).

12.143 Duty to re-house. Unless suitable alternative residential accommodation is otherwise available, on reasonable terms, a person displaced from land in consequence of a series of public actions will be entitled to re-housing from or arranged by— usually—the local authority (in some cases, from another public body such as a housing action trust, or new town corporation (Land Compensation Act 1973—"1973 Act"—s.39)).

12.144 The entitlement is not, however, to immediate permanent re-housing: the authority have do no more than their best, and if this means that the displaced occupant is provided with a series of short-life dwellings pending permanent re-housing, the authority will properly have discharged their duty (*R. v Bristol Corp Ex p. Hendy*, 1973).

12.145 Pre-conditions. The circumstances are:

1. displacement in consequence of compulsory purchase;

2. displacement in consequence of a housing order, i.e. a demolition order under Pt 9 of the 1985 Act (12.76–12.87), or a prohibition order under the 2004 Act Pt 1 (12.51–12.70).

3. displacement by an authority who have previously acquired the land, and who now decide to redevelop or improve it.

12.146 Additional conditions. For an occupier to qualify, displacement in consequence of improvement must be permanent (1973 Act s.39(6A)). So also must be displacement in consequence of an undertaking. An occupier claiming re-housing under (2) in the last paragraph must have been in occupation at the time the relevant order was made (1973 Act s.39(6)). An occupier claiming to be re-housed under (1) or (3), above, will not qualify unless he was in occupation when proceedings to purchase the land were commenced (1973 Act s.39(6)). Only a person in lawful occupation will qualify, not a trespasser, nor will there be qualification by someone to whom permission has been given to use the property pending demolition or improvement, i.e. short-life user (1973 Act s.39(3)). The 1973 Act contains provisions enabling the local authority to advance money to a displaced owner-occupier (1973 Act s.41); an owner-occupier who avails himself of this power cannot also claim the right to re-housing (1973 Act s.39(4)).

12.147 Caravan dwellers. Analogous re-housing provision is made for caravan dwellers displaced by the same public activities (1973 Act s.40).

12.148 Local authority tenants. Local authority tenants may qualify under (1) or (3) in 12.145, above, but as authorities will not usually be obliged (or able) to serve a demolition or prohibition order on themselves (12.02), they will not normally enjoy rights to re-housing under this provision (*R. v Cardiff CC Ex p. Cross*, 1983). The authority will, however, usually be obliged to offer alternative accommodation under the 1985 Act s.84 and Sch.2 Ground 10

(3.131), and duties under the 1996 Act Pt 7 will still apply (Chapter 10).

2. HOME LOSS PAYMENT

12.149 Availability. A home loss payment will be available in the same circumstances set out in 12.145, and also:

- in the event of permanent displacement of a housing association tenant on the carrying out of improvement to the dwelling or redevelopment of the land by the association, and

- to those evicted following an order under Ground 10 or 10A of the Housing Act 1985 (3.131) (1973 Act s.29(1));

12.150 While this payment will in the circumstances set out in 12.145 normally be paid by the local authority (even where one of the other public bodies has the re-housing obligation), displacement by a housing association under this additional ground results in payment by the association. Local authority tenants who normally not qualify under 12.145(2) ought to qualify instead under 12.145(3) (*R. v Corby D.C. Ex p. McLean*, 1975).

12.151 Pre-conditions. Home loss entitlement is limited to those with a legal interest in the dwelling, i.e. freeholders, leaseholders and tenants, statutory tenants, those with a restricted contract, and those with a right to occupy the dwelling under a contract of employment (1973 Act s.29(4)). The main limitation is that the claimant must have been in occupation of the dwelling for a minimum of one year, ending with the date of displacement (not of purchase proceedings or other action; *cf.* 12.146), and that occupation was:

- as or with a tenant or other person entitled to payment;

- as an only or main residence; and

- of the whole dwelling or a substantial part of it (1973 Act ss.29(2), 32(3)).

12.152 Additional conditions. Where the claimant has been in occupation of different rooms in the same building, e.g. a series of bedsitting-rooms, he is entitled to be treated as if he had remained in one room (1973 Act s.32(5)). Where there are two or more persons equally entitled to the payment, e.g. joint tenants (1.198–1.207), they each get an equal share (1973 Act s.32(6)). A spouse with home rights under the Family Law Act 1996 (9.16) may also claim (1973 Act s.29A).

12.153 In a case under 12.145(1), the claimant does not have to remain in occupation until required to leave by the authority: provided his qualifying period is fulfilled, he may leave at any time after the date when the authority were given consent to make the compulsory purchase, although not before (1973 Act s.29(3)).

12.154 Amount. The amount of the home loss payment, which must be claimed within six years of displacement (1973 Act s.32(7A)), is, in the case of an owner, 10 per cent of the market value of the interest, to a maximum of £15,000. In all other cases, the amount is £1,500.

3. DISTURBANCE PAYMENT

12.155 Availability. A disturbance payment is available in the same circumstances as a home loss payment, set out at 12.145. It is available from the same body (12.143) (1973 Act s.37(1)). The claimant must have been in lawful possession of the land: in a case within 12.145(1) at the date when notice was first published of the intention compulsorily to purchase; within 12.145(3), when proceedings towards the purchase were begun; or, within 12.145(2), at the date when the order was made, notice was served, or undertaking accepted (1973 Act s.37(3)).

12.156 No payment is made if the claimant is entitled to compensation for the making of a prohibition or demolition order (12.158). Displacement in consequence of an undertaking, or the carrying out of improvement, must be permanent (1973 Act s.37(3A)). Where there is no absolute entitlement under these provisions, and no compensation under any other enactment, the local authority have a discretion to make a disturbance payment in any event (1973 Act s.37(5)).

12.157 Amount. The amount of the disturbance payment is "the reasonable expenses of the person entitled to the payment in removing from the land from which he is displaced" (1973 Act s.38(1)). These words mean more than mere removal costs and include the costs of setting up in the new home. Many local authorities purport to fix amounts for disturbance payments, by scale, by *maxima*, or by limiting the matters for which payment will be made. There is no legal authority for this: the amount may be small or it may be large, and each case is to be judged on its facts. A dispute may be referred to the Lands Tribunal (1973 Act s.38(4)), which is one of the few tribunals for which legal aid is available.

4. COMPENSATION FOR CLOSING AND DEMOLITION ORDERS

12.158 Availability and amount. Where a prohibition (12.51) or demolition order (12.76) is made, every owner of the premises is entitled to compensation (1989 Act s.584A). The amount of compensation is determined on the day the order is made and is the diminution in the compulsory purchase value of the owner's interest as a result of the order being made. If a demolition order is subsequently substituted for the closing order, then the compensation already paid is to be deducted from that paid for the demolition order. Where the demolition or prohibition order is revoked, the recipient must, on demand, repay the compensation to the authority (1989 Act s.584B). Where the closing order is determined in relation to part only of the premises, provision is made for the amount repayable to be apportioned.

Occupier action

12.159 Judicial review. If an authority refused to take action under the provisions in this chapter despite receiving complaints from an occupier that showed that action should be taken, an occupier could compel the authority to take action by judicial review. It is not possible in this work to specify the circumstances in which an authority can be so compelled by the courts, but it should be noted that public bodies must act within the ambit of legislation, and that the courts will intervene (using their powers of judicial review) if authorities misunderstand or misapply the law, act in bad faith or otherwise fail to take relevant matters into account or disregard the irrelevant, or fail to take decisions in individual cases where they were obliged to do so. In such cases, the authority act ultra vires (outside their powers).

12.160 Limits of judicial review. It is imperative, however, to bear in mind that a court (other than a court given express powers on appeal) reviewing the conduct of a public body does not intervene because it disagrees with a decision entrusted by Parliament to that authority, nor because its (or the claimant's) view of what is reasonable is different from that of the authority, but because the authority have acted wrongly in one of the ways illustrated in the last paragraph, or so unreasonably that no reasonable authority, properly approaching the matter, could have so acted. For discussion of the principles in the context of homelessness, see also 10.182–10.194.

12.161   Human Rights Act.   The right to "respect for the home" as required by Art.8 of the European Convention on Human Rights may be breached by a person's home being in severe disrepair (*Lee v Leeds CC*, 2002). The steps which an authority are required to take to comply with Art.8, however, must be determined in each case, having regard not only to the needs of the occupiers but also to the limits on the resources available to the authority (*Lee*). Furthermore, in cases where there has been a severe interference, e.g. through environmental pollution, with an occupier's right to "respect for the home", the European Court of Human Rights has imposed a positive duty on Member States to take action (*Powell and Rayner v UK* (1990); *Lopes Ostra v Spain*, 1995). Thus, in cases involving extremely bad housing conditions, a failure to act by a local authority under one of the duties set out in this chapter may arguably be a breach of Art.8, which could be actionable under the Human Rights Act 1998 s.6.

12.162   Complaint to a J.P.   The 2004 Act, however, does provide the occupier with one, express and additional recourse: he may complain to a justice of the peace (magistrate) either that an individual dwelling-house or house in multiple occupation or that a whole area is unfit for human habitation (1985 Act s.4).

12.163   If the magistrate is satisfied that the complaint is correct, perhaps following a visit to the premises or area, he will in turn complain to the local authority's Medical Officer of Health or, if they have none, the proper officer of the authority. It is this officer's duty then to inspect the house or area, and report to his authority (or appropriate committee). That is as far as the obligation goes. There is no sanction. The officer or committee are free to disagree with the magistrate. The procedure is, however, a useful way of making the authority inspect, and, if the inspection reveals a Category 1 hazard they will be bound to take action (12.26).

CHAPTER THIRTEEN

Disrepair Under Environmental Law

Introduction

13.01 Scope. This chapter is concerned with a series of powers now to be found principally in the Environmental Protection Act 1990 ("1990 Act"), which consolidated much of the law formerly contained in the Public Health Act 1936 ("1936 Act") and the Public Health (Recurring Nuisances) Act 1969. It will also briefly consider some related powers to be found in the Building Act 1984 ("1984 Act") and in various Public Health Acts. It should be appreciated that in relation to housing, the Environmental Protection Act does not amount to a comprehensive or cohesive programme or policy. The provisions are not aimed exclusively at housing. The approach of this chapter is, accordingly, necessarily selective.

13.02 In addition, it may also be noted that before the introduction of the HHSRS (Chapter 12), local authorities' powers to regulate private sector housing conditions were much more limited. Many of the problems which previously could only be addressed using the powers considered below, if at all, can now more effectively be resolved using an authority's powers under the Housing Act 2004, e.g. the removal of vermin (13.71).

Outline

13.03 Preliminary matters

- Powers and duties to deal with environmental problems are imposed on local authorities.

- Authorities must inspect their area from time to time to detect statutory nuisances.

- Action under the Environmental Protection Act is not mutually exclusive to action under the Housing Act 2004.

- Authorities have powers of entry, which it is a criminal offence to obstruct.

13.04   Statutory nuisance

- The Environmental Protection Act 1990 applies to statutory nuisances, defined to include any premises in such a state as to be prejudicial to health or a nuisance.

- Where an authority are aware of a statutory nuisance they must serve an abatement notice on the person responsible.

- An abatement notice may be appealed to the magistrates' court.

- It is a criminal offence not to comply with an abatement notice.

- There is a special procedure for a "person aggrieved" to take action in the magistrates' court, which is available (among other circumstances) where the authority themselves are the person responsible for the nuisance.

- Notice of intention to take action must first be served on the person responsible for the nuisance.

- If the nuisance is proved, the court may make an abatement or works order, impose a fine, prohibit use of the premises for human habitation, or order works in default.

- The court may award an applicant his costs, and the case may be conducted by solicitors on a conditional fee basis; the court can also award compensation.

- There is a special procedure under the Building Act 1984 for urgent statutory nuisances.

13.05   Other controls

- There is a number of other statutory controls to deal with environmental problems:

    — dangerous buildings may be dealt with under the procedures in the Building Act 1984;

— there is a similar procedure under the 1984 Act to deal
with dilapidated buildings;
— some fire precaution measures are included in the Fire
Safety Order 2005;
— the provision and maintenance of sanitary accommodation is also regulated by the 1984 Act, as are drains
and sewers and the provision of adequate food storage;
— vermin can be controlled under the Public Health Act
1936;
— certain diseases are controlled by the Public Health
(Control of Disease) Act 1984.

Preliminary matters

13.06 Local authorities. As in the last chapter, and in the next,
we are here concerned primarily with duties imposed on local
authorities, rather than rights as between individuals. Local
authorities for these purposes are the same authorities who have
duties under the Housing Acts (12.11), save that in the area of a
housing action trust (3.243) some of these powers may be transferred to the trust, additional to or instead of the local authority
(Housing Act 1988 s.68).

13.07 Default powers. Where duties arise under the 1990 Act,
the Secretary of State for the Environment has power to declare
that an authority are in default of their duties, and may direct
them to carry out actions to remedy their default, or even take over
their obligations (1990 Act Sch.3).

13.08 Inspection. Authorities are obliged to inspect their districts with an eye to the performance of their duties in relation to
statutory nuisances, the main class of action with which we shall
be concerned in the present chapter (1990 Act s.79).

13.09 Overlapping powers. Action under the Housing Acts and
under the Environmental Protection Act is not mutually exclusive:
for example, statutory nuisance procedure is no substitute for
procedure under Housing Act 2004 (Chapter 12; *R. v Kerrier DC
Ex p. Guppy's (Bridport)*, 1985) and even though an area may be
declared a clearance area (12.76–12.86) under the Housing Act
1985 Pt 9, the authority will still be bound to take action under the
1990 Act if such action is called for (*Salford CC v McNally*, 1975).

13.10 Powers of entry. Whether the purpose of the entry is in
order to inspect premises, or in order to carry out works which

they are entitled to do, local authorities have a general power of entry into premises, which may be exercised at any reasonable hour (1990 Act Sch.3 para.2). At least 24 hours' notice must be given to the occupier of residential premises under this general power, although there is an additional power to apply to the magistrates' court for a warrant authorising entry, if necessary by force, which can be issued not only when entry has been sought and refused under the general power, but also when warning of a visit would defeat the purpose of the visit (1990 Act Sch.3 para.2(3), (4)). Authorities also have power to enter unoccupied premises in order to prevent them being or becoming a danger to public health (Local Government (Miscellaneous Provisions) Act 1982 s.29), although they are obliged to give an owner of the premises 48 hours' notice of intention of so doing.

13.11 Obstruction. Obstruction of an officer of the authority executing duties under the Acts is a criminal offence (1990 Act Sch.3 para.3).

Statutory nuisance

13.12 Definition. For the purposes of this work, a statutory nuisance means "any premises in such a state as to be prejudicial to health or a nuisance" (1990 Act s.79(1)). The limbs are alternative, so that statutory nuisance may be established by way of either:

- prejudice to health; or
- nuisance.

13.13 Prejudicial to health. Prejudicial to health is, in turn, defined as meaning "injurious or likely to cause injury to health" (1990 Act s.79(7)). The courts have attributed a narrow meaning this phrase so that there must be some feature in the premises which is, in itself, prejudicial to health, in that it is a source of possible infection or disease or illness. Examples include dampness, mould or dirt (*Oakley v Birmingham CC*, 2001).

13.14 Accordingly, the arrangement of the rooms in a house cannot mean that the house was prejudicial to health, notwithstanding that the arrangement could lead to the risk of cross-infection (*Oakley*). Likewise, a steep internal staircase which presents a serious risk of falling cannot be prejudicial to health (*R.*

v Bristol CC Ex p. Everett, 1999) nor can a flat with inadequate sound insulation (*R. (Vella) v Lambeth LBC and London and Quadrant Housing Association*, 2006).

13.15 Dampness, including condensation dampness, is capable of causing injury to health (*GLC v Tower Hamlets LBC*, 1983; *Dover DC v Farrar*, 1979; *Birmingham DC v Kelly*, 1985; *Birmingham DC v McMahon*, 1987; *Southwark LBC v Simpson*, 1998).

13.16 Sleeplessness could amount to injury to health for the purposes of the Act (*Lewisham LBC v Fenner*, 1995). The persons best equipped to determine prejudiciality to health are doctors and environmental health officers (*O'Toole v Knowsley MBC*, 1999). Whether or not premises are injurious to health, although a question of fact, may to an extent be a technical question, so that magistrates cannot (without controverting evidence) simply substitute their own opinions for those of a qualified person, unless, of course, they disbelieve the evidence (*Patel v Mehtab*, 1981); *cf.* the position where the complaint relates to a nuisance at common law (13.17–13.19). There can be a statutory nuisance even although the landlord is not in breach (see Chapter 11) of any repairing obligation (*Birmingham City DC v Kelly*, 1985).

13.17 Nuisance. To qualify as a nuisance within the definition, it must be shown that there is what is identifiable as a nuisance at common law (*National Coal Board v Thorne*, 1976). It follows (see also 8.94) that the nuisance must emanate from one set of premises, and create an effect in another. Thus, a leaking roof may be a nuisance to the occupier of the house, but unless it is injurious to his health it will not be a statutory nuisance. If, however, the effect of the leak spreads to the next-door property, there will be a nuisance, and as such a statutory nuisance, in the leaking premises, actionable in relation to the next door house.

13.18 In this connection, it should be noted that where what is occupied is a flat or a room, or anything less than a whole building, the common parts of the building will remain in the landlord's possession and for these purposes will constitute another set of premises, e.g. roof, halls, stairs, corridors. It is therefore important to define the premises which suffer the nuisance: where there was condensation throughout a block of flats, it was nonetheless each flat which suffered the nuisance, not the block as a whole (*Birmingham DC v McMahon*, 1987).

13.19 Not every activity which affects neighbouring land is a nuisance; only activity which unreasonably interferes with use of the neighbouring land is actionable. Whether interference is unreasonable, e.g. whether noise is so loud as to be unreasonable, is a question of fact and degree in each case, and a court is not bound by the expert opinion of environmental health officers on this issue (*R. (Hackney LBC) v Rottenburg*, 2007).

1. ABATEMENT PROCEEDINGS BY AUTHORITY

13.20 Whose responsibility? Once an authority are satisfied that there is a statutory nuisance, or that a nuisance is likely to recur, they are obliged to take action (1990 Act s.80). They must serve an abatement notice on the "person responsible" for the nuisance. This is the person to "whose act, default or sufferance" the nuisance is attributable (1990 Act s.79(7)). If that person cannot be found, then the authority may serve the notice on either the owner or the occupier although, if the abatement notice requires structural works, they can only serve the notice on the owner.

13.21 If it is clear that there is no fault on the part of either owner or occupier, and the authority cannot find the person responsible to serve an abatement notice on him, they may, instead of serving an abatement notice, carry out such works themselves as they consider necessary to abate the nuisance and to prevent its recurrence.

13.22 Owners. "Owner" is not defined in the 1990 Act, although under the Public Health Act 1936 it was defined in similar terms to a person having control under the Housing Acts (12.31) and that definition should still be applied (*Camden LBC v Gunby*, 1999). It is clear that in many cases this will be the authority themselves. In such a case, they cannot serve a notice on themselves (*R. v Cardiff CC Ex p. Cross*, 1983: 12.02), although the occupier will still be able to take his own proceedings against them (13.27–13.42).

13.23 Abatement notice. If the abatement can be effected without works, e.g. by the removal of some object causing the nuisance, the authority need do no more than require abatement of the nuisance; if works are needed, however, then the authority must specify what works they require (1990 Act s.80; *Kirklees MBC v Field*, 1997). The authority should allow a reasonable time for abatement, which they should state in the notice.

13.24 Appeal against abatement notice. A person who is served with an abatement notice may within 21 days appeal it to a magistrates' court (1990 Act s.80(3)). Appeal is by way of complaint and there is a further right of appeal to the Crown Court (1990 Act Sch.3). The grounds of appeal are set out in SI 1995/2644, and include that the notice was not justified, that it should have been served on another person and that the time given to comply was not long enough. On hearing the complaint, the magistrates' court may:

- quash the notice; or

- vary it in favour of the appellant; or

- dismiss the appeal (SI 1995/2644), reg.3(5)).

13.25 Prosecution for non-compliance. If without reasonable excuse the abatement notice is not complied with, and any appeal is unsuccessful, the recipient may be prosecuted. If found guilty, he may be fined up to Level 5 on the standard scale, and one tenth of that amount for each day the offence continues after conviction (1990 Act s.80(4), (5)). A nuisance is not abated just because the premises have been vacated (*Lambeth LBC v Stubbs*, 1980). Prosecution is a criminal proceeding, and does not lie within the residual civil jurisdiction of the magistrates' court: it should, accordingly, be commenced by information and summons, rather than by complaint (*R. v Newham East Justices Ex p. Hunt*, 1976).

13.26 Works in default. Where an abatement notice has not been complied with, the authority may, either additionally or instead of prosecution, abate the nuisance themselves and carry out any necessary works (1990 Act s.81(3)). Any expenses incurred may be recovered from the person by whose act or default the nuisance was caused (1990 Act s.81(4)). Where the expenses are recoverable from the owner, they become a charge on the premises, and may be repaid by instalments (1990 Act ss.81A and 81B).

2. PROCEEDINGS BY OCCUPIER

13.27 Person aggrieved. There is a special procedure which can be used by a private individual (1990 Act s.82). The individual must be a "person aggrieved" by the nuisance, i.e. someone suffering its effects, not - as it were - a mere busybody. A person cannot be aggrieved in relation to a whole block of flats, only in relation to the flat he occupies (*Birmingham DC v McMahon*, 1987).

13.28 Public funding. Public funding is not available for the prosecution of criminal offences, and is, accordingly, not available to an occupier seeking to use this provision. Initial assistance may be available under the "legal help" scheme, and solicitors are permitted to enter into conditional fee arrangements to take action under s.82 on the basis of recovering their costs under s.82(12) (13.40) (Courts and Legal Services Act 1990, as amended). If the person responsible appeals to the Crown Court against any order, the person aggrieved will be entitled to legal aid (*R. v Inner London Crown Court Ex p. Bentham*, 1988).

13.29 Local authority landlords. There are two circumstances in which an occupier is likely to want to use s.82: when the authority will not take action against a private landlord and, more commonly, when the landlord is the authority themselves. It is well-established that s.82 permits proceedings against a local authority, even the authority who would otherwise be responsible for taking action (*R. v Epping (Waltham Abbey) Justices Ex p. Burlinson*, 1948).

13.30 Procedure. Action is to be taken against the person responsible or the owner in the same way as with an abatement notice (13.23; 1990 Act s.82(4)). Prior to taking any proceedings under this section, the occupier must give 21–days' notice in writing to the proposed defendant (1990 Act s.82(6), (7)). Proceedings are commenced by "laying an information" before the magistrates.

13.31 Powers of court. Having heard the complaint, the magistrates' court may do one or more of the following:

- **Nuisance order**: make a nuisance order requiring the defendant to abate the nuisance and/or execute works to prevent its recurrence (1990 Act s.82(2));

- **Fine**: impose a fine not exceeding Level five on the standard scale (currently £5,000) (1990 Act s.82(2));

- **Prohibition of use**: if the nuisance renders the premises unfit for human habitation, prohibit the use of the premises for that purpose (1990 Act s.82(3));

- **Works in default**: where neither the person responsible for the nuisance nor the owner or occupier can be found, direct the local authority to do anything which the court would have ordered that person to do (1990 Act s.82(13)).

13.32 If without reasonable excuse the nuisance order is not complied with, further proceedings may be taken against the defaulter and he may be fined, continuing on a daily basis (1990 Act s.82(8)).

13.33 Types of work. The works to be included in a nuisance order can include structural works (13.20). There is, indeed, no express limitation on what works can be ordered, and cases under the Public Health Act 1936 will be relevant in this regard. In one case (*Dover DC v Farrar*, 1980), a magistrates' court ordered the installation of gas heating in place of electric heating, in premises suffering severely from condensation dampness. The Divisional Court quashed this order, because the reason the electric heating was not being used was not that it did not work but that the tenants could not afford to use it. It is quite clear from the case, however, that had the electric heating not worked, or had it been wholly unsuitable to eliminate such dampness even if fully and properly used by the tenants, that the order could have been regarded as a proper order, within the power of the magistrates.

13.34 Division of responsibility: landlord and tenant. In the *Dover* case, the landlord was held not to be responsible for the nuisance, as it was considered to be the fault of the tenants that the heating that had been provided was not being used (above, 13.20).

13.35 In another case (*GLC v Tower Hamlets LBC*, 1983), the GLC owned a corner flat situated on the ground floor of a block, but at a raised level, with three sides and the whole of its underneath open to the air, so that an exceptionally large part of the flat was exposed to the elements. Originally, the flat had an open solid fuel fire but this was subsequently blocked up and replaced with an electric heater, itself later removed. The flat suffered from severe condensation dampness. It was held that the flat was prejudicial to the health of the occupants because of dampness caused by the failure of the landlord to take necessary precautions, either by way of ventilation or insulation, or by providing any special form of heating, for a property wholly exceptionally vulnerable to condensation.

13.36 A landlord has to apply his mind to the need for ventilation, and, if need be, to insulation and heating, and must provide a combination of these factors to make a house habitable for the tenant. Once the landlord has done so, it is the tenant's responsibility to use the facilities, and if the cause of continuing condensation is the tenant's unwillingness to do so, then the landlord cannot be held responsible.

13.37 A landlord will also not be held responsible where the reason why works have not been done to abate the nuisance is refusal by the tenant to allow access (*Carr v Hackney LBC*, 1995).

13.38 Contents of order. An order should be as detailed and as specific as possible (*Salford CC v McNally*, 1975). The court has a relatively generous discretion as regards time. Thus, although the fact that Housing Act action is to be taken, e.g. by way of clearance (12.88–12.97), does not exclude the court's duty to make a nuisance order (13.31); it may still influence the amount of time allowed for compliance (*Nottingham Corporation v Newton*, 1974).

13.39 There is also a discretion as to extent of works: if the premises are shortly to be demolished, fewer works than otherwise may be ordered, provided what is ordered is sufficient to abate the nuisance for the period for which the property is likely to remain in use (*Lambeth LBC v Stubbs*, 1980; *Coventry CC v Doyle*, 1981). The fact that the premises are to be vacated does not, however, mean that the nuisance will be abated, for in the absence of an order prohibiting use (13.31) the premises might otherwise be used again in their current state of statutory nuisance (*Lambeth LBC v Stubbs*, 1980).

13.40 Expenses. The court has a discretion (1990 Act s.82(12)) to order a defendant to pay the person bringing the proceedings an amount it considers reasonably sufficient to compensate him for any expenses (including legal expenses) properly incurred in the proceedings, but only if the alleged nuisance existed at the date of making the complaint. Legal expenses can, however, only be recovered if there is a clear agreement by the person to pay the costs irrespective of outcome, but a conditional fee arrangement under the Courts and Legal Services Act 1990 is sufficient for this purpose.

13.41 When considering whether to make an order for costs, magistrates are entitled to take into account the failure of the person bringing the proceedings to allow the landlord access to the flat prior to the complaint being made and notice of intention to bring proceedings (13.30) being served (*Jones v Walsall MBC*, 2002).

13.42 Compensation. The court can also award compensation under the Powers of Criminal Courts (Sentencing) Act 2000 s.130

(formerly the Powers of Criminal Courts Act 1973 s.35) to a statutory maximum of £5,000 (*Botross v Hammersmith & Fulham LBC*, 1994). Where proceedings are instituted by a person, aggrieved compensation can only be awarded from the date of the period of the existence of the nuisance indicated in the summons, provided that date was not before whichever was the later of:

- the date when the statutory notice expired; and

- a date not more than six months before the complaint was made (*R. v Liverpool CC Ex p. Cooke*, 1996).

3.   URGENT STATUTORY NUISANCES

13.43   Unreasonable delay.   In view of the length of time which normal court proceedings can take, the local authority also have power to use a special, speedy procedure when it appears to them that premises are in such a defective state as to be a statutory nuisance, and that there would be unreasonable delay were the abatement procedure to be used (1984 Act s.76). In one case (*Celcrest Properties Ltd v Hastings BC*, 1979), the difference between four weeks under one of the Public Health Acts, and 11–12 weeks under normal abatement procedure, was upheld as an unreasonable delay, sufficient to justify use of the speedy procedure.

13.44   Notice and counter-notice.   The procedure commences with a notice of intent served by the authority on the same person as would an abatement notice be served (13.20). The notice has to state what works the authority intend to execute. The notice must be served at least nine days before commencement of works. During the seven days following service, the person served is entitled to serve on the authority a counter-notice, stating that he intends himself to remedy the defects which have been specified by the authority. The authority are then debarred from using this speedy procedure unless the person who has served the counter-notice does not commence or progress with the works within what appears to the authority to be a reasonable time.

13.45   Claim by authority.   The owner's remedy against use of this procedure is to do nothing: after the works have been completed, the authority will issue civil proceedings (generally in the county court) to recover their expenses; it is a defence to such a claim to show that no unreasonable delay would have flowed from use of the abatement procedure, and, if upheld, the authority recover none of their expenditure, even though the owner will have benefited to the extent of the works executed. The owner may also defend a claim for the authority's expenses if he served a counter-notice (13.44) but the authority entered to do works on the ground of unreasonable time, by proving to the court that the time taken to start or complete the works would not have been unreasonable.

13.46   Building preservation order.   The 1984 Act procedure is not available if the works would contravene a building preservation order under the Planning (Listed Buildings and Conservation Areas) Act 1990, designed for the protection of buildings of special historic or architectural interest. The 1984 Act procedure can be used, however, even though the works to be carried out could have been ordered by way of an improvement notice under ss.11 or 12 of the Housing Act 2004 (12.35–12.42).

4.   APPEALS

13.47   Courts.   Appeal lies from the magistrates' court to the Crown Court, although in certain circumstances it is possible for the appeal (on a point of jurisdiction) to lie by way of proceedings in the Divisional Court. Appeal lies from both a county court and the High Court to the Court of Appeal.

Other controls

1.   DANGEROUS BUILDINGS

13.48   Two procedures.   A dangerous building is any building in such a condition, or used to carry such a load, that it is dangerous (1984 Act s.77). Authorities have two means of dealing with dangerous buildings:

1. by normal procedure; and

2. by urgent procedure.

13.49   Normal procedure.   The normal procedure is by way of application by the authority to the magistrates' court, for an order requiring the owner (13.22), at his own election, either to carry out works to obviate the danger or to demolish the building or its dangerous part (1984 Act s.77).

13.50   Works to obviate the danger means something in the nature of a permanent or semi-permanent remedy, rather than shoring it up (*London CC v Jones*, 1912), or securing the doors against entry and excluding the tenants (*Holme v Crosby Corp*, 1949).

13.51 Though the court does not have to specify the exact works needed, it will need to specify a time for compliance, for no offence of non-compliance can arise until the time allowed has elapsed, nor will the authority acquire their rights to carry out the works in default (1984 Act s.77).

13.52 No provision is made for the removal, re-housing or compensating of tenants.

13.53 Urgent procedure. The urgent procedure is similar to that available in relation to urgent statutory nuisances (13.43–13.46). There is, however, no provision for counter-notice (13.44), and the authority need only serve notice of intention if it is reasonably practicable to do so (1984 Act s.78).

13.54 It is a defence to the authority's proceedings to recover their costs to show that the normal procedure (13.49) could reasonably have been used and, if successful, then again (*cf.* 13.45) the authority recover no part of their costs.

13.55 There is no provision for removal, re-housing or compensation of tenants.

2. DILAPIDATED BUILDINGS

13.56 Definition. For these purposes, a dilapidated building is one which is seriously detrimental to the amenities of the neighbourhood, e.g. unsightly or a health hazard, by reason of its ruinous or dilapidated condition (1984 Act s.79).

13.57 Procedure. Procedure is by way of notice requiring the owner (13.22) either to carry out works of repair or restoration or, at his own election, to demolish the building or a part of it. This procedure is subject to the special appeals and enforcement provisions contained in 1984 Act Pt 4, which permit the owner to challenge the notice by way of appeal on specified grounds, allow the authority to do works in default of compliance with the notice, and create offences of non-compliance.

13.58 No provision is made for removing, re-housing or compensating tenants.

3. FIRE PRECAUTIONS

13.59   Fire Safety Order. Fire is a prescribed hazard under the HHSRS (Chapter 12); and where residential premises are a fire risk, local authorities are likely to use their powers under the 2004 Act. Otherwise, there is not a great deal of legislation governing fire precautions in housing. The Regulatory Reform (Fire Safety Order) 2005 (SI 2005/1541), which repealed and replaced the Fire Precautions Act 1971, imposes duties on persons responsible for premises to take fire safety measures, which duties are enforceable by the fire service. The general provisions of the Order, however, do not apply to "domestic premises", i.e. private dwellings. Accordingly, the provisions do not apply to living accommodation although they do apply to the common parts of buildings containing flats or bed-sitting rooms (*Westminster CC v Select Managements*, 1985). The fire service may serve a prohibition notice restricting the use of such common parts (art.31).

4. SANITARY ACCOMMODATION

13.60   Powers. Inadequate provision for sanitation is a prescribed hazard under HHSRS (Chapter 12) and authorities can use their powers under the 2004 Act to require the installation of adequate sanitary facilities. In addition, however, local authorities have a duty to serve notice on an owner (13.22) of premises, requiring the provision of closets, when a building has insufficient sanitary accommodation, or when any part of the building occupied as a separate dwelling has insufficient sanitary accommodation (1984 Act s.64, as amended). They also have a duty to serve a similar notice if they are satisfied that such sanitary accommodation as exists is in such a state as to be prejudicial to health or a nuisance (13.13–13.19) and cannot be rendered satisfactory without reconstruction (1984 Act s.64).

13.61 For the purposes of the latter provision, local authorities not only enjoy their usual powers of entry (13.10), but are also entitled to apply tests or otherwise examine the closet's condition (1936 Act s.48).

13.62 If, on examination, the authority come to the conclusion that the closet can be rendered satisfactory without reconstruction, they serve notice requiring the execution of such works as may be necessary (1936 Act s.45). Such a notice may be served on either the owner or occupier.

13.63 Finally, the authority have power to require the replacement of earth or other (non-water) closets with water closets, even if the existing closets are in all other respects satisfactory (1936 Act s.47). This power can, however, only be used if there is a sufficient supply of water and sewer available. In the case of such a "substitution" order, the authority must pay half the costs of the installation; the authority have a choice between ordering the owner to execute the works and paying him half the costs, and doing the work themselves and recovering half the costs from the owner (1984 Act s.66).

13.64 Appeals, works in default and offences. These provisions are subject to the appeals procedure contained in the 1984 Act Pt 4 (13.47), which will entitle the person served to challenge a notice by way of appeal, but which also entitle the authority to carry out works in default, and which create offences of non-compliance.

13.65 In addition, there are three specific offences related to sanitary accommodation:

1. **Flushing or deodorizing**: failure to keep the convenience supplied with water for flushing, or in the case of an earth closet with dry earth or other suitable deodorising material (1936 Act s.51);

2. **Injury, fouling and obstruction**: when a convenience is used by more than one family, anyone who injures or improperly fouls the convenience, or anything used in connection with the convenience, or who wilfully or negligently obstructs the drain leading from the convenience, commits an offence (1936 Act s.52); and

3. **Insanitary state**: when a convenience is used by more than one family, leaving the convenience or the approach to the convenience in an insanitary state, for want of cleaning or attention, is also an offence (1936 Act s.52.).

5. DRAINS AND SEWERS

13.66 Powers and procedure. Local authorities enjoy wide powers to require owners (13.22) to make satisfactory provision for drainage and sewage, e.g. if a drain or sewer admits subsoil water, or is prejudicial to health or is a nuisance (1984 Act s.59). In addition, inadequate drainage is a prescribed hazard under HHSRS

(Chapter 12) in respect of which authorities may take enforcement action under the 2004 Act. In some circumstances, they may require remedial action by an occupier as well as, or instead of, by an owner, e.g. in the case of a blockage (Public Health Act 1961 Act s.17). In this last case, the authority can require removal of a blockage within 48 hours, in default of compliance with which they may themselves enter and carry out the works in default, recovering their expenses of so doing.

13.67 An authority may also secure repair of a drain or sewer, if they conclude:

- that it is not sufficiently maintained and kept in good repair; and

- that it could be repaired at a cost of less than £250 (Public Health Act 1961 Act s.17).

13.68 This power proceeds by way of notice of intention to carry out the works themselves, and recover the costs of so doing. There is no appeal against either of the last two classes of notice but in each case the authority's decision can be challenged by way of defence to the claim for recovery of expenses. Local authorities have additional discretionary powers to cleanse drains, at the request and cost of an owner or occupier (Public Health Act 1961 s.22).

6. FOOD STORAGE

13.69 Powers and procedure. Local authorities have power to require the provision of sufficient and suitable accommodation for the storage of food in houses, or in parts of a building occupied as separate dwellings (1984 Act s.70). The power proceeds by way of notice on the owner (13.22), who may challenge it under Pt 4 of the 1984 Act (13.47), which also gives the authority power to execute works in default and to recover the costs of so doing.

13.70 In addition, inadequate provision for the storage of food is a prescribed hazard under HHSRS (Chapter 12) and authorities may alternatively take enforcement action under the 2004 Act.

7. VERMIN

13.71 Powers. Vermin are harboured by filth. It follows that, not uncommonly, the property most in need of repair will be verminous, for everyday experience shows how impossible it is as a matter of practice for those living in shoddy property to keep the premises clean, and how little incentive there is constantly to clean up when the more serious problems of disrepair are never remedied. Exposure to pests is a prescribed hazard under HHSRS (Chapter 12) and authorities may take enforcement action under the 2004 Act. In addition, however, if the local authority are satisfied that premises are so filthy, or in such an unwholesome condition, as to be prejudicial to health (13.13) or verminous, they are bound to take action (1936 Act s.83, as amended).

13.72 Procedure. Action is by way of notice served on either the owner (13.22) or the occupier. The notice may require such steps as may be necessary to preventing the prejudice to health, or to remove and destroy the vermin, which steps can include, if necessary, the removal of wallpaper and other wall-coverings, papering or repapering, painting and distempering, at the option of the person served (1936 Act s.83, as amended). In the event of non-compliance, the authority may execute works in default, and seek to recover their costs from the person served, though it will be a defence to such an action to show either:

- that the notice was not necessary; or

- that as between owner and occupier, it is the other who should have been served (1936 Act s.83).

13.73 Gas attack. In some cases the premises may be in such a condition that a gas attack is called for. A gas attack is carried out by, and at the cost of, the authority, who must give notice to both owner and occupier of their intention to proceed. They may require the premises (and neighbouring premises) to be vacated during the attack, in which cases they must provide alternative temporary accommodation, free of charge (1936 Act s.83; Public Health Act 1961 s.36). A notice requiring the premises to be vacated may be appealed, but subject to the right of appeal it is an offence not to comply with it (1936 Act s.83).

8. DISEASE

13.74 Classes of disease. These provisions govern notifiable diseases, and infectious diseases. A notifiable disease means cholera, plague, relapsing fever, smallpox, typhus or any other disease specified in regulations (Public Health (Control of Disease) Act 1984 ss.10, 13).

(i) *Notifiable diseases*

13.75 Classes of offences concerning notifiable disease.
There are three classes of offence related to notifiable diseases:

1. **Enquiries by new occupier.** If a person seeking to rent
   premises asks whether there is, or during the preceding six
   weeks has been, anyone in the house suffering from a
   notifiable disease, it is a criminal offence, committed by
   anyone involved in letting the house, or showing the house
   with a view to its being let, or anyone who has recently
   ceased to occupy the house, to give an answer known to be
   false (Public Health (Control of Disease) Act 1984 s.29).

2. **Clearance certificates.** A person letting premises in which
   someone has suffered from a notifiable disease, without first
   securing a clearance certificate from the local authority or a
   registered G.P., commits an offence (Public Health (Control
   of Disease) Act 1984 s.29).

3. **Departing occupiers.** If notice has been given by the local
   authority both to the owner (13.22) and to an occupier,
   informing them of their obligations in relation to notifiable
   diseases, anyone who ceases to occupy premises in which, to
   his knowledge, anyone has, within the six weeks prior to his
   departure, suffered from a notifiable disease, may commit
   one of three further offences:

   (a) failing to have the house and any articles within it
       which are liable to retain infection disinfected and
       certified as such by an authority or a registered G.P.;
   (b) failing to give the owner of the premises notice of the
       existence of the disease;
   (c) giving a false answer to an owner who expressly asks
       whether anyone has been suffering from a notifiable
       disease during the six weeks before departure (Public
       Health (Control of Disease) Act 1984 s.30).

(ii) *Infectious diseases*

13.76 Cleansing of premises and property. If the Medical
Officer of Health, or proper officer of the authority, certifies that
premises need cleansing of infectious disease (which includes, but
is not limited to the specified notifiable diseases; *cf.* 13.74), or that
articles in the premises likely to retain infection require cleansing

or destruction, the local authority must give notice to the occupier that they intend to enter and cleanse or destroy, unless within 24 hours the occupier notifies them that he will himself execute all works as are specified in the notice, within a time to be stated for this purpose in the body of the notice (Public Health (Control of Disease) Act 1984 s.31).

13.77 If there is no counter-notice, or if the occupier fails to comply with his counter-notice, the authority may carry out the works in default of compliance and recover their costs. If the authority form the view that the occupier would in any event be unable to comply, they may dispense with the notice, and proceed directly to the works, but they must then bear the cost themselves.

13.78 Removal and vacating. The authority enjoy additional power to remove persons from the premises, with consent or on an order of a justice of the peace, but only if the Medical Officer of Health or proper officer has certified that this is necessary (Public Health (Control of Disease) Act 1984 s.32). The authority may also order the house to be vacated for the purpose of disinfecting it. In either event, the authority may provide, free of charge, alternative, temporary accommodation.

CHAPTER FOURTEEN

Overcrowding, HMOs and other local authority powers

Introduction

14.01 This chapter brings together a number of local authority powers to maintain proper management standards and maintenance of accommodation in their areas for the benefit not only of the occupiers but the community as a whole. First, we consider powers to control overcrowding under Pt 10 of the Housing Act 1985 ("1985 Act"). The levels of overcrowding permitted under the provisions are now somewhat out of date and are not commonly used. Further, overcrowding is now a hazard which may be dealt with under the HHSRS, Pt 1 of the Housing Act 2004 ("2004 Act") (12.20(11)), and authorities may now be able to impose stricter requirements using the provisions of that Act.

14.02 Secondly, we consider powers to regulate conditions in houses in multiple occupation ("HMO"). Authorities have long had powers to regulate HMOs. Formerly, those powers were contained in the 1985 Act Pt 11, which was repealed by the 2004 Act. In particular, the 2004 Act introduced licensing of HMOs (Pt 2), which fixes a permitted level of occupation for the HMO, and under which standards of management and maintenance can be imposed as conditions of the licence. Authorities must have a licensing scheme for certain "high-risk" HMOs, and can extend their scheme to other HMOs. Management standards in HMOs are also controlled by management regulations, and levels of occupation in unlicensed HMOs may be controlled by service of overcrowding notices.

14.03 In addition, the Act introduced licensing for other properties with the intention of regenerating areas of low housing demand (Pt 3).

14.04 If an appropriate licence holder cannot be found for either form of licence, the authority have power to assume management of a property under a management order.

14.05 Finally, we consider authorities' power to take over the management of properties which have been empty for over six months, by way of an empty dwelling management order.

Outline

14.06 Preliminaries

- It is local housing authorities as defined by the Housing Act 2004 who have primary responsibility for dealing with overcrowding and HMOs.
- Local housing authorities should inspect conditions in their area annually.
- Authorities have powers of entry for examining premises.

14.07 Overcrowding

- The overcrowding provision apply to "separate dwellings".
- There are two overcrowding tests:

  — the room standard is based on persons aged 10 or over, who are not husband and wife, having to sleep in the same room;

  — the space standard works by calculating the permitted number for a dwelling based on the number and size of the rooms.

- Even where there is statutory overcrowding, it may be licensed by the authority and it will not be unlawful if caused by family members staying temporarily or through natural growth.
- A number of offences may be committed in relation to overcrowding:

  — rent books must contain details of the overcrowding provisions, failure to comply with which requirement is an offence;

  — a landlord who permits overcrowding commits an offence;

  — an occupier who causes or permits overcrowding commits an offence.

- Local housing authorities have power to prosecute these offences.

- Rent Act protection is lost in the case of illegal overcrowding.

14.08   Houses in multiple occupation (HMOs)

- An HMO is a building or part of a building which meets one of a number of statutory tests: standard test, self-contained flat test and converted building test. A property can also be declared an HMO. Certain converted blocks of flats are HMOs.

- Local authorities must operate a licensing scheme for certain larger HMOs and have power to require other HMOs to be licensed (2004 Act Pt 2).

- The terms of an HMO licence regulate the level of occupation in an HMO and management standards.

- Management regulations impose duties on managers of HMOs to maintain proper management standards, and duties are also imposed on occupiers to ensure that managers can comply with those standards.

- An authority can control the level of occupation in an HMO that does not have to be licensed by service of an overcrowding notice.

14.09   Selective licensing

- Authorities may operate a licensing scheme for residential properties in areas of low housing demand (2004 Pt 3).

14.10   Enforcement of licensing

- There is a number of criminal offences related to licensing, including failure to obtain a licence and breach of license conditions.

- While a property is unlicensed, the landlord cannot recover possession against an assured shorthold tenant without establishing grounds for possession.

- An occupier or local authority can apply to the residential property tribunal for a rent repayment order requiring the landlord to pay back any rent or housing benefit paid while a property was unlicenced.

14.11 Management orders

- Where there is no appropriate person to be a licence holder for a property, the authority may assume management of it under a management order.

- There are two types of management order: interim and final. An interim order is designed to address immediate concerns about the property pending the grant of a licence. If no licence can be granted at the end of an interim order, a final management order must be made.

14.12 Empty-dwelling management orders

- An authority may assume control of a dwelling that has been empty for over six months.

- There are two types of management order: interim and final. Under an interim order, the authority may only let the property out with the owner's consent. Under a final order, consent is not required.

Preliminary matters

14.13 Local authorities. The authorities with responsibility for all of these provisions are the same as those who have responsibility under Pt 1 of the 2004 Act (12.11).

14.14 Inspection. The Housing Act duties to be considered in the present chapter are amongst those for the purposes of which the authority are bound to consider housing conditions in their districts on an annual basis (12.12; 2004 Act s.3(1)).

14.15 Ancillary powers. Local authorities have the same ancillary powers in relation to their functions under the provisions of the 2004 Act considered in this chapter as they have in relation to hazardous properties (12.13).

Overcrowding

1. DEFINITION

14.16 Use as a separate dwelling. The overcrowding provisions apply to premises used or suitable for use as a separate dwelling (1985 Act s.343). As much as a house could be over-crowded, or as little as a single room (see 3.17).

14.17 Alternative tests. There are alternative tests of over-crowding. If either is offended, the premises are overcrowded in law.

1. **Room standard.** There is overcrowding whenever there are so many people in a house that any two or more of those persons, being ten or more years old, and of opposite sexes, not being persons living together as husband and wife, have to sleep in the same room (1985 Act s.325). For these purposes, children under ten may be disregarded.

   A room means any room normally used in the locality as either a bedroom or a living room (1985 Act s.325). Kitchens used to be considered a living room, and might still so be held in this connection, at least if it is big enough to accommodate a bed (*Zaitzeff v Olmi*, 1952) as well as all the necessary kitchen utilities.

   The final point to note, which reduces the impact of this test, is that there is overcrowding not when two or more people do actually sleep in the same room, as prescribed, but when the number of rooms means that they have to do so. Thus, a couple, with two children of opposite sexes and 10 years old or more, with two living rooms, are not over-crowded, because the couple could occupy separate rooms, each with one of the children (of the appropriate sex).

2. **Space standard.** This standard works by the calculation of a permitted number for the dwelling in one of two ways: the lower number thus calculated is the permitted number for the dwelling (1985, s.326).

   One test is based on the number of living rooms in the dwelling (disregarding a room of less than 50 square feet):

   > one room, two persons;
   > two rooms, three persons;
   > three rooms, five persons;
   > four rooms, seven and a half persons;
   > five rooms or more, ten persons plus two for each room in excess of five rooms.

   The other test is based on floor areas of each room size:

   > less than 50 square feet, no one;
   > 50 to less than 70 square feet, half a person;

70 to less than 90 square feet, one person;
90 to less than 110 square feet, one and a half persons;
110 square feet or larger, two persons.

The reference to a "half person" is because, for these purposes, a child below the age of one counts not at all, and a child from one year old but who has not yet reached 10 counts as a half.

2. PERMISSIBLE OVERCROWDING

14.18 Categories. There are four circumstances in which over-crowding, although offending the above criteria, is still permissible:

1. **Licensed overcrowding.** On the application of an occupier, or an intending occupier, of a dwelling (but not on the application of the landlord, or of the local authority), a licence may be issued (in prescribed form), which lasts for no more than one year at a time (1985 Act s.330).

   The licence is issued by the local authority, having regard to exceptional circumstances, expedience and, where appropriate, seasonal increases in population.

   The licence must state how many people are to be permitted. A copy must be served on the landlord. It may be revoked at any time by one month's notice.

2. **Temporary overcrowding.** There is no overcrowding if additional members of the occupier's family are staying with him temporarily (1985 Act s.329).

3. **Natural growth.** Natural growth occurs when a child achieves a relevant age (14.17).

   If the occupier applies to the local authority for alternative accommodation, either before the child reaches the relevant age or before any prosecution is instigated (or possession proceedings; *cf.* 14.23), there will be no illegal overcrowding until either there is an offer of suitable alternative accommodation (14.19) by the authority, which the occupier fails to accept, or the opportunity arises (after the child reaches the relevant age) of asking someone else living in the house, who is not himself a member of the occupier's family, to leave, which opportunity the occupier fails to take (1985 Act s.328).

   An occupier need only ask someone else to leave if it is reasonably practicable for that person to do so, which is to be considered in all the circumstances, including whether or not there was suitable alternative accommodation available to him.

The exemption only continues to apply provided all the people sleeping in the house are those who were sleeping there at the date on which the child reached the relevant age, or their children.

4. **Original overcrowding.** This refers to premises overcrowded when the overcrowding provisions themselves first applied to the house (Housing (Consequential Provisions) Act 1985 Sch.4). As the provisions have applied throughout the country since at least 1935, this exemption is unlikely to be of relevance today.

14.19 Suitable alternative accommodation. Although this phrase is used in the Rent Act 1977 (5.169) and the Housing Acts 1985 (3.124) and 1988 (4.109–4.118), the term has its own meaning in the context of overcrowding (14.18(3)).

14.20 Alternative accommodation is only suitable for these purposes if:

- the occupier and family can live in the house without overcrowding;
- the authority certify it as suitable to his needs and the needs of his family as regards security of tenure, proximity to work, means, and otherwise; and
- if the house belongs to the authority, they can certify it as being suitable to his needs as regards extent of accommodation (1985 Act s.342).

They can only so certify extent if they provide a house with two bedrooms (note, not living rooms) for four people, three bedrooms for five, and four bedrooms for seven. It is, accordingly, a higher standard than that set by the overcrowding limits.

3. OFFENCES

14.21 Categories of offence. There are three sets of offences created by the overcrowding provisions:

1. **Rent book offences.** Every rent book or similar document must contain:

(a) a summary of the overcrowding offences;
(b) a statement of the power of the authority to licence overcrowding (14.18(1)); and
(c) a statement of the permitted number of occupants (14.17(2)) (1985 Act s.332).

Either the occupier or the landlord can ask the authority for a written statement of permitted number at any time. The authority can require the occupier to produce his rent book for inspection and—provided the occupier has it—it is an offence to fail to do so (1985 Act s.336). It is also an offence to fail to provide the summary and statements, although it is a defence to a charge based on the insertion of an incorrect permitted number that it was number provided by the authority (1985 Act s.332).

2. **Landlord's offences.** A landlord who causes or permits a dwelling to be overcrowded commits an offence (1985 Act s.331). This may occur when the landlord has reasonable cause to believe there might be illegal overcrowding, or by failing to make enquiries as to the number intending to occupy a dwelling, or, if the authority serve notice on the landlord that there is illegal overcrowding, by failing to take possession proceedings (14.16; 1985 Act s.331). Finally, unless the authority already know of the overcrowding, the landlord is obliged to notify the authority once he learns of it (1985 Act s.333).

3. **Occupier's offences.** The occupier commits an offence when he causes or permits premises to be illegally over-crowded (1985 Act s.327).

The authority have power to seek information from the occupier as to numbers in a dwelling, failure to comply with which demand, or providing an answer which the occupier knows to be false in a material particular, is also an offence (1985 Act s.335).

14.22 Prosecution of offences. The local authority may themselves commit an offence under these provisions. No one but a local authority may prosecute an overcrowding offence committed by a private individual, but a private individual may prosecute an authority, albeit only with the consent of the Attorney-General (1985 Act s.339); this will not easily be forthcoming.

4. POSSESSION PROCEEDINGS

14.23 Protection. Rent Act protection is lost to occupiers whose premises are illegally overcrowded (Rent Act 1977 s.101). It is, however, only illegal overcrowding that removes Rent Act protection, so that permissible overcrowding will allow the occupier to remain in the premises. The landlord must still determine the tenancy at common law (1.113–1.146). There is no equivalent lifting of Housing Act 1988 security for Housing Act assured tenants.

14.24 In addition, the authority may themselves bring proceedings for possession of premises illegally overcrowded, and recover their costs of doing so from the landlord (1985 Act s.338). The authority must serve prior notice on the occupier, giving the occupier 14 days within which to abate the overcrowding.

Houses in multiple occupation

1. DEFINITION

14.25 HMO. A building (or part of a building) is an HMO if it:

- satisfies the standard test;
- satisfies the self-contained flat test;
- satisfies the converted building test;
- an HMO declaration is in force in respect of it; or
- it is a converted block of flats, which satisfies certain requirements (2004 Act s.254).

14.26 The standard test. This includes the majority of HMOs that are encountered in practice, e.g. bedsitting-room accommodation and shared houses. Six conditions must be satisfied (2004 Act s.254(2));

1. **Not self-contained flats.** The premises must consist of one or more units of living accommodation which do not in themselves consist of a self-contained flat or flats. A self-contained flat is a separate set of premises which forms part of a building in which all the basic amenities are available for the exclusive use of its occupants. The basic amenities are:

    (a) a toilet;

(b) personal washing facilities, e.g. bathroom or shower-room; and

(c) cooking facilities.

2. **Not single household.** The living accommodation must be occupied by persons who do not form a single household. Occupiers includes tenants, licensees, statutory tenants and anyone with an interest in the premises. Persons do not form a single household unless they are either all members of the same family, or they fall within prescribed circumstances. Family members include: spouses; cohabitees who live together as husband and wife; same-sex couples who are in an equivalent relationship; parents; grandparents; children; grandchildren; brothers; sisters; uncles; aunts; nephews; nieces; and, cousins. Half-blood relationships are treated as full-blood relationships, and step-children are treated as children (2004 Act 258).

Regulations prescribe certain categories of person as being part of a single household even though they are not family members, e.g. carers, foster children and live-in employees, such as au pairs and nannies (Licensing and Management of Houses in Multiple Occupation and Other Houses (Miscellaneous Provisions) (England) Regulations 2006 (SI 2006/373) regs 3 and 4; or Licensing and Management of Houses in Multiple Occupation and Other Houses (Miscellaneous Provisions) (Wales) Regulations 2006 (SI 2006/1715) regs 3 and 4).

3. **Only or main residence.** The occupiers must occupy the living accommodation as their "only or main residence". The test is similar to the "only or principal home" residence condition for security of tenure under both the Housing Act 1988 and the Housing Act 1985 (3.32; 4.22).

Certain occupiers are deemed to be occupying property as their only or main residence (2004 Act s.259):

(a) students occupying the property for the purpose of undertaking a full-time course of further or higher education;

(b) occupiers of refuges; and

(c) any other occupiers specified in regulations, i.e. certain migrant or seasonal workers and asylum seekers (Licensing and Management of Houses in Multiple Occupation and Other Houses (Miscellaneous Provisions) (England) Regulations 2006 (SI 2006/373) reg.5; or Licensing and Management of Houses in Multiple Occupation and Other Houses (Miscellaneous Provisions) (Wales) Regulations 2006 (SI 2006/1715) reg.5).

4. **Sole use.** The occupiers' occupation of the living accommodation must constitute the only use of that accommodation. There is a rebuttable presumption that this is so. In some circumstances, the nature of the population of a property may fluctuate with the consequence that the property is not the only or main residence of every occupier, e.g. in hotels which accommodate holiday-makers but also provide hostel accommodation. To address this problem, authorities may declare a property to be an HMO, provided certain criteria are met (14.30).

5. **Consideration.** At least one of the occupiers must be liable either to pay rent or to provide other consideration for occupying the property.

6. **Sharing, or lack of, facilities.** Two or more of the households which occupy the living accommodation must share one or more basic facilities, i.e. toilet, personal washing facilities or cooking facilities or the living accommodation must be lacking in one or more of those facilities.

14.27 Self-contained flat test. The self-contained flat test is concerned with flats in multiple occupation. The only difference between the self-contained flat test and the standard test is that the relevant premises must be a self-contained flat rather than a building or part of a building. It is satisfied where a self-contained flat meets conditions (2) to (6), set out in 14.26 (2004 Act s.254(3)).

14.28 Converted building test. This test is concerned with buildings (or parts of buildings) which have been partly converted into self-contained flats but which also include living accommodation that is not a self-contained flat, i.e. because there is no front door providing access to all parts of the living accommodation (s.253(4)).

14.29 A converted building is a building (or part of a building) consisting of residential accommodation in which one or more units have been created since the building (or relevant part) was constructed. For a building to satisfy the converted building test:

- it must be a converted building;

- it must contain one or more units of living accommodation which are not self-contained flats (whether or not it also contains a self-contained flat or flats);

- the living accommodation must be occupied by persons who do not form a single household (14.26(2));

- the living accommodation must be occupied by those persons as their only or main residence (14.26(3));

- their occupation must constitute the only use of that living accommodation (14.26(4)); and

- at least one of the occupiers must be liable either to pay rent or to provide other consideration for occupying the property (14.26(5)).

14.30 HMO declaration. To satisfy any of the three tests set out above, it is necessary for the sole use of the living accommodation to be occupation by persons as their own or main residence. Where the nature of the property's population fluctuates, an authority may—to remove doubts about a property's status—make an HMO declaration (2004 Act s.255). Before making a declaration, the authority must be satisfied that:

- the standard test, the self-contained flat test, or the converted building test would be satisfied but for the fact that the sole use condition is not satisfied; and

- occupation as an only or main residence by persons who do not form a single household is a significant use of the property.

14.31 The authority must serve notice of their decision on (a) any person who has estate or interest in the premises (save a tenant under a lease with less than three years to run); (b) a person managing the premises (12.32); and (c) any person having control of the premises (12.31). That notice must inform the recipient of his right to appeal to the residential property tribunal within 28 days of the date of the authority's decision. There is no power to extend this time limit. If no appeal is brought in time, the declaration comes into force on the date specified in the notice.

14.32 Converted block of flats. A converted block of flats is a building (or part of a building) which has been converted into and consists of self-contained flats (2004 Act s.257(1)). The effect is to bring within the HMO regime properties which have inadequate fire separation between flats.

14.33 To be an HMO, a converted block of flats must satisfy two conditions:

1. **Conversion works.** The conversion works must fail to comply with the "appropriate building standards" (either, if the conversion was completed before June 1, 1992, the standards contained in the original form of the Building Regulations (SI 1991/2768) or, if completed later, the standards which applied at the date of completion).

2. **Low level of owner-occupation.** Less than two-thirds of the flats must be owner-occupied. A flat is owner-occupied if it is occupied by a freeholder, long leaseholder (1.15) or members of their families.

14.34 Exemptions. Certain properties are exempt for the purposes of the application of the licensing regime and the application of certain other local authority powers (2004 Act Sch.14). Such properties are only HMOs for the purposes of the application of HHSRS (Chapter 12). In general terms, exempt HMOs are buildings:

- managed by local authorities, registered social landlords or certain other specified public bodies;

- subject to the control of other, specified regulatory schemes, e.g. care homes;

- occupied by full-time students at specified educational institutions, where the person managing or having control of the building is the educational institution or another specified person;

- occupied by religious communities;

- predominantly occupied by owner-occupiers, i.e. freeholders and long leaseholders (1.15)—the building must be occupied by no more than two persons who are not owner-occupiers or members of their families; and

- occupied only by two persons who form two households.

2. LICENSING OF HMOS

14.35 Types of licensing. Local authorities must have a licensing scheme for certain types of HMO, which present the greatest risk of death by fire because of their size, and have power to impose licensing for other HMOs.

14.36 Effect. Failure to obtain a licence for an HMO which must be licensed may have serious consequences for the landlord: failure to obtain a licence for an HMO without a reasonable excuse is a criminal offence (14.99); while the HMO remains unlicensed, there are restrictions on the landlord's right to obtain possession (14.102); and the residential property tribunal may make a rent repayment order, which requires the landlord to repay rent or housing benefit which was paid during a period when the HMO should have been licensed (14.103).

14.37 Former registration schemes. Although there was no licensing of HMOs before the 2004 Act, authorities were—under the 1985 Act—able to make "registration schemes", which required registration of HMOs in their area. Such schemes could include control provisions limiting the number of households or occupiers in an HMO and/or special control provisions regulating management standards. Accordingly, many authorities were operating a de facto form of licensing before the 2004 Act. Detailed transitional provisions were made for converting such registration schemes into additional licensing schemes.

14.38 Local authority. Authorities are under general duties to make arrangements to secure effective implementation of the licensing regime and to ensure that all applications for licences are determined within a reasonable time (2004 Act s.55). As soon as reasonably practicable after a licence application is made, they must satisfy themselves as to whether they ought to take action under the HHSRS (Chapter 12). They must comply with the duty within five years of the date of the licence application.

14.39 Mandatory licensing. All authorities must operate a licensing scheme in respect of HMOs which:

- comprises three storeys or more;
- are occupied by at least five persons; and
- are occupied by persons living in two or more single households (14.19(2)) (Licensing of Houses in Multiple

Occupation (Prescribed Descriptions) (England) Order 2006 (SI 2006/371) or Licensing of Houses in Multiple Occupation (Prescribed Descriptions) (Wales) Order 2006 (SI 2006/1712)).

14.40 These regulations contain detailed provisions for the calculation of the number of storeys. Where the HMO is situated above or below business premises, the storeys comprised in the business premises are taken into account. A basement or attic is included where it is used wholly or partly as living accommodation, or it is has been constructed, converted or adapted for use wholly or partly as living accommodation. In addition, a basement is included if it is the only or principal means of entry into the HMO from the street; an attic is included if it is being used as an integral part of the HMO.

14.41 Additional licensing. Local authorities have power to require licensing of HMOs which are outside the mandatory licensing regime by making a designation. The power can be restricted in terms of location or in terms of particular categories of HMO.

14.42 Designation. To make a designation, the authority must consider that a significant proportion of the HMOs which they intend to include are being managed so ineffectively as to give rise, or to be likely to give rise, to problems either for the occupiers of the HMOs or for members of the public (2004 Act s.56(2)). Accordingly, additional licensing is not only about regulating the housing conditions but also about controlling the behaviour of occupiers of HMOs and their visitors. Before making a designation, the authority must take reasonable steps to consult persons who are likely to be affected by it, and must consider any representations made in response.

14.43 Authorities must ensure that any exercise of their power to require additional licensing is consistent with their overall housing strategy and must adopt a co-ordinated approach in dealing with the overlapping issues of homelessness, empty properties and antisocial behaviour in the private sector.

14.44 A designation must be confirmed by the Secretary of State or the National Assembly for Wales. Confirmation may either be specific or by way of a general approval. Following confirmation of the designation, the authority must take steps to publicise it, which are specified in regulations.

14.45 A designation must specify how long it is to last, to a maximum period of five years. The authority must periodically review its operation and may revoke it if they consider it appropriate to do so. If a designation is revoked, the authority must comply with certain prescribed publicity requirements.

14.46 Temporary exemption notice. A person having control of (12.31) or a person managing (12.32) an HMO which needs to be licensed may notify the authority of his intention to take steps to ensure that the house no longer requires to be licensed, e.g. by reducing the number of persons or households occupying the property (2004 Act s.62). If so, the authority may serve a "temporary exemption notice", the consequence of which is that the HMO does not have to be licensed while the notice is in force. A notice remains in force for three months but it can be extended for a further three months.

14.47 If the authority refuse to issue a temporary exemption notice, they must give the applicant written reasons for their decision and inform him of his right to appeal to the residential property tribunal within 28 days. There is no power to extend this time limit.

14.48 Application. A licence is required for each HMO to which the licensing requirements apply (2004 Act s.68). Licences are not transferable: on sale of the HMO, the new landlord has to apply for a new licence. An application for a licence must be made to the authority and must conform with any requirements which the authority may impose, including payment of a fee. Specified information must be contained in the application: Licensing and Management of Houses in Multiple Occupation and Other Houses (Miscellaneous Provisions) (England) Regulations 2006 (SI 2006/373) reg.7 and Sch.2, or Licensing and Management of Houses in Multiple Occupation and Other Houses (Miscellaneous Provisions) (Wales) Regulations 2006 (SI 2006/1715) reg.7 and Sch.2. In particular, the application must include:

- details about the person managing the HMO and the person having control (12.31) of the HMO;

- details about the layout of the HMO and facilities provided; and

- declarations that furniture and gas appliances in the HMO meet relevant safety requirements.

14.49 The form must also include questions designed to elicit information as to whether the proposed license holder and proposed manager are "fit and proper persons" (14.52). The applicant and the proposed licence holder (if different) must both sign the form, and their application must be accompanied by signed declarations as to the truth of its contents. A person knowingly supplying any information in the form which is false or misleading, or supplying such information reckless as to whether it is false or misleading, commits an offence (2004 Act s.238(1)).

14.50   Licence decisions. To grant a licence, the authority must be satisfied of five matters (2004 Act s.64(3):

1. The HMO must be reasonably suitable for occupation by not more than a specified maximum number of households or persons, or can be made so suitable by the imposition of conditions. (The maximum number is either that specified in the application or a number determined by the authority.)

2. The proposed licence holder must be a fit and proper person to be the licence holder and must be the most appropriate person to hold the licence.

3. The proposed manager must either be the person having control (12.31) of the HMO or his agent.

4. The proposed manager of the HMO must also be a fit and proper person.

5. The proposed management arrangements for the HMO must be otherwise satisfactory.

14.51   Suitability for multiple occupation. This is judged by standards prescribed by regulations: Licensing and Management of Houses in Multiple Occupation and Other Houses (Miscellaneous Provisions) (England) Regulations 2006 (SI 2006/373) Sch.3, or Licensing and Management of Houses in Multiple Occupation and Other Houses (Miscellaneous Provisions) (Wales) Regulations 2006 (SI 2006/1715) Sch.3. The regulations are detailed and prescribe the appropriate level of facilities, e.g. for cooking and washing, for a given number of occupiers, for fire safety requirements.

14.52   Fit and proper person. Both the proposed licence holder and the proposed manager must be "fit and proper" persons. In deciding this issue, authorities must take into account (2004 Act s.66(2)) evidence that the person in question:

- has committed any offence involving fraud or other dishonesty, or violence or drugs, or any offence listed in Sch.3 of the Sexual Offences Act 2003 (offences attracting notification requirements);

- has practised unlawful discrimination on grounds of sex, colour, race, ethnic or national origins or disability in connection with carrying out any business;

- has contravened any provision of the law relating to housing or of landlord and tenant; or

- has acted otherwise than in accordance with any applicable approved code of practice for the management of HMOs.

    Evidence of any such conduct by a person associated with, or formerly associated with, the proposed licence holder or manager must also be taken into account if it appears to be relevant to whether the person under consideration is a fit and proper person.

14.53 Management arrangements. In deciding whether other proposed management arrangements for the house are satisfactory, the authority must take into account (2004 Act s.66(5), (6)):

- whether any person proposed to be involved in the management of the HMO is sufficiently competent;

- whether any person proposed to be involved in the management is a fit and proper person; and

- whether any proposed management structures and funding arrangements are suitable.

14.54 Procedure. Detailed provision is made for the procedure for granting or refusing licences (2004 Act Sch.5 Pt 1). Before making a decision, the authority are obliged to consult "relevant persons", i.e. any other person who has an estate or interest in the HMO (other than a tenant under a lease of three years or less to run) or any other person managing (12.32) or person having control (12.31) of the HMO.

14.55 Grant of licence. On the grant or refusal of a licence, the authority must inform the applicant and any relevant person

(14.47) of their decision. There is a right of appeal to the residential property tribunal within 28 days, e.g. against a refusal or terms contained in the licence. The tribunal has power to extend this time-limit where it is satisfied that there is "good reason".

14.56 Licence conditions. Every licence must include certain conditions, and an authority have power to include other conditions which they consider appropriate for regulation of the management, use and occupation of the HMO and its condition and contents (2004 Act s.67).

14.57 Mandatory conditions. Every licence must include conditions requiring the licence holder:

- to produce to the authority a gas safety certificate of the annual inspection required under the Gas Safety (Installation and Use) Regulations 1998;

- to keep electrical appliances and furniture provided by him in a safe condition and to supply the authority, on demand, with a declaration by him as to their safety;

- to install smoke alarms and keep them in proper working order and to supply the authority, on demand, with a declaration as to their safety; and

- to supply the occupiers with a written statement of the terms under which they occupy.

14.58 Discretionary conditions. Illustrations of other conditions that the authority may impose are to be found in the Act:

- restrictions or prohibitions on the use or occupation of particular parts of the HMO;

- requirements for taking reasonable and practicable steps to prevent or reduce antisocial behaviour by occupiers or their visitors;

- provisions for facilities and equipment in the HMO to meet prescribed standards;

- obligations to keep such facilities and equipment in repair and proper working order;

- time-limits for carrying out such works of repair; and

- a requirement for the licence holder or manager to undertake training courses in relation to the standards which may be set out in an approved code of practice.

14.59 A defect in an HMO may constitute a Category 1 or Category 2 hazard under HHSRS against which the authority could take enforcement action (Chapter 12) but which could also be dealt with by imposing license conditions. In general terms, authorities should deal with Category 1 or Category 2 hazards by enforcement action rather than by imposing licence conditions (2004 Act s.68).

14.60 Duration. The licence comes into force on the date specified in the licence and, unless the licence holder dies or the licence is revoked, remains in force for a maximum of five years.

14.61 Variation and revocation. A licence may be varied or revoked at any time. An authority may revoke a licence either by agreement with the licence holder or in the following circumstances (2004 Act s.70):

- where the authority consider that the licence holder or any other person has committed a serious breach of a condition of the licence or repeated breaches of such a condition;

- where the authority no longer consider that the licence holder is a fit and proper person;

- where the authority consider that the management of the HMO is no longer being carried out by persons who are fit and proper persons;

- where the HMO ceases to be an HMO which needs to be licenced;

- where the authority consider that, were the licence to expire they would, for a reason relating to the management structure for the HMO, refuse to grant a new licence to the licence holder on similar terms to the existing licence.

14.62 Procedure. As with licensing decisions, detailed provision is made for the procedure to be adopted before a licence can be varied (2004 Act Sch.5). Before making a decision, consultation must take place with the licence holder and any relevant person (14.54). The authority must give reasons for their decision; there is a right of appeal to the residential property tribunal within 28 days (which may be extended for good reason).

3. MANAGEMENT REGULATIONS

14.63 Proper standards of management. Under the 2004 Act the s.234, regulations ("Management Regulations") may be issued to ensure that the person managing (12.32) an HMO observes proper standards of management. The current management regulations are contained in the Management of Houses in Multiple Occupation (England) Regulations 2006 (SI 2006/372) and the Management of Houses in Multiple Occupation (Wales) Regulations 2006 (SI 2006/1713).

14.64 The regulations require the manager of the house to:

- provide contact details to all occupiers and display these in the house;

- take safety measures, including fire safety measures;

- maintain the water supply and drainage;

- supply and maintain gas and electricity, including ensuring that appliances are tested and that certificates are provided to the local housing authority upon request;

- maintain common parts, fixtures, fittings and appliances;

- maintain living accommodation; and

- provide waste disposal facilities.

14.65 Duties are imposed on those living in the house to ensure that the manager can effectively carry out these requirements.

14.66 Failure to comply with a regulation without reasonable excuse is an offence punishable by a fine not exceeding Level 5 on the standard scale (currently £5,000) (2004 Act s.234(3)).

4. OVERCROWDING CONTROLS

14.67 Overcrowding notice. A licence for an HMO specifies a permitted level of occupation (2004 Act s.64). Authorities have power through service of overcrowding notices to regulate the level of occupation in HMOs outside their licensing scheme.

14.68 An authority may serve notice in respect of an HMO which appears to them to accommodate, or be likely to accommodate, an excessive number of persons (2004 Act s.139). The notice must specify the maximum number who are to sleep in reach room in the HMO. The notice may also state that some rooms are unsuitable for use as bedrooms. The maximum stated may be age-related.

14.69 A notice may be served on one or more "relevant persons" (14.54).

14.70 The notice must contain one of two further classes of prohibition.

1. **Immediate reduction.** The person served must not:

(a) permit a room to be occupied other than in accordance with the notice; or
(b) allow so many people to live in the house that it is impossible for them to occupy without offending the notice, or without sleeping in parts of the house which are not rooms, or without two persons of the opposite sex and over the age of 10, not living together as man and wife, being obliged to sleep in the same room.

2. **Natural reduction.** The person served must not:

(a) permit a room to be occupied by a new resident, other than in accordance with the notice; or
(b) permit a new resident to occupy any part of the premises if it is not possible to do so without offending the notice, or without sleeping in parts of the house which are not rooms, or without two persons of the opposite sex and over the age of 10, not living together as man and wife, being obliged to sleep in the same room.

14.71 Breach of either class of notice is a criminal offence (2004 Act s.139(7)), punishable by a fine on standard scale 4 (currently £2,500). It is a defence that the person has a reasonable excuse for contravening the notice.

14.72 Procedure. At least seven days before serving an over-crowding notice, the authority must inform every relevant person (14.54) of their intention to serve the notice. At the same time, the authority must try to ensure that every occupier is also told of their intention.

14.73 Appeals. A person aggrieved by an overcrowding notice, e.g. landlords or occupiers, may appeal to the residential property tribunal within the 21 days of service. The effect of an appeal is to suspend the operation of the notice pending the outcome.

14.74   Power to revoke or vary. The notice may be revoked or varied by the authority at any time on the application of any relevant person (14.54) (2004 Act s.144). A refusal to revoke or vary may also—within 21 days—be appealed to the residential property tribunal.

5.   CODES OF PRACTICE

14.75   Codes of practice. Codes of practice may be issued laying down standards of conduct and practice to be followed with regard to the management of HMOs, including exempt HMOs (2004 Act 233). Failure to comply with a provision of a code does not of itself render a person liable to any civil or criminal proceedings, but a code may be relevant in a number of circumstances, e.g. failure to comply with a provision of a code is relevant to whether a proposed licence holder is a fit and proper person. At the time of writing, the only codes of practice which have been issued relate solely to accommodation for students in halls of residence and other university buildings

Selective licensing

14.76   Policy. Selective licensing of residential accommodation (2004 Act Pt 3) is intended to address problems in areas of low housing demand. In some areas, an absence of owner-occupiers has led to an influx of speculative landlords, who have little interest in either maintaining proper standards of accommodation for their tenants or exercising any control over their tenants' behaviour. Part 3 allows authorities to designate areas within their district as being subject to selective licensing. All houses and flats within the designation area and to which the designation applies must be licensed.

14.77   Failure to obtain a licence for a property which must be licensed may have serious consequences for the landlord. Failure to obtain a licence without a reasonable excuse is a criminal offence (14.99). While the property remains unlicensed, there are restrictions on the landlord's right to obtain possession (14.102). Furthermore, the residential property tribunal may make a rent repayment order, which requires the landlord to repay rent or housing benefit paid during the period when the property should have been licensed (14.103).

14.78 Application of scheme. A selective licensing scheme applies to "houses" but this is defined so as to include flats (2004 Act s.99). The scheme only applies to premises which are let out, although not necessarily under a single tenancy or licence (2004 Act s.79). An HMO which has to be licensed under Pt 2 does not, however, also have to be licensed under Pt 3 (2004 Act s.85).

14.79 No licence is necessary where any part of the house is let under an "exempt tenancy" (2004 Act s.79), i.e. a tenancy or licence granted by a registered social landlord or a tenancy or licence specified in regulations. Specified exempt tenancies include:

- tenancies or licences of houses managed by local authorities and certain other specified public bodies;

- long leases (1.15) where the occupier is either the tenant under the lease, or his successor in title, or a family member of the landlord;

- service tenancies and service occupancies; and

- tenancies or licences granted by a resident landlord.

14.80 Designation. An authority may designate either the whole or part of their area as subject to a selective licensing scheme. Before making a designation, the authority must be satisfied that one of two conditions is met (2004 Act s.80).

14.81 The first condition is that the area is, or is likely to become, an area of low housing demand and that making a designation will contribute to improvement of the social or economic conditions in the area.

14.82 The alternative condition is that the area is experiencing a significant and persistent problem caused by antisocial behaviour, which at least some of the landlords in the area are failing to address and that—in the authority's opinion—will be eliminated or reduced by the designation.

14.83 Before making a designation, the authority must take reasonable steps to consult persons who are likely to be affected by it and consider any representations made in response, and must ensure that any exercise of their power to require selective licensing is consistent with their overall housing strategy.

14.84   A designation must be confirmed by the Secretary of State or the National Assembly for Wales. Confirmation may either be specific or by way of a general approval. Following confirmation of the designation, the authority must take steps to publicise it, which steps are specified in regulations.

14.85   The designation may last up to a maximum of five years (2004 Act s.84). The authority must periodically review its operation, and they may revoke it if they consider it appropriate to do so. Any revocation must be publicised in accordance with prescribed requirements.

14.86   Temporary exemption notice.   A person having control (12.31) of, or a person managing (12.32), a property which needs a licence may notify the authority that he intends to take action to ensure that it no longer does so (2004 Act s.86). The authority may serve a "temporary exemption notice", the consequence of which is that the house does not have to be licensed while the notice is in force. A temporary exemption notice lasts for three months but can be extended for a further three months.

14.87   If the authority refuse to issue a temporary exemption notice, they must give the applicant written reasons for their decision and inform him of his right to appeal to the residential property tribunal within 28 days (2004 Act s.86(6)). There is no power to extend this time limit.

14.88   Licence applications.   A licence is required for each property which is subject to a designation (2004 Act s.68). Licences are not transferable; on sale, the new landlord has to apply for a new licence.

14.89   An application must conform with any requirements which the authority may impose, including payment of a fee. Regulations specify information which is to be contained in the application, including details of the person managing (12.32) the property and the person having control (12.31) of it. The application must also include questions designed to elicit information as to whether the proposed license holder and proposed manager are fit and proper persons (14.91). The applicant and the proposed licence holder (if different) must both sign the application, which must be accompanied by signed declarations as to the truth of its contents. It is an offence knowingly or recklessly to include information in the form which is false or misleading (2004 Act s.238(1)).

14.90 Licence decisions. The authority may grant a licence where they are satisfied of four matters (2004 Act s.88):

1. The proposed licence holder must be a fit and proper person to be the licence holder, and must be the most appropriate person to hold the licence.

2. The proposed manager must either be the person having control (12.31) of the house or his agent or employee.

3. The proposed manager of the property must also be a fit and proper person.

4. The proposed management arrangements must be satisfactory.

14.91 Fit and proper persons. To grant a licence, the authority must be satisfied that both the proposed licence holder and the proposed manager are "fit and proper" persons. In deciding this issue, authorities must take into account evidence that the person in question (2004 Act s.89):

- has committed any offence involving fraud or other dishonesty, or violence or drugs, or any offence listed in Sch.3 of the Sexual Offences Act 2003 (offences attracting notification requirements); or

- has practised unlawful discrimination on grounds of sex, colour, race, ethnic or national origins or disability in connection with carrying out any business; or

- has contravened any provision of the law relating to housing or of landlord and tenant.

  Evidence of such conduct by a person associated with, or formerly associated with, the proposed licence holder or manager must also be taken into account if it appears to be relevant to whether the person under consideration is a fit and proper person.

14.92 Management arrangements. In deciding whether proposed management arrangements are satisfactory, the authority must have regard to:

- whether any person proposed to be involved in the management of the property is sufficiently competent to do so;

- whether any person proposed to be involved in the management (other than the manager) is a fit and proper person; and

- whether any proposed management structures and funding arrangements are suitable (2004 Act s.89(6)).

14.93 Procedure. The procedure governing the grant or refusal of a licence is identical to that for HMO licences (14.54).

14.94 Licence conditions. Every licence must include certain conditions, and an authority have power to include other conditions to regulate the management, use and occupation of the house concerned (2004 Act s.90).

14.95 The conditions which must be included in every licence are the same as those that must be included in every HMO licence (14.57). The Act provides that additional conditions may include:

- regulation of the use of parts of the property by occupiers;

- requirements for the licence holder to take action to prevent or reduce antisocial behaviour by occupiers or their visitors;

- provision of facilities and equipment for meeting the standards to be prescribed by regulations;

- obligations to keep such facilities and equipment in repair and proper working order; and,

- time limits for carrying out works of repair.

14.96 An inadequacy or defect may constitute a Category 1 or Category 2 hazard under HHSRS, against which the authority could take enforcement action (Chapter 12) but which could also be dealt with by imposing license conditions. In general terms, authorities should deal with Category 1 or Category 2 hazards by enforcement action rather than by licence conditions (2004 Act s.90(5)).

14.97 Duration. The licence comes into force on the date specified in it and, unless the licence holder dies or the licence is revoked, remains in force for a maximum of five years.

14.98 Variation and revocation. A licence may be varied or revoked at any time. The procedure for variation or revocation of a

Pt 3 licence is identical to that for variation of an HMO licence (14.62). A licence may be revoked with the licence holder's agreement or where:

- the authority consider that the licence holder or any other person has committed a serious breach of a licence condition or repeated breaches of such a condition;

- the authority no longer consider that the licence holder is a fit and proper person;

- the authority consider that the management of the house is no longer being carried out by fit and proper persons;

- the house ceases to be a house to which the selective licensing scheme applies; or

- the authority consider that if the licence were to expire they would refuse to grant a new licence to the licence holder on similar terms in respect of it because of the management structure applying to the property (2004 Act s.93)

Failure to licence: consequences

1. CRIMINAL OFFENCES

14.99 Failure to obtain licence. If an HMO or house is not licensed when it should be, the person having control of (12.31) or managing (12.32) the property commits an offence (2004 Act s.72(1) if an HMO; s.95(1) if selective licensing). No offence is committed if the defendant has an outstanding application for a licence or temporary exemption notice or an outstanding appeal at the relevant time. It is also a defence that the defendant had a reasonable excuse. The offence is punishable by a maximum fine of £20,000.

14.100 Over-occupation. In relation to HMOs, a person having control of (12.31) or a managing (12.32) the HMO commits an offence if he knowingly permits someone to occupy the HMO so that the house is occupied by more households or persons than is permitted under the licence (2004 Act s.72(2)). It is a defence that the defendant had a reasonable excuse for permitting the person to occupy the house. The offence is punishable by a maximum fine of £20,000.

14.101 Breach of conditions. Failure to comply with a licence condition is an offence (2004 Act s.72(3) if an HMO; s.95(2) if selective licensing). The offence is committed by the person on whom the condition is imposed (usually the licence holder). A defence is available if there was a reasonable excuse for failing breaching the condition. The offence is summary only and punishable by a fine not exceeding Level 5 on the standard scale (currently £5,000).

2. RESTRICTION ON POSSESSION

14.102 Most tenants of HMOs or Pt 3 houses are assured shorthold tenants; a landlord is therefore entitled to recover possession provided he has served a notice in accordance with s.21 of the Housing Act 1988 (6.16). As long as an HMO or house which needs a licence remains unlicensed, however, the landlord may not serve a s.21 notice (2004 Act s.75 if an HMO; s.98 if selective licensing). There is nothing to prevent the tenancy being brought to an end by other means. Accordingly, the landlord may recover possession by serving a notice under s.8 of the 1988 Act and relying on grounds for possession contained in the Housing Act 1988 Sch.2, as he could do were the tenancy not shorthold (4.84–4.125); or, the tenant may end the tenancy by notice to quit or surrender (1.113–127).

3. RENT REPAYMENT ORDERS

14.103 Failure to obtain a license when one is necessary can have serious financial consequences for landlords as it can lead to the making of a "rent repayment order". Such an order is made on application to the residential property tribunal, and may require the landlord to repay rent (or other payments) to the occupier, or, if the occupier was in receipt of housing benefit, to repay the benefit to the local authority.

14.104 An application may be made by the local authority or by an occupier. It may be made against the "appropriate person", defined as the person who was entitled to receive payments "on his own account", i.e. usually the landlord rather than a managing agent (2004 Act s.73(10) if an HMO; s.96(10) if selective licensing).

14.105 Authority's application. On an authority's application, the tribunal must, before making an order, be satisfied of three matters:

>   1. At any time within the period of 12 months ending with the date of the notice of intended proceedings, the appropriate

person had committed the offence of failing to obtain a licence (14.99). It is not, however, necessary for any prosecution proceedings to have been taken.

2. Housing benefit had been paid whether to the appropriate person or someone else. (Whether the housing benefit has been passed on is relevant to the amount of the repayment.)

3. Notice of intended proceedings had been served by the authority and the authority must have considered any representations made in response (2004 Act s.73(6) if an HMO; s.96(6) if selective licensing).

14.106 Notice of intended proceedings. This warns the landlord of the authority's intention to make the application, and invites representations within 28 days. The notice must give reasons for making the application and provide a calculation for the money sought.

14.107 Occupier's application. Where the application is made by an occupier, the tribunal must be satisfied of three matters:

1. The appropriate person must either:

   (a) have been convicted of an offence of failing to obtain a licence (14.99); or
   (b) there must be an existing rent repayment order in respect of housing benefit, i.e. the authority have already successfully obtained a rent repayment order.

2. The occupier had made payments to a person having control of (12.31) or a person managing (12.32) the property during the relevant time.

3. The application is made within 12 months of the date of the conviction or order. If there has been both a conviction and a rent repayment order, the time limit runs from the later date (2004 Act s.73(8) if an HMO; s.96(8) of selective licensing).

14.108 Amount. On an authority's application, the tribunal must order repayment of the total amount of housing benefit paid during the relevant period, if satisfied that:

- a person has been convicted for failure to obtain a licence (14.99); and

- housing benefit was paid during the period when the offence was being committed (2004 Act s.74(2) if an HMO; s.97(2) if selective licensing).

14.109 This is subject to three limitations:

1. If the total amount received by the appropriate person is less than the housing benefit paid, e.g. because the tenant or managing agent did not pay the housing benefit over to the landlord, the amount of the repayment is limited to what was received.

2. The repayment cannot exceed the amount which the tribunal is satisfied that, by reason of exceptional circumstances, it would be unreasonable for the appropriate person to pay.

3. The order cannot require repayment of an amount payable more than twelve months before the date of the notice of intended proceedings.

14.110 In addition, no benefit which is recoverable from the landlord under the ordinary provisions for recovering overpaid housing benefit may be the subject of an order (Rent Repayment Orders (Supplementary Provisions) (England) Regulations 2007 (SI 2007/572) reg.2).

14.111 In the case of any other application, i.e. by an occupier, or where there has been no conviction for failure to obtain a licence, the amount of the repayment is such amount as the tribunal considers to be reasonable in the circumstances. In considering this, the tribunal must consider:

- the amount paid during the time when it appears that an offence of failure to licence was being committed;

- the extent to which that amount consisted of housing benefit and was actually received by the appropriate person;

- whether the appropriate person has been convicted of an offence of failing to licence;

- the conduct and financial circumstances of the appropriate person; and

- where the application is made by an occupier, the occupier's conduct.

14.112 On an occupier's application, the order cannot require repayment of an amount payable more than 12 months before the date of application.

Management orders

14.113 A management order allows an authority to take over the management of an HMO or a house which should be licenced under Pt 3. Usually, a management order is made because the authority consider that there is no reasonable prospect of granting a licence. The general effect of a management order is that the authority take possession of the property, although do not acquire any legal interest in it. Existing tenancies and licences are binding on the authority and, in some circumstances, the authority are able to grant tenancies or licences of the property. The provisions governing management orders are contained in Chapter 1, Pt 4 of the Housing Act 2004.

14.114 There are two forms of management order: interim and final. An interim order lasts for a maximum of 12 months. Its purpose is to secure that any necessary immediate steps are taken to protect the health and safety or welfare of the occupiers and to secure proper management of the house pending the grant of a licence or the making of a final management order. A final management order lasts a maximum of five years. Its purpose is to secure the proper management of the property on a long-term basis in accordance with a management scheme contained in the order.

14.115 Conditions: interim order. An interim order must be made:

- If the property is an unlicensed HMO or Pt 3 house and the authority consider that:

  — there is no reasonable prospect of it becoming licensed in the near future; or
  — an order is necessary to protect the health, safety or welfare of the occupiers, or persons occupying, or having an estate or interest in, any premises in the vicinity (2004 Act s.102).

14.116 Conditions: final order. Where the authority consider that on expiry of the interim order they will still be unable to grant a licence under Pts 2 or 3, they must replace an interim order with a final order (2004 Act s.113). The authority have power to make a final order where it is necessary for the protection of the health, safety, or welfare of occupiers or persons in the vicinity of the premises. On expiry of a final order, a further final order must be made if the authority are still unable to grant a licence under Pts 2 or 3 and, in any event, may be made if it is necessary to do so to protect the health, safety, or welfare of occupiers or persons in the vicinity of the premises.

14.117   Special orders.   In some cases, an authority can make an order in relation to premises which do not need to be licensed. Such an order must be authorised by the residential property tribunal. In the case of an HMO, authorisation can only be given if the order is necessary to protect the health, safety, or welfare either of the occupiers or of persons in the HMO's vicinity. In the case of other premises, the tribunal must also be satisfied that the antisocial behaviour of the occupiers is causing significant problems in the area and that the landlord is failing to take action against it.

14.118   Consultation.   The authority must consult any relevant persons (14.54) and provide them with copies of the proposed order including the management scheme (14.122) (2004 Act Sch.6).

14.119   Powers.   While a management order is in force, the authority have power to do anything which anyone else in possession of the premises could (2004 Act ss.107, 116). They may discharge their functions through managing agents. If they have assumed control from a person who was a lessee, they are treated as if they were that lessee. They may take over responsibility for any furniture in the property. They can take over the landlord's responsibility under contracts relating to the property and can carry on legal proceedings brought by or against him (2004 Act s.125).

14.120   While a management order is in force, the authority have the right to enter any part of the house for the purpose of carrying out works (2004 Act s.131). If an occupier prevents them from carrying out the works, the authority may obtain an order from the magistrates' court ordering him to permit them to be done. A person who fails to comply with such an order commits an offence.

14.121   Rights of occupation.   In relation to existing tenancies, Housing Act 1988 and Rent Act security will continue notwithstanding the control order. Any new tenancies granted by the authority will not be secure or introductory but will be assured (2004 Act s.124).

14.122 During an interim order, the authority can only grant a new tenancy with the consent of the person whom they have replaced as landlord (2004 Act s.107). Once a final order is in force, however, consent is not required unless the tenancy is a fixed-term tenancy (1.109), which would expire after the proposed expiry date for the final order, or it is a periodic tenancy (1.109) determinable by more than four weeks (2004 Act s.116).

14.123 Management scheme. A final management order must contain a "management scheme", which must set out how the authority intend to ensure proper management of the property and include details of any proposed works (2004 Act s.119).

14.124 Provision is made for detailed accounts to be drawn up and maintained by the authority (2004 Act s.119(7)) and for payment of compensation to certain persons affected by the order (2004 Act s.128(1)).

14.125 Procedure. As soon as practicable after making a management order (interim or final), the authority must serve the occupiers with a copy of the order together with a notice (2004 Act Sch.6 para.7). Within seven days, the authority must also serve a copy on each relevant person (14.54) together with a notice which informs him of his right to appeal to the residential property tribunal within 28 days. If the authority are assuming control from a person who is a lessee, there is additional provision for service of a notice on the superior landlord so that the authority can take over liability under the lease.

14.126 Variation and revocation. An order may be varied or revoked at any time. A relevant person (14.54) has a right to request variation or revocation. There is detailed provision governing the procedure to be adopted (2004 Act Sch.6 Pt 2). Any relevant persons (14.54) must be consulted before a decision to vary or revoke the order is taken. A decision to vary or revoke, or to refuse to vary or revoke, must be served on any relevant person. Reasons for the decision must be given and the authority must inform the recipient of the 28–day time limit for appealing to the residential property tribunal. If there is an appeal, the variation or revocation is suspended pending its outcome.

Empty Dwelling Management Orders (EDMOs)

14.127 Policy. The purpose of an EDMO is partly to bring vacant dwellings in the private sector back into occupation at a time when demand for accommodation is high, and partly to address the impact that empty dwellings can have on a neighbourhood, e.g. because they attract vandals. The scheme for EDMOs is similar to that for other management orders. As with other management orders, there are two forms of EDMO: interim and final. The crucial difference is that an interim EDMO only allows the authority to let out the dwelling with the owner's consent, whereas a final EDMO allows them to let the dwelling without the owner's consent. Before making an interim EDMO, the authority must obtain authorisation from the residential property tribunal. If at the end of the interim order (which lasts for a maximum of 12 months) the authority consider that an order is still required to ensure that the property becomes or remains let out, they may make a final order.

14.128 Dwelling. An EDMO can only be made in respect of a "dwelling", which is:

- a building intended to be occupied as a separate dwelling (3.17); or

- a part of a building intended to be occupied as a separate dwelling which may be entered otherwise than through any non-residential accommodation in the building, i.e. a flat is a dwelling unless entry to it is through commercial accommodation (2004 Act s.132).

14.129 If an EDMO is made, the authority assume the position of "the relevant proprietor", i.e. the freeholder or, if let, the lessee who is the lowest in any chain of leases who has an unexpired term of seven years or more (2004 Act s.132).

14.130 Exempt relevant proprietors. An EDMO cannot be made where the relevant proprietor is one of the following:

- a local housing authority;

- a registered social landlord;

- a police authority;

- a fire and rescue authority; or

- a health service body (2004 Act s.133).

14.131 Exempt properties. Regulations prescribe a number of circumstances in which an EDMO cannot be made, including where the relevant proprietor is absent because of ill health or serving in the armed forces or where the property is a holiday home or is usually used for tied accommodation (Housing (Empty Dwelling Management Orders) (Prescribed Exceptions and Requirements) (England) Order 2006 (SI 2006/367) reg.3.

14.132 Authorisation. Before making an EDMO, the authority must obtain authorisation from the residential property tribunal. This can only be given if the tribunal considers that the property has been "wholly unoccupied" for at least six months. It is not necessary for the property to be occupied lawfully: a property that has been squatted in the past six months cannot be made the subject of an EDMO (2004 Act s.133). In addition, the tribunal must be satisfied that no exemptions apply (14.130) and that there is no real prospect of the property being let unless an order is made.

14.133 Effect. The position under an EDMO is similar to that under any other management order and the discussion in relation to other management orders in relation to the authority's powers (14.118), rights of occupation (14.120), powers of letting (14.121), accounting obligations (14.123) and variation and revocation (14.125) all apply equally to EDMOs.

INDEX

LEGAL TAXONOMY
FROM SWEET & MAXWELL

This index has been prepared using Sweet and Maxwell's Legal Taxonomy. Main index entries conform to keywords provided by the Legal Taxonomy except where references to specific documents or non-standard terms (denoted by quotation marks) have been included. These keywords provide a means of identifying similar concepts in other Sweet & Maxwell publications and online services to which keywords from the Legal Taxonomy have been applied. Readers may find some minor differences between terms used in the text and those which appear in the index. Suggestions to *sweetandmaxwell.taxonomy@thomson.com*.

(All references are to paragraph numbers)